D0787540

The Economics of Globalization
Policy Perspectives from Public Economics

The increasing economic openness expressed in the globalization of independent economic systems has created problems as well as opportunities that cross formal borders in new and unexpected ways. Professors Assaf Razin and Efraim Sadka have compiled and edited a series of essays based on lectures delivered at the 1996 Congress of the International Institute of Public Finance that explore the ramifications of globalization in selected areas of public finance. Eight main topics are covered by the sixteen essays in the volume: the international mobility of technology; capital flows and exchange-rate misalignments; tax incentives and patterns of capital flows; income redistribution and social insurance in federal systems; tax harmonization and coordination; political-economy aspects of international tax competition; the migration of skilled and unskilled labor; and the fiscal aspects of monetary unification.

Assaf Razin is Mario Henrique Professor of Public Economics at Tel Aviv University, Research Associate at the National Bureau of Economic Research, Cambridge, and Research Fellow at the Centre for Economic Policy Research, London. He is also a Fellow of the Econometric Society and a frequent visiting scholar at the International Monetary Fund in Washington, D.C. Professor Razin's major previous publications include *Fiscal Policies and Growth in the World Economy*, third edition (MIT Press, with Jacob Frenkel and Chi-Wa Yuen), *Population Economics* (MIT Press, with Efraim Sadka), *The Economy of Modern Israel: Malaise and Promise* (University of Chicago Press, with Efraim Sadka), *International Taxation* (MIT Press, with Jacob Frenkel and Efraim Sadka), and *A Theory of International Trade under Uncertainty* (Academic Press, with Elhanan Helpman), and *Current Account Sustainability* (International Finance, Princeton University).

Efraim Sadka is Henry Kaufman Professor of International Capital Markets at Tel Aviv University. From 1982 to 1985 he served as chairman of the Eitan Berglas School of Economics, Tel Aviv University, and from 1987 to 1989 he served as the director of the Sapir Center for Economic Development there. In addition to being the author or coauthor of six books, three of which are cited above, and editor or coeditor of four others, Professor Sadka has published articles in the *American Economic Review*, the *Quarterly Journal of Economics*, the *Review of Economic Studies*, *Econometrica*, the *Journal of Political Economics*, the *Journal of Public Economics*, and the *Journal of International Economics*.

The Economics of Globalization

Policy Perspectives from Public Economics

Edited by

ASSAF RAZIN

EFRAIM SADKA

CAMBRIDGE
UNIVERSITY PRESS

PUBLISHED BY THE PRESS SYNDICATE OF THE UNIVERSITY OF CAMBRIDGE
The Pitt Building, Trumpington Street, Cambridge, United Kingdom

CAMBRIDGE UNIVERSITY PRESS
The Edinburgh Building, Cambridge CB2 2RU, UK
http://www.cup.cam.ac.uk
40 West 20th Street, New York, NY 10011-4211, USA   http://www.cup.org
10 Stamford Road, Oakleigh, Melbourne 3166, Australia

© Assaf Razin, Efraim Sadka 1999

First published 1999

Printed in the United States of America

Typeset in Times Roman 10/12 pt, Quark XPress[TH][BTS]

*A catalog record for this book is available from
the British Library.*

Library of Congress Cataloging-in-Publication Data
The economics of globalization: policy perspectives from public
  economics / edited by Assaf Razin, Efraim Sadka.
     p. cm.
  ISBN 0-521-62268-9 (hb)
     1. Finance, Public – Congresses.   2. Competition, International –
Congresses.   3. International economic relations – Congresses.
I. Razin, Assaf.   II. Sadka, Efraim.
HJ113.E347   1999
336 – dc21   97-52781
                                                                    CIP

ISBN 0 521 62268 9 hardback

In memory of Ofair Razin

Contents

Preface

Ofair Razin died at the age of thirty after an almost lifelong struggle with multiple sclerosis. On the basis of his Ph.D. dissertation, "Exchange Rate Misalignments and Economic Growth," submitted to the Georgetown University Department of Economics, his adviser, Susan M. Collins, prepared a chapter for this volume. Although only a budding researcher in economics, Ofair Razin was a mature fighter for dignity in a life lived under adverse conditions. We dedicate this book to his memory.

Contributors

Julian S. Alworth, *Università Luigi Bocconi, Milan, Italy*
Roel Beetsma, *Economic Policy Directorate, Ministry of Economic
    Affairs, The Hague*
A. Lans Bovenberg, *CPB, Netherlands Bureau for Economic
    Policy Analysis and Center for Economic Research, Tilburg
    University*
Nancy H. Chau, *Southern Illinois University, Carbondale, Illinois*
Susan M. Collins, *Georgetown University and The Brookings Institution*
Helmuth Cremer, *IDEI (Institut d'Economie Industrielle) and
    GREMAQ, University of Toulouse and Institut Universitaire de
    France*
Andreas Haufler, *University of Konstanz, Konstanz*
Elhanan Helpman, *Harvard University, Tel Aviv University, and the
    Canadian Institute for Advanced Research*
Ephraim Kleiman, *The Hebrew University of Jerusalem*
Ben Lockwood, *University of Warwick and The Center for Economic
    Policy Research*
Carlo Perroni, *University of Warwick*
Pierre Pestieau, *CREPP, University of Liege; CORE, University of
    Louvain; and DELTA, Paris*
Assaf Razin, *Tel Aviv University, NBER and CEPR*
Ofair Razin, *Georgetown University*
Gilles Saint-Paul, *Universitat Pompeu Fabra, Barcelona and CEPR*
Kimberley A. Scharf, *Warwick University and Institute for Fiscal
    Studies (affiliated with University College, London)*
Guttorm Schjelderup, *Institute of Economics, Norwegian School of
    Economics and Business Administration, Bergen, and the
    Norwegian Research Centre in Organization and Management
    (LOS), Bergen*
Hans-Werner Sinn, *Munich University*

xi

Bent Sørensen, *Brown University*
Lars Sørgard, *Norwegian School of Economics and Business
Administration, Bergen-Sandviken*
Oded Stark, *University of Oslo and University of Vienna*
Vito Tanzi, *International Monetary Fund*
Oved Yosha, *Eitan Berglas School of Economics, Tel Aviv University*
Chi-Wa Yuen, *School of Economics and Finance, University of
Hong Kong*

Introduction

Assaf Razin and Efraim Sadka

The past two decades have witnessed a growing trend toward economic openness. The fading of borders between independent economic systems – local, state, national, and otherwise – has had immense implications for economic policies in each of these systems. Capital, firms, and labor are now able to move more freely across regions, states, and countries and can better exploit differences in opportunities (employment, savings, investment, etc.) and in technological and economic environments, as well as in fiscal and monetary stances. For instance, the tax base has increasingly become more global, and its allocation among the various tax jurisdictions more responsive to the tax policies in each of these jurisdictions. As succinctly put by *The Economist* (May 31, 1997):

Globalisation is a tax problem for three reasons. First, firms have more freedom over where to locate. . . . This will make it harder for a country to tax [a business] much more heavily than its competitors. . . . Second, globalisation makes it hard to decide where a company should pay tax, regardless of where it is based. . . . This gives them [the companies] plenty of scope to reduce tax bills by shifting operations around or by crafty transfer-pricing. . . . [Third], globalisation . . . nibbles away at the edges of taxes on individuals. It is harder to tax personal income because skilled professional workers are more mobile than they were two decades ago. [pp. 17–18]

Similarly, capital can move from regions where its return is low and labor costs are high to regions where its return is high and labor costs are low. Furthermore, real–exchange-rate misalignments affect the degrees of utilization of capital, labor, and other inputs in one country relative to another and, correspondingly, the international location of economic activity. Such misalignments are often caused by cross-country differences in monetary policies that induce short-term interest-rate disparities and international flows of financial capital.

Another important aspect of globalization is the cross-country diffu-

1

sion of technology. International mobility of skilled labor, international trade in goods and services, and foreign direct-investment flows are all important vehicles for the international mobility of technology. This makes the global (worldwide) economic value of a technological innovation much higher than the national value, which itself is significantly higher than the return to the firm developing the innovation. Thus there is a two-tier spillover effect of technological innovations, with increased globalization amplifying the top-tier effect.

1   International Mobility of Technology

The spillover effects of technological innovations have strong implications for an issue that has recently been much debated, the issue of (per-capita) output convergence across developing and developed economies. This question inspired Robert Lucas (1988) in his study on endogenous growth. He posed the issue of accounting for the observed diversity in the levels and rates of growth of per-capita income across countries as being *the* problem of economic development. On the one hand, developing countries tend to accumulate capital much more rapidly than their counterparts among the developed countries, thereby narrowing the per-capita income gap. On the other hand, as observed by Elhanan Helpman, research-and-development (R&D) expenditures, which have enormous rates of return, are heavily concentrated within a small number of industrialized countries. If R&D expenditures do not significantly spill over to the developing countries, then these expenditures will tend to widen the income gap.

This issue prompted Helpman to raise the question whether the international distribution of the *benefits* of R&D expenditures is as skewed as the expenditures themselves or whether the substantial international spillover effects of R&D expenditures cause the international distribution of the benefits to be more spread out. Such spillovers can mitigate the effect of R&D in widening the income gap. In Chapter 1, Helpman tentatively concludes that the R&D spillover "effects are important and that there exist significant cross-country links that are driven by foreign trade and [foreign direct] investment. Since foreign trade and investment are also important for a variety of other reasons, international-productivity links that are driven by R&D make them all the more important."

2   Capital Flows and Exchange-Rate Misalignment

Nowadays, with increasing international integration of capital markets, one often encounters significant deviations of exchange rates from their long-term stable levels. These phenomena are referred to as exchange-rate misalignments. In Chapter 3, Ofair Razin and Susan Collins construct indicators of real–exchange-rate misalignments employing a stochastic version of the Mundell-Fleming open-economy model (Frenkel, Razin, and Yuen, 1996). The model allows both perfect price flexibility and partial price flexibility. Misalignment is defined in terms of the deviation of the level of the real exchange rate under price rigidity from its equilibrium real level under perfect price flexibility.

Typically, a sharp fiscal expansion in a large economy puts upward pressure on its domestic interest rates, and that soaks up capital from the rest of the world. As emphasized by Rudiger Dornbusch (1976), the predominance of wage and price rigidities can induce excessive realignments of exchange rates. Such was the effect of the 1981 fiscal expansion in the United States that triggered a significant overvaluation of the U.S. dollar. Observing that and other similar episodes, Hans-Werner Sinn, in Chapter 2, offers a fresh look at the global effects of the German unification. In order to raise, almost instantly, the income level of East German workers to that of their West German counterparts, a massive west–east transfer took place, generating an enormous fiscal expansion, with the primary structural budget deficit reaching a record high of 3.1% of gross domestic product (GDP) in 1991. European capital and other capital flowed into Germany, and the deutsche mark appreciated excessively. Because of the rigid currency arrangement of the European Monetary System (EMS), other European currencies followed suit. That culminated in the EMS crisis of 1992, when some of the EMS countries (United Kingdom, Italy) quit and allowed downward adjustments of their currencies, whereas some other countries (Spain, Portugal, Ireland) followed a similar course of action within the confines of the EMS. Sinn attempts to determine whether or not further realignments of European currencies will be needed before they are frozen permanently in 1999 into the Maastricht currency union.

In Chapter 3, Razin and Collins further examine empirically the effects of real exchange-rate misalignments on long-term growth. They present evidence that this effect is not symmetric: Overvaluation is harmful to growth, but undervaluation is not closely related to growth.

3   Tax Incentives and Patterns of Capital Flows

Some of the most important changes in world capital markets that have taken place in recent decades have been the increasing flows of portfolio investments and foreign direct investments and the growth of multinational enterprises (MNEs). The patterns of capital flows and trade in goods are affected by direct taxes (on capital and labor), in addition to the obvious influence of taxes on trade (such as import tariffs).

The efficiency aspects of taxation in an open economy are conveniently grouped into two categories. The first deals with the broadly defined concept of production efficiency. This concept refers not only to the standard efficiency of allocation of inputs in domestic production but also to the efficient temporal and intertemporal allocation of production between home and abroad (via international trade). The second category deals with the match between consumers' willingness to pay for their consumption bundles and the opportunity costs of their production. Ideally, one would like to achieve both kinds of efficiency, but that is impossible in our second-best world, where distortionary taxes are inevitable. Still, the modern public-finance literature emphasizes the desirability of production efficiency over consumption efficiency (Diamond and Mirrless, 1971).

Production efficiency requires an economy to adopt the *residence principle* of taxation (Frenkel, Razin, and Sadka, 1991). This principle states that the place of residence of the taxpayer is the basis for assessment of tax liability. Residents of a country are taxed uniformly on their worldwide income, regardless of the source of that income (domestic or foreign). Similarly, a country does not tax nonresidents on their income originating in that country. In this way, the marginal return to capital in the home country is equated to the world rate of return to capital, ensuring a maximum value for the national capital stock. (Production efficiency can still be maintained when nonresidents are taxed, provided that they receive a full tax credit in their countries of residence.)

Nevertheless, there are important cases of international capital-market failures that may require a deviation from the residence principle. In Chapter 4, Assaf Razin, Efraim Sadka, and Chi-Wa Yuen study three major vehicles for international capital flows: portfolio debt flows, portfolio equity flows, and foreign direct-investment flows. Because of information asymmetries between domestic and foreign investors (e.g., because of "home-court advantage" for domestic investors), the various types of international capital flows can be suboptimal. This necessitates a fresh look at the issue of tax treatment for the various vehicles of capital flows in order to provide proper investment incentives to correct the market failures. In particular, depending on the type of capital flow, it may be efficient to tax or subsidize these flows in a manner that differs from the residence principle.

A very important form of international capital flow is foreign direct investment, especially by MNEs. A key public-finance aspect of the behavior of MNEs that has been thoroughly researched in the literature on MNEs is transfer pricing. Typically, this research has focused on the role of transfer pricing in shifting profits from high-tax to low-tax jurisdictions. A standard assumption in this context is that the MNE determines not only the transfer prices for trade among its affiliates but also the prices for the final products sold by those affiliates in their domestic markets. In Chapter 5, Guttorm Schjelderup and Lars Sørgard note that in many cases the MNE determines only the transfer prices, with the decisions about the prices of the final products sold by them in their domestic markets being delegated to the affiliates. Furthermore, they assume that the affiliates do not exercise full monopoly power, but rather strategically interact with domestic competitors. They show that because the transfer-pricing policy usually affects the strategic behavior of the affiliates, the MNE can no longer rely on transfer prices to shift profits from high-tax to low-tax jurisdictions. Rather, a transfer-pricing policy by the MNE may reduce the total profits of the MNE. Thus, Schjelderup and Sørgard show that the incentive to use transfer pricing for tax-saving purposes is dampened.

4 Limits to Income Redistribution in Federal Systems

An economic union has two layers of government: one supranational government and many national governments. A similar two-level structure of government exists in a federation: one central (federal) government and many state governments. Parallel to this two-layer structure, there are two layers of social insurance and income redistribution: interstate and intrastate insurance and redistribution. The issue of redistribution typically arises when not all members of the federation are equal according to certain socioeconomic characteristics and/or when not all the individuals within a member state are equal according to such characteristics. The issue of social insurance arises even when, ex ante, all states are alike and all individuals within a state are alike, provided that the risks they (the states and the individuals) face are not perfectly correlated, so that risk sharing is desirable.

In an economic union that has two levels of governments (one central government and many local governments), the conventional public-finance wisdom provides a strong case for assigning the income redistribution role to the central (federal) government. First, factor mobility gives rise to tax competition among state governments if they are assigned the role of redistribution, often resulting in suboptimal redistribution because of the "disappearing taxpayer" phenomenon. Second, only the federal government can redistribute income across states, an important role when labor is immobile. In Chapter 6, to focus on this issue of the interstate redistribution role of the central government, Helmuth Cremer and Pierre Pestieau abstract from the issue of tax competition by assuming factor immobility. They also assume some informational asymmetry between the central government and the state governments, which, in effect, allows only state governments to redistribute income among their residents. The federal government can only observe the aggregate redistributive effort of each state (as measured, say, by its total gross tax collections) and base its interstate redistribution policy on this variable. Therefore, the redistribution policy of the central government weakens the incentive of the relatively rich state governments to redistribute income among their residents, because a state government that is engaged in such a redistribution is "punished" by the federal government. This creates a trade-off between interstate and intrastate income redistributions. Whereas the optimal incentive-comparable redistribution policy of the central government typically reduces the extent of the (internal) income redistribution of a relatively rich state, Cremer and Pestieau show that the effect on a relatively poor state is not clear: Both insufficient redistribution as well as excessive (internal) redistribution can arise.

The globalization that brought about cross-border flows of capital provides an important mechanism for sharing idiosyncratic output risk. A gross domestic product (GDP) shock is no longer fully transmitted into a gross national product (GNP) shock. Because national consumption is more closely related to GNP than to GDP, a GDP shock likewise is not transmitted fully to consumption. Asdrubali, Sorensen, and Yosha (1996) have found that this channel of risk sharing (i.e., cross-border ownership of capital) is very important and that it has risen significantly over time in the United States: 27% of shocks to state output were absorbed through the capital market in the 1960s; the figure rose to 48% in the 1980s. Sala-i-Martin and Sachs (1992) have pointed out that a progressive-tax transfer system also contributes to risk sharing within a federation. In Chapter 7, Bent Sørensen and Oved Yosha advance this outlook by attempting to measure the contributions of the various federal insurance mechanisms (such as unemployment insurance, old-age social security, etc.) to interstate sharing of idiosyncratic output risk. They examine the degree to which the state output is negatively correlated with the net federal transfer it receives. They find a significant role for federal social insurance in interstate risk sharing in the United States. Among the various forms of this insurance, unemployment contributions and benefits are singled out as the most cost-effective. The lesson they draw from this conclusion, as it pertains to the European Union (EU), is that with a relatively small budget for an EU-wide unemployment insurance system, the EU can achieve significant risk sharing among its members.

5 Tax Harmonization, Tax Coordination, and the "Disappearing Taxpayer"

With the increasing international integration of financial and economic activities, issues such as taxation of incomes of multinational enterprises and treatment of foreign-source income of residents and domestic-source income of nonresidents are increasingly occupying the agendas of tax-policy scholars and practitioners. Without more intensive cooperation among national fiscal authorities (e.g., transfer of information, harmonization and coordination of tax rates and bases) it will become increasingly difficult to tax mobile factors. Nowadays, not only are financial capital and physical capital mobile, but also skilled labor and professional labor and even unskilled labor are becoming more mobile. Thus, without international cooperation, the national tax bases may seriously shrink. Furthermore, the global as well as the national efficiency of the tax system could be severely hampered. For these and other reasons, Vito Tanzi, in Chapter 8, raises and discusses the issue of a need for a world tax organization. Such an organization could also deal with cross-border environmental spillovers and other international externalities, tax arbitration among countries, technical assistance on fiscal matters, accounting standards for tax purposes, and so forth.

In Chapter 9, Julian Alworth further strengthens the case for a world tax organization by elaborating on the challenges posed to taxation in integrated financial markets by the ever-spreading derivative financial instruments (DFIs). He highlights "the near impossibility of applying a source-based gross withholding tax to many DFIs . . . and the possibility that taxpayers may seek to disguise otherwise-taxable transactions as DFIs for the purpose of avoiding tax at source." A world tax organization could help the individual countries (through the exchange of information among them) to implement the residence principle, possibly with some elements of source-based taxation, with credit for foreign taxes paid.

It is most often the case that fiscal separation is maintained within an economic union. Such is, for instance, the case with the EU, as well as the case analyzed by Ephraim Kleiman in Chapter 11: the economic integration between Israel and the Palestinian entity. International tax cooperation through some supranational body, such as Tanzi's world tax organization, is then needed. According to the Israeli-Palestinian accord of 1994, a combination of elements from both a customs union and a free-trade area has been put in place. A common external tariff envelope embraces both entities, with free movements of goods and capital between the two entities, without tax-border checkpoints, and with somewhat more managed movements of labor. In this case, one encounters the need to establish criteria for revenue sharing and clearance. For instance, as pointed out by Kleiman in Chapter 11, most of the imports to the Palestinian entities pass through Israeli harbors and airports, with indirect taxes (such as a value-added tax, VAT) and tariffs collected there by the Israeli fiscus. Similarly, because of the large Palestinian import surplus in its trade with Israel, the VAT revenues collected by the Israeli fiscus on the consumption of Israeli commodities by Palestinians exceed the VAT revenues collected by the Palestinian fiscus on the consumption of Palestinian commodities by Israelis (given the similarity in VAT rates). In all of these cases, some form of either revenue sharing or clearance has to be agreed upon.

The issues of the global efficiency and national efficiency of the tax system have occupied the international public-finance literature for some time. For instance, when cross-border taxation can be effectively enforced, noncooperative tax competition among small, market-powerless countries may be second-best efficient (Razin and Sadka, 1991); that is, even though taxes by themselves are distortionary, coordination and/or harmonization of tax policy cannot improve efficiency. International tax cooperation may enhance enforcement, especially when economic borders (e.g., border checkpoints) are removed, as has been the case in the EU since 1992. However, when economies are large enough to exert some market powers, and when they actually so behave, then noncooperative tax competition is inefficient in a manner akin to the suboptimal outcome of the prisoner-dilemma game.

International terms-of-trade manipulation through direct trade taxes and subsidies was shown long ago by Harry Johnson (1953–54) to be inefficient. Such outright trade wars have by now largely ceased and have completely vanished from the EU and other free-trade areas. In Chapter 10, Ben Lockwood considers economies in which governments employ non-trade-related taxes (e.g., indirect consumption taxes, such as the consumption-type VAT) in order to meet certain revenue requirements. As by-products, these taxes serve also as weapons in trade wars because they influence the patterns of domestic consumption and production and consequently the patterns of international trade and the terms of trade. He shows how and under what circumstances commodity-tax harmonization (such as the European Commission 1993 directive on minimum VAT and excise tax rates) can be Pareto-improving in the sense that all countries gain either actually or potentially (after some compensations from actual gainers to actual losers).

6 Political-Economy Aspects of International Tax Competition

Traditional public-finance models presuppose that economic policy is derived from an optimization process by a benevolent government or social planner according to well-defined criteria such as a Bergson-Samuelson social-welfare function. However, in practice we often encounter the failure of such models to explain actual economic policies in general and tax policies in particular. For example, there is no clear evidence that effective capital income tax rates have substantially and *uniformly* declined in the EU countries over the recent period of increased capital-market integration, as theory suggests. This deviation between optimization-based policy and actual policy has motivated the emergence of political-economy-based models of international or inter-jurisdictional tax competition. In these models, policy is the outcome of a political balance either among lobby and pressure groups or directly among the voters (as in a direct representative democracy).

As pointed out earlier, when the residence principle cannot be implemented (because taxes on foreign-source income of residents cannot be effectively enforced), an optimization-based tax policy typically will call for low taxes on capital income. Under certain circumstances (such as the availability of a broad range of alternative tax bases), capital-income taxation vanishes altogether. In Chapter 12, Andreas Haufler suggests an alternative model of tax-policy determination based on a political balance between capital and labor. Increased integration of capital markets raises the efficiency cost of capital taxation when enforcement of taxes on foreign-source income is costly. When the distributional aspects dominate the efficiency aspects in the political equilibrium, the result (a converging-vanishing tax on capital income) is overturned. When capital markets are integrated, workers generally lose and capital-owners gain from *outflows* of capital; workers gain and capital-owners lose from *inflows* of capital. Therefore a capital-exporting country will change the equilibrium mix between capital and labor taxes so as to raise the tax on capital income and lower the tax on labor income. The opposite occurs in a capital-importing country, giving rise to an international divergence of tax rates on capital income.

In Chapter 13, Carlo Perroni and Kimberley Scharf discuss the effects of tax competition on the political-equilibrium tax policy in a variety of models of political processes. For instance, they suggest that lobbying by domestic firms and labor unions could help explain why tax-competing countries follow the (inefficient) source principle, in contrast to the predictions of the traditional optimization-based models. Similarly, whereas the latter models suggest that coordination can enhance efficiency (e.g., by avoiding trade wars), in political-economy equilibria, coordination may be harmful.

7   Migration of Skilled and Unskilled Labor

In the presence of frictionless international factor mobility, factors of production will move from locations where their marginal product is low to other locations where their marginal product is high. Thus, when factor mobility is not constrained, eventually each factor of production will generate the same marginal product wherever it is employed. (In fact, with identical constant-returns-to-scale technologies everywhere, and with two factors – capital and labor – that equalize the marginal product of every factor everywhere, it suffices that one factor be freely mobile.) Even though factor mobility in general, and more specifically here migration, raises global output and also per-capita output everywhere, the gain is not shared by everyone. There are certain sectors, both in the home country and in foreign countries, that actually lose. With perfect, nondistortionary redistribution mechanisms, the gain could be spread to all.

Nevertheless, in practice one often finds widespread resistance to migration, both in the foreign (destination) country and in the home (source) country. Such resistance can introduce frictions into the migration process and mitigate the global gain. Similarly, imperfect information can generate obstacles to migration.

Labor mobility is much more common among the various regions of a single country or among the various states in a federation than across political borders. Importantly, labor mobility closely interacts with labor laws, unionism, unemployment, and social insurance. In Chapter 14, Gilles Saint-Paul notes that Germany and Italy offer key recent examples of interregional migration (east–west in Germany, south–north in Italy). In both cases, one region (the west in Germany and the north in Italy) is more abundant in human capital (high-skill labor) than the other and also politically dominates the national union of low-skill labor. In the long run, labor mobility tends to equalize factor prices across regions through a flow of low-skill labor from the poor region to the rich one and a flow of high-skill labor in the opposite direction. Saint-Paul develops a model in which a wage-setting union of low-skill labor is politically dominated by the insiders in the rich region. If the wage for low-skill labor in the poor region is raised closer to the wage level in the rich region, then unemployment of low-skill labor in the poor region will jump in the short run and later on peter down. Such a wage hike in the poor region will therefore increase the flow of unemployed low-skill labor from the poor region to the rich region. This will be bad news for the insiders of the low-skill labor union in the rich region. At the same time, it will weaken the incentive for high-skill labor in the rich region to migrate to the poor region. That will be good news for the aforementioned insiders. Saint-Paul argues that the incentive for the rich-region insiders to equalize wages for low-skill labor across regions will be greater the larger the migration cost of low-skill labor relative to high-skill labor, which is an empirically plausible assumption.

Employment opportunities for migrants in a destination country are adversely affected by lack of perfect information in the destination country regarding the migrants' skills. Specifically, in Chapter 15, Nancy Chau and Oded Stark model this asymmetric information between employers in the source and destination countries in order to study the implications for the dynamics of migration, including return migration. In the initial stage, before any migration occurs, employers in the destination country can make no distinction between skilled and unskilled would-be migrants. In that case, all migrants are offered the same wage – their average marginal product, as in Akerlof's market for lemons (Akerlof, 1970). (A similar mechanism is employed in Chapter 5.) However, as exposure breeds familiarity, with a continuous flow of migration the employers in the destination country will observe the productivity of already-employed migrants and gradually become able to discern the skill levels of would-be migrants. Wages offered to would-be migrants will no longer be uniform, and the wages received by already-employed migrants will gradually converge to match their true productivity. These changes in the wage structure will have three effects. First, they will enhance migration of the more skilled and discourage unskilled migration. Second, they will hasten return migration of unskilled workers. Third, they will strengthen the incentive to acquire skills in the source country. The latter effect may offset the adverse consequences of the brain drain on those left behind in the source country.

8   Fiscal Aspects of Monetary Unification

In a monetary union, national governments obviously are in charge of fiscal policies only. Thus, whereas in the presence of independent national monetary and fiscal policies country-specific output shocks can be stabilized through both monetary and fiscal adjustments, the stabilization role of a national government in a monetary union is left to fiscal policy alone.

One channel of interaction between monetary policy and fiscal policy available to a national government that is lost in a monetary union is seigniorage as a source of revenue alternative to explicit (generally distortionary) taxation (Phelps, 1973; Helpman and Sadka, 1979). In Chapter 16, Roel Beetsma and Lans Bovenberg study the reduced stabilization role of monetary policy and the consequent increased stabilization role of fiscal policy in a monetary union and their implications for the behaviors of central banks and national fiscal authorities and for national welfare. They show that the optimally designed central bank, à la Rogoff (1985), is more conservative in the sense that it attaches a higher priority to price stability than does society. The results are, on the one hand, lower inflation, but, on the other hand, reduced output and reduced public spending – the net effect on welfare being negative. This decline in welfare can be mitigated by a properly designed mechanism for transfers among the monetary union's members (see also Chapter 8).

9 Conclusions

The selection of topics in this volume does not reflect an attempt to cover all aspects of economic and financial integration. Nevertheless, it brings together many issues of economic and financial integration from the point of view of economic policy in general and public finance in particular. The following is a representative sampling of the topics covered in this volume: international R&D spillovers, the role of exchange rates in economic integration, the interaction between international taxation and capital flows, the division of the role of redistribution between the supranational government and the national governments, the effects of integration on the political-economy equilibrium tax on labor and capital, union wage-setting in the presence of migration, and the increased stabilization role of fiscal policy in a monetary union.

REFERENCES

Akerlof, G. (1970). The market for lemons: qualitative uncertainty and the market mechanism. *Quarterly Journal of Economics* 84:488–500.

Asdrubali, P., Sørensen, B. E., and Yosha, O. (1996). Channels of interstate risk sharing: United States 1963–1990. *Quarterly Journal of Economics* 111: 1081–110.

Diamond, P. A., and Mirrlees, J. (1971). Optimal taxation and public production. *American Economic Review* 61:8–17, 261–78.

Dornbusch, R. (1976). Expectations and exchange rate dynamics. *Journal of Political Economy* 84:1161–76.

Frenkel, J. A., Razin, A., and Sadka, E. (1991). *International Taxation in an Integrated World*. Massachusetts Institute of Technology Press.

Frenkel, J. A., Razin, A., and Yuen, C.-W. (1996). *Fiscal Policies and Growth in the World Economy*. Massachusetts Institute of Technology Press.

Helpman, E., and Sadka, E. (1979). The optimal financing of the government's budget: taxes, bonds or money. *American Economic Review* 69:152–60.

Johnson, H. G. (1953–54). Optimum tariffs and retaliation. *Review of Economic Studies* 22:142–53.

Lucas, R. A., Jr. (1988). On the mechanics of economic development. *Journal of Monetary Economics* 22:3–42.

Phelps, E. S. (1973). Inflation in the theory of public finance. *Swedish Journal of Economics* 75:67–82.

Razin, A., and Sadka, E. (1991). International tax competition and gains from tax harmonization. *Economics Letters* 37:69–76.

Rogoff, K. (1985). The optimal degree of commitment to an intermediate monetary target. *Quarterly Journal of Economics* 99:1169–89.

Sala-i-Martin, X., and Sachs, J. (1992). Fiscal federalism and optimum currency areas: evidence for Europe from the United States. In: *Establishing a Central Bank: Issues in Europe and Lessons from the U.S.*, ed. M. Canzoneri, P. Masson, and V. Grilli, pp. 195–219. Cambridge University Press.

PART I

International Mobility of Technology

CHAPTER 1

R&D and Productivity:
The International Connection

Elhanan Helpman

... we may say that certainly since the second half of the nineteenth century, the major source of economic growth in the developed countries has been science-based technology – in the electrical, internal combustion, electronic, nuclear, and biological fields, among others. [Kuznets, 1966, p. 10]

No matter where these technological and social innovations emerge – and they are largely the product of the developed countries – the economic growth of any given nation depends upon their adoption. ... Given this worldwide validity and transmissibility of modern additions to knowledge, the transnational character of this stock of knowledge and the dependence on it of any single nation in the course of its modern economic growth become apparent. [Kuznets, 1966, p. 287]

1   Introduction

Ninety-six percent of the world's research and development (R&D) is carried out in a handful of industrial countries. The remaining 4% is conducted in a large number of developing countries, though among them only 15 countries perform significant R&D (Coe, Helpman, and Hoffmaister, 1997). This raises the question whether or not the distribution of the benefits of R&D is as skewed as the distribution of expenditures.

Why should we be interested in this question? First, because R&D is an important activity. True, the industrial countries spend only 1.5–3% of gross domestic product (GDP) on R&D, but the rates of return on R&D are so high that even that investment can have a significant impact on output growth. Second, if the benefits of R&D are distributed across

Based on a lecture delivered to the 52nd Congress of the International Institute of Public Finance in Tel Aviv and on the Gilbert Lecture at the University of Rochester. I thank the National Science Foundation for financial support and Jane Trahan for editorial assistance.

17

countries as unevenly as the expenditures, disparities in income per capita will tend to widen. As it happens, these disparities are large already. Income per capita in the United States, for example, is 20 times higher than in many developing countries, and many more times higher than in some of the poorest countries of the world.

Patterns of capital accumulation tend to compensate for differences in income per capita. But R&D raises productivity, which in turn encourages capital accumulation. Therefore, large differences in R&D benefits counteract the equalizing effects of capital accumulation, and they can trigger cumulative processes that will greatly widen the disparities in income per capita (Grossman and Helpman, 1991, ch. 8).

2   Is R&D Important?

It is sometimes taken for granted that R&D is an important activity that drives some of the most dynamic sectors of modern economies. But this is by no means a universal attitude. Mankiw (1995), for example, has recently argued that one can understand economic growth by focusing on education and capital accumulation, disregarding the determinants of technological progress.[1] In my view, the evidence that inventive activities play a key role in modern economic growth is overwhelming. Education is, of course, very important, and so is capital accumulation, but they do not diminish the role of technological progress as a major force in expanding income per capita. The importance of inventive activities can be argued in three parts.

First, numerous historical studies have examined particular inventions and innovations and the role of technological progress more generally in the long-term evolution of national economies (e.g., Schmookler, 1966; Landes, 1969; Rosenberg, 1982; Mokyr, 1990). Historical studies are particularly relevant in this context, because it is often necessary to take a long-term view of technological improvements in order to understand their impact. The steam engine, which provided a reliable source of energy, is a case in point (von Tunzelmann, 1978). The dynamo, which enabled flexible use of electricity in manufacturing plants, is another (Du Boff, 1967; David, 1991). In both cases it took many years for the full economic impact of the new technology to work itself out. For example, it was not until 40 years after the invention of the dynamo that electrification substantially raised total factor productivity in U.S. manufacturing (David, 1991). It is therefore unfortunate that macroeconomic

---

[1] See, however, Klenow and Rodriguez-Clare (1997) for a criticism of this position within the frame of its own premises.

analysis too often loses sight of the relevant time frame for technological progress. What the detailed historical studies have taught us is that over the past 200 years inventions and innovations have played a central role in raising our standard of living (Rosenberg and Birdzall, 1986).

Second, studies have found high rates of return on R&D investment in the postwar period (Griliches, 1979). To begin with, these rates are high for individual companies. In the United States, for example, the average rate of return on R&D investment is more than twice the rate of return on investment in capital equipment. In some countries it is more than twice as high (Mohnen, 1992). But the social rate of return is higher still; spillovers across firms that operate in the same sector double the rate of return. And the rate of return rises further when measurement takes account of the spread of benefits from R&D-performing sectors to technologically related user sectors (Terleckyj, 1980; Scherer, 1982; Griliches, 1992; Mohnen, 1992). In those instances, the rates of return can exceed 100%. All in all, rates of return on R&D investment appear to be consistently high.

Third, studies of national economies have provided estimates of the extent to which R&D contributes to the total factor productivity of the performing countries (Coe and Helpman, 1995; Park, 1995; Hejazi and Safarian, 1996; Nadiri and Kim, 1996; Engelbrecht, 1997). Coe and Helpman (1995) have reported particularly high rates of return (e.g., 85% for small industrial countries). Their estimates most likely overstate the true rates of return, but they are not out of line with the findings in other studies that have taken intersectoral spillovers into account (e.g., Terleckyj, 1980; Scherer, 1982).[2]

Taken together, these three arguments suggest that inventive activities are very important indeed.

Having established that R&D is important, we shall now examine how R&D investment in one country affects other economies. For this purpose it is necessary to understand how countries interact with one another in the international marketplace and in what ways they become interdependent through such interactions.

3   International Links

National economies operate in a global system. Each country depends on its trade partners for its supply of consumer goods, intermediate

---

[2] Engelbrecht (1997) shows that these estimates are somewhat exaggerated, because they do not take into account differences in education. Park (1995) has also found lower rates of return. Finally, Nadiri and Kim (1996), who used a different approach, have reported much smaller rates of return for the G7 countries.

inputs, and machines and equipment. In addition, trade partners supply a country with markets in which it can sell its products and services. And trade partners sometimes adopt one another's manufacturing methods, modes of organization, product design, and product development.

The traditional literature originally emphasized gains from trade that stem from comparative-advantage-based specialization, where comparative advantage derives from technological differences or differences in factor endowments (Dixit and Norman, 1980). Later, economies of scale and variety choice were added to the sources of gains from trade (Helpman and Krugman, 1985). Finally, dynamic scale economies and learning mechanisms have been incorporated into the analysis (Grossman and Helpman, 1991, 1995). Whereas improvements in the terms of trade raise a country's total factor productivity, the theoretical literature has emphasized four additional channels through which the productivity levels of various countries are interrelated.

First, international trade enables a country to consume products and to use inputs that were developed and perfected in other countries, items that it cannot manufacture on its own. Such inputs may differ in quality from those available at home, or they may perform functions that complement domestic inputs. Second, international trade and direct foreign investment provide opportunities for cross-border learning in the normal course of business, requiring no special effort or investment of resources. This sort of learning applies to manufacturing techniques, organizational methods, and market conditions. In all of those cases the acquired knowledge improves domestic productivity. Third, international trade and investment provide opportunities for a deliberate effort to imitate foreign products and methods. Imitation is widespread in developing countries. But it is not free.[3] It is, for example, quite costly to reverse-engineer a sophisticated product. Nevertheless, this is an important channel through which technology transfer takes place. Some of the most rapidly growing economies have relied on it extensively, such as Japan in the immediate postwar era and, more recently, the newly industrializing countries of East Asia. Fourth, international economic relations that provide learning opportunities reduce innovation and imitation costs, making it easier to raise total factor productivity in the future.

Theory thus suggests two broad ways in which trade and investment contribute to total factor productivity: by making available products and services that embody foreign knowledge, and by providing foreign technologies and other types of knowledge that would otherwise be unavail-

---

[3] See Mansfield, Schwartz, and Wagner (1980), who have reported that imitation costs exceed half the value of innovation costs.

able or very costly to acquire. Productivity-transmission channels of this sort are particularly important for developing countries, but they also play a significant role in industrial countries.[4]

To conclude, international trade and direct foreign investment have the potential to carry productivity gains via flows of goods and knowledge across national borders. If such flows prove to be important in practice, then the existing patterns of R&D investment are not producing equally skewed patterns of benefits. It is therefore of value to know the size of such international spillovers.

4   Productivity Growth and Stocks of Knowledge

To estimate the extent of international R&D spillovers we need to identify a variable that will correctly reflect their influence. Total factor productivity (TFP) seems to be particularly suited for this purpose. Simple measures of TFP do not adjust, however, for the quality of capital and labor, and both are important. Unfortunately, such adjustments are difficult to make, especially for large samples of countries. As a result, most studies have attempted to explain variations in simple measures of TFP, but have included available proxies for human capital among the explanatory variables.

The relationships among productivity, education, trade, and R&D have been studied for almost 100 countries. About 20% of them are industrial, and the rest are developing. They vary greatly in terms of productivity growth, R&D investment, levels of education, trade, and direct foreign investment.

Table 1.1 shows some of these differences for three industrial countries and four developing countries, as well as averages for developing countries on two continents: Asia and Africa. Over a period of 20 years, from 1971 to 1990, TFP increased by 10% in the United States, by 30% in Ireland, and by 70% in Japan. Ghana, on the other hand, suffered a decline of 6% in TFP. In other words, the efficiency with which Ghana's economy was able to utilize resources declined by 6%. The fate of Zaire was even worse; its TFP declined by 36%. But two of the remaining developing countries in the table did extremely well: Mauritius doubled its TFP, and Taiwan increased its TFP by 87%.

---

[4] According to Lockwood (1954), direct learning played an important role in Japan when it opened up to the rest of the world in the second half of the nineteenth century. It also played an important role in South Korea during the early stages of its recent industrialization, as reported in the case studies by Rhee, Ross-Lauson, and Purcell (1984). Finally, Irwin and Klenow (1994) have reported significant international spillovers in the modern semiconductor industry.

Table 1.1. *Rates of growth, 1971–90*

Country	TFP (%)	R&D stock (%)
United States	10	100
Ireland	30	270
Japan	70	320
Zaire	−36	
Ghana	−6	
Taiwan	87	
Mauritius	100	
Africa	2	
Asia	31	

Source: Coe and Helpman (1995, table 1) for the first three rows; Coe, Helpman, and Hoffmaister (1997, table 1) for the rest.

For the industrial countries, the table also shows rates of increase in the stock of R&D investment (i.e., a cumulative measure of how much R&D a country carried out over those years). This stock doubled in the United States, more than tripled in Japan, and almost tripled in Ireland.

More generally, among the industrial countries Japan had the fastest rate of productivity growth. It also experienced the highest growth in the stock of R&D investment among the G7 economies (Coe and Helpman, 1995). Among a group of 77 developing countries for which calculations were made, about half had very small changes in TFP over those years. But for about a dozen countries, TFP increased by more than 50%. In contrast, another dozen countries suffered serious declines in TFP over the same 20 years (Coe et al., 1997). And countries in Asia did, on average, much better than countries in Africa. As shown in Table 1.1, developing countries in Africa hardly made any productivity gains during those years, whereas developing countries in Asia gained 31%.

Table 1.2 reports a measure of openness to foreign trade and a measure of human capital for the four developing countries in Table 1.1. The former is represented by imports of machinery and equipment from industrial countries as a share of the developing country's GDP, and the latter by the secondary-school enrollment ratio (the ratio of students in secondary schools to the population in the relevant age group). Evidently, Taiwan and Mauritius, which experienced high rates of productivity growth, had both more exposure to foreign trade and a better-

Table 1.2. *Averages, 1971–90*

Country	Import share (%)	Secondary enrollment (%)
Zaire	5	24
Ghana	4	36
Taiwan	10	47
Mauritius	8	46

Source: Coe, Helpman, and Hoffmaister (1997, table 1).

educated labor force than did Zaire and Ghana, which suffered declines in TFP.

The differences in degrees of openness and secondary-school enrollment ratios seen in Table 1.2 are not particularly extreme within the sample of 77 developing countries studied by Coe et al. (1997). In their sample, the lowest import share of machinery and equipment was 1% for India. The highest was 38% for Singapore. Whereas Singapore is an outlier, India is not; a number of countries had import shares of 2%. In fact, about half the countries had import shares that did not exceed 5%, and only 13 had import shares larger than 10%. Considerable variation also existed in the secondary-school enrollment ratios, whose sample average was 31%. Whereas some countries, such as Jordan, had enrollment ratios in excess of 70%, a number of African countries, such as Chad, had enrollment ratios of less than 10%.

Using this sort of data, one can estimate the impacts of education, trade, direct foreign investment, and R&D on TFP, including cross-country effects.

5 Quantitative Assessment I

What do these estimates show? To begin with, education has a significant impact on TFP. Estimates from macroeconomic data only confirm known findings from more detailed microeconomic studies. But after controlling for education, R&D investment shows up as a potent force for productivity growth, the more so for countries that are more involved in foreign trade and investment. Countries that perform R&D reap large benefits from this investment. But a fraction of these benefits also spills over to other countries.

Table 1.3 shows estimates for the elasticity of TFP with respect to domestic and foreign R&D capital stocks; all the estimates are positive

Table 1.3. *Elasticity of TFP with respect to R&D stocks*

Country	Domestic	Foreign[a]
G7	0.234	$0.294 m_{GS}$
Small industrial	0.078	$0.294 m_{GS}$
Developing		$0.837 m_{ME}$

[a] m_{GS} represents imports of goods and services as a fraction of GDP; m_{ME} represents imports of machinery and equipment from industrial countries as a fraction of GDP.
Source: Coe and Helpman [1995, table 3, col. (iii)] for the first two rows; Coe, Helpman, and Hoffmaister [1997, table 2, col. (x)] for the third row.

and significant. The elasticity with respect to foreign R&D capital is proportional to import shares – the import share of goods and services for the industrial countries, and the import share of machinery and equipment for developing countries. Because developing countries engage in little R&D activity, the impact of their R&D on TFP has not been estimated.

For the purpose of estimating these elasticities, domestic R&D capital stocks were constructed by accumulating real R&D investment, allowing for depreciation (Griliches, 1979). Foreign R&D capital stocks were constructed as the trade-weighted average of trade partners' domestic R&D capital stocks, using import shares as weights. Evidently, the elasticities with respect to domestic R&D capital stocks are large. This elasticity also appears to be much larger in the G7 countries than in the smaller industrial countries. Elasticities with respect to foreign R&D capital stocks also appear to be large. A G7 country that has an import share of goods and services of 25% (such as Canada in 1990) has a foreign R&D elasticity of 0.075, which is about the same as the elasticity with respect to the domestic R&D capital stocks of the smaller industrial countries.[5] On the other hand, a developing country that has

---

[5] An import share of 25% is not unusual for the industrial countries. West Germany and the United Kingdom had somewhat larger import shares in 1990, and a number of the smaller industrial countries (such as Ireland) had import shares more than twice as large. As noted before, Engelbrecht [1997, table 1, col. (iv)] reported somewhat lower elasticities for the industrial countries, after controlling for differences in education levels. His elasticities of TFP with respect to the domestic R&D capital stock were 0.237 for the G7

an import share of machinery and equipment of 7% (the group's average) enjoys a TFP elasticity with respect to foreign R&D capital of close to 0.06, which is substantial.

These estimates imply that the own rate of return on R&D investment is about 120% in G7 countries and about 85% in the smaller industrial countries (Coe and Helpman, 1995). Because the calculation of these rates of return is sensitive to the initial stocks of R&D, however, and these stocks are very imperfectly estimated, one should treat these findings with great caution. Nevertheless, they do suggest that R&D investment is highly profitable (at the national level) in the industrial countries.

These estimates also suggest that there are substantial international R&D spillovers. In addition to the domestic rate of return, R&D investment in G7 countries produces an extra 30% return by raising TFP in the smaller industrial countries. And particularly encouraging is the finding that developing countries also gain from R&D performed in the industrial countries.

We conclude that a country's TFP depends not only on how much R&D it does but also on how much R&D is done in other countries with which it engages in trade and investment. The larger a country's exposure to the international economy, the more it gains from R&D activities in other countries.

Two channels appear to be major carriers of these cross-country benefits: international trade and direct foreign investment. At the moment, we know more about the role of trade than about the role of direct foreign investment. But ongoing research undoubtedly will provide better information on the relative importance of these transmission mechanisms.

6   Quantitative Assessment II

Elasticity estimates of the type reported in Table 1.3 can be evaluated in more than one way. We have thus far gauged their importance by examining implied rates of return on R&D investment. Those calculations are incomplete, however, because they do not take into account a variety of changes that are induced by higher levels of R&D, such as shifts in pat-

countries and 0.055 for the smaller industrial countries, and his elasticity with respect to the foreign R&D capital stock was $0.220\,m_{GS}$. On the other hand, Hejazi and Safarian [1996, table 3, col. (a)], who added direct foreign investment flows from the United States as an additional channel of international R&D spillovers, reported (for the industrial countries) similar elasticities with respect to the domestic R&D capital stock and higher elasticities with respect to the foreign R&D capital stock.

terns of capital accumulation and in terms of trade. An alternative way to evaluate the significance of these elasticities is to embody them in a fully fledged econometric model of the world economy and to trace out by means of this model the dynamic implications of an increase in R&D investment. This sort of evaluation has been carried out by Bayoumi, Coe, and Helpman (1996) using the MULTIMOD model of the International Monetary Fund (IMF).

MULTIMOD consists of 13 linked econometric models that cover the entire globe. Bayoumi et al. (1996) used a version that dropped the oil-exporting developing countries. The remaining coverage consisted of one model for each of the G7 countries, one model for the remaining industrial countries, and four regional models for non-oil-exporting developing countries: those in Africa, those in the Western Hemisphere, the Asian newly industrialized economies (NIEs) (Hong Kong, Korea, Singapore, and Taiwan), and the remaining Asian developing countries (Bayoumi, Hewitt, and Symanski, 1995).

Some features of MULTIMOD make it particularly suitable for a long-run analysis of economic growth.[6] First, output is determined by a standard production function for labor and capital. Second, consumption is derived in a consistent way from a reasonable structure of preferences (of the Blanchard type), implying that in the long run consumption is proportional to wealth. In addition, care is taken to include in "wealth" the expected stream of labor and capital income, as predicted by the model. As a result, expectations are self-fulfilling in the long run. Third, the investment function is derived from the theory of investment in the presence of costs of adjustment. Fourth, countries are linked via trade with endogenous adjustments to the terms of trade. Finally, although the developing countries face balance-of-payments constraints, the industrial countries do not, and the world interest rate is determined so as to equate world savings with world investment.

The IMF's version of MULTIMOD treats TFP as exogenous. Bayoumi et al. (1996) changed this feature by incorporating into the model a set of equations, estimated by Coe and Helpman (1995) and Coe et al. (1997), that provide linkage among TFP, trade, and domestic and foreign R&D capital stocks. These equations have the R&D elasticities reported in Table 1.3. Using that augmented version of MULTIMOD, they traced out the dynamic responses of all countries and regions to increases in R&D investment.

It takes a long time to reach a steady state in a neoclassical model,

---

[6] MULTIMOD has a number of Keynesian features in the short run that appear to me to be unreliable for predictions of short-run growth.

Table 1.4. *United States raises R&D by 0.5% of GDP: long-run rates of growth*

Country	TFP (%)	GDP (%)	Consumption (%)
United States	7.3	9.5	7.1
Industrial	1.7	2.8	4.0
Developing	2.3	3.4	3.3

Source: Bayoumi, Coe, and Helpman (1996, table 1, last column).

and MULTIMOD is no exception. Expansion of R&D investment, which is the main focus of our attention, takes about 80 years to reach its full impact. But the fact of the matter is that the impact is large early on and very small in the last phases of the growth process. In particular, about half of the quantitative effects are obtained after 15 years (Bayoumi et al., 1996). In what follows, we focus on the long run.

Table 1.4 shows the simulated effects of an increase in R&D investment in the United States of 0.5% of GDP; the new level of investment is maintained throughout. This raises the U.S. TFP by 7.3%. But it also raises TFP by 1.7% in the industrial countries and by 2.3% in the developing countries. So, clearly, other countries stand to gain much from an expansion of U.S. R&D. There exists, however, an additional multiplier effect. As TFP rises, it becomes more profitable to invest in machines, equipment, and structures. This additional investment flow raises the capital stock, thereby raising output. As a result, GDP rises, not only because the economy becomes more productive but also because it invests more. The induced accumulation of capital raises output growth by about one-third of the rise in TFP. Therefore output in the United States rises in total by 9.5%, in the industrial countries by 2.8%, and in the developing countries by 3.4%. Finally, consumption rises by 7.1% in the United States, by 4.0% in the other industrial countries, and by 3.3% in the developing countries. Evidently, consumption rises by less than output in the United States and by more than output in the other countries. This difference reflects terms-of-trade movements. As U.S. output expands in response to larger R&D investment, its terms of trade deteriorate, while the terms of trade for its trade partners improve. A comparison of the last two columns in Table 1.4 reveals that changes in the terms of trade have lesser effects on the developing countries than on the industrial countries.

Table 1.5 shows the changes in TFP, output, and consumption that

Table 1.5. *Industrial countries raise R&D by 0.5% of GDP: long run rates of growth*

Countries	TFP (%)	GDP (%)	Consumption (%)
Industrial	13.2	17.5	16.1
Developing	7.6	10.6	13.0

Source: Bayoumi, Coe, and Helpman (1996, table 1, last column).

result from a coordinated expansion of R&D by 0.5% of GDP in all industrial countries. Now the quantitative impact is very large indeed. TFP rises by 13.2% in the industrial countries and by 7.6% in the developing countries. After accounting for the induced accumulation of capital, output rises by 17.5% in the industrial countries and by 10.6% in the developing countries. Clearly, the output multipliers for R&D investment are large, with major international ramifications. And again, consumption rises by less than output in the R&D-expanding countries and by more than output in their trade partners (consumption rises by 16.1% in the industrial countries and by 13.0% in the developing countries). Now developing countries make a significantly larger gain in consumption than in output as a result of improvement in their terms of trade, whereas the industrial countries gain in consumption significantly less than in output as a result of the deterioration in their terms of trade.

7   Conclusions

It is apparent from the reported estimates that R&D is an important activity that has a major impact on the performing countries as well as on their trade partners. We may not yet have precise estimates of these impacts, both because of difficulties with available data and because of some unsettled methodological issues. But it is safe to draw a tentative conclusion, namely, that these effects are important and that there exist significant cross-country links that are driven by foreign trade and investment. Because foreign trade and investment are also important for a variety of other reasons, international productivity links that are driven by R&D make them all the more important. This means that we have reason to be optimistic about recent trends toward tighter integration of national economies. And it means that technological developments in industrial countries that have been perceived by many to be detrimental to the developing countries may in fact be good for them after all.

REFERENCES

Bayoumi, T., Coe, D. T., and Helpman, E. (1996). R&D spillovers and global growth. CEPR discussion paper 1467, Centre for Economic Policy Research, London. Forthcoming in the *Journal of International Ecomomics*.

Bayoumi, T., Hewitt, D., and Symanski, S. (1995). MULTIMOD simulations of the effect on developing countries of decreasing military spending. In: *North-South Linkages and International Macroeconomic Policy*, ed. D. Currie and D. Vines. Cambridge University Press.

Coe, D. T., and Helpman, E. (1995). International R&D spillovers. *European Economic Review* 39:859–87.

Coe, D. T., Helpman, E., and Hoffmaister, A. W. (1997). North–south R&D spillovers. *Economic Journal* 107:134–49.

David, P. (1991). Computer and dynamo: the modern productivity paradox in a not-too-distant mirror. In: *Technology and Productivity: The Challenge for Economic Policy*, pp. 315–48. Paris: Organization for Economic Cooperation and Development.

Dixit, A., and Norman, V. (1980). *Theory of International Trade*. Cambridge University Press.

Du Boff, R. B. (1967). The introduction of electric power in American manufacturing. *Economic History Review* 20:509–18.

Engelbrecht, H. J. (1997). International R&D spillovers, human capital and productivity in OECD economies: an empirical investigation. *European Economic Review* 41:1479–88.

Griliches, Z. (1979). Issues in assessing the contribution of research and development in productivity growth. *Bell Journal of Economics* 10: 92–116.

Griliches, Z. (1992). The search for R&D spillovers. *Scandinavian Journal of Economics* 94:29–47.

Grossman, G. M., and Helpman, E. (1991). *Innovation and Growth in the Global Economy*. Massachusetts Institute of Technology Press.

Grossman, G. M., and Helpman, E. (1994). Endogenous innovation in the theory of growth. *Journal of Economic Perspectives* 8:23–44.

Grossman, G. M., and Helpman, E. (1995). Technology and trade. In: *Handbook of International Economics*, vol. 3, ed. G. M. Grossman and K. Rogoff, pp. 1279–337. Amsterdam: Elsevier.

Hejazi, W., and Safarian, E. (1996). Trade, investment and United States R&D spillovers. Working paper 65. Toronto: Canadian Institute for Advanced Research.

Helpman, E., and Krugman, P. R. (1985). *Market Structure and Foreign Trade*. Massachusetts Institute of Technology Press.

Irwin, D., and Klenow, P. (1994). Learning-by-doing spillovers in the semiconductor industry. *Journal of Political Economy* 102:1200–27.

Klenow, P., and Rodriguez-Clare, A. (1997). The neoclassical revival in growth economics: has it gone too far? *NBER Macroeconomic Annual 1997* 12:73–103.

Kuznets, S. (1966). *Modern Economic Growth*. New Haven: Yale University Press.

Landes, D. (1969). *The Unbound Prometheus*. Cambridge University Press.

Lockwood, W. (1954). *The Economic Development of Japan: Growth and Structural Change. 1868–1938*. Princeton University Press.

Mankiw, G. (1995). The growth of nations. *Brookings Papers on Economic Activity* 25:275–326.

Mansfield, E. Schwartz, M., and Wagner, S. (1980). Imitation costs and patents: an empirical study. *Economic Journal* 91:907–18.

Mohnen, P. (1992). *The Relationship Between R&D and Productivity Growth in Canada and Other Major Industrial Countries*. Ottawa: Economic Council of Canada.

Mokyr, J. (1990). *The Lever of Riches*. Oxford University Press.

Nadiri, M. I., and Kim, S. (1996). International R&D spillovers, trade and productivity in major OECD countries. NBER working paper 5801. Washington, DC: National Bureau of Economic Research.

Park, W. G. (1995). International R&D spillovers and OECD economic growth. *Economic Inquiry* 33:571–91.

Rhee, Y. W., Ross-Lauson, B., and Purcell, G. (1984). *Korea's Competitive Edge: Managing Entry into World Markets*. Baltimore: Johns Hopkins University Press.

Rosenberg, N. (1982). *Inside the Black Box*. Cambridge University Press.

Rosenberg, N., and Birdzall, L. (1986). *How the West Grew Rich*. New York: Basic Books.

Scherer, F. M. (1982). Inter-industry technology flows and productivity growth. *Review of Economics and Statistics* 64:627–34.

Schmookler, J. (1966). *Innovation and Economic Growth*. Cambridge, MA: Harvard University Press.

Terleckyj, N. (1980). Direct and indirect effects of industrial research and development on the productivity growth of industries. In: *New Developments in Productivity Measurement and Analysis*, ed. J. Kendrick and B. Vaccara, pp. 359–77. University of Chicago Press.

von Tunzelmann, G. N. (1978). *Steam Power and British Industrialization to 1860*. Oxford: Clarendon Press.

PART II

Capital Flows and
Exchange-Rate Misalignment

CHAPTER 2

International Implications
of German Unification

Hans-Werner Sinn

1   Introduction

The unification of Germany has not been solely an internal affair; it has accelerated the unification of Europe as a whole, and its economic consequences have severely affected the rest of Europe, if not the rest of the world. The acceleration of European unification has occurred because of the widely held belief that only a tight integration of Germany into the European Community would make it possible to control and influence the economic power center thought to have been created by German unification. Nicholas Ridley, the British secretary of commerce, who had publicly expressed the opposite view that European integration was a German trick aimed at controlling the rest of Europe, had to resign immediately after making his statement. The official policy of Europe's governments was for, not against, tighter integration of Germany.

The unification of Germany has also had a very direct effect on the Maastricht treaty. When Chancellor Kohl and President Mitterand announced in early 1990 that there would be a government conference in Maastricht, Mitterand also promised his support for the unification of Germany. That was a surprising step, given that in late 1989 Mitterand had tried his utmost to prevent that unification. He had tried hard to stabilize the East German regime and to persuade Gorbachev to veto the unification, but without success. It is an open secret that

This study was prepared for the 52nd Congress of the International Institute of Public Finance in Tel Aviv, Israel, August 26–29, 1996, and revised in May 1997 with the then-available data. The author gratefully acknowledges careful research assistance and useful comments by Helge Berger, Holger Feist, Ronnie Schöb, Ulrich Sch ten, Claudio Thum, and Alfons Weichenrieder.

Germany had to buy the consent of France by sacrificing the deutsche mark (DM).

Ironically, the ease with which the unification of Germany has swept away the political barriers to a European currency union contrasts sharply with the economic obstacles that unification may have created for such a union. The economic unification of Germany probably has been the greatest shock to the world economy since Reagan's tax reform in 1981. Germany has been soaking up resources from all over the world to feed the eastern Germans, who are still a long way from earning their own living, and as a result the exchange-rate volatility has been substantial.

This study describes how Germany and its trading partners were affected by these events, compares the German-unification shock with the shock created by Reagan's policies, and analyzes the impacts of the German-unification shock on interest rates, exchange rates, and the performance of the European monetary system (EMS). An attempt is made, focusing on considerations of purchasing-power parity, to determine which currencies have survived the German-unification shock in sufficiently good condition for them to enter into a currency union, as contrasted with those currencies that need to be realigned before entering. Arguably, the question whether or not the exchange rates between the deutsche mark and other currencies are in line with purchasing-power parities is more important for the decision about creating a monetary union than are the debt criteria whose importance has been overly stressed in the public policy debate.

This study also comments on the widely held belief that a European currency union would cause problems similar to those caused by the German currency union.

Because so much has already been written about these issues of German unification, Europe, and the exchange markets, this study cannot claim full originality. The basic point, that the revaluation of the deutsche mark was caused by German unification, has been made by various authors,[1] and there have even been allusions to Reagan's tax reforms in this context by Branson (1993, 1994) and Sinn and Sinn (1992, pp. 44–51, esp. p. 51). However, these issues seem sufficiently important to justify a synthesis and broader analysis using the statistical information available in 1997. This is particularly so as the realization of the Maastricht treaty

---

[1] Cf., e.g., Issing (1992), Svensson (1994), or Deutsche Bundesbank, *Monatsbericht*, Mai 1996, p. 55.

approaches, and decisions about the countries joining the union will have to be made soon.

2 Thirsty as a Giant

Although Germany is the largest country in the European Community (EC), with one-quarter of its population, it is not a giant. Russia's population is 80% larger; Turkey will have reached Germany's population within a decade; China's population would make almost 15 Germanies. However, Germany is as thirsty as a giant, because eastern Germany absorbs far more resources than it produces.

Figure 2.1 shows the development of eastern German economic absorption since the unification occurred. The extent of absorption has more than doubled in the 6 years that have elapsed, and currently its rate is still about 50% larger than the eastern German gross domestic product (GDP). In 1996 the eastern German economy absorbed DM 235 billion more in terms of consumption, investment, and public expenditure on goods and services than it produced. About one-third of the excess absorption stemmed from private capital imports into the eastern German economy, with two-thirds being public transfers, primarily for unemployment benefits, pensions, and public infrastructure investment. The total amount of public funds pumped into the eastern German economy in the first 6 years since unification approximates DM 800 billion. This sum excludes the deficit of the Treuhandanstalt, the government-controlled resolution trust for the industries of the old *Länder*. If the Treuhand deficit is added, the total sum of public-resource transfers increases to about DM 1,000 billion.

These sums are truly large, especially if they are compared with the capital imports for other eastern countries. From 1990 through 1995, the accumulated net inflow of capital into *all* other former Comecon countries amounted to no more than DM 115 billion,[2] and the accumulated inflow of direct investment was only about DM 60 billion.[3] In 1995 the net per-capita import of resources into eastern Germany was more than

---

[2] Estimation based on European Bank for Reconstruction and Development, *Transition Report*, 1995, London, Annex 11.1, and European Bank for Reconstruction and Development, *Transition Report Update*, London, April 1996. For some smaller eastern economies the data for 1990 and 1991 are not available.

[3] UN/ECE, *East-West Investment News*, Summer 1996 (2). European Bank for Reconstruction and Development, *Transition Report*, 1994, London, p. 123. The foreign-direct-investment figure excludes Armenia, Azerbaijan, Georgia, Kyrgyzstan, Turkmenistan, Uzbekistan, and Tajikistan.

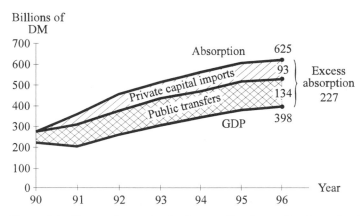

Figure 2.1. Excess absorption in the new *Länder* and its financing. The new *Länder*'s nominal GDP is augmented by net imports to calculate absorption. Net imports include not only the trade deficits with foreign countries but also those with the old *Länder* (former Federal Republic of Germany). It therefore can be interpreted as the excess absorption of the new *Länder*. Net public transfers are measured as the sum of the transfers to the new *Länder* made by central and local governments and include special subsidy programs and social insurance. The deficit of the Treuhandanstalt is not included. The transfers are measured net of taxes and fees from the new *Länder*. The residual of excess absorption and public transfers is private capital imports (and private transfers). Excess-absorption data for 1995 and 1996 are estimates. Sources: Bundesbank, *Monatsbericht*, October 1996, Frankfurt/Main, p. 19; Deutsches Institut für Wirtschaftsforschung, *DIW Wochenbericht*, 27–28/95 and 30/95, Berlin 1995, pp. 464 and 524, and additional information; Statistisches Bundesamt, *Fachserie* 18, Reihe 1.2, Konten und Standardtabellen, Vorbericht 1995, Wiesbaden, p. 76.

160 times the per-capita import of resources into all other former Eastern-bloc countries, and by 1995 direct investment per capita was about 100 times as large in eastern Germany as in the other eastern European countries.[4]

The public transfers that explain two-thirds of eastern Germany's

---

[4] The "net import of resources" is the current-account deficit, and direct investment is greenfield investment plus foreign acquisitions. For the purpose of this comparison, eastern Germany is treated like a separate country; i.e., the imports include those from western Germany. Sources: *DIW Wochenbericht*, 3/95, table 1; *Jahresabschluß der Treuhandanstalt*, 31 December 1994; UN/ECE, *Statistical Survey of Recent Trends in Foreign Investment in East European Countries*, November 1995, p. 72. Cf. also Sinn and Weichenrieder (1997).

excess absorption reflect Germany's current problems. East Germans were promised the West German living standard, but the naive belief that the promise could be kept simply by raising eastern German wages to the western level has led to the virtual destruction of the eastern German manufacturing industry. Four out of five jobs that were available in manufacturing before unification have disappeared, without being replaced. Manufacturing output has declined by two-thirds and is recouping only gradually. Union wages are now basically at the western German level, but unemployment benefits, social aid, and public pensions are the expensive consequences for the German government budget.

Most of the public funds involved in such transfers have been borrowed by the German government. Chancellor Kohl had made something like President Bush's "read my lips" promise in 1990, excluding tax increases as a means of financing unification. As a consequence, there have been no major tax increases in Germany since the time of unification. On the contrary, in 1993 the so-called location-preservation law (*Standortsicherungsgesetz*) was passed, and that implied a substantial reduction of business taxes. As a result of the divergence between public expenditure and revenue, the German public debt jumped from DM 928.8 billion in 1989 to DM 1,994.5 billion by the end of 1995, and the ratio of debt to GDP has climbed from 41.8% to 57.7%. By the end of 1996 the ratio had grown to 61%, violating even the Maastricht criterion (Figure 2.2).

The public and private resources that Germany needed for its new *Länder* could, in principle, have been financed by belt tightening (i.e., with increased private savings). However, that did not happen. German households obviously knew little about Ricardian equivalence and did not react to the foreseeable future tax burden that the public borrowing was likely to necessitate (i.e., they did not curtail their consumption levels).[5]

So the necessary resources in fact had to come from abroad. In 1989 Germany had a current-account surplus of DM 107 billion, which was then the largest current-account surplus in the world.[6] As Figure 2.3 shows, with unification that situation changed rapidly. From 1991 onward

---

[5] Alternatively, they may have been Ricardians with more sophisticated expectations. For example, they may have expected that the service of public debt would be financed with public-expenditure cuts, rather than tax increases, or they may have expected a future increase in the value-added tax and thus substituted away from expensive future consumption to cheap present consumption.

[6] One-third of that surplus (DM 36.9 billion) consisted of voluntary transfers to other countries, and two-thirds of net capital exports.

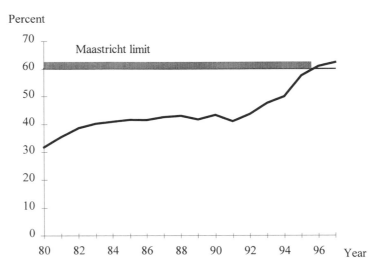

Figure 2.2. German debt–GDP ratio for Germany's public sector. Treuhand debt is included starting in 1995; 1996 and 1997 are OECD projections. Sources: Bundesbank, *Monatsberichte* (various issues), Frankfurt/Main, table "Verschuldung der öffentlichen Hand"; Statistisches Bundesamt, *Statistisches Jahrbuch* (various issues), table "Volkswirtschaftliche Gesamtrechnung"; OECD, *Economic Outlook* 59, annex of table 61.

the current account has been persistently negative, and Germany has turned into a capital-importing country. The change in the current account relative to the year 1989 was about DM 160 billion, which just happens to equal the amount of the current flow of public funds from western to eastern Germany.

The resources that Germany needed came primarily from the other EC countries, which are Germany's major trading partners. In 1991 they financed two-thirds of the current-account deficit, and in 1995 nearly all of it. Figure 2.4 illustrates the situation.

Despite being a net importer of resources, Germany has positive current accounts with some countries, in particular with the United States. In 1995, Germany's current-account surplus with the United States was about DM 17 billion. The United States, too, has been in a situation that has required a substantial amount of resource absorption, and there are in fact startling similarities to the state of affairs following German unification. To understand the situation of the United States, we need to look back to the year 1981.

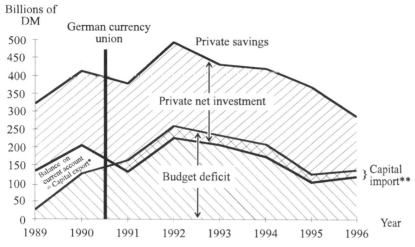

Figure 2.3. The squeeze on the current-account balance. The government budget deficit includes the borrowing for the German Unity Fund and the deficit of the GDR budget. Until 1994 the government budget deficit included the net borrowing and the sales proceeds of the Treuhandanstalt. The debt of the Treuhandanstalt was transferred to the Erblastentilgungsfonds in 1995. Thus the 1995 figure includes the change in the net debt of the Erblastentilgungsfonds. Sources: Bundesbank, *Monatsberichte* (various issues), Frankfurt/Main; Statistisches Bundesamt, *Volkswirtschaftliche Gesamtrechnung*, Fachserie 18, Reihe 3; Deutsches Institut für Wirtschaftsforschung, *DIW Wochenbericht*, 46/91, 34/92, 46/94, 7/96, Berlin; Treuhandanstalt, various press releases; information from Bundesanstalt für vereinigungsbedingte Sonderaufgaben of July 19, 1996.

3   Reagan's Tax Reforms: A Historically Similar Experiment

In 1981, President Reagan persuaded the U.S. Congress to pass a tax-reform package that may well have been the most radical in U.S. history. Despite the occasional hope for a Laffer-curve effect, the tax cuts associated with that reform brought about a rapid increase in the U.S. federal budget deficit that, over a period of 5 years, was estimated to amount to some $160 billion (Sinn, 1984).

Even more important than the budget effects may have been the incentive effects of the so-called accelerated cost-recovery system (ACRS), which was the most important part of the reform package. The ACRS implied a dramatic shortening of the write-off periods for invest-

Figure 2.4. Germany's current account, the EC, and the rest of the world. The graph shows Germany's current-account surplus against all states that joined the EC up to the end of 1994 and against all other countries. The sum of the balances defines Germany's whole current-account surplus. The downward-sloping curve through the origin has a slope of −1. Points on this curve are characterized by a German current-account surplus of zero. Source: Bundesbank, *Zahlungsbilanzstatistik*, table "Leistungsbilanz nach Ländern und Ländergruppen," various volumes, Frankfurt/Main.

ment projects and provided a massive investment stimulus. Combined with the investment tax credit, the stimulus was approximately equal to an immediate write-off. With tax rates in the neighborhood of 50%, as they were at the time, the switch from economic depreciation to an immediate write-off implied that investment projects could survive a doubling of the rate of interest without becoming unprofitable. In other words, the investment demand curve was shifted upward to twice its original level. The reform actually carried out did not quite have such a dramatic effect, because some acceleration of tax depreciation had previously been allowed. Nevertheless, it is estimated (Sinn, 1984) that the long-run cumulative effect of the ACRS on U.S. capital imports was about $1,000–1,500 billion. Reagan's tax reforms of 1981 have partly been reversed by the subsequent reforms of 1986, but they have had long-lasting effects on the trade relationships between the United States and the rest of the world.[7]

U.S. interest rates rose sharply after the recession of 1982 and reached a historical peak in 1994. The implication was that the dollar became a very attractive investment currency and climbed to a peak value of DM 3.45 in February 1985. The U.S. current account, which before the 1981 reform had been balanced, turned strongly negative. In the first 5 years after the reform, the accumulated capital import of the United States was $390 billion more than in the 5 years before the reform, and by the end of 1995 it had increased to $1,320 billion, about what had been predicted.

Undoubtedly, the 1981 U.S. tax reform was a major shock to the world economy, and the shock waves were felt everywhere. Whereas foreign exporters were happy about the business they could do with a high value of the dollar, debtors all over the world were running into problems because they had to pay higher interest rates. In Europe, the construction industries collapsed, and in all likelihood even the world debt crisis was triggered off by the rising interest rates.[8]

The resource demand that the German unification produced for the world economy was not very different from that created by Reagan's tax reforms. Despite the fact that the two events had their own idiosyncratic causes, the common elements were the sharp increase in the public budget deficit and a special stimulus for private investment. In the United States, that stimulus came from the ACRS; in Germany it came from the new investment opportunities in the new *Länder*.

Surprisingly, even the magnitudes of the resource demands for the two events were rather similar. In the first 5 years after German unification, the accumulated effect on the German current account amounted to a differential capital import of $338 billion relative to the 5 years before unification. This amount is of the same order of magnitude as the $390 billion that is the measure of the accumulated impact of Reagan's reforms in the 5 years after 1981. Figure 2.5 illustrates the striking similarity in the magnitudes of U.S. and German capital imports following the two different historical events.

---

[7] A comparison of the 1981 and 1986 reforms has been published (Sinn, 1988).

[8] During the 1970s, the developing countries had been able to borrow at negative real rates of interest. After the U.S. tax reform, the real rates jumped by 5 percentage points to a level of about 4% which many developing countries were unable to bear. Starting with Mexico in 1982, many of them declared their inability to service their debts. See Sinn (1993) for details.

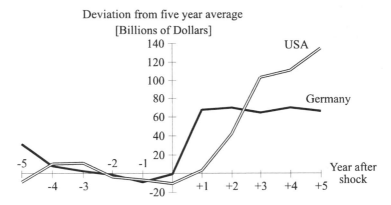

Figure 2.5. Net resource imports following two shocks: Reagan's tax reforms and German unification. The additional net resource import after the shock has been calculated from current-account data. The curves have been adjusted so that the average in the 5 years before the shock is zero. In the United States, the shock was in 1981; in Germany, the shock was in 1990. Sources: OECD, *Main Economic Indicators: Historical Statistics, 1969–1988*, 1990, p. 91; OECD, *Economic Outlook*, July 1996, pp. A40 and A53.

4   The Revaluation of the Deutsche Mark and the European Currency Crisis

The unification of Germany, too, was a shock, and it likewise produced a crisis – not a world debt crisis, but a crisis for the EMS. The high public and private demands for capital increased German interest rates relative to those in other countries, increased the deutsche mark's attractiveness as an investment currency, and created strong appreciation pressure. Initially, the EMS prevented the deutsche mark from appreciating after unification. Despite the Bundesbank's offer to revalue the deutsche mark within the system, a political decision was made to defend the existing exchange rates. However, the EMS was only temporarily able to prevent the flood of capital that had been attracted. Economic forces were stronger than political will. Only 2 years after unification, the EMS broke down, and the deutsche mark became free to revalue.

The following figures show what happened. Figure 2.6 shows the development of the German interest rates and those in the other EMS countries. Before unification, there had been persistent interest differentials between Germany and the other EMS countries of 400 base points and more. Those differentials shrank rapidly after unification. The

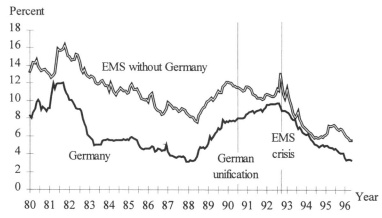

Figure 2.6. Daily interest rates: Germany vs. EMS. The broken curve shows the weighted daily interest rates of the EMS countries without Germany. Weights are based on 1980 GDP figures. EMS countries include Austria, Belgium, Denmark, Spain, France, Italy, Ireland, The Netherlands, Portugal, and the United Kingdom. Because of lack of data, some country series start later than 1980. Weights have been adjusted accordingly. Sources: Bundesbank, *Monatsberichte* (various issues), Frankfurt/Main, Table IV.4; letter from Bundesbank of July 11, 1996; OECD, *National Accounts*, Paris, 1996, Table 3, p. 158; own calculations.

high demand for funds in the German capital market that resulted from the boom brought about by unification produced a textbook-like response by the interest rates.

The interest response was not limited to short-term rates or to European currencies. Figure 2.7 shows the development of German long-term rates compared with long-term rates in the United States and in western Europe's largest countries. The picture is always the same: Unification pulled the traditionally low German interest rates upward against the rates in other countries. The figure shows that German and U.S. interest rates in particular have coincided closely since unification. For the 1980s, the unusual circumstances in the United States explain an American interest lead of more than 200 base points. In the 1990s, the unusual circumstances in Germany and the United States have balanced out, and their long-term interest rates are more or less the same.

There is only one important exception to the general trend of shrinking interest differentials – the EMS crisis itself. In the second half of 1992, various European central banks made desperate attempts to defend their

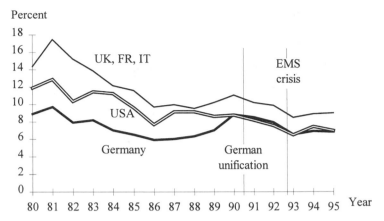

Figure 2.7. Long-term interest rates. The series UK, FR, IT is the unweighted mean of the respective country interest rates. Source: OECD, *Main Economic Indicators* (various issues), Paris.

currencies against devaluations by artificially increasing their short-term interest rates. Figure 2.8 shows this for Sweden and Ireland. Sweden was not a member of the EMS, but had unilaterally tried to peg its krona to the EMS currencies. Ireland was a member. In both countries the daily interest rates were pushed to astronomical heights. Because Figure 2.8 shows the monthly averages of the daily interest rates, it understates the actual development. On September 17 the Swedish discount rate was 500%.

The temporary increase in short-term interest rates was an exception to the post-unification trend, and it indicates how strong the market forces must have been. Both Sweden and Ireland lost the game. Like so many other currencies, their currencies were devalued relative to the deutsche mark.

The crisis in the EMS reached a climax on "Black Wednesday," September 16, 1992. On that day the membership of the British pound in the EMS was temporarily suspended, and the lira followed the next day. A period of successive devaluations of various currencies against the deutsche mark began, and in the end both the United Kingdom and Italy were forced to leave the system. Sweden and Norway gave up their attempts to maintain fixed exchange rates with the EMS currencies.

The successive devaluations added up to a substantial revaluation of the deutsche mark. Figure 2.9 demonstrates the revaluation effect by

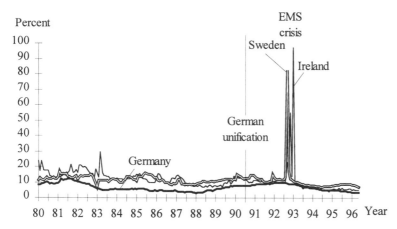

Figure 2.8. Desperate attempts to defend the exchange rate. All rates are monthly averages of daily interest rates. Sources: Bundesbank, *Monatsberichte* (various issues), Frankfurt/Main, Table IV.4; letter from Bundesbank of July 11, 1996.

comparing the trade-weighted exchange value of the deutsche mark with its trade-weighted purchasing-power parity (PPP), as measured by the Organization for Economic Cooperation and Development (OECD). The abscissa of the diagram shows the ratio of these two values. A value of unity indicates an exchange rate equal to the OECD PPP. The data refer to 14 countries that together account for two-thirds of Germany's foreign trade,[9] and they include all countries that are or were members of the EMS. With regard to the EMS countries, the revaluation of the deutsche mark between January 1992 and April 1995 was 20% in real terms. The respective revaluation figure for all countries that were considered was about 16%.

These figures are significantly smaller than the respective figures for the revaluation of the dollar in the 1980s, which in trade-weighted real terms was about 50%,[10] but they are nevertheless large if one takes into account the fact that the German economy is much more integrated into the world economy and is less self-sustaining than the U.S. economy. In the 1980s the export share in the U.S. GDP was about 9%, whereas

---

[9] The rest are as follows: developing countries, including OPEC, 13%; transition countries, including China, 10.5%; Switzerland, 5%; others, 6.5%.

[10] See Sinn (1988, p. 39), where a diagram with unpublished International Monetary Fund (IMF) data is shown.

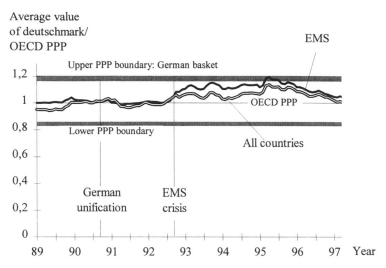

Figure 2.9. Real value of the deutsche mark: 14 countries. The EMS series is constructed as the weighted average of the ratios of exchange rates and OECD PPPs of EMS countries. Exchange rates are monthly, and PPPs are annual data. Both indicate the value of a deutsche mark (i.e., they use the respective foreign currency as the numeraire). Weights are based on 1989 trade flows following the external-value concept of the Bundesbank. EMS countries include Austria, Belgium, Denmark, Spain, France, Italy, Ireland, The Netherlands, Portugal, and the United Kingdom. "All countries" are EMS countries plus Finland, Sweden, Japan, and the United States. A series takes the value 1 if the weighted average of the exchange rates equals the weighted average of the OECD PPPs. The higher limit of the upper boundary gives the weighted mean of the PPPs based on the German basket relative to the PPP according to the OECD basket for all countries. The lower limit of the upper boundary gives the respective PPP value for the EMS countries. As a rule, German-basket PPPs are above OECD-basket PPPs. The limits of the lower boundary are the inverses of the respective limits of the upper boundary. Sources: OECD, *Main Economic Indicators*, Paris, 1996, p. 201; OECD, *National Accounts*, Paris 1996, table 3, p. 158; Statistisches Bundesamt, *Statistisches Jahrbuch für das Ausland*, Wiesbaden 1995, Table 16.3, pp. 342–3; letter by Bundesbank of July 11, 1996; Bundesbank, *Monatsbericht*, April 1989, Frankfurt/Main, p. 46; own calculations.

Germany's current export share is 21.2%. Even a 16% revaluation for the deutsche mark is a dramatic amount that severely threatens the competitiveness of the German economy. In 1969, a furious debate about a revaluation by 8.5% preceded the collapse of a German government.

5 Alternative Explanations for the Currency Crisis

The unification shock seems an obvious explanation for the EMS crisis and the subsequent revaluation of the deutsche mark. However, there are other possible explanations, and this section will briefly screen them.

A popular explanation favored by many German politicians sees the revaluation of the deutsche mark as proof of Germany's strength, of the soundness of its economic policy, and of the confidence of international investors.[11] That explanation is wishful thinking. It may describe investors' expectations about what other investors believe, but it certainly does not describe the economic fundamentals underlying those expectations. German economic policy after unification has not been sound. It has failed to prevent disastrous wage increases, and with massive subsidies of a size previously unknown in the history of industrialized nations it has created nothing more than a straw fire in the east. The jump in the German debt ratio and the failure to satisfy the Maastricht criterion do not provide a basis for confidence in the strength of the German economy or in German economic policy.

If the interpretation advanced in this study is correct, it was the weakness, not the strength, of the German economy that created the currency crisis and forced the revaluation of the deutsche mark. The high capital demand, particularly by the public sector, raised German interest rates, which in turn attracted foreign capital and thus induced the revaluation. If there had been a less destructive policy for eastern Germany, the German resource demand, interest level, and exchange rate would all have been lower.

Another possible explanation for the revaluation often advanced in Germany refers to the apparently low German inflation rate. The excess of foreign inflation over German inflation, so the argument goes, built up a revaluation potential for the deutsche mark and created the pressure that led to the breakdown of the EMS in 1992.[12] That argument likewise is not convincing. Why it is not convincing is obvious from Figure 2.9, which shows that before the EMS crisis the value of the deutsche mark was approximately equal to the OECD PPP, and there was no

---

[11] According to the Bundesbank (*Geschäftsbericht*, 1992, Frankfurt/Main, p. 82), the "true reason" for the breakdown of the EMS was the "failure to correct the exchange rates according to the accumulating differences in the development of prices, costs, budget deficits, and current accounts" (my translation).

[12] See the foregoing quotation. For a similar line of reasoning, compare Eichengreen and Wyplosz (1993, p. 64).

apparent tendency for that value to fall below the OECD PPP, which might perhaps have justified a revaluation.[13]

A major reason for that was the "franc-fort" policy of the French central bank, which had in fact implied that for some years the French inflation rate had been lower than the German rate. Because France is Germany's most important trading partner, the franc-fort policy explains a substantial part of the flat trend of the real exchange value of the deutsche mark before the currency crisis.

Admittedly, the OECD PPP is not the only basis for making a judgment about a revaluation potential. The horizontal upper boundary in Figure 2.9 indicates the PPP value for the German consumption basket published by the Statistisches Bundesamt. Judged by the German-basket PPP, there was indeed a revaluation potential that might explain the EMS crisis. However, there are at least two counterarguments to that interpretation. One is that in early 1995 the value of the deutsche mark in terms of the EMS currencies went even beyond the German-basket PPP value. This indicates an additional cause for a revaluation.

The second counterargument denies the validity of a PPP comparison based on only one country's currency basket. In general, the PPP value of a currency is high when it is calculated on the basis of that country's basket of commodities, because commodities that are cheap there have a high weight. This is simply a result of the relative-price effect. If the lira is evaluated on the basis of the American consumption of gasoline, its purchasing-power value is low, but so is the value of the dollar if it is evaluated on the basis of Italian wine consumption. Thus, if the baskets of other countries are chosen, then, in general, a rather low PPP value of the deutsche mark should be found. Statistical information about the United Kingdom and Sweden (reported later in Figure 2.11) confirms this. Thus a comparison based on the OECD basket, which is an average of the various country baskets, seems best suited for a judgment, and this comparison lends no support for the "undervaluation thesis."[14]

---

[13] Even if the exchange rate had fallen relative to the PPP, that would not necessarily have indicated a revaluation potential, because it could have resulted simply from the Balassa effect. With the integration of poor eastern Germans in the German economy, the price level of nontraded goods has fallen, and hence an appropriately calculated PPP value should have risen after unification, which is the same as saying that the exchange rate should have fallen relative to the OECD PPP. The fact that such obviously was not the case (Figure 2.9) strengthens the argument put forward here that the deutsche mark was not undervalued before the crisis.

[14] Unfortunately, only information about the PPPs based on the OECD and German baskets is available for all countries. So the lower PPP boundary that would result from using Germany's trading partners' baskets is unknown. However, in a symmetrical situ-

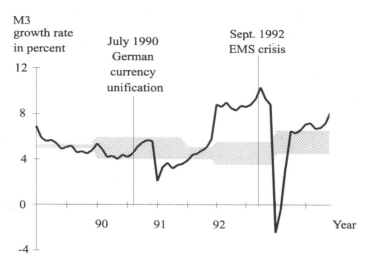

Figure 2.10. Did the Bundesbank cause the EMS crisis? The growth targets are announced by the Bundesbank on an annual basis. After 1990, a growth zone instead of a single target rate was announced. The target variable is M3. Following the Bundesbank's methodology, the actual growth rates are monthly changes of M3 as compared with the average stock in the last quarter of the previous year translated into annualized rates. Sources: Bundesbank, *Geschäftsbericht* 1995, Frankfurt/Main, p. 79; Bundesbank, *Saisonbereinigte Wirtschaftszahlen – Beihefte zum Monatsbericht*, April 1993, 1995, Frankfurt/Main, Table I.1, p. 6.

A third possible explanation for the EMS crisis that competes with the one argued for here refers to the Bundesbank's monetary policy during the time before the crisis (De Grauwe, 1994, p. 152). The Bundesbank has been severely criticized for a too-restrictive monetary policy before Black Wednesday. That argument is that it had put German price stability above the survival of the EMS and had artificially created the demand for deutsche marks in the foreign-exchange markets by reducing the money supply and boosting German interest rates. That argument reflects the anger of the other central banks when faced with the floods of capital leaving their countries, but it is false. Figure 2.10 shows that the Bundesbank did not carry out a contractionary policy; on the contrary, it tried to provide liquidity to the German banking system so as to keep the German interest rates down.

ation, its relative distance to the OECD PPP should be the same as that of the PPP based on the German basket. The "Lower PPP boundary" illustrated in Figure 2.9 reflects this assumption.

From the end of 1991, and right through the crisis, the actual growth rate of M3 exceeded by more than 4 percentage points the target zones that the Bundesbank had originally announced, and only after the crisis, in late spring 1993, did the Bundesbank make an attempt to correct the excessive growth of the money supply. To read anything into Figure 2.10 that could be interpreted as a criticism of the Bundesbank would be courageous, to say the least.

The only possible explanation for the EMS crisis that, in my opinion, merits confidence is the speculative-attack theory advanced by Eichengreen and Wyplosz (1993). According to this theory, pegged exchange rates like those in the EMS invite speculative attacks by investors, because there is nothing to lose if an attack fails, but much to gain if it succeeds. Pegged exchange rates are inherently unstable. The incentive to buy a currency is higher the greater the number of speculators who have already made the decision to buy, because the more people buy, the larger the probability that the central banks will be unable to defend the exchange rate.

Although their theory is an important part of the mosaic that contributes to a picture of what has happened, it cannot explain why a speculative attack begins and the direction such an attack takes. It is a theory that explains the amplification of an existing shock, and nothing more. The view that the unification of Germany caused the currency crisis harmonizes very well with this theory.

6   Implications for the Maastricht Treaty

On January 1, 1999, the Bundesbank will have lost its sovereignty, and the deutsche mark will no longer be a separate currency – it will be only a subunit of the "euro," just as a pfennig is a subunit of the deutsche mark. By the end of 2001, deutsche-mark coins and banknotes will have disappeared. The destinies of the other currencies joining the EMS will be similar, but precisely which currencies will be affected cannot be known at the time of this writing. France, Austria, The Netherlands, and Luxembourg will definitely be members. The rest is unclear. However, in all likelihood Germany and France will not be able to exclude many of the other countries that violate the Maastricht criteria even if they want to, because Germany and France themselves do not meet those criteria. In nearly all cases it will be necessary to stretch article 104c of the Treaty of Maastricht to make membership possible.

It seemed for a long time that the problem with the treaty would be that Germany's unification shock will not have been fully absorbed when the exchange rates are irrevocably fixed in 1998.[15] The fear was that the exchange rates would be frozen at a level that would be appropriate for the current need to pump economic resources into Germany, but not appropriate for a more normal future, when eastern Germany has recovered and Germany's thirst has been quenched.[16] Under the European Monetary Union (EMU), adjustments of the exchange rates can occur in real terms only through diverging inflation rates or diverging deflation rates. Thus either a deflation in Germany or an inflation in other European countries would be necessary to balance the trade flows, neither of which would be compatible with the goals of the EMU.

Fortunately, however, the situation has eased substantially in the meantime. Figure 2.9 shows that in the period from the first quarter of 1995 through the first quarter of 1997, exchange rates came down substantially. With regard to all of Germany's trading partners, the trade-weighted real exchange rate of the deutsche mark has returned to the OECD PPP value, and with regard to the EMS countries only a slight overvaluation of 4% remained by April 1997, the time this study was last updated. The reasons for this include the appreciation of the lira in 1996 and the strong appreciations of the dollar and the pound in the first quarter of 1997.

It is true that despite this exchange-rate adjustment, potential danger remains insofar as the accumulation of foreign debt due to the public transfers to eastern Germany will result in an increase in the flow of interest payments to (or a reduction in the flow from) foreigners. This increase will have to be financed with a trade surplus, which in turn will require an undervaluation. However, this is a second-order effect that is likely to wash out over a long period of time. It seems likely that the necessary undervaluation can easily be achieved with only a slight inflation differential between Germany and its trading partners, and this should not be a matter of major concern.[17]

---

[15] Indeed, that was so when the first version of this study was presented in the summer of 1996 in Tel Aviv.

[16] An economic model that predicts the rise and fall of the deutsche mark's value has been provided by Adams, Alexander, and Gagnon (1993). However, because of its Ricardian nature, that model abstracts fully from the effects of the increased public deficit that explains more than two-thirds of eastern Germany's excess absorption (cf. Figure 2.1).

[17] Wyplosz (1991) used a similar kind of argument to demonstrate that German unification would result in a depreciation of the deutsche mark right from the beginning. National investors, so his argument went, would know the long-run equilibrium of the exchange rate and would therefore anticipate that value in the current exchange rate. The revaluation of the deutsche mark has proved that argument wrong. Obviously, financial investors are not as farsighted as Wyplosz assumed.

A more important concern is the question whether all the country-specific exchange rates have returned to their long-run equilibrium values or whether it is only Germany's average exchange rate that has become normalized. An answer is given in Figure 2.11, which breaks up the country-specific information that was used to calculate the aggregate EMS exchange rate depicted in Figure 2.9. Figure 2.11 shows time paths for the actual market exchange rate, the OECD PPP, the PPP according to the German basket, and, if available, the PPP based on the respective foreign baskets. To allow a plausible judgment to be made, it will be assumed that an exchange rate is acceptable for entry into the EMU if it is within the PPP bounds, where the upper bound is defined by the German baskets, the lower bound by the respective foreign baskets, and the middle by the OECD basket.

Obviously, there is no problem with Austria and Belgium. The exchange rates have been stable and lie in the neighborhood of either the German PPP or the OECD PPP, which are anyway close to one another.

The Danish exchange rate has been stable, but is below the German PPP and the OECD PPP. The krone seems to be slightly overvalued, judged by the OECD PPP criterion, but if a PPP based on the Danish basket were available, it is likely that the krone would still be within the PPP bounds.

The Finnish markka was strongly overvalued before the EMS crisis. After some initial overshooting of the exchange rate, its value is now in the neighborhood of the OECD PPP. Sometimes the volatility of the markka is seen as an indication that Finland may not yet be suitable for the union. However, in light of Figure 2.11, that interpretation would seem completely wrong, because the "volatility" was in fact a one-step adjustment that corrected the previous overvaluation. There can be little doubt that Finland is well suited to join the EMU.

The value of the Irish pound seemed correct before the EMS crisis, but since then it has moved farther away from the OECD PPP, even leaving the PPP bounds. By now, however, the deviation has been partly corrected, and the exchange rate is again below the German PPP. It seems that Ireland can join the currency union even though some further revaluation might be useful before membership becomes effective.

A revaluation will definitely be necessary for the lira. The lira was strongly devalued during the currency crisis, and even more so in 1995, when a political crisis was added. In the meantime the devaluation has been partly reversed, and the lira was even able to return to the EMS by the end of 1996. However, despite that, the lira has remained outside the PPP bounds. In order to satisfy the German PPP, the deutsche mark would have to cost about 880 lire, but to satisfy the OECD PPP only 750 lire. In fact, however, it costs about 1,000 lire. Until the undervaluation of the lira is corrected, the lira will have difficulties in participating in the currency union.

France and The Netherlands face no problems whatsoever. Both exchange rates have been stable, and both have been close to the respective PPPs. If anything, the franc is slightly undervalued. However, the margins are so small that it is clear that France and The Netherlands can safely join a currency union.

That may not be so for Portugal and Spain. The escudo was undervalued both before and after the currency crisis. During the crisis its value was within the PPP bounds, and only recently has it touched the German PPP value again, which, however, is a long way from the OECD PPP. The peseta was within the bounds before the crisis, but after the crisis its value collapsed like that of the Italian lira, and it has stayed outside the bounds ever since. Whereas the escudo's chronic undervaluation may partly be attributed to the Balassa effect, the values of the peseta and the lira deviate too much for such an explanation to make sense. After all, the two countries are well developed. There rather seems to be an idiosyncratic Mediterranean deviation from the respective PPPs, which makes it more than doubtful that these currencies can be integrated into the currency union without a substantial realignment.

The Swedish picture is reminiscent of that for Finland: Before the crisis the krona was overvalued, but now its value seems right. The exchange rate approximates the OECD PPP, and currently it just equals the Swedish-basket PPP, which itself is very close to the OECD basket. Sweden, too, could join the EMU at the current exchange rate, notwithstanding the fact that Sweden has declared that it will stay outside the system for the time being.

For a long time the United Kingdom was a major problem for the EMU, because the pound was strongly overvalued after the currency crisis. The recent strong revaluation of the pound has corrected all that. The pound is still undervalued relative to the OECD PPP, but in April 1997 it was clearly within the PPP bounds. Thus there is little doubt that the United Kingdom could join the EMU at the going exchange rate if it wished to do so.

To summarize this section, it seems that the German-unification shock has been overcome just in time for the EMU to begin. Most of the countries considered can join the EMU without problems. Only Italy and Spain, and to a limited extent Portugal, raise some doubts. If judged by the PPP criterion, their currencies need devaluations before they can be exchanged for the euro. These devaluations would then be able to correct

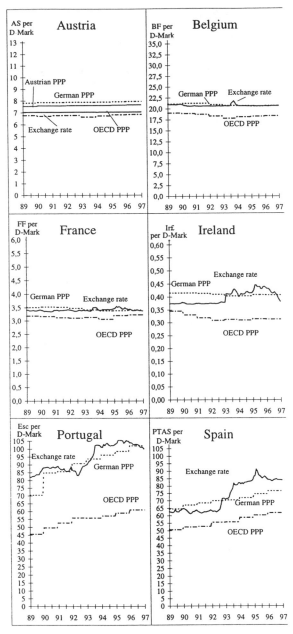

Figure 2.11. Exchange rates and PPPs: a comparison for 12 countries. The exchange rates (monthly) and the PPPs (annually) are defined as the value of a deutsche mark in terms of the respective foreign currency (i.e., a higher rate implicates a stronger deutsche mark). The "German PPP" is based on the German basket, and the "OECD PPP" on the OECD basket. Specific country PPPs are based on the respective

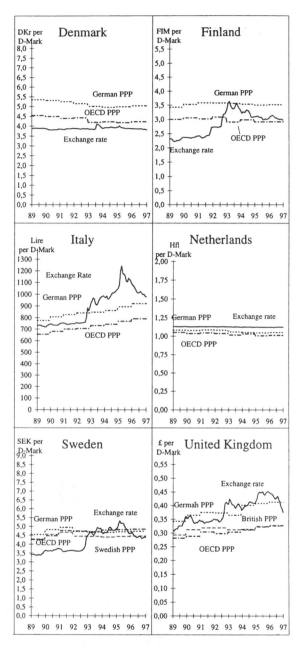

Caption to Figure 2.11 (cont.) national baskets. Sources: OECD, *Main Economic Indicators*, Paris, 1996, p. 201; OECD, *National Accounts*, Paris, 1996, table 3, p. 158. Statistisches Bundesamt, *Statistisches Jahrbuch für das Ausland*, Wiesbaden, 1995, table 16.3, pp. 342–3; letter from Bundesbank of July 11, 1996; own calculations.

the 4% overvaluation of the deutsche mark with regard to all EMS currencies that, as Figure 2.9 showed, persisted in early 1997.

7   The German Currency Union as a Warning for Europe?

Karl Otto Pöhl, the former president of the Bundesbank, warned the European Parliament not to agree to a currency union, because that would be a "disaster" as, in his opinion, the German currency union was.[18] Pöhl was right about the German currency union, but wrong about the European one. The similarity between the two currency unions is very limited.

A major reason that the German currency union turned out to be disastrous for eastern German industry was that it was combined with a real revaluation of the eastern German price level by 340%. Because all prices and wages were fixed in numerical terms (while debt contracts were cut in half), eastern German products became 4.4 times more expensive for western German buyers than before the currency union.

Before unification, a big hole in the iron curtain always existed for the purpose of active intra-German trade. That trade took place at special prices that were equivalent to an exchange rate between ostmarks (East Germany) and deutsche marks (West Germany) of 4.3:1. The East German economy had been competitive at that rate, delivering many commodities to the West German market through West Germany's trade chains. The currency unification simply equated one ostmark to one deutsche mark, thus destroying eastern Germany's competitiveness overnight.

The currency union not only destroyed eastern German industry but also turned out to be a major obstacle to subsequent recovery because it paved the way for additional wage increases. The unification made it possible for western German trade unions and western German employers' associations to open offices in the east and to negotiate eastern German wages. Because both parties were more interested in the safety of western German workplaces than in a quick recovery for eastern German industry, they were happy to agree to overly generous wage contracts for their eastern German competitors that implied full equalization of union wages by 1996. The currency union and the subsequent proxy negotiations for eastern German firms had the effect of a 10-fold increase in eastern German wages in terms of deutsche marks. East

---

[18] In a speech delivered to the economic and monetary section of the European Parliament, January 7, 1991.

German wages used to be 7% of West German wages (in terms of deutsche marks); now they are about 70%. They would be even higher if many eastern German firms and workers had not in the meantime rejected the wage decree of their western colleagues, as indeed they have.

Fortunately, none of these effects will endanger a European currency union. The exchange rates are basically correct now, and there is no risk that successive wage negotiations will create an unemployment problem. There will be no way German trade unions could enforce their wages on Portuguese workers after a European currency union is created. Each country will retain its own sovereignty. Proxy negotiations of the German type are unthinkable in the European context.

8   Conclusions

The German-unification shock created substantial difficulties for Germany's trading partners and triggered the crisis of the EMS. For a while, a large number of currencies were undervalued relative to a long-run equilibrium that presumably lies in the neighborhood of PPP values. However, recent revaluations have largely eliminated those deviations. Judged by various PPP criteria, only the Mediterranean currencies seem to need modest revaluations before they can join without exporting deflationary pressures to the other member countries.

Thus, in contrast to the time when the first version of this study was written (early 1996), the way toward a European currency unification seems to be open. Horrors of the type created by Germany's internal currency unification do not have to be feared, because European currency unification will not be accompanied by realignment shocks or cross-border wage dictates. The European economies are ready for the euro.

REFERENCES

Adams, G., Alexander, L., and Gagnon, J. (1993). German unification and the European Monetary System: a quantitative analysis. *Journal of Policy Modelling* 15:353–92.

Branson, W. (1993). Comment [on Eichengreen and Wyplosz (1993)]. *Brookings Papers on Economic Activity* 1:125–39.

Branson, W. (1994). Comments [on Rose and Svensson: European exchange rate credibility before the fall (same issue)]. *European Economic Review* 38: 1217–20.

De Grauwe, P. (1994). Towards EMU without the EMS. *Economic Policy* 18: 147–85.

Eichengreen, B. J., and Wyplosz, C. (1993). The unstable EMS. *Brookings Papers on Economic Activity* 1:51–143.

Issing, O. (1992). The impact of German unification on the members of the European Community. In: *Auszüge aus Presseartikeln* (Deutsche Bundesbank) 75:3–6.

Sinn, G., and Sinn, H.-W. (1992). *Kaltstart. Volkswirtschaftliche Aspekte der deutschen Vereinigung*, 2nd ed. Tübingen: Mohr. (First German edition 1991; first English edition 1993: *Jumpstart. Economic Aspects of German Unification*. Massachusetts Institute of Technology Press).

Sinn, H.-W. (1984). Die Bedeutung des Accelerated Cost Recovery System für den internationalen Kapitalverkehr. *Kyklos* 37:542–76.

Sinn, H.-W. (1988). United States reform 1981 and 1986: impact on international capital markets and capital flows. *National Tax Journal* 41:327–40.

Sinn, H.-W. (1993). American economic policy and the international debt crisis. *Journal of International and Comparative Economics* 2:207–26.

Sinn, H.-W., and Weichenrieder, A. J. (1997). Foreign direct investment, political resentment and the privatization process in eastern Europe. *Economic Policy* 24:179–210.

Svensson, L. (1994). Fixed exchange rates as a means to price stability: What have we learned? *European Economic Review* 38:447–68.

Wyplosz, C. (1991). On the real exchange rate effect of German unification. *Weltwirtschaftliches Archiv* 127:1–17.

CHAPTER 3

Real-Exchange-Rate Misalignments and Growth

Ofair Razin and Susan M. Collins

1   Introduction

Real-exchange-rate (RER) misalignment refers to a situation in which a country's actual RER deviates from some notion of an implicit "ideal" RER. An exchange rate is labeled "undervalued" when it is more depreciated than this ideal, and "overvalued" when it is more appreciated than this ideal. Such misalignments are widely believed to influence economic behavior. In particular, overvaluation is expected to hinder economic growth, and undervaluation is sometimes thought to provide an environment conducive to growth. But unless the ideal is explicitly specified, the concepts of RER misalignment remain subjective. The objectives of this chapter are (1) to develop and construct explicit measures of RER misalignment and (2) to explore systematically the relationships between misalignment and economic growth.

Conceptually, an RER is misaligned when it deviates from the underlying RER that would have prevailed in the absence of price rigidities, frictions, and other short-term factors. A more structured definition of misalignment uses the notion of an "equilibrium RER." This typically refers to the theoretical RER that would prevail if the economy were simultaneously in internal and external balance. "Internal balance" refers to the economy operating at full employment and at full-capacity output. "External balance" refers to a sustainable current-account position given a country's desired capital position as a net lender or borrower. RER misalignment can then be defined as the deviation of the actual RER from this equilibrium RER.

Several empirical studies have attempted to measure RER misalign-

The research presented in this chapter is work that Ofair Razin completed for his doctoral dissertation. It was a pleasure to advise him in his doctoral work and to prepare this chapter for publication, in his memory.

ments by operationalizing the theoretical concept of an equilibrium RER. This literature includes Williamson (1995), Bayoumi et al. (1994), Borenzstein (1995), Edwards (1989, 1995), Elbadawi (1995), Cottani, Cavallo, and Kahn (1990), and Ghura and Grennes (1993). See Razin (1996, ch. 1) for additional discussion of this literature. Those empirical studies have included very different types of analysis for developed countries and for developing countries. Analyses for developed countries typically have taken advantage of both extensive available data and the findings from large multicountry macro-scale models (e.g., the IMF's MULTIMOD). Such models can simulate equilibrium RERs that are consistent with constructed proxies for external and internal balances. Both types of information can then be used to provide benchmark RERs for policy-makers. The study by Williamson (1995) is one example of this literature.

Such extensive information is not available for the less developed countries (LDCs). Their data are much less detailed and usually incomplete, and there are no comparable dynamic-simulation models. The existing empirical studies of LDCs have been done mostly at a cross-country level, using pooled data and estimating cross-country regressions. Further, such analysis typically is done for relatively small samples of countries. For example, Edwards (1995) developed a model for a small economy. He showed how both nominal and real factors play roles in determining the RER[1] in the short term, whereas only real factors influence the (steady-state) "equilibrium exchange rate." Edwards estimated a version of his model using pooled data for a panel of 12 LDCs. His results provide support for the model – RER movements do respond to both nominal and real disturbances, and inconsistent macroeconomic policies tend to generate RER overvaluation.

A key objective of this chapter, therefore, is to develop and empirically implement a method for constructing RER-misalignment indicators for a very large sample of both industrial economies and developing economies. The study focuses on the misalignment that arises as a result of short-term price rigidity. A stochastic, open-economy macrolevel model provides a unified framework for analysis. As shown later, an estimable equation was derived from the model's structural solution for the RER. The resulting estimates were then used to construct RER-misalignment measures for 93 countries over 16–18-year periods since 1975. These misalignment indicators were then used as explanatory variables in growth regressions.

There are at least two possible channels through which RER mis-

---

[1] Edwards defines the RER as the relative prices of tradables and nontradables.

alignments might influence growth. First, they could influence domestic and foreign investment, thereby influencing the capital-accumulation process. Capital accumulation is a well-established "engine of growth." Second, an RER that is out of line could affect the tradables sector and the competitiveness of that sector vis-à-vis the rest of the world. That sector's performance is also generally thought to be an important component of the economy's overall growth.

Misalignment volatility could also have an impact on growth. Theoretical and empirical research has shown that a volatile economic environment (e.g., volatility of the terms of trade, exchange rates, money supply, productivity) has harmful effects on economic performance (e.g., Campa, 1993; Dixit and Pindyck, 1994; Gavin, Hausmann, and Leiderman, 1995; Leahy and Whited, 1995). Misalignment volatility is possibly another such factor.

This chapter is organized as follows. Section 2 focuses on RER misalignments. It begins by outlining the theoretical framework that provides the basis for the study. It then uses the framework to construct indicators of RER misalignment. Section 3 uses the standard method of growth regressions to explore the effects of RER misalignment on growth. An innovative element of this analysis is its consideration of potentially nonlinear relationships between key variables. The final section contains concluding remarks.

2   RER Misalignment

The empirical analysis herein implements the stochastic version of the Mundell-Fleming open-economy model (Clarida and Gali, 1994; Frenkel et al., 1996, ch. 3). The model consists of a set of simple equations that represent linear approximations to underlying behavioral equations. This model is particularly appropriate for use in constructing indicators of RER misalignment because its solution distinguishes between an RER that is affected by short-term rigidities and an RER that would obtain in the absence of such rigidities. As noted earlier, this is precisely what is meant here by "misalignment." The model also explicitly distinguishes between perfect capital mobility and full capital controls. This provides a structure for exploring differences between industrial countries and developing counties, which typically differ in the extent of capital restrictions. The discussion that follows highlights key features of the model and then focuses on the implied solutions for the RER that are used in the estimations. Readers are referred to Razin (1996a) and Frenkel et al. (1996) for a detailed presentation of the model and a derivation of the solution.

2.1   *Theoretical Framework*

The model is based on the standard IS-LM model of a small open economy that produces a single traded good. Aggregate demand depends on the RER and on real interest rates. Equilibrium is determined simultaneously in the goods and money markets. This basic framework is extended in two ways. First, output supply, money supply, and domestic demand are assumed to be stochastic processes, through the introduction of independent and identically distributed (iid) shocks.

Second, price rigidities are introduced by specifying the price level as an average of the free-market (*flex*) price and a one-period contract price set in period $t - 1$ based on expectations about the market-clearing price in period t. Thus the model has both the standard *flex-price solution*, which assumes that prices are fully flexible, and a *full-fledged solution*, which incorporates the price rigidities.

Just as for a standard IS-LM structure, this model can be solved under different assumptions about the extent of international capital mobility. Of particular interest in the current context is that the determinants of the RER are somewhat different in the perfect-capital-mobility case than they are in the full-capital-controls case.

The empirical analysis in this chapter is based on the solutions for the equilibrium RER that result from the model outlined earlier (Frenkel et al., 1996; Razin, 1996a). All variables (except interest rates) are expressed in logarithms.

We define the RER as follows: $q_t = s_t + p_t - p_t^*$, where s is the foreign-currency price of domestic currency, and p and p^* are domestic and foreign price levels, respectively. Note that exchange rates have been defined so that increases in their values imply appreciation. It can be shown that the *full-fledged* solution for the RER is the *flex-price* solution $g(\ )$ plus a linear combination of stochastic shocks $f(\ )$:

$$\text{capital mobility:} \qquad q_t = g_1\!\left(y_t^s,\, d_t,\, i^*\right) + f_1\!\left(\varepsilon_{mt},\, \varepsilon_{yt}\right) \qquad (3.1)$$

$$\text{capital controls:} \qquad q_t = g_2\!\left(y_t^s,\, d_t^X\right) + f_2\!\left(\varepsilon_{mt},\, \varepsilon_{yt},\, \varepsilon_{dt}^A\right) \qquad (3.2)$$

where f_1, f_2, g_1, and g_2 are all linear functions, y^s is output supply, i^* is the world interest rate, d is the exogenous component of aggregate demand, and ε_y and ε_m are stochastic shocks to output and money supply. In the capital-controls case, aggregate demand has been decomposed into domestic absorption and the trade balance. Thus, d^X is the exogenous component of demand for net exports, and ε_d^A is the stochastic shock to domestic absorption.

Equation (3.1) shows the determinants of the RER under perfect capital mobility. The *flex-price* solution g_1 depends on the fundamental determinants of domestic supply and aggregate demand, as well as on world interest rates. In the absence of price rigidities, the RER will appreciate in response to higher output or higher world interest rates, but will depreciate in response to higher aggregate demand. The function $f(\ )$ shows how the RER will deviate from its flex-price level given price rigidities – money-supply shocks will cause short-term real appreciations, and output-supply shocks will cause short-term real depreciations.

Under full capital controls, the RER must adjust so as to maintain external balance. Thus, in the solution for the RER given in equation (3.2), conditions in world capital markets no longer determine the flex-price solution. Instead of total aggregate demand, it is now the exogenous component of demand for net exports that matters. As before, increased long-term output supply is associated with an RER appreciation. Because of short-term price rigidities, the RER will deviate from this flex-price solution because of money and output shocks, as in the capital-mobility case. In addition, positive shocks to domestic absorption will cause a temporary RER appreciation.

The model thus provides a clear distinction between a flex-price RER and the model's full-fledged RER solution. The flex-price RER is determined by fundamental (or long-term) variables related to domestic supply, demand, and the external economy. In the empirical analysis, deviations of the actual RER from (an estimated) flex-price level will be taken as indicators of exchange-rate misalignment. As shown earlier, these deviations arise from short-term rigidities and are associated with various types of shocks.

The model also distinguishes between high and low capital mobility. Two key differences between the two that arise in the solution for the RER are considered in the empirical analysis. First, factors related to external balance are important determinants of the flex-price RER under capital controls, but not under full capital mobility. Second, domestic-absorption shocks cause deviations from the flex-price RER under capital controls, but not under full capital mobility.

Finally, we should note that an attractive feature of this model is its relative simplicity. The RER solutions are well defined, and yet general enough to provide a useful framework for empirical implementation. However, one drawback is that the model does not provide a fully dynamic framework and thus cannot capture dynamic, forward-looking behavior. See Elbadawi (1995) for an argument for such models in this context.

2.2   *Empirical Implementation*

The solutions for the full-fledged RER provide the basis for construction of indicators of RER misalignment. A country's actual annual RER is assumed to be a linear function of two sets of determinants. In equation (3.3), W denotes long-term (or fundamental) variables that would determine its RER in the absence of any rigidities. Z denotes key shocks. The error term is included to capture additional shocks omitted from Z. It also reflects unobserved fundamentals.

$$q_{it} = W_{it}\alpha + Z_{it}\beta + \gamma_{it} \qquad (i = 1, \ldots, M, \; t = 1, \ldots, T) \qquad (3.3)$$

As before, q_{it} is the log of the RER of country i at time t, W_{it} is a vector of variables for country i at time t that capture longer-term factors and thus are relevant for the flex-price RER, Z_{it} is a vector of variables for country i at time t that proxy short-term shocks, and γ_{it} is an iid error term for country i at time t.

This equation was estimated separately for developed countries and developing countries. In both cases the empirical analysis tested whether the appropriate specification was random effects or fixed effects (by country). Two additional econometric issues were raised, but not pursued: the potential non-stationarity of the RER (Razin, 1996a) and the potential endogeneity of variables chosen as long-term factors.

Misalignment indicators were then constructed for each country at each time period, where misalignment was defined as

$$Mis_{it} = (q_{it} - W_{it}\alpha) = (Z_{it}\beta + \gamma_{it}) \qquad (3.4)$$

Thus a misalignment is the deviation of the actual RER from a linear combination of variables that proxy the flex-price RER. It arises from the short-term shock proxies and the error term of the regression.

The analysis was undertaken for a total of 93 countries over the period 1975 to 1992. However, shorter time periods were used for some countries. The sample was divided into two subpanels: one with 20 developed countries and a total of 322 observations, and the other with 73 developing countries and a total of 1,190 observations (Appendix A lists the total sample).

2.1.1   The RER

Implementation required a measure of the RER for a very large panel of developed countries and LDCs. Previous analyses of this type had either focused on developed economies or used smaller groups of LDCs. In particular, previous work by Razin (1996a) used data on real effective exchange rates from Morgan Guaranty for 19 developed countries and 23 developing countries.[2]

The procedure followed here was to use data on the prices of consumption goods (and services) from the PENN *World Tables*. The PENN is attractive for use in this context because it is available for such a large cross section of countries and years and because it was constructed to be internationally comparable.[3] Taking higher consumption-goods prices as reflecting more appreciated exchange rates, the data for each country were then indexed (1987 = 100).[4]

Table 3.1 reports means and standard deviations of the log RER (LRER) for developed and developing countries. The figures illustrate the well-known fact that there is considerably more exchange-rate volatility among developing countries than among industrial countries. Note that the similarity of the means for the two country groups reflects the indexation procedure.

2.2.2 Long-Term Versus Short-Term Factors: The *W* and *Z* Matrices

The next step was to specify the right-hand-side variables. As discussed earlier, the variables included in the *W* matrix should reflect underlying fundamentals or longer-term variations, and those included in the *Z* matrix should proxy short-term shocks. The model also suggested that somewhat different variables were relevant depending on the degree of capital mobility – both sets will be considered in the analysis. [Note: All data discussed here are from the World Bank (1996) *World Tables*.]

---

[2] Earlier we had explored links between the misalignment indicators constructed from Morgan Guaranty real effective exchange rates (REERs) and economic growth. Overall, the results were similar to those reported here. However, in some instances the relatively small sample size made it difficult to draw conclusive results.

[3] See Summers and Heston (1991) for further discussion of these data, and Bosworth, Collins, and Chen (1996) for additional discussion of this series as a measure of RERs. Note that this measure of domestic prices relative to foreign prices is consistent with the form of the RER assumed in the model. Edwards (1995) followed an alternative approach, specifying the RER as the domestic price of tradable goods relative to non-tradable goods.

[4] Indexing does remove much of the cross-country variation. However, the within-country variation in the data proved insignificant in the regression analysis when nonindexed series were used. Indexing the RERs lessens the influence of the between-country average (although it is still relatively strong) and gives substantially more sensible estimates for constructing misalignments. There is a second justification for the indexation. It is well known that the consumption-price series from the PENN World Tables is systematically related to country income level. See Bosworth et al. (1996) for further discussion. Various procedures have been used to adjust for this bias. The use of indices (1987 = 100) here was one means of adjustment.

Table 3.1. *Variables for the* X *matrix: long-term factors*

Variable	Definition	Developing countries		Developed countries	
		Av.	SD	Av.	SD
LRER	log of the yearly constructed RER	2.0669	0.1591	2.0030	0.0327
TOT5	5-year MA[a] of the log of yearly terms of trade	2.0602	0.0851	1.9909	0.0516
RBY5	5-year MA of the ratio of resource balance to GDP	−0.0720	0.1056	0.0031	0.0324
MG5	5-year MA of the money-supply growth minus GDP growth	0.0079	0.0288	0.0019	0.0113
KY5	5-year MA of the ratio of net long-term capital inflows to GDP	0.0424	0.0384	0.0019	0.0327
GYL5	5-year growth of GDP per worker	0.0147	0.0642	0.0282	0.0242

[a] MA, moving average.

For the *W* matrix the theoretical model points to variables related to output supply, the exogenous components of demand in general, and the trade balance more specifically, and world interest rates. Accordingly, five variables were chosen as candidates for *W*. Both to incorporate a longer-term perspective and to reduce potential endogeneity problems, each of these variables was specified as a 5-year moving average. Table 3.1 shows means and standard deviations for the two groups of countries.

The variable GYL5, growth in output per worker, was used as an indicator of trends in labor productivity – a fundamental determinant of domestic-output supply. As shown in Table 3.1, productivity growth was somewhat slower, on average, among developing countries, but exhibited considerably greater variability.

MG5, the annual money growth in excess of output growth, was the variable taken as an indicator of the overall stance of monetary policy. Thus it was interpreted as an underlying determinant of domestic demand. Not surprisingly, this indicator implied that LDCs maintained considerably looser monetary policy, on average, than did the industrial countries.

Table 3.2. *Variables for the Z matrix: shocks*

Variable	Definition	Developing countries		Developed countries	
		Av.	SD	Av.	SD
SHOCKY	Yearly log of GDP minus the 5-year MA[a] of the series	0.0280	0.0329	0.0231	0.0140
SHOCKA	Yearly log of absorption minus the 5-year MA of the series	0.0264	0.0438	0.0262	0.0264
SHOCKM	Yearly log of the money supply minus the 5-year MA of the series	0.2122	0.2438	0.1024	0.0631

[a] MA, moving average.

In addition, three variables were included as potential indicators of external conditions: TOT5, the (log of the) terms of trade; KY5, the annual long-term capital inflows as a share of GDP; RBY5, the annual resource balance (exports minus imports of goods and nonfactor services), also as a share of GDP. Table 3.1 shows that LDCs, as a group, enjoyed much larger long-term capital inflows, but ran much larger external deficits. If, as postulated, industrial economies exhibit greater capital mobility than do LDCs, then those variables related to external balance should be important in the estimated equation for LDCs.

The Z matrix should include variables that proxy short-term shocks to output, absorption, and money supply. Thus, the three indicators considered were SHOCKY, SHOCKA, and SHOCKM, which represent, respectively, yearly deviations of (the logs of) GDP, absorption, and money supply from fitted ARMA(1, 1) processes. Again, the model implies that we should expect to see differences between the high-capital-mobility developed countries and the lower-capital-mobility LDCs. Domestic-absorption shocks should matter more for the LDCs, whereas output-supply and money-supply shocks should be relevant for both groups. Means and standard deviations for these variables are given in Table 3.2. A key difference between LDCs and industrial economies was seen in the average sizes of monetary shocks. There was also much more variability for all three variables in the LDC sample.

Table 3.3. *RER regressions (for construction of misalignment indicators)*

Variable	Developing countries	Developed countries
Constant	Fixed effect	1.76484
		(21.4)
RBY5	−0.18774	
	(−3.72)	
TOT5	0.389938	0.121548
	(9.30)	(2.92)
KY5	0.835939	
	(7.47)	
MG5	0.48991	
	(4.94)	
GYL5		−0.10682
		(−1.28)
SHOCKY	−0.71121	
	(−4.34)	
SHOCKA	0.473968	0.249905
	(4.29)	(2.57)
SHOCKM		−0.07161
		(−1.94)
Adj. R^2	0.664	0.378

Note: Dependent variable is LRER; t statistics in parentheses; critical values = 1.28 (10%), 1.96 (2.5%), 2.57 (0.5%).

2.3   *RER Regression Results*

The results from the panel regressions of LRER on long-term factors and shocks are reported in Table 3.3. Note that the specifications for each country group were chosen on the basis of the significance of estimated coefficients and the robustness to outliers, though certainly future research should explore alternative explanatory variables and specifications. The results reported here are quite interesting and are broadly consistent with the model developed earlier. In particular, there are significant differences between the estimated coefficients for developed countries versus LDCs, and many of these can be interpreted in terms of the more extensive capital controls among LDCs. However, there are also some surprises.

Using a Hausman-Wu test, it was found that the fixed-effects specification could be rejected for developed countries, but not for developing countries. Overall, the fit was considerably better for LDCs than for developed countries. This most likely reflects both the use of fixed effects and the fact that the right-hand-side variables exhibited significantly more variation for the LDC sample.

We consider first the role of long-term factors in determining RER movements. As expected, variables directly related to external balance were much more important for LDCs than for developed countries. Indeed, both long-term trends in net trade relative to GDP (RBY5) and long-term capital inflows relative to GDP (KY5) were strongly significant in the LDC equation, but insignificant for developed countries. Greater net trade surpluses in LDCs were associated with more-depreciated RERs, and greater long-term capital inflows were associated with more-appreciated RERs. The terms of trade (the variable TOT5) entered significantly in both regressions – terms-of-trade improvements were associated with more-appreciated RERs. However, the terms of trade had both greater statistical significance and a larger coefficient estimate for LDCs.

The results for other long-term variables were somewhat surprising. GDP per worker (GYL5), a proxy for productivity growth, did not enter significantly in either regression. The growth of money relative to GDP (KY5) entered only for LDCs and had an unexpected sign (it was positive). Especially given these surprising results for money shocks (MG5) (it did not enter for LDCs, although it had a negative sign for developed countries), it would be interesting to explore other proxies for the long-term and short-term monetary variables.

We consider next the role of shocks. As discussed earlier, the model implies that absorption shocks should be more important in developing countries, to the extent that they are characterized by less capital mobility. Table 3.3 shows that although positive absorption shocks were associated with RER appreciation in both groups, the coefficient was larger and more significant for LDCs. The model also implies that output and money shocks should be relevant for both country groups. Again, as shown in Table 3.3, output shocks appeared to matter only for LDCs (positive shocks were associated with RER depreciations). Finally, recall that money shocks entered only in the developed-country equation – as expected, a positive money shock was associated with RER depreciation.

2.4   *Misalignment Indicators*

The next step was to construct misalignment indicators for each country in each time period. Recall that "misalignment," as defined in equation (3.4), is the deviation of the actual RER from a linear combination of variables that proxies the flex-price RER. It arises from the short-term shock proxies and the error term of the regression. A positive value signifies an overvaluation of the actual RER relative to the flex-price RER, and a negative value signifies an undervaluation. Thus, annual misalignment indicators were constructed using the coefficient estimates reported in Table 3.3. See Razin (1996a) for an extensive discussion of the behavior of similarly constructed misalignment indicators in a number of individual countries.

The growth analysis in the next section required country characteristics, including RER misalignment over longer time periods. Thus the annual data were divided into two subperiods: 1975–77 to 1983 (period 1), and 1984 to 1990–92 (period 2). The earlier period includes the years leading up to the international debt crisis, and the latter period encompasses the aftermath and early recovery. For each country and subperiod, averages and standard deviations of the yearly values were constructed. The resulting 170 observations were each characterized by a country and a period. The values for both variables were multiplied by 100 to convert them to percentages.

Table 3.4 provides some statistics on RER misalignments in each time period, with the LDCs divided into six regional groupings. According to the indicator developed and constructed here, RERs were overvalued in most of the LDC regions during the earlier period, with the misalignments most pronounced in sub-Saharan Africa, southern Asia, and especially Europe and central Asia. In contrast, RERs were relatively undervalued in all regions, on average, in the later period. Of course, such broad regional and time-period averages can mask significant differences among individual countries and over time.

3   Growth Analysis

This section explores the link between RER misalignment and economic growth, using regression analysis.[5] Many previous growth studies had included RER indicators as explanatory variables, typically finding RER instability to be associated with significantly slower growth (e.g., Gavin et al., 1995). These previous studies used RER proxies directly, without attempting to construct measures of misalignment. Arguably, it is mis-

---

[5] For further discussion of the large and growing literature using growth regressions, see Barro and Lee (1994), Collins and Bosworth (1996), and Levine and Renelt (1992). Note that one drawback to the growth-regression approach is the difficulty in addressing dilemmas related to the potential endogeneity of explanatory variables other than initial conditions.

Table 3.4. *Summary statistics for the constructed misalignments*

Type	Region	Period	No. of observations	Average	Standard deviation
Developing countries	Sub-Saharan Africa	1	27	2.698	7.854
		2	27	−5.121	7.572
	Eastern Asia and Pacific	1	7	1.816	6.698
		2	9	−4.328	5.425
	Latin American and Caribbean	1	20	1.479	6.238
		2	17	−1.872	6.620
	Middle East and North Africa	1	4	−0.4007	4.972
		2	9	−1.726	4.649
	Southern Asia	1	3	2.501	1.464
		2	4	−6.026	1.394
	Europe and Central Asia	1	3	4.706	2.169
		2	3	−4.7065	2.1691
Developed countries		1	20	−1.441	4.909
		2	17	−0.948	2.454

alignment, not the level or variability of the RER per se, that should be associated with slower growth.

The approach followed here was to add misalignment measures to the right-hand-side variables that are now standard in this literature. Indeed, the choice of explanatory variables was heavily influenced by the classic analysis in Barro and Lee (1994). As in their work, these variables include indicators for initial conditions, the external environment, and macroeconomic policy. In this context, the actual RER (level, change, or standard deviation) has frequently been included as an indicator of macroeconomic policy. The finding that RER volatility (measured by the standard deviation) is negatively associated with growth has been interpreted as evidence that "unsustainable" macroeconomic policies cause exchange-rate misalignments and hinder growth. But volatility may be a poor proxy for RER misalignment. Furthermore, any misalignments should reflect not only policy variables, such as monetary and fiscal policies, but also the effects of various shocks. Thus the analysis reported here included among these variables the measure of RER misalignment constructed earlier.

A difference between the analysis presented here and those by Barro and Lee (1994) and others is the relatively short time period considered here. The intent in the analysis presented here was to select a time period that would be short enough for the misalignment indicator to be meaningful, but long enough to eliminate cyclic factors as the primary determinants of growth.

Summary statistics for the variables used in the growth regressions are reported in Table 3.5, where observations are averaged over both time periods, but disaggregated by region. The dependent variable was *gypc* – average annual growth in per-capita GDP. The four indicators of initial conditions were all for 1970. These were *gdp*, *life*, *prim*, and *sec*, defined respectively as per-capita GDP in U.S. dollars, life expectancy at birth, and primary-school and secondary-school enrollments (as percentages of total relevant age group). Initial income was included to capture "catch-up," and the other variables were taken as measures of the initial levels of health and education.[6] Changes in the terms of trade, *gtot*, and standard deviations in the terms of trade, *sdtot*, were included to capture cross-country differences in the relevant external environment. Finally, government consumption as a percentage of GDP, *govcon*, was included as an indicator of fiscal policy.[7] As with misalignment, these variables were measured as percentages. The variables constructed for each country were for the same subperiods as the misalignment measures. Data, taken from the World Bank *World Tables*, were available for 152 of the 170 observations.

3.1   *Growth Regressions*

Table 3.6 presents the basic results. All the observations were pooled, and regional dummies were included. Consider first the results of regression 1. All the variables, except possibly the initial conditions for primary and secondary schooling, had the expected signs. The variable *govcon*

---

[6] Barro (1991) and Barro and Lee (1994) showed the importance of *conditional* convergence of growth rates of countries with different initial incomes – initial income is negatively associated with growth when accounting for other initial conditions (such as initial human capital). The data are 1970 values of GDP (in constant 1985 dollars), life expectancy when born (years), primary- and secondary-school enrollment rates (ratios of actual number of students to number of children in the relevant age group).

[7] Barro and Lee (1994) stressed that government size is potentially associated negatively with growth.

Table 3.5. *Summary statistics for variables used in growth regressions*

Variable	Sub-Saharan Africa	Eastern Asia and Pacific	Latin America and Caribbean	Middle East and North Africa	Southern Asia	Europe and central Asia	Developed countries
gypc (%)	−0.1907[a]	1.720	0.0583	0.3839	1.207	0.8334	0.8381
	(0.9908)[b]	(1.293)	(0.8967)	(1.752)	(0.2402)	(0.4845)	(0.3919)
gtot (%)	−0.8075	−0.7786	−0.8718	−0.9821	−0.7855	−0.1171	−0.0571
	(1.563)	(1.337)	(1.575)	(1.2457)	(0.7672)	(1.557)	(0.8476)
sdtot	17.65	13.47	19.73	18.06	10.09	8.625	6.201
	(14.60)	(8.656)	(12.31)	(12.13)	(5.124)	(5.522)	(3.792)
govcon (%)	15.02	13.35	11.84	19.26	11.22	12.51	18.38
	(5.358)	(5.582)	(4.330)	(6.749)	(1.148)	(5.095)	(4.077)
life (years)	43.90	56.81	59.98	58.30	48.37	65.97	72.17
	(6.003)	(6.87)	(6.36)	(8.27)	(2.30)	(6.60)	(1.32)
prim (%)	56.86	87.14	97.34	80.80	56.00	104.4	101.4
	(27.92)	(18.19)	(15.41)	(16.84)	(16.53)	(5.31)	(10.24)
sec	8.40	28.28	28.93	35.18	16.72	50.85	75.73
	(6.19)	(14.62)	(13.52)	(19.17)	(8.98)	(16.49)	(10.36)
gdp	1180	1605	2987	3330	990.2	3200	8889
	(868.4)	(638.4)	(1838)	(2858)	(203.1)	(835.7)	(2328)
No. of observations	43	14	33	13	5	7	37

[a] Average.
[b] Standard deviation.
Source: World Bank (1996).

Table 3.6. *Growth regressions, basic results*

Variable	Definition	Regression 1	Regression 2
govcon	Percent age of government consumption in GDP	−0.0424 (−2.66)	−0.0443 (−2.80)
gtot	Growth of TOT (%)	0.0470 (1.10)	0.0599 (1.40)
sdtot	Standard deviation of TOT	−0.0067 (−0.97)	−0.0051 (−0.75)
life	Life expectancy at birth in 1970 (years)	0.0493 (3.28)	0.0458 (3.05)
prim	Primary-school enrollment rate in 1970 (%)	−0.0072 (−1.49)	−0.0059 (−1.23)
sec	Secondary-school enrollment rate in 1970 (%)	−0.0028 (−0.35)	−0.0025 (−0.32)
gdp	GDP per capita in 1970 ($)	−0.0001 (−3.35)	−0.0001 (−3.57)
Dummies			
SSA	Sub-Saharan Africa	−0.7690 (−1.34)	−0.5436 (−0.94)
EAP	Eastern Asia and Pacific	0.6901 (1.07)	0.9363 (1.44)
LAC	Latin America and Caribbean	−0.7800 (−1.20)	−0.5162 (−0.78)
MENA	Middle East and North Africa	−0.1651 (−0.24)	−0.0727 (−0.10)
SA	Southern Asia	0.1516 (0.22)	0.3650 (0.53)
ECA	Europe and central Asia	−0.1471 (−0.20)	0.1695 (0.23)
DED	Developed countries	0.4437 (0.64)	0.7331 (1.05)
Mis	Average misalignment (%)	−0.0213 (−1.73)	
1. 90 observations with undervaluations	Absolute value of average misalignment		−0.0143 (−0.65)
2. 62 observations with overvaluations	Average misalignment		−0.0647 (−2.56)
SD Mis	Standard deviation of yearly misalignments	−0.0309 (−1.34)	−0.0206 (−0.87)
No. of observations		152	152
Adj. R^2		0.403	0.415

Note: Dependent variable is *gypc*; t statistics in parentheses; critical values = 1.28 (10%), 1.96 (2.5%), 2.57 (0.5%).

had a significant negative coefficient, which accords with the arguments made by Barro and Lee (1994). The initial conditions of life expectancy and income level were significantly associated with growth, as expected. Although schooling had a somewhat surprising negative coefficient, the estimate for primary schooling was only marginally significant, whereas that for secondary schooling was insignificant.[8] Whereas the coefficients of the dummies for eastern Asia and the developed countries were positive (although not significant), those for sub-Saharan Africa and Latin America were negative and marginally significant. Somewhat surprisingly, the external conditions did not enter significantly.

Regression 1 also shows that the average misalignments and the standard deviations of misalignments were negatively associated with growth. However, that result was only weakly significant. The remainder of this chapter explores the possibility that this weak finding was due to nonlinearities in the relationship.

3.1.1 Overvaluation versus Undervaluation

One hypothesis suggested by the research reported here is that misalignments can have very different effects on growth depending on whether they reflect overvaluations or undervaluations of the RER. To test this hypothesis, the misalignment variable was split into two pieces. Those observations in which misalignment was positive were labeled "overvaluation," and those in which it was negative were labeled "undervaluation."

As shown by the results for regression 2 (Table 3.6), overvaluation had a negative and statistically significant effect on economic growth. The effect was also economically significant – the estimated coefficient implies that a 10% overvaluation of a country's RER is associated with a decline in real per-capita output growth of 0.6 percentage point. Interestingly, the estimation did not find a significant relationship between RER undervaluation and growth. These findings motivated a closer look at various groupings of the data, as discussed next.

3.1.2 Additional Nonlinearities

The final part of the analysis entailed a search for additional nonlinearities in the relationships between growth and both misalignment and the volatility of misalignment. This attempt should be viewed as exploratory.

---

[8] See Collins and Bosworth (1996) for additional discussion of the links between education and growth and for further references.

The approach taken was to subdivide further the groups of 90 overvalued RERs (misalignment > 0) and 62 undervalued RERs (misalignment < 0) into low, medium, high, and very high categories. In each case, "low" referred to a relatively small misalignment (near zero), and "very high" referred to the observations with the greatest percentage misalignments. Similarly, the observations for the standard deviation of RER misalignment were divided into four groups, with "low" referring to those with the most stable misalignment indicator, and "very high" referring to those with the greatest volatility in RER misalignment.

In creating these subdivisions, the intent was to identify meaningful differentiations among groups with respect to the variable in question while ensuring that the subgroups were of similar sizes. For the four undervalued RER groups and the four standard-deviation groups, that was accomplished by division into quartiles. For the four overvalued-RER groups, the observations were first divided according to the overall average, and then each of the resulting groups was split in half.

In the resulting groups, the undervaluations ranged from 1.2% in the "low" group to 10% in the "very high" group. Those observations indicating high undervaluation were primarily from the later time period, but included all regions. Overvaluations ranged from 0.9% in the "low" group to 11.7% in the "very high" group. Those indicating high overvaluation were predominantly from the earlier time period and were concentrated in sub-Saharan Africa and Latin America. Standard deviations ranged from an average of 2.2% in the "low" group to 13.9% in the "very high" group. Observations with very high standard deviations of misalignment were concentrated in Africa and Latin America. However, they came from both time periods and included observations with undervaluation and overvaluation.

Estimations are reported in Table 3.7. The column for regression 3 shows the results when all 12 misalignment indicators were included. It is perhaps not surprising that most did not enter significantly. However, the results show that the previously reported finding that overvaluations were correlated with slow growth was due to the influence of observations with very high overvaluations. Smaller amounts of overvaluation did not appear to have significantly deleterious effects. The column for regression 4 shows the results when only a subset of these misalignment indicators were included in the equation. This subset resulted from a stepwise elimination of variables, based on the sizes of their t statistics. Although these results should be viewed as preliminary, they are quite provocative. In addition to the strong negative effect of very high overvaluation, the results suggest that "high" (but not "very high") undervaluations may help to promote growth. However, this analysis has failed

Table 3.7. *Growth regressions, additional results*

Variable	Regression 3	Regression 4
govcon	−0.0490 (−3.27)	−0.0458 (−3.21)
gtot	0.0459 (1.08)	0.0547 (1.34)
prim	0.0057 (−1.16)	−0.0059 (−1.31)
life	0.0467 (3.83)	0.0415 (4.51)
gdp	−0.0001 (−3.68)	−0.0001 (−4.00)
Dummies		
SSA	−0.5724 (−2.49)	−0.6426 (−3.26)
EAP	0.7356 (2.49)	0.8297 (2.98)
LAC	−0.6635 (−2.67)	−0.6401 (−2.67)
DED	0.6548 (1.82)	0.7749 (2.35)
Mis, undervalued		
1. Low	0.0804 (0.34)	
2. Medium	−0.0921 (−0.82)	
3. High	0.0586 (0.94)	0.0940 (2.31)
4. Very high	−0.0266 (−0.97)	
Mis, overvalued		
1. Low	−0.3080 (−1.11)	
2. Medium	−0.1027 (−1.12)	
3. High	−0.0059 (−0.10)	
4. Very high	−0.0773 (−2.54)	−0.0625 (−2.67)
SD Mis		
1. Low	−0.1197 (−0.72)	−0.0633 (−0.84)
2. Medium	−0.0103 (−0.09)	
3. High	−0.0199 (−0.03)	
4. Very high	−0.0221 (−0.59)	−0.0190 (−1.23)
Extreme no. of observations	152	152
Adj. R^2	0.440	0.452

Note: Dependent variable is *gypc*; *t* statistics in parentheses; critical values = 1.28 (10%), 1.96 (2.5%), 2.57 (0.5%).

to find a significant relationship between the volatility of misalignment and economic growth.

4   Conclusions

This chapter has empirically explored the relationship between RER misalignment and economic growth for a large sample of developed and developing countries. It has sought to make two contributions to the existing literature. First, it developed and implemented an indicator of RER misalignments. That indicator was based on a well-structured but simple extension of an IS-LM model of an open economy. The framework introduced short-term price rigidities and showed that the solution for the RER can be decomposed into an RER that would obtain if prices were fully flexible and a deviation from that level that arises because of various short-term shocks. That framework was then used as the basis for construction of an RER regression. Interestingly, the estimation results were consistent with key model predictions about the differences between RER determinations for industrial countries with relatively high capital mobility and RER determinations for developing economies with relatively extensive capital restrictions. The estimation results were then used to construct indicators of misalignment.

We then reported the use of growth-regression analysis in a study of the determinants of economic growth. In addition to the standard explanatory variables – initial conditions, external environment, and fiscal-policy stance – the level and standard deviation of RER misalignment were introduced among these factors. These variables were conceptually preferable to simply including the change or standard deviation in the RER, as various other studies have done. While recognizing the problems arising from potential endogeneity of the policy and RER indicators, the results are provocative. The analysis reveals that there are important nonlinearities in the relationship between misalignment and growth. In particular, only very high overvaluations appear to be associated with slower economic growth. Furthermore, moderate to high (but not very high) undervaluations appear to be associated with more rapid economic growth.

APPENDIX A: COUNTRIES USED IN THE GROWTH ANALYSIS

1. Sub-Saharan Africa
   Benin
   Burkina Faso
   Cameroon
   Central African Federation
   Chad
   Côte d'Ivoire
   Gabon
   Gambia
   Kenya
   Madagascar
   Mali
   Mauritania
   Mauritius

   Nigeria
   Rwanda
   Senegal
   Sierra Leone
   South Africa
   Sudan
   Togo
   Zaire
   Zambia
   Zimbabwe

2. Middle East and North Africa
   Algeria
   Cyprus

Egypt
Iran
Israel
Kuwait
Morocco
Syria
Tunisia

3. Eastern Asia and the Pacific
China
Indonesia
Korea
Malaysia
Papua New Guinea
Philippines
Singapore
Thailand

4. Latin America and the
   Caribbean
Bolivia
Brazil
Chile
Costa Rica
Dominican Republic
Ecuador
El Salvador
Guatemala
Guyana
Honduras
Jamaica
Mexico
Nicaragua
Paraguay
Peru
Trinidad and Tobago
Uruguay
Venezuela

5. Southern Asia
Bangladesh

India
Pakistan

6. Europe and central Asia
Greece
Poland*
Portugal
Turkey

7. Developed countries
Australia
Austria
Belgium
Canada
Denmark
England
Finland
France
Germany
Iceland
Ireland
Italy
Japan
New Zealand
Norway
Spain
Sweden
The Netherlands
United States

8. Additional countries (not in
   the growth analysis)
Argentina
Colombia
Congo
Ghana
Malawi
Myanmar
Somalia
Sri Lanka

* Poland was not part of the dummy for Europe and central Asia.

REFERENCES

Barro, R. (1991). Economic growth in a cross section of countries. *Quarterly Journal of Economics* 106:407–43.

Barro, R., and Lee, J. W. (1994). Sources of economic growth. *Carnegie-Rochester Conference Series on Public Policy* 40:1–46.

Bayoumi, T., Clark, P., Symanski, S., and Taylor, M. (1994). The robustness of equilibrium exchange rate calculations to alternative assumptions and methodologies. In: *Estimating Equilibrium Exchange Rates*, ed. J. Williamson, pp. 19–59. Washington, DC: Institute for International Economics.

Borenzstein, E. (1995). Long run exchange rate developments in Korea. Unpublished paper, International Monetary Fund, Washington, DC.

Bosworth, B., Collins, S. M., and Chen, S. (1996). Accounting for differences in economic growth. In: *Structural Adjustment and Economic Reform: East Asia, Latin America and Central and Eastern Europe*, ed. A. Kohsaka and K. Ohno, pp. 47–120. Tokyo: Institute of Developing Economies.

Campa, M. (1993). Entry by Foreign Firms in the U.S. under Exchange Rate Uncertainty. *Review of Economics and Statistics* 75:614–22.

Clarida, R., and Gali, J. (1994). Sources of real exchange rate fluctuations: How important are nominal shocks? *Carnegie-Rochester Conference Series on Public Policy* 41:1–56.

Collins, S. M., and Bosworth, B. (1996). Economic growth in East Asia: accumulation versus assimilation. *Brookings Papers on Economic Activity* 2:135–203.

Cottani, J., Cavallo, D., and Khan, S. (1990). RER behavior and economic performance in LDCs. *Economic Development and Cultural Change* 39:61–76.

Dixit, A., and Pindyck, R. (1994). *Investment under Uncertainty*. Princeton University Press.

Edwards, S. (1989). Real exchange rates in developing countries: concepts and measurement. NBER working paper 1950. Washington, DC: National Bureau of Economic Research.

Edwards, S. (1995). Real and monetary determinants of real exchange rate behavior: theory and evidence from developing countries. In: *Estimating Equilibrium Exchange Rates*, ed. J. Williamson, pp. 61–91. Washington, DC: Institute for International Economics.

Elbadawi, I. (1995). Estimating long-run equilibrium exchange rates. In: *Estimating Equilibrium Exchange Rates*, ed. J. Williamson, pp. 93–131. Washington, DC: Institute for International Economics.

Frenkel, J., Razin, A., and Yuen, C.-W. (1996). *Fiscal Policies and Growth in the World Economy*, 3rd ed. Massachusetts Institute of Technology Press.

Gavin, M., Hausmann, R., and Leiderman, L. (1995). The macroeconomics of capital flows to Latin America: recent experience and policy issues. OCE working paper, Inter-American Development Bank, New York.

Ghura, D., and Grennes, T. (1993). The RER and macroeconomic performance in sub-Saharan Africa. *Journal of Development Economics* 42:155–74.

Leahy, J. V., and Whited, T. M. (1995). The effect of uncertainty on investment: some stylized facts. NBER working paper 4986. Washington, DC: National Bureau of Economic Research.

Levine, R., and Renelt, D. (1992). A sensitivity analysis of cross-country growth regressions. *American Economic Review* 82:942–63.

Razin, O. (1996a). Real exchange rate misalignments and growth. Ph.D. dissertation, chapter 1, Department of Economics, Georgetown University, Washington, DC.

Razin, O. (1996b). Real exchange rate misalignments and growth. Ph.D. dissertation, chapter 2, Department of Economics, Georgetown University, Washington, DC.

Summers, R., and Heston, A. (1991). The PENN World Table (mark 5): an expanded set of international comparisons, 1950–1988. *Quarterly Journal of Economics* 106:327–68.

Williamson, J. (1995). Estimates of FEERs. In: *Estimating Equilibrium Exchange Rates*, ed. J. Williamson. Washington, DC: Institute for International Economics, pp. 177–243.

World Bank (1996). *World Tables*. Washington, DC: Johns Hopkins University Press.

PART III

Tax Incentives and
Patterns of Capital Flows

CHAPTER 4

Implications of the Home Bias:
A Pecking Order of Capital Inflows
and Corrective Taxation

Assaf Razin, Efraim Sadka, and Chi-Wa Yuen

1   Introduction

Even though financial markets today show a high degree of integration, with large amounts of capital flowing across international borders to take advantage of rates of return and risk-diversification benefits, the world capital market is still far from the textbook story of perfect capital mobility. As an example of the limited degree of capital mobility, Tesar and Werner (1995) found that despite the recent increase in U.S. equity investment abroad (including investment in emerging stock markets), the U.S. portfolio remains strongly biased toward domestic equity.[1] Likewise, Huberman (1997) reports evidence of "home bias" within the United States: American investors have a strong preference toward firms located in their states over out-of-state firms.

Capital immobility has been explained not only on the basis of capital controls but also on the basis of the informational problems associated with international investment. Because of adverse selection and moral-hazard problems, real rates of return across countries are not fully equalized.[2] Capital-market regulations and better rules of disclosure, as

We thank Tamim Bayoumi, Jon Eaton, Liam Ebrill, Robert Feenstra, Se-Jik Kim, John Montgomery, Soren Bo Nielsen, Vito Tanzi, Kei-Mu Yi, and the participants in the 1996 NBER Summer Institute at Cambridge and the 1996 Congress of the International Institute of Public Finance at Tel Aviv and the EPRU workshop at the Copenhagen Business School for useful comments, and Gal Hochman for research assistance.

[1] They reported that equity-portfolio flows to Western Europe, as a fraction of the capitalized value of the U.S. equity markets, rose from only 0.3% in 1976 to about 2.2% in 1990. The share invested in Canada remained fairly constant, at less than 1%.

[2] See Obstfeld and Rogoff (1996, ch. 6) for further discussion.

applied to information about the profitability of domestic firms, can alleviate some of these asymmetric information problems. The stationing of managers from the headquarters of multinational firms at their foreign direct investment establishments in the destination countries is one way to monitor closely the operation of such establishments, thus circumventing some of these informational problems.

It is well known that in a perfectly functioning world capital market, the efficient international tax principle is the residence principle. That is, foreign-source and domestic-source incomes of residents are taxed at equal rates, and nonresidents' incomes are fully tax-exempt.[3] In a less-than-perfect world capital market, the residence principle may no longer be efficient, however, and the optimal tax structure may also require substantial modifications. The failure to have a tax scheme under which rates of return across countries are equated can lead to inefficient capital flows across countries. Such investment inefficiency results from interactions between market imperfections and the tax system.[4] The purpose of this study is to highlight some key sources of market failure (particularly asymmetric information) in the context of international capital flows and to provide guidelines for efficient tax structure in the presence of capital market imperfections.

In general, capital flows can be in the form of either direct investment or portfolio investment. Depending on the specific types of securities involved, we can further subdivide the latter into portfolio debt investment and portfolio equity investment. In this chapter we attempt to provide a synthesis of these three types of capital inflows: foreign direct investment (FDI), foreign portfolio debt investment (FPDI), and foreign portfolio equity investment (FPEI). In particular, we want to examine how the optimal tax treatment of the capital incomes of both domestic and foreign residents can vary across these three forms of foreign investment.

According to Claessens (1995), portfolio flows now account for about a third of the net resource flows to developing countries. To

---

[3] The residence principle means that the home country does not levy additional taxes on incomes of nonresidents over and above what they will have to pay in their country of residence. In case the latter country offers credits for foreign taxes (i.e., for the taxes paid by these nonresidents in the home country), then the home country will levy on nonresidents only a tax that is equal to what they will be liable to pay (before the credit) in their country of residence. Therefore, the "zero-tax" reference point for nonresidents would mean "same tax" as the tax levied on nonresidents in the country of residence.

[4] For an application of the interaction between taxation and inflation, see Bayoumi and Gagnon (1996).

Table 4.1. *Aggregate net long-term resource flows to developing countries, 1990–5 (in billions of U.S. dollars)*

Flows	1990	1991	1992	1993	1994	1995
Aggregate net resource flows	103.5	129.2	159.7	212.8	212.9	233.3
Official development finance	57.2	64.4	55.3	52.5	44.9	71.5
Official grants	28.8	36.9	31.6	28.5	27.6	27.0
Official loans	28.4	27.5	23.7	24.0	17.3	44.5
Bilateral	13.2	12.6	10.9	9.4	7.1	32.6
Multilateral	15.2	15.0	12.8	14.6	10.2	11.9
Total private flows	46.3	64.8	104.4	160.3	168.0	161.8
Private-debt flows	16.2	20.5	42.4	45.8	56.1	53.5
Commerical banks	1.1	3.9	14.3	−2.6	15.1	17.0
Bonds	3.1	12.4	12.9	39.9	38.0	33.0
Others	12.0	4.2	15.2	8.5	3.0	3.5
Foreign direct investment	26.3	36.7	47.8	67.6	77.3	86.1
Portfolio equity flows	3.8	7.6	14.2	46.9	34.6	22.2

Source: World Bank, Debtor Reporting System.

provide a sense of their relative importance, Table 4.1 gives the breakdown among the various kinds of capital flows. It shows that although equity flows to developing countries have risen rapidly in recent years, they still compose a much smaller fraction of the total portfolio flows than do debt instruments (such as bonds, certificates of deposit, and commercial paper). A striking feature can be seen in this table: FDI makes up more than half of private flows, followed by debt finance, whereas equity flows are relatively unimportant. Indeed, our model suggests some reasons, associated with asymmetric information, as to why this pattern occurs.

This ranking of capital inflows is somewhat similar to the "pecking order of capital structure" in corporate finance. Recall that in corporate finance the hypothesis maintains that firms prefer internal finance (retained earnings: the analogue of our FDI) to external finance. If the latter is required, then firms will issue the safest security (debt: the analogue of our FPDI), and they will issue new equity (the analogue of our FPEI) only as a last resort.[5] The pecking order of capital inflows can be stated in terms of the magnitudes of those flows in, for example, 1995. Table 4.1 shows the dominance of FDI ($86.1 billion) compared with

---

[5] See Myers (1984) for an explanation based on asymmetric information.

private-debt flows ($53.5 billion) and portfolio equity flows ($22.2 billion). In terms of percentages of total private flows, the numbers are 53.2%, 33.1%, and 13.7%, respectively.

Contrary to the efficiency implications of the residence principle in international taxation as emphasized by the literature (e.g., Gordon and Varian, 1989; Frenkel, Razin, and Sadka, 1991), our main finding is that it is generally efficient to have different tax treatments for these three types of international capital flows. First, we show that for both FPDI and FPEI, deviations from residence-based taxation may be called for on efficiency grounds, whereas efficient taxation of FDI is compatible with the residence principle. Second, whereas it is efficient to subsidize nonresidents on their investments and to tax domestic corporate income in the case of FPEI, as shown by Gordon and Bovenberg (1996), it is still efficient to grant nonresidents a favorable tax treatment over residents (but not necessarily to actually subsidize foreign investment) in the case of FPDI. In the latter case, it remains efficient to tax domestic corporate income and interest income of residents.

The organization of this chapter is as follows. Section 2 develops the asymmetric information framework used herein. This is first applied to FPDI. The other kind of portfolio flow, FPEI, is recast in the same framework in Section 3. In Section 4 we look at FDI. Section 5 provides a quantitative assessment of the allocative and welfare effects as well as the corrective tax implications of these three different forms of finance in terms of simulations. Conclusions and possible extensions are provided in Section 6. The two-period analysis of this study is extended to a dynamic growth context in Appendix B so as to examine the implications of the information problems for long-term capital accumulation under the FPDI and FPEI regimes.

2   Foreign Portfolio Debt Investment (FPDI)

Throughout this chapter we assume a small, capital-importing country, referred to as the home country. In this section it is assumed that capital imports are channeled solely through borrowing by domestic firms from foreign banks and other lenders. The economy is sufficiently small that in the absence of any government intervention, it faces a perfectly elastic supply of external funds at a given risk-free world rate of interest r^*. In the absence of capital flows, this r^* is assumed to be lower than the domestic marginal productivity of capital, and so there can be welfare gains from capital imports.

We follow Gordon and Bovenberg (1996) in modeling the risk in this economy and the asymmetry in information between foreign investors and domestic investors.[6] Consider a two-period model with a very large number N of ex-ante-identical domestic firms. Each firm employs capital input K in the first period in order to produce a single composite good in the second period. For simplicity, we assume that capital will have depreciated fully at the end of the production process in the second period. Output in the second period is equal to $F(K)(1 + \varepsilon)$, where $F(\cdot)$ is a production function exhibiting diminishing marginal productivity of capital, and ε is a random productivity factor. The latter has zero mean and is independent across all firms (ε is bounded from below by -1, so that output is always nonnegative). Given the very large size of N and the independence of ε across firms (which allow for complete diversification of such idiosyncratic risks through optimal portfolio decisions at the household level), consumer-investors will behave in a risk-neutral way.

In the first period, the firms commit their investment in the planning stage, but the actual investment and its funding are delayed to the implementation stage. Investment decisions are made by the firms before the state of the world (i.e., ε) is known. Because all firms face the same probability distribution of ε, they all choose the same level of investment (K). They then issue debt, either at home or abroad, to finance the investment. At this stage, domestic lenders are better informed than foreign lenders. There are many ways to specify the degree of this asymmetry in information. In order to facilitate the analysis, however, we simply assume that domestic lending institutions, being "close to the action," observe ε before they make their loan decisions; but foreign lending institutions, being "far away from the action, " do not.

Throughout this study we consider three tax instruments: a corporate income tax (at the rate θ), a tax on the capital income of residents (at the rate τ), and a tax on the capital income of nonresidents (at the rate τ^*). However, with debt financing, a corporate tax is essentially a tax on pure profits (rents) and therefore does not affect corporate behavior (see Appendix A, section A.1). To simplify notations, therefore, we set θ equal to zero in this section. In practice, the neutrality of this tax in the presence of debt finance makes it efficient to set it at a high rate. For simplicity, we assume that the foreign (capital-exporting) country is tax-free.

---

[6] In this chapter, the three modes of finance (i.e., FPDI, FPEI, and FDI) are considered separately. They are blended together in Razin, Sadka, and Yuen (1998c).

Competition among the borrowing firms and among the lending institutions, both domestic and foreign, ensures that there will be a unique interest rate charged to all the domestic borrowing firms. We denote this domestic interest rate by r. As in the study of Stiglitz and Weiss (1981), a firm may choose to default on its debt if its future cash flow falls short of its accumulated debt. Given its investment decision (K), a firm will default on its debt if the realization of its random productivity factor is low, so that its output $F(K)(1 + \varepsilon)$ is smaller than $K(1 + r)$. Thus, there is a cutoff value ε_0, such that all firms that realize a value of ε below ε_0 will default, and all other firms (i.e., firms with $\varepsilon > \varepsilon_0$) will fully repay their debt. This cutoff level of ε is defined by

$$F(K)(1+\varepsilon_0) = K(1+r) \tag{4.1}$$

We denote the cumulative probability distribution of ε by $\Phi(\cdot)$. Then $N\Phi(\varepsilon_0)$ firms default on their debt, and the other $N[1 - \Phi(\varepsilon_0)]$ firms remain solvent.

Recall that domestic lenders are able to observe the value of ε before making their loan decisions. Therefore they will not lend money to a firm that has realized a value of ε lower than ε_0. But foreign lenders cannot observe ε, and so they will advance loans to all firms, because all firms look identical to them. Thus, foreign lenders will give loans to all the $N\Phi(\varepsilon_0)$ firms that will become bankrupt and to some fraction (say, β) of the $N[1 - \Phi(\varepsilon_0)]$ firms that will remain solvent. (The other fraction, $1 - \beta$, of the firms that will remain solvent is financed by domestic lenders.) Foreign lenders therefore receive a total of $\beta N[1 - \Phi(\varepsilon_0)]K(1 + r)$ from the solvent firms. Each bankrupt firm can pay back only its gross output [i.e., $F(K)(1 + \varepsilon)$]. Thus, foreign lenders receive a total of $N\Phi(\varepsilon_0)F(K)(1 + e^-)$ from the bankrupt firms, where e^- is the mean value of ε realized by the bankrupt firms:

$$e^- \equiv E(\varepsilon/\varepsilon \leq \varepsilon_0) \tag{4.2}$$

That is, e^- is the conditional expectation of ε given that $\varepsilon \leq \varepsilon_0$. For later use, we also define e^+, the conditional expectation of ε given that $\varepsilon \geq \varepsilon_0$:

$$e^+ \equiv E(\varepsilon/\varepsilon \geq \varepsilon_0) \tag{4.3}$$

Note that the weighted average of e^- and e^+ must yield the average value of ε; that is,

$$\Phi(\varepsilon_0)e^- + [1 - \Phi(\varepsilon_0)]e^+ = E(\varepsilon) = 0 \tag{4.4}$$

The latter equation also implies that $e^- < 0$ and $e^+ > 0$ [i.e., the expected value of ε for the "bad" ("good") firm is negative (positive)].

Altogether, foreign lenders receive the following sum before domestic taxes are levied on their total loans (FPDI) made to the domestic firms:

$$A \equiv \beta N[1 - \Phi(\varepsilon_0)]K(1+r) + N\Phi(\varepsilon_0)F(K)(1+e^-) \tag{4.5}$$

where the amount of loans is given by

$$\text{FPDI} = \beta N[1 - \Phi(\varepsilon_0)]K + N\Phi(\varepsilon_0)K \tag{4.6}$$

They thus accumulate a capital income of $A - \text{FPDI}$, which is subject to domestic taxation at the rate τ^*. Net of tax, their FPDI yields $A - \tau^*(A - \text{FPDI})$. This amount must be equal to $\text{FPDI}(1 + r^*)$, as foreign lenders can earn a return of r^* in their own countries. Consequently,

$$\text{FPDI}[1 + r^*/(1 - \tau^*)] = A \tag{4.7}$$

The rationale for the latter equality is straightforward: Foreign lenders must earn a before-tax rate of return of $r^*/(1 - \tau^*)$ on their FPDI so that their after-tax rate of return will remain r^*, the rate of return they can earn in their own countries. As a result, the tax that our small economy imposes on their capital income is fully shifted to the domestic borrowers. Substituting for the values of A and FPDI from equations (4.5) and (4.6), equation (4.7) becomes

$$\{\beta N[1 - \Phi(\varepsilon_0)]K + N\Phi(\varepsilon_0)K\}[1 + r^*/(1 - \tau^*)]$$
$$= \beta N[1 - \Phi(\varepsilon_0)]K(1+r) + N\Phi(\varepsilon_0)F(K)(1+e^-) \tag{4.8}$$

Let us now examine the debt-financed investment decision of a representative firm. This firm invests K in the first period and expects to receive an output of $E[F(K)(1 + \varepsilon)] = F(K)$ in the second period. It also knows that if ε turns out to be smaller than ε_0, it will default on its debt. This firm expects then to pay back its accumulated debt [i.e., $K(1 + r)$] with probability $1 - \Phi(\varepsilon_0)$. It expects to default, paying only $F(K)(1 + e^-)$, with probability $\Phi(\varepsilon_0)$. Thus the expected value of its cash receipts in the second period is

$$F(K) - [1 - \Phi(\varepsilon_0)]K(1+r) - \Phi(\varepsilon_0)F(K)(1+e^-) \tag{4.9}$$

Maximizing the latter expression with respect to K yields the following first-order condition:

$$F'(K) = \frac{[1 - \Phi(\varepsilon_0)](1+r)}{1 - \Phi(\varepsilon_0)(1+e^-)} \tag{4.10a}$$

Because $1 + e^- < 1$, it follows that

$$F'(K) < 1 + r \qquad (4.10b)$$

Knowing that if it has a "bad" realization of ε (when $\varepsilon \leq \varepsilon_0$) it will not fully repay its loan, the firm invests beyond the level where the unconditionally expected net marginal productivity of capital [viz., $F'(K) - 1$] is just equal to the interest rate (viz., r).[7] Note that, unlike the case of FPEI to be discussed in the next section, we cannot assert here that $F' > 1 + r^*/(1 - \tau^*)$. However, as expected, because of the default possibility, foreign lenders charge an ex ante interest rate (r) higher than what they will be satisfied with $[r^*/(1 - \tau^*)]$ given that the alternative return at home is r^*. This difference is a reflection of the risk premium.[8]

We abstract from income-distributional equity considerations, implicitly assuming that the government can optimally redistribute income via lump-sum transfers, à la Samuelson (1956). This means that, with no loss of generality, we can assume that there is one representative individual consumer in the economy. She has an initial endowment of I_1 in the first period and I_2 in the second period. She consumes c_1 in the first period and c_2 in the second period. Her saving earns an after-tax rate of return of $(1 - \tau)r$, so that her net discount factor is equal to[9]

$$q \equiv [1 + (1 - \tau)r]^{-1} \quad \text{or} \quad \tau \equiv (rq - 1 + q)/rq \qquad (4.11)$$

We denote her net wealth (i.e., the present value of her after-tax lifetime income) by W. As we assume that the government can levy lump-sum taxes, it essentially controls W. The consumer budget constraint is given by $c_1 + qc_2 = W$. Maximization of her utility subject to this constraint gives rise to an indirect utility function $v(W, q)$ and consumption demand functions $c_1(W, q)$ and $c_2(W, q)$ in the first and second periods, respectively.

[7] Eaton and Gersovitz (1989) considered related interactions in the context of foreign investment with sovereign debt.

[8] More specifically, we can show [by substituting (4.1) into (4.8)] that $[1 + r^*/(1 - \tau^*)]/(1 + r) = \alpha + (1 - \alpha)(1 + e^-)/(1 + \varepsilon_0)$, where $\alpha = \beta[1 - \Phi(\varepsilon_0)]/\{\Phi(\varepsilon_0) + \beta[1 - \Phi(\varepsilon_0)]\}$. Thus $[1 + r^*/(1 - \tau^*)]/(1 + r)$ is a weighted average of 1 and $(1 + e^-)/(1 + \varepsilon_0)$. Because $(1 + e^-)/(1 + \varepsilon_0) < 1$, it follows that $1 + r^*/(1 - \tau^*) < 1 + r$. This implies that $r^*/(1 - \tau^*) < r$.

[9] Her saving is deposited either with domestic intermediaries (banks, etc.) that channel it to the firms or in government bonds that also yield a before-tax rate of return of r. Assuming, as we are, that the government can levy lump-sum taxes in each period to balance its budget makes these bonds superfluous.

In the first period, the economy faces a resource constraint, stating that FPDI must suffice to cover the difference between domestic investment (viz., NK) and national savings [viz., $I_1 - c_1(W, q) - G_1$, where G_1 is public consumption financed through lump-sum taxes]:

$$\text{FPDI} = NK - [I_1 - c_1(W, q) - G_1] \tag{4.12}$$

No matter what taxes are levied by the home country on FPDI, foreigners will be able to extract from the home country an amount of $1 + r^*$ units of output in the second period for each unit that they invest in the first period. Therefore the home country faces the following second-period budget constraint:[10]

$$NF(K) - (1 + r^*)\text{FPDI} + I_2 = c_2(W, q) + G_2 \tag{4.13a}$$

That is, gross *national* output $[NF(K) - (1 + r^*)\text{FPDI}]$ and the initial endowment (I_2) must suffice to support private consumption (c_2) and public consumption (G_2). Employing (4.12), we can rewrite (4.13a) in present-value terms as

$$I_1 + I_2/(1 + r^*) + NF(K)/(1 + r^*)$$
$$= c_1(W, q) + c_2(W, q)/(1 + r^*) + G_1 + G_2/(1 + r^*) + NK \tag{4.13b}$$

We are now in a position to formulate an optimal tax policy for the government. Because we concentrate on tax policy, we can consider the public expenditure variables (i.e., G_1 and G_2) as exogenous, with no loss of generality. (This means that our results will be valid whether or not the government expenditure policy is optimal.) The aim of our benevolent government is to maximize the utility $v(W, q)$ of the representative individual. There are nine endogenous variables: K, r, ε_0, β, τ^*, τ, q, W, and FPDI. There are also seven constraints that combine real resource constraints [i.e., (4.12) and (4.13a)], market equilibrium constraints [i.e., (4.1), (4.6), and (4.8)], an optimizing-agent behavioral constraint [i.e., (4.10a)], and a definition of the consumer's discount factor [i.e., (4.11)].

It turns out, however, that the optimal policy problem can be simplified a great deal. To accomplish this, notice that the objective function [$v(W, q)$] and the present-value resource constraint (4.13b) contain only three endogenous (control) variables: W, q, and K. Thus we can first

---

[10] Note that the expected value of output is $E[NF(K)(1 + \varepsilon)] = NF(K)$, because $E(\varepsilon) = 0$.

choose these three variables so as to maximize the individual utility function subject to the present-value resource constraint (4.13b). The Lagrangian expression for this optimization problem is

$$L = v(W, q) + \lambda[I_1 + I_2/(1+r^*) + NF(K)/(1+r^*)$$
$$- c_1(W, q) - c_2(W, q)/(1+r^*) - G_1 - G_2/(1+r^*) - NK] \qquad (4.14)$$

where $\lambda \geq 0$ is a Lagrange multiplier. Having solved for the optimal values of W, q, and K, we can then employ the remaining six constraints [(4.1), (4.6), (4.8), (4.10a), (4.11), and (4.12)] to solve for the optimal values of the remaining six control variables (i.e., r, ε_0, β, τ^*, τ, and FPDI).

There are three main policy conclusions that we wish to emphasize here. First, the optimal level of investment is such that the expected net marginal product of capital [i.e., $F'(K) - 1$] is equal to the world rate of interest (i.e., r^*):

$$F'(K) = 1 + r^* \qquad (4.15)$$

[Note that it then follows from (4.10b) that $r > r^*$, i.e., the domestic rate of interest stays above the world rate of interest.] Equation (4.15) is essentially a corollary of the familiar aggregate production efficiency theorem of welfare economics: A small open economy should equate all of its marginal rates of transformation to the corresponding world prices. In our case there is only one marginal rate of transformation [the intertemporal rate $F'(K)$], and the corresponding world price is $1 + r^*$. The proof of (4.15) follows immediately upon differentiating L in (4.14) with respect to K and setting the derivative equal to zero.

Second, the optimal policy calls for a tax on the capital income of the residents (i.e., $\tau > 0$). To prove this, observe that with the availability of lump-sum, nondistortionary taxes, it is optimal to follow the Pareto-efficiency rule of equating the marginal rate of substitution between present consumption and future consumption (q^{-1}) to the gross marginal product of capital [$F'(K) = 1 + r^*$]:

$$q^{-1} = 1 + r^* \qquad (4.16)$$

(See Appendix A, section A.2, for a formal proof.) Substituting (4.16) into (4.11) yields

$$1 + (1 - \tau)r = 1 + r^*$$

Given $r^* < r$, this implies that

$$\tau = 1 - r^*/r > 0 \tag{4.17}$$

Third, the rate of tax on nonresidents' capital income (τ^*) must be lower than the rate of tax on residents' capital income (τ). To prove this, substitute (4.1) into (4.8) to get

$$\{\beta N[1 - \Phi(\varepsilon_0)]K + N\Phi(\varepsilon_0)K\}[(1 + r^*)/(1 - \tau^*)]$$

$$= \beta N[1 - \Phi(\varepsilon_0)]K(1 + r) + N\Phi(\varepsilon_0)K(1 + r)(1 + e^-)(1 + \varepsilon_0)^{-1}$$

Rearrangement of terms yields

$$\frac{(1 + r^*)/(1 - \tau^*)}{1 + r} = \frac{\beta[1 - \Phi(\varepsilon_0)] + \Phi(\varepsilon_0)(1 + e^-)/(1 + \varepsilon_0)}{\beta[1 - \Phi(\varepsilon_0)] + \Phi(\varepsilon_0)} < 1$$

The inequality follows from $e^- < \varepsilon_0$. By (4.17), this implies that

$$\tau^* < (1 - r^*)/r = \tau \tag{4.18}$$

In fact, τ^* may even be negative. It is worth emphasizing that the two tax instruments (τ and τ^*) support a first-best allocation.

The rationale behind the optimal tax policy (i.e., $\tau > 0$, and $\tau^* < \tau$) is quite straightforward. First, given the possibility of default, in which case firms would not fully repay their loans, they tend to overinvest relative to the domestic interest rate that they face: The expected net marginal product of capital $[F'(K) - 1]$ is driven below the domestic rate of interest (r) [see condition (4.10b)]. In order to ensure that firms do not drive their expected net marginal product of capital below the world rate of interest (r^*), the government must positively tax domestic interest so as to maintain the domestic rate of interest above the world rate. Second, by the small-country assumption, any tax levied on foreign lenders must be shifted fully to domestic borrowers. Therefore, foreign lenders must earn an expected return of $r^*/(1 - \tau^*)$ on their loans. Because the interest cannot be fully recouped in the case of default, they must initially charge domestic borrowers a rate of interest higher than $r^*/(1 - \tau^*)$. As a result, the domestic rate of interest (r) that is charged by all lenders, both foreign and domestic, must be higher than $r^*/(1 - \tau^*)$. In other words, $r > r^*/(1 - \tau^*)$, or $r(1 - \tau^*) > r^*$. This means that if the nonresident tax rate (τ^*) were to be applied to residents, their net-of-tax interest rate $[(1 - \tau^*)r]$ would have to be higher than the world rate of interest (r^*). But Pareto efficiency requires that the net-of-tax domestic interest rate $[(1 - \tau)r]$ be equal to the world rate of interest. Therefore, residents must be levied a tax rate on their capital income higher than that for nonresidents.

3   Foreign Portfolio Equity Investment (FPEI)

In this section we assume that capital flows are channeled solely through foreign portfolio equity investment (FPEI). Officially, FPEI is defined as buying less than a certain small fraction (say, 10–20%) of shares of a firm. However, from an economic point of view, the critical feature of FPEI is the lack of control of the foreign investor over the management of the domestic firm, because of the absence of foreign managerial input. For our purposes, we shall simply assume that foreign investors buy shares in existing firms without exercising any form of control or applying their own managerial input.

This is also why we assume, in complete analogy to the information asymmetry assumed in the model of FPDI, that foreign investors do not observe the actual value of ε when they purchase shares in existing firms. Domestic investors, on the other hand, do observe the value of ε at that stage. As before, we continue to assume that ε is not known to the firm or to anyone else when capital investment is made. This is precisely the model that was developed by Gordon and Bovenberg (1996). For the sake of completeness, we employ the analytical apparatus that we developed in the preceding section in order to derive optimal policy prescriptions in this case. These policy prescriptions are different from those obtained in the preceding section in the case of FPDI.

As before, all firms choose the same level of K in the first period, because ε is unknown to them at this stage. All firms are originally owned by domestic investors who equity-finance their capital investment K. After this capital investment is made, the value of ε is revealed to domestic investors, but not to foreign investors. The latter buy shares in the existing firms at a total amount of FPEI. They expect their investment to appreciate in the second period to an amount FPEI $[(1 + r^*)/(1 - \tau^*)]$, as the capital gains are taxed at the rate τ^*, and foreign investors must earn a net-of-tax rate of return of r^*, which is the alternative rate of return they could earn by investing in their home countries.

Being unable to observe ε, foreign investors will offer the same price for all firms, reflecting the average productivity for the group of low-productivity firms they purchase. On the other hand, domestic investors who do observe ε will not be willing to sell at that price the firms that have experienced high values of ε. (Equivalently, domestic investors will outbid foreign investors for these firms.) As before, there will be a cutoff level of ε, say ε_0 (possibly different from the one under FPDI), such that all firms that experience a value of ε lower than the cutoff level will be purchased by foreigners. All other firms will be retained by domestic investors. The cutoff level of ε is then defined by

$$[(1-\theta)F(K)(1+e^-)]/[(1+r*)/(1-\tau*)]$$
$$=[(1-\theta)F(K)(1+\varepsilon_0)]/[1+(1-\tau)r] \tag{4.19}$$

The value of a typical domestic firm in the second period is equal to its output minus corporate profit taxes [i.e., $(1-\theta)F(K)(1+\varepsilon)$].[11] Because foreign equity investors will buy only those firms with $\varepsilon \le \varepsilon_0$, the expected second-period value of a firm they buy is $(1-\theta)F(K)(1+e^-)$, which they then discount by the factor $1 + r*/(1-\tau*)$ to determine the price they are willing to pay in the first period. At equilibrium, this price is equal to the price that a domestic investor is willing to pay for the firm that experiences a productivity value of ε_0. The cutoff price is equal to the output of the firm minus corporate profit taxes discounted at the rate domestic investors can earn on bonds issued by their own government [i.e., $(1-\tau)r$].[12] This explains the equilibrium condition (4.19). Rearranging terms, equation (4.19) reduces to

$$(1+e^-)/[(1+r*)/(1-\tau*)] = (1+\varepsilon_0)/[1+(1-\tau)r] \tag{4.1'}$$

As $e^- < \varepsilon_0$, an equilibrium with both foreigners and residents having nonzero holdings in domestic firms requires that the foreigners' net-of-tax rate of return $[r*/(1-\tau*)]$ be lower than the residents' net-of-tax rate of return $[(1-\tau)r]$. In some sense, this means that foreign investors are overcharged for their purchases of domestic firms. They outbid domestic investors who are willing to pay *on average* only a price of $(1-\theta)F(K)(1+e^-)/[1+(1-\tau)r]$ for the low-productivity firms. Because there are $\Phi(\varepsilon_0)N$ firms purchased by foreign investors, the amount of FPEI is given by

$$\text{FPEI} = [\Phi(\varepsilon_0)N(1-\theta)F(K)(1+e^-)]/[(1+r*)/(1-\tau*)] \tag{4.6'}$$

---

[11] Strictly speaking, the corporate tax rate (θ) applies to profits, $F(K) - K$, i.e., output minus depreciation, and not to output, $F(K)$. However, there is a one-to-one relation between the tax base $F(K) - K$ and the tax base $F(K)$. We therefore follow Gordon and Bovenberg (1996) in levying a tax at a rate θ on output, $F(K)$, which simplifies the notation a great deal.

[12] Here again, government bonds are superfluous, but we retain them in order to establish a possibility for the consumer to lend money and assign some meaningful value for a net-of-tax domestic interest rate, namely, $(1-\tau)r$.

Consider now the capital investment decision of the firm that is made before ε becomes known. The firm seeks to maximize its market value, net of the original investment (K). There is a probability $\Phi(\varepsilon_0)$ that it will be sold to foreign investors, who will pay $(1 - \theta)F(K)(1 + e^-)/[1 + r*/(1 - \tau*)]$. There is a probability $[1 - \Phi(\varepsilon_0)]$ that it will be sold to domestic investors, who will pay, on average, $(1 - \theta)F(K)(1 + e^+)/[1 + (1 - \tau)r]$. Hence the firm's expected market value, net of the original capital investment, is

$$-K + \Phi(\varepsilon_0)(1 - \theta)F(K)(1 + e^-)\big/[(1 + r*)/(1 - \tau*)]$$
$$+ [1 - \Phi(\varepsilon_0)](1 - \theta)F(K)(1 + e^+)\big/[1 + (1 - \tau)r] \qquad (4.9)'$$

Maximizing this expression with respect to K yields the following necessary and sufficient first-order condition:

$$\Phi(\varepsilon_0)(1 - \theta)F'(K)(1 + e^-)\big/[(1 + r*)/(1 - \tau*)]$$
$$+ [1 - \Phi(\varepsilon_0)](1 - \theta)F'(K)(1 + e^+)\big/[1 + (1 - \tau)r] = 1 \qquad (4.10a)'$$

Unlike the debt-finance case of the preceding section, the corporate tax in this equity-finance case *does* affect the firm's behavior, as expected and as can be seen immediately from $(4.10a)'$. Because the firm knows, when making its capital investment decision, that it will be sold to foreign investors at a "premium" if faced with low-productivity events, it tends to overinvest relative to the net-of-tax rate of return to domestic investors and underinvest relative to the net-of-tax rate of return to foreign investors:

$$(1 + r*)/(1 - \tau*) < (1 - \theta)F'(K) < 1 + (1 - \tau)r \qquad (4.10b)'$$

(A formal proof of these inequalities is provided in Appendix A, section A.3.)

The remaining equations of the FPEI model are essentially similar to those of the FPDI model in the preceding section. Equation (4.11), which defines the consumer's discount factor, stays intact. In equation (4.12), we have to replace FPDI by FPEI. Accordingly,

$$\text{FPEI} = NK - [I_1 - c_1(W, q) - G_1] \qquad (4.12)'$$

Equation (4.13b), the present-value resource constraint, remains unchanged.

The public finance objective is again to maximize $v(W, q)$ subject to six constraints: $(4.1)'$, $(4.6)'$, $(4.10a)'$, (4.11), $(4.12)'$, and $(4.13b)$. There are nine control (endogenous) variables: $K, r, \varepsilon_0, \tau*, \tau, \theta, q, W$, and FPEI.

Note that we have the same number of variables as before, but one less constraint. This is not surprising, as τ and r cannot be uniquely determined. Because the only lending/borrowing activity here is carried out between the government and the (homogeneous) household sector, what matters is the net-of-tax rate of interest [i.e., $(1 - \tau)r$], not τ and r separately. An analytical procedure similar to that in the preceding section is applied here.

The optimal policy prescriptions are as follows:[13]

1. As in the FPDI case, the expected net (of depreciation) marginal product of capital $[F'(K) - 1]$ must be equated to the world rate of interest ($r*$), so that

    $$F'(K) = 1 + r* \qquad (4.15)$$

    This means that the capital investment per firm is the same in the two cases (FPDI and FPEI).
2. The optimal policy calls for a subsidy to foreign investment. That is,

    $$\tau* < 0 \qquad (4.18)'$$

    To get this, observe first that, as in the preceding section, we can show that $1 + (1 - \tau)r = 1 + r*$ [equation (4.16)]. Substituting this equality into (4.10b)' yields $(1 + r*)/(1 - \tau*) < 1 + r*$, which implies (4.18)'.
3. It is optimal to levy a positive tax on corporate income. That is,

    $$\theta > 0 \qquad (4.20)$$

    To see this, substitute (4.15) and (4.16) into (4.10b)' to get $(1 - \theta)(1 + r*) < 1 + r*$, which implies that $\theta > 0$.

Indeed, by using the optimal tax instruments, we obtain again the first-best allocation, as in the preceding section. Thus the volume of optimal foreign investment is the same in both cases: FPDI = FPEI. The difference lies in the mix of policy tools:

1. In the debt-flow case, the corporate income tax (θ) is a neutral tax that could be set at any (arbitrarily high) level. In the equity-flow case, we find a well-defined tax $\theta > 0$.
2. In the debt-flow case, the capital income of residents should be positively taxed (i.e., $\tau > 0$). In the equity-flow case, τ is irrelevant.

---

[13] These are precisely the policy prescriptions derived by Gordon and Bovenberg (1996).

3. In the debt-flow case, the tax on capital income of nonresidents (τ^*) should be lower than the corresponding tax on residents (τ); that is, $\tau^* < \tau$. In the equity-flow case, foreign investment should actually be subsidized (i.e., $\tau^* < 0$), and τ is irrelevant.

In concluding our discussion of the two indirect flows of capital, let us emphasize that the real system with fixed corporate, domestic, and foreign-investment tax rates fits closely the first-best equilibrium that is achieved in the full-information setup.

4   Foreign Direct Investment (FDI)

In this section we consider international capital flows in the form of foreign direct investment (FDI). In a formal sense, foreign acquisition of shares in domestic firms is classified as FDI when the shares acquired exceed a certain fraction of ownership (say, 10–20%). From an economic point of view, we look at FDI not just as a purchase of a sizable share in a company but, more importantly, as an actual exercise of control and management. We thus view FDI as a tie-in activity, involving an inflow of both capital and managerial input.

This combination of inputs accords foreign investors the same kind of home-court advantage (with respect to, say, business information) that domestic investors have, but foreign-portfolio (debt and equity) investors lack. Specifically, foreign direct investors can learn about the state of the world (i.e., the realization of the productivity factor ε) at the same time as domestic investors. The asymmetric information feature of the two preceding sections is thus circumvented by FDI.[14]

A foreign direct investor purchases a domestic company from scratch, at the "greenfield" stage (i.e., before any capital investment has been made). In fact, the foreign direct investor makes the capital investment decision herself and imports capital input K^* from her country. Output in the second period is $F(K^*)(1 + \varepsilon)$. If J firms are purchased by foreign

---

[14] Caballero and Hammour (1996) identified a potentially important cost associated with foreign direct investment. They viewed FDI as a specific relation between domestic and foreign inputs that, to the extent that FDI is irreversible, creates specific quasi rent that may not be divided ex post according to the parties' ex ante terms of trade. The ex post bilateral monopoly, known in the literature as the holdup problem, requires prior protection through comprehensive and enforceable long-term contracts. The problem is that such contracts are not easily implementable in actual practice. The consequent undersupply of FDI may warrant favorable tax treatment by the host country. Furthermore, the shortage of FDI is exacerbated by the existence of technological spillovers.

direct investors, for a price of V^* per firm, then the total volume of FDI is given by

$$\text{FDI} = J(K^* + V^*) \tag{4.21}$$

The output of a domestically owned firm that invests a capital input of K continues to be $F(K)(1 + \varepsilon)$. As foreign investors and domestic investors are equally informed, the expected value of ε is the same for both investors (i.e., zero).

If a firm is sold to foreign direct investors, its expected second-period cash receipts, net of corporate taxes, will be $(1 - \theta)F(K^*)$,[15] which, in the first period, will be worth

$$(1 - \theta)F(K^*)/[(1 + r^*)/(1 - \tau^*)]$$

to the foreign investors. Subtracting the original capital investment from the preceding value yields the following as the market value of a firm purchased by foreign direct investors:

$$V^* = -K^* + (1 - \theta)F(K^*)/[(1 + r^*)/(1 - \tau^*)] \tag{4.22}$$

Similarly, the market value of a domestically owned firm is given by

$$V = -K + (1 - \theta)F(K)/[1 + (1 - \tau)r] \tag{4.23}$$

Thus, a firm is sold to foreign direct investors if (4.22) exceeds (4.23) (when K^* and K are optimally chosen). At an equilibrium with a positive number of firms owned by both types of investors, we must therefore have equality between (4.22) and (4.23); that is,

$$V^* = -K^* + (1 - \theta)F(K^*)/[(1 + r^*)/(1 - \tau^*)]$$
$$= -K + (1 - \theta)F(K)/[1 + (1 - \tau)r] = V \tag{4.1}''$$

Optimizing behavior on the part of all firms [i.e., maximization of (4.22) with respect to K^*, and (4.23) with respect to K] yields

$$F'(K^*) = (1 + r^*)/(1 - \bar{\tau}^*) \tag{4.10a}''$$

$$(1 - \theta)F'(K) = 1 + (1 - \tau)r$$

The total effective tax rate levied by the home country on the capital income of nonresidents at both the corporate and individual levels, denoted by $\bar{\tau}^*$, is defined implicitly by

---

[15] We continue to ignore depreciation in calculating the corporate tax base, with no loss of generality.

$$(1+r*)/(1-\bar{\tau}*) \equiv [(1+r*)/(1-\tau*)]/(1-\theta)$$

In this case of fully symmetric information, the optimal fiscal policy conclusions are quite straightforward (formal proofs are relegated to Appendix A, section A.4).

First, it will still be optimal to follow the aggregate production efficiency rule, which requires that

$$F'(K*) = 1 + r* \qquad (4.15)'$$

Comparing (4.15)' to (4.10a)″ implies that nonresidents' incomes should not be taxed; that is,

$$\bar{\tau}* = 0 \qquad (4.24)$$

Thus, the residence principle of international taxation should be followed in this case. FDI, which circumvents the asymmetric information distortion, restores the efficiency of the residence-based taxation on international flows of factors of production (see Frenkel et al., 1991).[16]

Note also that aggregate production efficiency requires that the net-of-depreciation marginal product of capital of the non-FDI domestic firm $[F'(K) - 1]$ be equal to the world rate of interest $(r*)$; that is,

$$F'(K) = 1 + r* \qquad (4.15)$$

Comparing (4.15)' to (4.15) implies that the firm owned by the foreign direct investor finds it profitable to carry the same capital investment as the domestically owned firm (i.e., $K* = K$). Also comparing (4.15) to (4.10a)″ implies that domestic tax rates must be set in such a way as to satisfy

$$1 + (1-\tau)r = (1+r*)(1-\theta) \qquad (4.25)$$

That is, there should be no tax distortions on the corporate profits of the non-FDI firms. [Recall from equation (4.10a)″ that the term on the left-hand side of (4.25) is the corporate return factor, net of all taxes, at both the individual level and the corporate level.][17]

---

[16] It is worth emphasizing that this strong result of no taxation of nonresidents' income holds whether or not the government can levy lump-sum taxes or transfers, i.e., whether or not a first-best allocation is attained. Thus, even when the government must resort to distortionary taxation on residents' incomes (i.e., $\tau > 0$) in order to meet its revenue needs, it will still be efficient to exempt nonresidents.

[17] In addition, aggregate production efficiency requires that the number of firms sold to foreign direct investors be such that the net economic value of a firm in the hands of foreign direct investors must be equal to the net economic value of a firm remaining under domestic control and management; that is,

To avoid distortions on the consumption side (i.e., to achieve MRS = $1 + r^*$), we must have $1 + (1 - \tau)r = 1 + r^*$. Hence, $(1 - \tau)r = r^*$.[18] Then (4.25) implies that $\theta = 0$.

5 Corrective Tax Experiments and Welfare Analysis: Some Simulation Results

In this section, we compare quantitatively the benchmark laissez faire FPDI and FPEI regimes with the (financial) autarky and FDI (first-best) regimes on the one hand, and with three optimal tax regimes on the other. Among the latter, the first corresponds to the first-best corrective tax regime while the second and third correspond to different second-best tax regimes. Between the two second-best regimes, one assumes a single distortionary tax instrument whose proceeds are rebated in a lump-sum fashion (assuming the other two tax instruments are not available); the other assumes the use of only distortionary tax instruments in the absence of lump-sum taxes/transfers.[19]

5.1 Tax Experiments Under FPDI

Let us first recapitulate the sources of inefficiencies under FPDI, and then quantitatively examine their allocative and welfare effects and corrective tax implications. Recall from (4.10b) above that $F'(K) < 1 + r$, implying that the domestic stock of capital is larger than what domestic consumer-savers are willing to pay for in terms of forgone present consumption – that is, domestic oversaving or production-consumption inefficiency. Recall also that because of the default possibility, foreign lenders will charge an ex ante interest rate (r) that is higher than what they will be satisfied with $[r^*/(1 - \tau^*)]$, given that their alternative return

$$F(K^*)/(1 + r^*) - K^* = F(K)/(1 + r^*) - K \quad (4.26)$$

Indeed, when the residence principle of international taxation is fulfilled and the domestic tax rates are set as in equation (4.25), then condition (4.26) must also be satisfied. This can be seen by substituting the optimal tax rules (4.24) and (4.25) into (4.1)" and comparing the outcome to (4.26). Obviously, (4.26) implies that $K = K^*$, a result that we have also established from (4.15)' and (4.15).

[18] Because there is no borrowing/lending except from/to the government, τ and r are not relevant separately. All that matters is that $(1 - \tau)r = r^*$, as in the FPEI case.

[19] Obviously, when the tax proceeds from one tax instrument have to balance those from another to satisfy the government budget constraint (as in the second of our second-best tax regimes), one of the taxes must be negative while the other must be positive.

at home is r^* – the difference being a reflection of the risk premium. Together with (4.7), this means that we are likely to get $F'(K) >$ $1 + r^*$, implying foreign underinvestment or aggregate production inefficiency.

The comparison between the unfettered FPDI with autarky reveals the magnitude of these inefficiencies. When we move from autarky to the FPDI regime, the aggregate production inefficiency measure is reduced from 64.8% to 44.3% and, as a by-product, the production-consumption inefficiency measure (which was nonexistent under the former regime) becomes −20.1%. As a result of this tradeoff, the welfare loss – defined as a permanent decrease in consumption in the second period, interpretable as the reduction in consumption for the second half of the current generation[20] – from shutting down these FPDI flows is a mere 0.06%. This suggests that the information asymmetry between domestic and foreign investors (a by-product of the liberalization of capital flows) creates so large a distortion that the net gains from opening up the international capital market are almost negligible.

As shown in Section 2, Pareto inefficiency can be restored by employing a positive tax on the capital income of the residents (i.e., $\tau > 0$), coupled with a lower tax (possibly at a negative rate – i.e., a subsidy) on the capital income of the nonresidents (i.e., $\tau^* < \tau$). (As previously stated, because the corporate tax is neutral in the FPDI case, we have set θ to zero in all these experiments.) Indeed, Table 4.2 reveals that the first-best taxes are $\tau = 5.1\%$ and $\tau^* = 4.7\%$ (given $\theta = 0$ due to the neutrality of the corporate income tax), respectively. The importance of the corrective tax package is highlighted by the significant increase in the share of FPDI in total investment from 0.10 to 3.99. Concomitantly, the fraction of good firms financed by FPDI (β) rises from 0.04 to 4.17. Since the debt flows finance not only firm investment but also private consumption, both measures of foreign capital ($FPDI/K$ and β) exceed unity. Domestic investment then rises by 16%. Evidently, the two kinds of inefficiencies vanish, resulting in a welfare gain of 1.57%.

When a single tax instrument is employed, welfare can still be improved; but naturally full Pareto efficiency cannot be restored. Interestingly enough, the welfare-improving change in a single-tax instrument can be in a direction opposite to the corresponding change in this instru-

---

[20] One reason why we focus on welfare changes in the *second* period is that, in our setup, all taxes are levied only in that period. Another reason is that in our simulations, we treat one period as half of a generation (30 years). Therefore, heavy discounting is applied to consumption changes in the second period if we define welfare in terms of compensating changes in *present* (i.e., first-period) consumption.

Table 4.2. *The effects of tax changes on FPDI and welfare*

Regime	θ	τ	τ^*	FPDI/K	K/K^0	β	Production inefficiency (%)	Production-consumption inefficiency (%)	Welfare gains (%)
Laissez faire	0	0	0	0.10	1	0.04	44.3	−20.1	0
Autarky	0	0	0	0	0.93	0	64.8	0	−0.06
First best	0	0.051	0.047	3.99	1.16	4.17	0	0	1.57
Second best (i.1)	0	0	0.12	0.42	1.01	0.38	40.0	−20.1	0.21
Second best (i.2)	0	−0.020	0	3.36	1.23	3.51	−18.2	−27.0	1.54
Second best (ii)	0	−0.028	0.08	0.27	1.04	0.22	32.7	−29.9	0.11

[a]The utility function is $U(c_2,c_1) = \ln(c_1) + \delta\ln(c_2)$, where $\delta = (0.9)^{30}$, representing a discount rate of 11%, with each of the two periods lasting 30 years.

[b]The production function is $F(K) = BK^a$, where B = 5 and $\alpha = 0.2$.

[c]The distribution of ε, $\Phi(\varepsilon)$, is assumed to be uniform over the interval $[-0.9, 0.9]$.

[d]The values for the other exogenous parameters are: $N = 1$, $l_1 = 9.4$, $l_2 = 9.0$, $1 + r^* = 1/\delta = (1.11)^{10}$.

[e]K^0 is the laissze faire (no-tax) level of the stock of domestic capital.

[f]The two distortion measures of aggregate production inefficiency and production-consumption inefficiency are given by $100[F'(K) - (1+r^*)]$ and $100[F'(K) - (1 + (1 - \tau)r)]$, respectively.

[g]The welfare gains are defined in terms of a compensating change in second-period consumption, $100\Delta\%$, with Δ given implicitly by $U[c_1^0, c_2^0(1 + \Delta)] = U(c_1,c_2)$, where (c_1^0, c_2^0) is the no-tax consumption bundle.

[h]Between the two second-best tax regimes, (i) involves a single distortionary tax/subsidy instrument financed by lump-sum taxes/transfers while (ii) involves two distortionary tax instruments without any lump-sum taxes/transfers.

ment as a component of the optimal package of all tax instruments. Rows 4 and 5 of Table 4.2 describe the effects of a single tax change, assuming all other tax rates are set to zero and the proceeds are distributed in a lump-sum fashion.

Consider first a change in the tax on the capital income of nonresidents (τ^*). Recall that as a component in the first-best tax package, τ^* has to be smaller than τ. Here, even though τ is set equal to zero, the welfare-maximizing τ^* ($=12\%$) is positive and warrants only a negligible welfare gain of 0.21%. As mentioned earlier, in the no-tax case, there are two distortions: aggregate production inefficiency and production-consumption inefficiency. A positive tax on the capital income of nonresidents, τ^*, serves to mitigate the negative impact of both inefficiencies. First, as τ^* must be fully shifted to domestic borrowers, this is achieved by a higher share of FPDI in total investment and a higher fraction (β) of "good" firms financed by FPDI [see (4.8)]. In our simulation, β rises from 0.04 in the no-tax case to 0.38 at the welfare-maximizing level of τ^*, and the fraction of the stock of capital financed by FPDI rises from 0.10 to 0.42. The increase in FPDI enhances welfare by a moderate 0.21% (because $F' > 1 + r^*$).

Consider next the effect of a change in the tax on the capital income of the residents (τ). In this case, we find that the welfare-maximizing rate is negative. A small subsidy of 2% for domestic saving generates a sizable welfare gain amounting to an increase of 1.54% in second-period consumption and gets the economy fairly close to the first-best optimum. The rationale behind this outcome is as follows. The government cannot directly affect FPDI through τ alone. It therefore subsidizes domestic saving, thereby raising the post-subsidy return to saving (i.e., $(1 - \tau)r$) and lowering the pre-subsidy return (i.e., r). Observing that with constant returns to scale production technology, ε_0 and hence $\Phi(\varepsilon_0)$ are not affected by policy variables [see (4.8) and (4.9)], this fall in r will raise the demand for capital by the firms, which will in turn bring in more FPDI. In fact, the welfare-maximizing subsidy τ raises the stock of capital by 23% and the flow of FPDI from 0.10 to 3.36, resulting in foreign over- (rather than under-) investment. Note from Table 4.2 that the τ instrument raises welfare more than does the τ^* instrument, as it brings in more FPDI, thereby more effectively mitigating the aggregate production inefficiency.

In the alternative second-best tax regime with purely distortionary taxes, $\tau = -2.8\%$ and $\tau^* = 8\%$. Here, again, the optimal tax package differs radically from its first-best counterpart. This tax mix does not induce a substantial rise in FPDI flows, and, as a result, the welfare gain is a meager 0.11%. Notice that in this case, the mitigation of the effect of the aggregate production inefficiency is achieved at the cost of exacerbating the production-consumption distortion.[21] However, the aggregate production efficiency principle generally dominates the production-consumption inefficiency.

5.2   Tax Experiments under FPEI

As in the previous subsection, let us first recapitulate the sources of in-efficiencies under FPEI, and then quantitatively examine their allocative and welfare effects and corrective tax implications. Referring once more to (4.10b)', $(1 + r^*)/(1 - \tau^*) < (1 - \theta)F'(K) < 1 + (1 - \tau)r$, which implies

$$1 + r^* < F'(K) < 1 + r \qquad (4.10b)'$$

under laissez faire (i.e., in the absence of taxes). The first inequality $(1 + r^* < F')$ indicates foreign underinvestment or aggregate production inefficiency. The second inequality $[F'(K) < 1 + r]$ indicates domestic oversaving or production consumption inefficiency.

Similar to Table 4.2, Table 4.3 compares the benchmark laissez faire FPEI regime with the (financial) autarky regime and the first- and second-best tax regimes (remembering that τ is set to zero in this section). The comparison between the unfettered FPEI and autarky reveals the magnitude of the inefficiency. When we move from autarky to the FPEI regime, the aggregate production inefficiency measure is reduced from 64.8% to 64.3%, and, as a by-product, the production-consumption inefficiency measure (which was nonexistent under the former regime) becomes -0.23%. As a result of this tradeoff, the welfare loss from shutting down these FPEI flows is a mere 0.01% (smaller than in the case of the laissez faire FPDI flows). Even more so than the FPDI case, this suggests that information asymmetry creates a distortion so large that the net gains from opening up the international capital market are negligible.

As shown in Section 3, Pareto inefficiency (i.e., $r^* = F' - 1 = r$) can be restored by a package of tax instruments in which $\theta > 0$ and $\tau^* < 0$. Indeed, Table 4.3 reveals that the first-best taxes are $\theta = 37\%$ and $\tau^* = -96\%$ (given $\tau = 0$ due to the neutrality of the capital income tax on the after-tax return for residents in this case), respectively. The importance of the corrective tax package is highlighted by the significant increase in the share of FPEI in total investment from 0.019 to 3.99. These equity flows finance not only firm investment but also private consumption

---

[21] In principle, second-best tax reforms can reduce distortions at some margin while increasing distortions at other margins. That is why, in Table 4.2 (as well as in Table 4.3), the absolute values of the two inefficiency measures are not necessarily smaller under the second-best regimes, relative to the laissez-faire regime.

Table 4.3. *The effects of tax changes on FPEI and welfare*

Regime	θ	τ	τ°	FPEI/K	K/K^0	Production inefficiency (%)	Production-consumption inefficiency (%)	Welfare gains (%)
Laissez faire	0	0	0	0.019	1.000	64.3	-0.23	0
Autarky	0	0	0	0	0.999	64.8	0	-0.0117
First best	0.37	0	-0.96	3.99	1.250	0	0	1.6237
Second best (i.1)	0	0	-0.83	2.60	1.660	-84.9	-100	1.3612
Second best (i.2)	0	0	0	0.019	1.000	64.3	-0.23	0
Second best (ii)	0.377	0	-0.96	4.02	1.240	-69.0	282.1	1.6236

Note: The preferences and technology as well as other parameter values are identical to those described in Table 4.2.

through short sales of domestic equity to foreigners. Domestic investment then rises by 25%. Evidently, the two kinds of inefficiencies vanish, resulting in a welfare gain of 1.62%.

Table 4.3 also illustrates what can be done when only one tax instrument is employed. Consider first the nonresident tax τ^* as the single instrument (with $\theta = 0$). In this case, we still wish to subsidize the capital income of the nonresidents (i.e., to set a negative τ^*) in order to attract more FPEI. This policy raises the total stock of capital but by a smaller amount than the increase in FPEI, so that domestic saving actually declines. The optimal subsidy to the capital income of the nonresidents is indeed found to be rather high, 83% (i.e., $\tau^* = -0.83$), resulting in foreign over- (rather than under-) investment and a fairly substantial welfare gain, equivalent to a 1.36% increase in half-generation consumption.

Consider next the corporate tax (θ) as a single tax instrument (with $\tau^* = 0$). In this case, the corporate tax reduces the return to investors, both foreign and domestic, and does not operate directly on production efficiency. It turns out that the welfare-maximizing rate for this tax is zero; thus, it coincides with the original laissez faire FPEI equilibrium.

If, however, the tax package involves only two distortionary taxes $(\theta$ and $\tau^*)$ but no lump-sum taxes/transfers, the second-best tax mix is almost indistinguishable from the first-best tax mix, and the welfare gain is only a tiny bit below that of the first best. In other words, the absence of the lump-sum tax/transfer instrument is insignificant here. Interestingly, such a tax package results in domestic undersaving and foreign overinvestment.

5.3   FDI versus FPDI and FPEI: The Costs of Asymmetric Information

In Section 4, we assume that foreign direct investors purchase domestic companies at the "greenfield" stage before any capital investment has been made. This aspect of FDI accords foreign investors with the same kind of "home court" advantage (with respect to, say, business information) that domestic investors have but foreign portfolio (debt and equity) investors lack. Specifically, foreign direct investors can learn about the state of the world (i.e., the realization of the productivity factor ε) at the same place as domestic investors do. The asymmetric information feature of the two preceding sections is thus circumvented by FDI. As a result, the laissez faire FDI allocation is Pareto-efficient and identical to the

Table 4.4. *The cost of asymmetric information*[a]

Type of capital flows	Deviation in capital stock (%)[b]	Deviation in capital imports (%)[c]	Deviation in savings rates (%)[d]	Welfare cost/(%)[e]
FPDI	−13.9	−97.8	0.770	1.55
FPEI	−19.5	−99.6	0.774	1.60

[a] Preferences, technology, and parameter values are as in Table 4.2.
[b] This is measured by $100(K^i - K^{FDI})/K^{FDI}$, where K^i is the domestic capital stock in case i = FPDI and FPEI, with no taxes.
[c] This is defined in a similar way as in *b*.
[d] This is measured by $100[(I_1 - c_1^i)/I_1 - (I_1 - c_1^{FDI})/I_1] = 100(c_1^{FDI} - c_1^i)/I_1$, where c_1^i is the first-period consumption and $100[(I_1 - c_1^i)/I_1]$ is the savings rate in case i = FPDI and FPEI, with no taxes.
[e] This is measured by 100Δ with Δ defined implicitly by $U(c_1^i, c_2^i) = U[c_1^{FDI}, c_2^{FDI}(1 - \Delta)]$, where i = FPDI and FPEI, with no taxes.

allocation achieved in the FPDI and FPEI cases with a full package of tax instruments.[22]

Table 4.4 compares this FDI symmetric information allocation with the laissez faire asymmetric information FPDI and FPEI allocations. It illustrates the large magnitude of foreign underinvestment (98–99%) and the relatively small magnitude of domestic oversaving (only 77 basic points of GNP) in both the FPDI and the FPEI cases, relative to the Pareto-efficient FDI case. Correspondingly, the stock of domestic capital is too low (by about 13.9% in the FPDI case and 19.5% in the FPEI case, relative to the FDI case). The overall welfare cost associated with the asymmetric information is sizable, amounting to a permanent fall of 1.55% in half-generation consumption in the FPDI case and 1.60% in the FPEI case, relative to the Pareto-efficient FDI case. Notice that the asymmetric information problem is more severe in the case of FPEI than in the case of FPDI. Tables 4.2 and 4.3 indicate, however, that the different corrective tax packages are more likely to

---

[22] In Razin, Sadka, and Yuen (1998a), we analyze a different asymmetric information structure in which the owner-managers of the firms are better informed about their productivity levels than are the outside suppliers of funds (both domestic and foreign). In that case, the exercise of control and management by the FDI investors accords them with informational advantages over foreign and domestic savers so that, in contrast to this case, the FDI equilibrium there will not be first best.

produce significant welfare gains in the case of FPEI than in the case of FPDI.

To summarize, the simulation exercise indicates that the market failures caused by the information asymmetry between domestic and foreign suppliers of investment funds are quite severe, slightly more so with equity flows than with debt flows. These inefficiencies can, nonetheless, be corrected by a mix of tax-subsidy instruments. However, when only a partial set of instruments is available in practice, the prescription for each tax instrument can change radically and may even be reversed. This may occur even though the welfare gains can be fairly substantial and sometimes close to the first-best optimum. This partial set of instruments seems to be more effective in handling market failures in the case of equity flows than in the case of debt flows.

Obviously, the first-best tax regime generates larger welfare gains than do second-best tax regimes. In comparing the two kinds of second-best regimes – that is, (i) single distortionary tax/subsidy instruments financed by lump-sum transfers/taxes and (ii) two distortionary tax/subsidy instruments without lump-sum taxes/transfers – we cannot draw a definite conclusion as to which regime welfare-dominates which. While regime (i) is welfare-superior in the FPDI case, the opposite is true in the FPEI case.

6   Conclusions

This chapter has considered optimal tax design by a small host country that is characterized by asymmetric information problems: Domestic investors are better or earlier informed about the profitability of investment projects than are prospective foreign investors. We have sequentially analyzed debt, equity, and direct-investment finance. For each financing vehicle we have determined the set of taxes that will be selected by the host government in order to maximize welfare in the host country. The main policy conclusions for the three forms of capital inflows are summarized in Table 4.5, which emphasizes the efficiency of a nonuniform treatment of the various vehicles of international capital flows.

In simulations based on this model, we have computed welfare-maximizing taxes in both the first- and second-best senses. There we have also found a welfare ranking among the three types of capital flow regimes in the absence of corrective taxes, which is consistent with the pecking order mentioned in the introduction; that is, FDI comes first, followed by FPDI flows, and lastly by FPEI flows. (See Table 4.4.)

Table 4.5. *Tax treatment of foreign investment*

	Type of foreign investment		
Type of tax	FPDI	FPEI	FDI
Corporate tax (θ)	High	Positive	Zero
Tax on capital income of residents (τ)	Positive	Irrelevant	Irrelevant
Tax on capital income of nonresidents (τ^* or $\bar{\tau}^*$)	Lower than on residents	Negative	Zero

Among other conclusions of our study, the reader may query the idea that subsidies should be provided to the ignorant. The foreign investors in our treatment have no incentive to invest in information-gathering, because they receive a rate of return on their investment that is the same as the rate of return they obtain elsewhere. In political correctness terminology, they are not informationally challenged, especially because there is a cost to acquiring information in reality.

Also, on political-economy grounds one may object to our conclusion of providing subsidies to foreign investors. Although the political-economy equilibrium is likely to be dominated by domestic pressure groups, it must incorporate the efficiency costs associated with the asymmetric information problems that we highlight in this chapter. This problem is reflected in the undersupply of foreign capital, which the subsidies help to alleviate.

Even if we take it for granted that foreign capital should be subsidized, do we actually observe subsidization of capital inflows in the real world? There is some evidence that regional governments and states compete for foreign capital through subsidies. But whether or not capital inflows effectively receive favorable tax treatment in the real world should, in our view, be a subject for future inquiries.

The aforementioned issues aside, our analysis in this study is by no means complete. Because our analysis has been confined to a small open economy, one may wonder if the findings here will carry over straightforwardly to large open economies. In the large economies case, will international policy coordination necessarily welfare-dominate policy competition? Will there be situations in which "policy cooperation among benevolent governments may be undesirable," as Kehoe (1989) suggests? Will the conclusions depend on the timing convention of the tax policies – in particular, whether taxes are set before or after investment decisions are made by the domestic and/or foreign investors?

Obviously, our study abstracts from discussions of many related issues in the taxation of foreign investment. One such issue is the existence of insured domestic financial intermediaries, as in the case of the central bank (or the government) bailing out troubled commercial banks and savings and loan institutions. If these intermediaries are not excluded from international transactions, the essentially domestic moral hazard problem may also plague international capital inflows. That problem, however, calls for applying policy instruments different from the ones analyzed in this study.

Concerning the asymmetric information structure, we have assumed that the domestic savers are better informed than their foreign counterparts. In another study (Razin, Sadka, and Yuen, 1998a, 1998b) we assume an alternative information structure in which the domestic firms ("insiders") possess an information advantage about their own productivity levels over and above the domestic and foreign suppliers of funds ("outsiders").[23] In reality, there may exist two levels of information asymmetry whereby the domestic firms are better informed than the domestic savers, who are in turn better informed than the foreign savers. In future research, we plan to examine the implications of this more realistic asymmetric information structure for capital flows and the efficiency in the allocation of world savings and investment.

In addition to informational asymmetry, there are other differences between foreign portfolio investment (FPI) and foreign direct investment (FDI). One noticeable difference lies in the degree of reversibility of these investment decisions: Whereas FDI is almost irreversible, FPI is not. How would this difference in lock-in effects affect the time consistency of the Pareto-efficient tax policies and international tax principles?

If we broaden the definition of investment to include human capital, then the issues of whether or not to subsidize foreign students and to tax foreign labor more heavily become relevant. Will the optimal tax impli-

---

[23] Obviously, differences in the nature of asymmetric information structures give rise to different kinds of market failure and different implications for corrective taxes. In particular, we find that (1) whereas the debt market is efficient, the scope of the equity market is too narrow – thus calling for a lump-sum subsidy to firms that equity-finance their investment, and (2) there exist foreign overinvestment and domestic undersaving in the FDI-equity case that call for a tax on the capital income of nonresidents and a subsidy to corporate income (Razin, Sadka, and Yuen, 1998a, 1998b).

cations depend on whether or not knowledge spillovers are generated by the inflow (or outflow) of workers?[24] These important issues and those mentioned in the preceding paragraphs are left for future research.

APPENDIX A

A.1 PROOF THAT THE CORPORATE INCOME TAX IS NONDISTORTIONARY IN THE CASE OF FPDI

Expression (4.9) describes the expected (second-period) cash receipts of the firm before any corporate taxes. If a corporate tax θ is levied on the firm, and assuming full loss offset, the expected tax liability will be

$$\theta\{F(K)-K-[1-\Phi(\varepsilon_0)]Kr-\Phi(\varepsilon_0)[F(K)(1+e^-)-K]\} \quad (4.A1)$$

The tax is levied on net output [i.e., $F(K) - K$, allowing for depreciation] minus interest expenses, which are either Kr with probability $1 - \Phi(\varepsilon_0)$ in the no-default case or $F(K)(1 + e^-) - K$ with probability $\Phi(\varepsilon_0)$ in the default case. Subtracting (4.A1) from (4.9) yields the net-of-tax expected cash receipts of the firms:

$$(1-\theta)\{F(K)-[1-\Phi(\varepsilon_0)]K(1+r)-\Phi(\varepsilon_0)F(K)(1+e^-)\} \quad (4.A2)$$

Because the after-tax objective function of the firm [i.e., (4.A2)] differs from its pre-tax objective function [i.e., (4.9)] by only a multiplicative factor (i.e., $1 - \theta$), it follows that, with a full loss offset, the tax has no effect on the firm's behavior.

A.2 PROOF OF EQUATION (4.16)

Differentiate L [equation (4.14)] with respect to W and q to get

$$v_1 - \lambda c_{11} - \lambda c_{21}/(1+r^*) = 0 \quad (4.A3)$$

and

$$v_2 - \lambda c_{12} - \lambda c_{22}/(1+r^*) = 0 \quad (4.A4)$$

where $v_1 = \partial v/\partial W$, $v_2 = \partial v/\partial q$, $c_{11} = \partial c_1/\partial W$, $c_{12} = \partial c_1/\partial q$, $c_{21} = \partial c_2/\partial W$, and $c_{22} = \partial c_2/\partial q$. Substituting Roy's identity

$$v_2 = -c_2 v_1 \quad (4.A5)$$

---

[24] Some of these issues are dealt with by Razin and Yuen (1997).

and the Hicks-Slutsky equations

$$c_{i2} = \bar{c}_{i2} - c_2 c_{i1} \quad (i = 1, 2) \tag{4.A6}$$

where $\bar{c}_{i2}$ is the Hicks-compensated derivative of c_i with respect to q, into (4.A4) yields

$$-c_2[v_1 - \lambda c_{11} - \lambda c_{21}/(1+r^*) - \lambda \bar{c}_{12} - \lambda \bar{c}_{22}/(1+r^*) = 0 \tag{4.A7}$$

Substitute (4.A3) into (4.A7) to get

$$\bar{c}_{21} - \bar{c}_{22}/(1+r^*) = 0 \tag{4.A8}$$

where use is made of the symmetry of the Hicks-substitution effects: $\bar{c}_{12} = \bar{c}_{21}$. Substituting the Euler equation

$$\bar{c}_{21} + q\bar{c}_{21} = 0 \tag{4.A9}$$

into (4.A8) implies $q^{-1} = 1 + r^*$.

A.3 PROOF OF EQUATION (4.10b)′

Substitute for $(1 + e^-)[(1 + r^*)/(1 - \tau^*)]$ from (4.1)′ into (4.10a)′ and rearrange terms to get

$$\Phi(\varepsilon_0)(1-\theta)F'(K)(1+\varepsilon_0) + [1 - \Phi(\varepsilon_0)](1-\theta)F'(K)(1+e^+) = 1 + (1-\tau)r \tag{4.A10}$$

Because $1 + \varepsilon_0 > 1 + e^-$, it follows from (4.A10) that

$$1 + (1-\tau)r > (1-\theta)F'(K)\{\Phi(\varepsilon_0)(1+e^-) + [1 - \Phi(\varepsilon_0)](1+e^+)\}$$
$$= (1-\theta)F'(K),$$

given the term in the curly brackets is equal to unity [see equation (4.4)]. This proves the inequality in the right end of (4.10b)′. Substitute for $1 + (1 - \tau)r$ from (4.1)′ into (4.10a)′ and rearrange terms to get

$$\Phi(\varepsilon_0)(1-\theta)F'(K)(1+e^-) + [1 - \Phi(\varepsilon_0)](1-\theta)$$
$$F'(K)(1+e^+)(1+e^-)(1+\varepsilon_0)^{-1} = (1+r^*)/(1-\tau^*) \tag{4.A11}$$

Because $(1 + e^-)(1 + \varepsilon_0)^{-1} < 1$, it follows from (4.A11) that

$$(1+r^*)/(1-\tau^*) < (1-\theta)F'(K)\{\Phi(\varepsilon_0)(1+e^-)$$
$$+ [1 - \Phi(\varepsilon_0)](1+e^+)\} = (1-\theta)F'(K),$$

which completes the proof of (4.10b)′.

A.4 PROOF OF EQUATION (4.26)

The objective of the government is to choose K, K^*, q, W, and J so as to maximize $v(W, q)$ subject to the present-value resource constraint:

$$(I_1 + I_2)/(1 + r^*) + (N - J)F(K)/(1 + r^*)$$
$$+ JF(K^*)/(1 + r^*) = c_1(W, q) + c_2(W, q)/(1 + r^*)$$
$$+ G_1 + G_2/(1 + r^*) + (N - J)K + JK^* \qquad (4.13b)'$$

Then the other six control variables – FDI, $V, \tau, r, \bar{\tau}^*, \theta$ – are determined by the constraints (4.21), (4.1)″, (4.10a)″, (4.11), and the first-period resource constraint

$$\text{FDI} = JK^* + (N - J)K - [I_1 - c_1(W, q) - G_1] \qquad (4.12)''$$

The Lagrangian expression is

$$L = v(W, q) + \lambda[(I_1 + I_2)/(1 + r^*) + (N - J)F(K)/(1 + r^*)$$
$$+ JF(K^*)/(1 + r^*) - c_1(W, q) - G_1 - c_2(W, q)/(1 + r^*)$$
$$- G_2/(1 + r^*) - (N - J)K - JK^*] \qquad (4.14)''$$

The first-order conditions establish the familiar aggregate production efficiency results:

$$F'(K^*) = 1 + r^* \qquad (4.15)'$$

$$F'(K) = 1 + r^* \qquad (4.15)$$

In addition, differentiating L with respect to J and setting the derivative equal to zero yields

$$F(K^*) - (1 + r^*)K^* = F(K) - (1 + r^*)K$$

This proves (4.26).

APPENDIX B: THE INFINITE-HORIZON MODEL

The two-period analysis in the main text has a natural extension to an infinite horizon. For simplicity, we assume that the random productivity factor is serially uncorrelated and that there is no information-gathering or learning over time, so that the same asymmetric information problem will repeat itself period after period. In this appendix we consider only the laissez faire cases (i.e., the analogue of Sections 2 and 3 without taxes) and focus only on that part of the analysis that differs somewhat from the two-period analysis in the text.

B.1 LOAN AND DEBT FINANCE (FPDI)

In the case of FPDI, two extreme kinds of credit-market arrangements that span the whole spectrum of financing possibilities can be considered. In one extreme, the firm is allowed to use as collateral its expected future value $E[V(K')]$ (where the prime denotes next-period value). In the other extreme, collaterals are not allowed.

Assuming full distribution of current profits to the households every period (i.e., no past-accumulated profits by the firms), the cutoff level of ε_0' when the firm cannot use its expected future value as collateral is determined by

$$F(K')(1+\varepsilon_0')=[K'-(1-\delta)K](1+r') \tag{4.B1}$$

where the rate of capital depreciation, δ, is allowed to be less than unity here, so that the total firm loan equals its investment, $K' - (1 - \delta)K$.

The objective function of the firm becomes

$$E[V(K)] = \max_{K'} \{F(K') + E[V(K')]$$
$$- [1 - \Phi(\varepsilon_0')][K' - (1 - \delta)K](1 + r')$$
$$- \Phi(\varepsilon_0')F(K')(1 + e^{-'})\}/(1 + r')$$

The first-order condition and envelope condition from the firm's optimal investment decision imply that

$$F'(K') = \left(\frac{1 - \Phi(\varepsilon_0')}{1 - \Phi(\varepsilon_0')(1 + e^{-'})}\right)\left[(r' + \delta) + (1 - \delta)\left(\frac{\Phi(\varepsilon_0'') - \Phi(\varepsilon_0')}{1 - \Phi(\varepsilon_0')}\right)\right] \tag{4.B2}$$

where the two primes indicate two-period-ahead values. In the steady state, where $\Phi(\varepsilon_0') = \Phi(\varepsilon_0'')$, (4.B2) implies that $F'(K') < r' + \delta$, since $e^- < 0$. Note that given the assumed constancy of the foreign interest rate r^*, the domestic capital stock and the cutoff level of the random (serially uncorrelated) productivity factor will attain their steady-state values in one period, so that $\Phi(\varepsilon_0') = \Phi(\varepsilon_0'')$ and $F'(K') < r' + \delta$, as in the two-period model of Section 2. As the domestic interest rate r' represents the willingness of the domestic savers to forgo current consumption in return for future consumption, this inequality implies domestic oversaving.

On the other hand, the possibility of foreign underinvestment [i.e., $F'(K') > r^{*'} + \delta$, as the foreign interest rate $r^{*'}$ represents the country's external cost of funds] can be established in a way that is similar to the two-period case (see footnote 8) and will not be repeated here. As a result, the capital stock can very likely be underaccumulated and thus lower than its Pareto-efficient level.

Overall, the multiperiod extension does not change the efficiency implications of the information asymmetry from the two-period case. The story can be very different, however, when the firm can use its future value as collateral. We now turn to that case.

In the alternative case in which the firm is allowed to borrow against its expected future value, the cutoff value of ε'_0 is determined by the following condition:

$$F(K')(1 + \varepsilon'_0) + E[V(K')] = [K' - (1 - \delta)K](1 + r') \qquad (4.B1)'$$

The objective function of the firm can be specified by the Bellman equation:

$$
\begin{aligned}
E[V(K)] = \max_{K'} \{ &F(K') + E[V(K')] \\
&- [1 - \Phi(\varepsilon'_0)][K' - (1 - \delta)K](1 + r') \\
&- \Phi(\varepsilon'_0)[F(K')(1 + e^{-'}) + E[V(K')]] \}/(1 + r')
\end{aligned}
$$

Observe that the term $E[V(K')]$ appears twice in the firm's objective function. Its first appearance is for the period after next, for, whether or not it defaults, that is its expected future value to its owner; it appears for the second time under the default situation in the next period, because the firm is allowed to use its expected future value as collateral.

Combining the first-order condition with the envelope condition, we have

$$F'(K') = \left(\frac{1 - \Phi(\varepsilon'_0)}{1 - \Phi(\varepsilon'_0)(1 + e^{-'})} \right) [(r' + \delta)\, \Phi(\varepsilon''_0)(1 - \delta)] \qquad (4.B2)'$$

Because $e^{-} < 0$, it follows from (4.B2)' that $F'(K') < r' + \delta$; that is, the asymmetric information problem will lead to domestic oversaving only if $\Phi(\varepsilon'_0)$ is close to zero or δ is close to unity. Note that equation (4.B2)' is different from its two-period analogue (4.10a) because of the inclusion of the term $\Phi(\varepsilon''_0)(1 - \delta)$, which is equal to the expected marginal future value of the firm from one unit of investment, $E[V'(K')]$ – interpretable as the marginal penalty due to seizure of the collateral if the firm chooses to default. Obviously, this term is absent in the two-period framework where the second period is terminal and $\delta = 1$. As the firm's liability will no longer be limited by its current output in the case of default, domestic undersaving may occur if such penalty is large (as when the default probability is high and/or when the capital depreciation rate is small). Because $r > r*$ (see footnote 8), it is still likely to have foreign underinvestment and hence underaccumulation of capital relative to the Pareto-efficient level, whether we have domestic oversaving or undersaving.

B.2 EQUITY FINANCE (FPEI)

In the case of equity finance, the value to the foreign equity investors who purchase only low-productivity firms is given by

$$V^-(K) = \{F(K')(1+e^{-'}) + E[V(K')]\}/(1+r^{*'})$$
$$- [K' - (1-\delta)K]$$

Similarly, the value to the marginal domestic investors who purchase the lowest-ε firms in the high-productivity group is given by

$$V^0(K) = \{F(K')(1+\varepsilon'_0) + E[V(K')]\}/(1+r')$$
$$- [K' - (1-\delta)K]$$

The cutoff level for ε is defined by equating $V^-(K)$ to $V^0(K)$, which can be simplified as follows:

$$\frac{F(K')(1+e^{-'}) + E[V(K')]}{1+r^{*'}} = \frac{F(K')(1+\varepsilon'_0) + E[V(K')]}{1+r'} \quad (4.B3)$$

The firm's expected market value, net of capital investment, is

$$E[V(K)] = \max_{\{K'\}} \Phi(\varepsilon'_0) \frac{F(K')(1+e^{-'}) + E[V(K')]}{1+r^{*'}}$$
$$+ [1 - \Phi(\varepsilon'_0)] \frac{F(K')(1+\varepsilon'_0) + E[V(K')]}{1+r'} - [K' - (1-\delta)K]$$

Combining the first-order condition with the envelope condition, we have

$$1 = \Phi(\varepsilon'_0) \frac{F'(K')(1+e^{-'}) + (1-\delta)}{1+r^{*'}}$$
$$+ [1 - \Phi(\varepsilon'_0)] \frac{F'(K')(1+e^{+'}) + (1-\delta)}{1+r'} \quad (4.B4)$$

To address the issue of foreign underinvestment and domestic oversaving, we have to compare the net marginal productivity of capital $[F'(K') - \delta]$ with the foreign and domestic interest rates ($r^{*'}$ and r').

Substituting for $1/(1 + r^{*\prime})$ from (4.B3) into (4.B4) and rearranging terms, we get

$$\Phi(\varepsilon_0')[F'(K')(1+e^{-\prime})+(1-\delta)]z'$$
$$+[1-\Phi(\varepsilon_0')][F'(K')(1+e^{+\prime})+(1-\delta)]=1+r'$$

where

$$z' = \{F(K')(1+\varepsilon_0')+(1-\delta)K' + E[V(K')]\}/$$
$$\{F(K')(1+e^{-\prime})+(1-\delta)K' + E[V(K')]\} > 1$$

because $\varepsilon_0 > e^-$. It therefore follows that

$$1+r' > [F'(K')+(1-\delta)]\{\Phi(\varepsilon_0')(1+e^{-\prime})+[1-\Phi(\varepsilon_0')](1+e^{+\prime})\}$$
$$= F'(K')+(1-\delta)$$

because the term in curly brackets is equal to unity [see equation (4.4)]. This implies, in turn, that

$$F'(K') < r' + \delta$$

Substituting for $1/(1 + r')$ from (4.B3) into (4.B4) and rearranging terms, we get

$$\Phi(\varepsilon_0')[F'(K')(1+e^{-\prime})+(1-\delta)]$$
$$+[1-\Phi(\varepsilon_0')][F'(K')(1+e^{+\prime})+(1-\delta)]/z' = 1+r^{*\prime}$$

Because $z' > 1$ (given $\varepsilon_0 > e^-$), it follows that

$$1+r^{*\prime} < [F'(K')+(1-\delta)]\{\Phi(\varepsilon_0')(1+e^{-\prime})+[1-\Phi(\varepsilon_0')](1+e^{+\prime})\}$$
$$= F'(K')+(1-\delta)$$

which implies in turn that

$$F'(K') > r^{*\prime} + \delta$$

Together, the two preceding inequalities [i.e., $F'(K') < r' + \delta$, and $F'(K') > r^{*\prime} + \delta$] imply that

$$r^{*\prime} < F'(K') - \delta < r'$$

The first inequality implies foreign underinvestment, and the second implies domestic oversaving. In other words, the asymmetric information leads to underaccumulation of capital in the FPEI case relative to the Pareto-efficient stock of capital.

The multiperiod extension of the FDI (full and symmetric information) case is straightforward and so will not be discussed here. Obviously, the equilibrium it generates will remain first-best efficient. If we allow for active learning and information-gathering on the part of the foreign portfolio investors, however, the inefficiencies associated with the information asymmetry in the FPDI and FPEI cases may vanish over time. This means that the inefficient accumulation of capital may be only a short-run transitional phenomenon that will not necessarily carry over to the long-run steady-state equilibrium.

REFERENCES

Bayoumi, T., and Gagnon, J. (1996). Taxation and inflation: a new explanation for capital flows. *Journal of Monetary Economics* 38:303–30.
Caballero, R. J., and Hammour, M. L. (1996). The macroeconomics of specificity. Unpublished manuscript, Department of Economics, Massachusetts Institute of Technology.
Claessens, S. (1995). The emergence of equity investment in developing countries: overview. *World Bank Economic Review* 9:1–18.
Eaton, J., and Gersovitz, M. (1989). Country risk and the organization of international capital transfer. In: *Debt, Stabilization, and Development: Essays in Memory of Carlos Diaz-Alejandro*, ed. G. A. Calvo et al. London: Blackwell.
Frenkel, J. A., Razin, A., and Sadka, E. (1991). *International Taxation in an Integrated World Economy*. Massachusetts Institute of Technology Press.
Gordon, R. H., and Bovenberg, A. L. (1996). Why is capital so immobile internationally? Possible explanations and implications for capital income taxation. NBER working paper 4796. Washington, DC: National Bureau of Economic Research.
Gordon, R. H., and Varian, H. (1989). Taxation of asset income in the presence of a world security market. *Journal of International Economics* 26:205–26.
Huberman, G. "Familiarity breeds investment." Columbia University Business School, mimeo.
Kehoe, P. J. (1989). Policy cooperation among benevolent governments may be undesirable. *Review of Economic Studies* 56:289–96.
Myers, S. C. (1984). The capital structure puzzle. *Journal of Finance* 39:575–85.
Obstfeld, M., and Rogoff, K. (1996). *Foundations of International Macroeconomics*. Massachusetts Institute of Technology Press.
Razin, A., Sadka, E., and Yuen, C.-W. (1998a). Channeling domestic savings into productive investment under asymmetric information: The essential role of foreign direct investment. Unpublished manuscript.
Razin, A., Sadka, E., and Yuen, C.-W. (1998b). Capital flows with debt- and equity-financed investment: Equilibrium structure and efficiency implications. Unpublished manuscript.

Razin, A., Sadka, E., and Yuen, C.-W. (1998c). Why debt flows may crowd out home-biased equity flows? Unpublished manuscript.

Razin, A., and Yuen, C.-W. (1997). Income convergence within an economic union: the role of factor mobility and coordination. *Journal of Public Economics* 66:225–45.

Samuelson, P. A. (1956). Social indifference curves. *Quarterly Journal of Economics* 70:1–22.

Stiglitz, J. E., and Weiss, A. (1981). Credit rationing in markets with imperfect information. *American Economic Review* 71:393–410.

Tesar, L. L., and Werner, I. M. (1995). U.S. equity investment in emerging stock markets. *World Bank Economic Review* 9:109–30.

CHAPTER 5

Transfer Pricing as a Strategic Device for Decentralized Multinationals

Guttorm Schjelderup and Lars Sørgard

1   Introduction

In the literature on multinational enterprises (MNEs) it has been recognized that an MNE encountering differing tax and tariff schedules can shift profits to low-tax countries by altering transfer prices (Copithorne, 1971; Horst, 1971). There are two crucial assumptions in the literature on transfer pricing: First, the MNE's price or quantity decisions are made at a central level; second, the MNE exercises monopoly power in national markets. Many MNEs, however, delegate decision-making, such as output price decisions, to national affiliates. This is common in the automobile industry, where the parent company, which is the producer, determines the export price (transfer price) to importing foreign affiliates, but leaves the responsibility of deciding on the final price to consumers to the importing affiliate. Moreover, in most industries, including the automobile and oil industries, MNEs interact with other firms. Hence the monopoly-power assumption in the conventional literature is often violated. The purpose of this study is to analyze whether or not an MNE's transfer-pricing policy, which is decided upon at a central level, changes if the foregoing two assumptions are relaxed.

It is well known in the industrial-organization literature that a principal can gain extra benefit by hiring an agent and giving that agent an incentive to maximize something other than the welfare of the principal. Thus, if an MNE's affiliates face oligopolistic competition, it may be beneficial to the MNE to direct the incentives away from maximizing the MNE's global profits; provided that the MNE's competitors in the

We are indebted to Jack Mintz and two anonymous referees for extremely valuable comments.

123

national markets react favorably. In particular, if an MNE sets the transfer price at a central level, but delegates decisions about prices or quantities in national markets to national affiliates, the MNE may gain from such a strategy. Under Cournot competition, for example, setting a low transfer price to an importing affiliate will turn the importing affiliate into a low-cost firm that will behave aggressively by selling a large quantity. Such aggressive behavior will encourage its rival to behave softly by selling a low quantity. A soft response from the rival will be beneficial to the MNE, thus suggesting that delegation of decision-making has strategic value.[1]

If MNEs interact strategically with other firms in some national markets, and if the affiliates of the MNEs in these markets can independently choose their optimal quantities or prices, then the price for intrafirm traded goods (the transfer price) – which is set at a central level – will be a function of (1) the nature of the competition and (2) the tax and tariff rates. In the industrial-organization literature on MNE behavior, both delegation of authority to local affiliates and strategic interaction are discussed.[2] The focal point in that literature on MNEs, however, is on foreign direct investments, not on profit shifting through transfer pricing. The analyses typically examine whether an MNE should produce a good in the foreign market or establish a foreign affiliate to import the good from the national market where the MNE's headquarters are located (Horstman and Markusen, 1992; Motta, 1992; Cordella and Vannini, 1993; Markusen and Venables, 1995). In contrast, we assume that the affiliate in the foreign market is importing its good from the MNE's home country.

We incorporate delegation of authority and strategic interaction into the conventional literature on the microeconomics of transfer pricing, where the question of how profits can be shifted from one country to

---

[1] The gains from delegation were first discussed by Schelling (1960) and further elaborated by Vickers (1985), Sklivas (1987), and Fersthman and Judd (1987). For a survey of the literature, see Shapiro (1989), Katz (1989), and Basu (1993, ch. 14). The focal point in those studies was that an owner can gain by delegating decisions to the firm's manager. This is the same kind of mechanism that we are discussing, where the MNE delegates output decisions to its affiliates. Notice that Janeba (1996) incorporated competition into the context of multinationals, but did not focus on the strategic aspect of transfer pricing. Elitzur and Mintz (1996) modeled multinational-firm behavior in a principal–agent setting, but in their model the transfer price was not a strategic variable.

[2] Hirshleifer (1957) proved that in the absence of tax and tariff rates, the efficient transfer price when the individual divisions of the MNE were run as separate profit centers equaled the marginal cost of the exporting division. That early attempt to enrich the literature on transfer pricing by MNEs seems to have been overlooked by most later authors.

another through transfer pricing is at the heart of the analysis. The structure of the chapter is as follows: Section 2 constructs the model and discusses some of the underlying assumptions. Sections 3 and 4 examine strategic interaction by assuming that either Cournot competition or Bertrand competition prevails in one of the national markets. Section 5 examines a numerical example, and Section 6 offers some concluding remarks.

2   Some Preliminaries

The model is one of horizontally integrated trade in secondary processed goods along the lines of Horst (1971). Initially we assume that the MNE has affiliates with monopolistic power in two countries: country 1 and country 2. The MNE's objective is to maximize net global profits. The affiliate in country 1 produces quantities s and S_1 and has a cost function of $c(s + S_1)$, where $c' \geq 0$ and $c'' \geq 0$. Quantity s is sold in country 1 at a price $p(s)$, yielding revenue $r(s)$, where $r'' \leq 0$ and $p' < 0$. Quantity S_1 is exported to the affiliate in country 2 at a transfer price q and is resold in country 2 at a price $P(S_1)$, earning revenue $R(S_1)$ (in the absence of competition), with $P' < 0$ and $R'' \leq 0$. It is assumed that the MNE is able to practice systematic price discrimination between the domestic market and the foreign market. Then

$$\pi_1 = [r(s) - c(s + S_1) + qS_1] \quad \text{and} \quad \pi_2 = [R(S_1) - q(1 + \tau)S_1]$$

where τ is an ad valorem tariff on imports in country 2.

We assume that the affiliates are separate and independent entities, so that they are subsidiaries and thus are taxed at source. The MNE is faced with proportionate profit taxes of t and T in countries 1 and 2. The importing affiliate repatriates its profits to the affiliate in country 1. The taxation of repatriated profits varies across countries. A number of capital-exporting countries give a tax credit, upon repatriation, for foreign taxes paid.[3] When $t \geq T$, full credit is given, whereas when $t < T$, the credit is equal to the home-country tax on foreign profits, so that income earned in country 2 is effectively exempt from taxation upon repatriation. These two cases are discussed next.[4] To illustrate the tax-shifting motive, it is initially assumed that all decisions are made at a central level.

---

[3] See OECD (1977) for an elaboration of how repatriated profits are taxed.
[4] Alternatively, $t < T$ could be interpreted as the source principle of taxation, and the case $t \geq T$ as the residence principle with full credit for foreign taxes paid.

Case 1.   When $t < T$, foreign-source income is exempt from taxation because the credit for foreign taxes paid is limited to the domestic tax due on foreign-source income. The MNE's global after-tax profits are[5]

$$\Pi = (1-t)\pi_1 + (1-T)\pi_2 \tag{5.1}$$

Note that equation (5.1) is applicable only if profits in both countries are nonnegative, because negative profits would not be taxed.

In the absence of strategic interaction, the transfer price takes on the role of a pure profit-shifting device. In this case the transfer-pricing policy of the MNE depends on the sign of the following equation:

$$\frac{\partial \Pi}{\partial q} = S_1(1-T)[\theta - \tau] \tag{5.2}$$

where $\theta \equiv (T - t)/(1 - T)$ is the relative differential in tax rates between the importing country and the exporting country. From (5.2) it can be seen that when $\theta > \tau$, profits can be increased by raising the transfer price; that is, the MNE reduces the total tax payment by charging a high transfer price (above marginal cost) on exports to country 2. Similarly, when $\theta < \tau$, a low transfer price is desirable. Thus the tax motive for setting the transfer price is determined by differences in national tax and tariff rates.

Case 2.   When $t \geq T$, taxes paid in country 2 are refunded to the MNE, but profits in country 2 are subject to taxation in country 1 upon repatriation. Then:

$$\Pi = (1-t)[\pi_1 + \pi_2] \tag{5.3}$$

The transfer-pricing policy of the MNE depends on the sign of the following equation:

$$\frac{\partial \Pi}{\partial q} = \tau S_1(1-t) < 0 \tag{5.4}$$

so that when full credit is given, the MNE will always choose a low transfer price in order to save the cost of the tariff.

Thus far we have outlined the role of the transfer price as a profit-shifting device when decisions about the transfer price and quantities (or prices) are set at a central level. In the next sections the assumption about monopoly in national markets is relaxed by introducing oligopolistic competition in country 2. In addition, it is assumed that decisions

---

[5] This profit expression is similar to that of Samuelson (1982).

about quantities (or prices) in national markets are delegated to national affiliates.

The introduction of competition in country 2 means that when setting the transfer price on exports from country 1 to country 2, the MNE must take into account the fact that the affiliate in country 2 faces a local rival. For example, a low transfer price encourages the affiliate in country 2 to behave aggressively. When the local rival observes a low transfer price, it anticipates that the affiliate will behave aggressively, and it responds by changing its own behavior. Notice that the strategic effect of the transfer price (i.e., its effect on the local rival's behavior) is crucially dependent on the fact that the rival can observe the transfer price of the MNE.[6] Competition in country 1 is not allowed for, and it can be shown that the qualitative results from this model are not affected by allowing for competition in both countries. Restricting competition to country 2, however, is of importance for the magnitude of the strategic effect.[7]

3   Optimal Transfer-Pricing Policy under Cournot Competition

Suppose now that the affiliate in country 2 faces a local rival. Let S_2 denote the quantity sold by the local rival. Furthermore, let us assume that Cournot competition prevails and that the two competing firms are thus quantity-setters.[8] Sales in country 2 bring the MNE a revenue of

---

[6] Because the competing firms set their choice variables (either prices or quantities) simultaneously, the local rival cannot observe the affiliate's actual behavior before setting its own quantity (or price). Hence, by observing the transfer price, it anticipates the affiliate's actual behavior. Observability of the transfer price may seem a strong assumption. However, import prices are public information in many countries because of the calculation of tariff payments. And in the automobile industry, for example, import prices and thus transfer prices are public information. For a discussion of the role of observability, see Katz (1991).

[7] To understand this, it should be instructive to investigate the following example: Suppose the multinational firm has increasing marginal costs of production and that there is Cournot competition in both countries. As shown in Section 3, the optimal transfer price in the absence of tax and tariff policies is to set a low transfer price on exports to country 2. A low price encourages the affiliate in country 2 to behave aggressively and thus to sell a large quantity. A large quantity sold, however, will increase the marginal costs of production for sale in country 1. The increase in marginal costs is therefore disadvantageous for the affiliate from a strategic point of view, and it dampens the multinational firm's incentive to set a low transfer price. Only in the case of constant marginal costs of production is this effect of no importance.

[8] Although technically we assume that the firms set quantities, we can interpret the nature of competition as simultaneous capacity-setting, followed by simultaneous price-setting (Kreps and Scheinkmann, 1983).

$R(S_1, S_2)$, with $\partial^2 R/\partial S_1^2 \leq 0$ and $\partial R/\partial S_2 < 0$. The latter implies that the two firms' products sold in country 2 are substitutes.

The discussion will now proceed along two lines. We shall first examine how the transfer price should be set when $t < T$ and a limited tax credit applies, and then we shall discuss how the optimal transfer price is set when $t \geq T$ and full credit is given for foreign taxes paid.

3.1   Transfer Pricing When $t < T$

The global profit-maximizing function of the firm is now

$$\Pi = (1-t)\pi_1 + (1-T)\pi_2$$
$$= (1-t)[r(s) - c(s+S_1) + qS_1] + (1-T)[R(S_1, S_2) - q(1+\tau)S_1] \quad (5.5)$$

Under delegation of authority, the MNE chooses q at a central location in order to maximize net global profits, but it delegates decisions about price or quantities in local markets to its affiliates. The maximization procedure has two stages: At the first stage, a central authority within the MNE sets q. At the second stage, the firm in country 1, the affiliate in country 2, and its competitor set the quantities $s^* = s^*(q)$, $S_1^* = S_1^*(q)$, and $S_2^* = S_2^*(q)$.

A marginal change in q will affect the global profit of the MNE as follows:

$$\frac{\partial \Pi}{\partial q} = (1-t)\left[\left(\frac{\partial r}{\partial s} - \frac{\partial c}{\partial s}\right)\frac{\partial s}{\partial S_1}\frac{\partial S_1}{\partial q} - \left(\frac{\partial c}{\partial S_1}\frac{\partial S_1}{\partial q}\right) + S_1 + q\frac{\partial S_1}{\partial q}\right]$$
$$+ (1-T)\left[\left(\frac{\partial T}{\partial S_1} - q(1+\tau)\right)\frac{\partial S_1}{\partial q} + \left(\frac{\partial R}{\partial S_2}\frac{\partial S_2}{\partial q}\right) - (1+\tau)S_1\right] \quad (5.6)$$

Because both affiliates take the transfer price as exogenous, their first-order conditions are

$$\frac{\partial \pi_1}{\partial s} = (1-t)\left[\frac{\partial r}{\partial s} - \frac{\partial c}{\partial s}\right] = 0 \quad (5.7)$$

$$\frac{\partial \pi_2}{\partial S_1} = (1-T)\left[\frac{\partial R}{\partial S_1} - (1+\tau)q\right] = 0 \quad (5.8)$$

As explained in the preceding section, a change in q affects the affiliate's optimal sale and thereby the rival's optimal sale. Put differently, q affects S_2 indirectly through its effect on S_1. We call this the strategic effect of a change in the transfer price. Following Tirole (1988, p. 326), the strategic effect, $\partial S_2/\partial q$, can be rearranged in the following way:[9]

---

[9] See also Brander (1995, p. 1408), where the strategic effect is substituted into equation (3.16). Brander used the cross-derivative of the profit function ($\partial^2 \Pi/\partial S_2 \, \partial S_1$) to define

$$\frac{\partial S_2}{\partial q} = \frac{\partial S_2}{\partial S_1} \frac{\partial S_1}{\partial q} \tag{5.9}$$

After substitution of (5.7), (5.8), and (5.9) into (5.6), the MNE has the following first-order condition:

$$\frac{\partial \Pi}{\partial q} = (\theta - \tau)S_1 + \frac{\partial S_1}{\partial q}\left[\frac{(1-t)}{(1-T)}\left(q - \frac{\partial c}{\partial S_1}\right) + \left(\frac{\partial R}{\partial S_2}\frac{\partial S_2}{\partial S_1}\right)\right] = 0 \tag{5.10}$$

The MNE will increase q until the marginal benefits equal marginal costs; that is,

$$q - \frac{\partial c}{\partial S_1} = \frac{(1-T)}{(1-t)}\left[\frac{(\tau - \theta)S_1}{(\partial S_1/\partial q)} - \left(\frac{\partial R}{\partial S_2}\frac{\partial S_2}{\partial S_1}\right)\right] \tag{5.11}$$

Equation (5.11) shows that the transfer price under strategic interaction differs from the marginal cost. This is contrary to the conventional literature, where the transfer price in the absence of tax and tariff rates is equal to the marginal cost of the exporting division (Hirshleifer, 1956; Eden, 1985). In particular, the sign of $(q - \partial c/\partial S_1)$ depends on the last term inside the large brackets. Assuming Cournot competition, it is well known that for a large class of demand functions, $\partial S_2/\partial S_1 < 0$ (i.e., firm 2's optimal response to an increase in firm 1's sales is to reduce its own sales).[10] Because by assumption the two products are substitutes, it follows that $\partial R/\partial S_2 < 0$, and we can conclude the following:

Proposition 1. *If tax and tariff rates equal zero and Cournot competition prevails, then the MNE sets $q < c'$.*

Proposition 1 makes it clear that under Cournot competition the strategic effect alone dictates a transfer price below the marginal costs of the exporting firm. The idea is that a low transfer price makes the importing affiliate sell a larger quantity than it otherwise would. The competitor anticipates this, and its best response is to limit its own sales. Hence, a low transfer price will indirectly force the local rival to behave less aggressively. As a result, profits are increased in country 2 and, at the same time, for the whole MNE as well.

We now turn to examine how taxes and tariffs influence the transfer-pricing policy of the MNE. We have the following:

what we call the strategic effect. That method is equivalent to the method of Tirole (1988). Notice that the term $\partial S_2/\partial S_1$ must not be interpreted as though the local rival can change its output in response to changes in S_1. Because both firms set their sales simultaneously, $\partial S_2/\partial S_1$ captures the complex reasoning of both firms following a change in q.

[10] For example, a sufficient condition is that both demand and cost functions be convex (Bulow, Geanakoplos, and Klemperer, 1985).

Proposition 2. *Under Cournot competition and* $\theta < \tau$, *the MNE sets* $q < c'$.

Note that when $\theta < \tau$, we know from equation (5.2) that profit-shifting dictates a low transfer price. Because, other things not considered, the forces of competition induce the firm to set a low transfer price, the introduction of tax policy in this case simply reinforces the argument for a low transfer price. Put differently, when $\theta < \tau$, the profit-shifting motive and the strategic effect work in the same direction, necessitating a transfer price below the marginal costs of exporting.

The immediate consequence of Proposition 2 is that if the firm is to switch to a high-transfer-price policy (i.e., set $q > c'$), then the tax-shifting argument must go in the opposite direction from the strategic argument and override the strategic effect.

Proposition 3. *Under Cournot competition and* $\theta > \tau$, *the requirement for* $q > c'$ *is*

$$\tau - \theta < \frac{\partial R}{\partial S_2} \frac{\partial S_2}{\partial S_1} \frac{\partial S_1}{\partial q} \frac{1}{S_1}$$

Proposition 3 states the requirement for the case in which the profit-shifting motive dominates the strategic effect.[11] In general, the relative strengths of the strategic effect and the tax-shifting effect cannot be determined from Proposition 3, but depend on the demand and cost characteristics. In Section 5, a numerical example will show that the strategic effect can be significant and can even outweigh the incentive to shift profits to country 1 in order to reduce the overall tax burden for the MNE.

3.2   *Transfer Pricing When $t \geq T$*

The global profit function in this case is given by

$$\Pi = (1-t)[\pi_1 + \pi_2]$$
$$= (1-t)\{[r(s) - c(s + S_1) + qS_1] + [R(S_1, S_2) - q(1+\tau)S_1]\} \qquad (5.12)$$

By the same procedure as before, we find that the optimal transfer price is given by

---

[11] Both sides of the inequality are negative. For a high transfer price to be chosen, the right-hand side must be less negative than the left-hand side, i.e., the strategic effect is less important for the firm.

$$q - \frac{\partial c}{\partial S_1} = \left[\frac{\tau S_1}{(\partial S_1/\partial q)} - \left(\frac{\partial R}{\partial S_2} \frac{\partial S_2}{\partial S_1} \right) \right] \qquad (5.13)$$

Thus, we can state the following:

Proposition 4. *When full credit is granted for foreign taxes paid and Cournot competition prevails, the MNE sets $q < c'$.*

Because income abroad and income at home face the same corporate tax rate, the MNE will always want to charge a low transfer price in order to save tariff payments. As a consequence, the profit-shifting motive and the strategic effect work in the same direction, dictating a transfer price below the marginal costs of exporting.

4   Optimal Transfer-Pricing Policy Under Bertrand Competition

In the Cournot model the firm's choice variables are quantities; however, it seems equally natural to consider what happens to the optimal transfer-pricing strategy if the firms in country 2 are price-setters. In addition, we assume that the two firms' products in country 2 are imperfect substitutes.[12]

4.1   *Transfer Pricing When $t < T$*

The global profit function is now

$$\begin{aligned}
\Pi &= (1-t)\pi_1 + (1-T)\pi_2 \\
&= (1-t)\{r(p) - c[s(p) + S_1(P_1, P_2)] + qS_1(P_1, P_2)\} \\
&\quad + (1-T)[R(P_1, P_2) - q(1+\tau)S_1(P_1, P_2)] \qquad (5.14)
\end{aligned}$$

where $P_i = P_i(q), i = 1, 2$, and $p = p\{S_1[P_1(q), P_2(q)]\}$. The effect on global profits from a change in q is

$$\begin{aligned}
\frac{\partial \Pi}{\partial q} &= (1-t)\left[\left(\frac{\partial r}{\partial p} - \frac{\partial c}{\partial s} \frac{\partial s}{\partial p} \right) \frac{\partial p}{\partial S_1} \frac{dS_1}{dq} - \frac{\partial c}{\partial S_1} \frac{dS_1}{dq} + S_1 + q \frac{dS_1}{dq} \right] \\
&\quad + (1-T)\left[\left(\frac{\partial R}{\partial P_1} - q(1+\tau)\frac{\partial S_1}{\partial P_1} \right) \frac{\partial P_1}{\partial q} \right. \\
&\quad \left. + \left(\frac{\partial R}{\partial P_2} - q(1+\tau)\frac{\partial S_1}{\partial P_2} \right) \frac{\partial P_2}{\partial q} - (1+\tau)S_1 \right] \qquad (5.15)
\end{aligned}$$

---

[12] If the products are perfect substitutes and there are no capacity constraints (constant marginal costs), it is well known in the industrial-organization literature that price equals

where

$$\frac{dS_1}{dq} = \frac{\partial S_1}{\partial P_1}\frac{\partial P_1}{\partial q} + \frac{\partial S_1}{\partial P_2}\frac{\partial P_2}{\partial q}$$

Because each affiliate maximizes local profits and decides on optimal price, the first-order conditions for profit maximization are

$$\frac{\partial \pi_1}{\partial p} = (1-t)\left[\left(\frac{\partial r}{\partial p} - \frac{\partial c}{\partial s}\frac{\partial s}{\partial p}\right)\right] = 0 \tag{5.16}$$

$$\frac{\partial \pi_2}{\partial P_1} = (1-T)\left[\left(\frac{\partial R}{\partial P_1} - q(1+\tau)\frac{\partial S_1}{\partial P_1}\right)\right] = 0 \tag{5.17}$$

Following Tirole (1988), the strategic effect can be expressed in the same manner as previously; that is,

$$\frac{\partial P_2}{\partial q} = \frac{\partial P_2}{\partial P_1}\frac{\partial P_1}{\partial q} \tag{5.18}$$

Substituting (5.16), (5.17), and (5.18) into (5.15) and rearranging, we obtain the condition for the optimal transfer-price–marginal-cost margin as

$$q - \frac{\partial c}{\partial S_1} = \frac{(1-T)}{(1-t)}\frac{1}{dS_1/dP_1}\left[\frac{(\tau-\theta)S_1}{\partial P_1/\partial q} - \eta\frac{\partial P_2}{\partial P_1}\right] \tag{5.19}$$

where

$$\eta \equiv \frac{\partial R}{\partial P_2} - q(1+\tau)\frac{\partial S_1}{\partial P_2} \quad \text{and} \quad \frac{dS_1}{dP_1} = \frac{\partial S_1}{\partial P_1} + \frac{\partial S_1}{\partial P_2}\frac{\partial P_2}{\partial P_1}$$

If tax and tariff rates are zero, the first term inside the large brackets on the right-hand side is zero. Thus the sign of $q - c'$ depends on the last term inside the brackets as well as dS_1/dP_1. Bertrand competition implies that for a large class of demand and cost functions, $\partial P_2/\partial P_1 > 0$ (Bulow et al., 1985); $\eta > 0$, because an increase in P_2 will increase π_2. Finally, an increase in P_1 will reduce S_1 (i.e., $dS_1/dP_1 < 0$). Using these properties, we can now state the following:

Proposition 5.   *If tax and tariff rates equal zero and Bertrand competition prevails, then the MNE sets* $q > c'$.

Proposition 5 makes it clear that under Bertrand competition the strategic effect dictates a high transfer price (above marginal cost). The

marginal cost for the most inefficient firm and that the most efficient firm serves the whole market (Tirole, 1988, ch. 5). In such a case there is no scope for strategic transfer pricing.

rationale is that a high transfer price will induce the affiliate in country 2 to set a high price on its sales in country 2. The local rival will anticipate that, and its best response will be to set a high price. Such a non-aggressive response from the local rival is beneficial to the affiliate in country 2.

If we include tax and tariff rates, inspection of (5.19) leads us to state the following:

Proposition 6.   *Under Bertrand competition and $\theta > \tau$, the MNE sets $q > c'$.*

In contrast to the case of Cournot competition, here the profit-shifting motive and the strategic motive work in the same direction when $\theta > \tau$. Hence, strategic considerations reinforce the tax-policy argument for setting a high transfer price. However, it is ambiguous whether or not the transfer price should be above marginal costs when $\theta < \tau$:

Proposition 7.   *Under Bertrand competition and $\theta < \tau$, the requirement for a low transfer price ($q < c'$) is*

$$\tau - \theta > \eta \frac{\partial P_2}{\partial P_1} \frac{\partial P_1}{\partial q} \frac{1}{S_1}$$

For the MNE to set a transfer price below marginal costs, the tax-shifting motive must be sufficiently strong to outweigh the benefit from using a high transfer price as a strategic variable. In general, the total effect is ambiguous and depends on the relative magnitudes of the two effects. In the next section we show that it can indeed be the case that forces of competition will be sufficiently strong to dampen, or even reverse, the profit-shifting motive.

4.2   *Transfer Pricing When $t \geq T$*

Now the global profit function can be stated as

$$\begin{aligned}
\Pi &= (1-t)[\pi_1 + \pi_2] \\
&= (1-t)\{r(p) - c[s(p) + S_1(P_1, P_2)] + qS_1(P_1, P_2)\} \\
&\quad + (1-t)[R(P_1, P_2) - q(1+\tau)S_1(P_1, P_2)]
\end{aligned} \tag{5.20}$$

The condition for the optimal transfer-price–marginal-cost margin is given as

$$q - \frac{\partial c}{\partial S_1} = \frac{1}{dS_1/dP_1}\left[\frac{\tau S_1}{\partial P_1/\partial q} - \eta \frac{\partial P_2}{\partial P_1}\right] \tag{5.21}$$

	Cournot	Bertrand
$\theta = \tau = 0$	$q < c'$	$q > c'$
$\theta > \tau$	?	$q > c'$
$\theta < \tau$	$q < c'$	?

Figure 5.1. $t < T$.

	Cournot	Bertrand
$\tau = 0$	$q < c'$	$q > c'$
$\tau > 0$	$q < c'$	?

Figure 5.2. $t > T$.

We have the following:

Proposition 8. *When full credit is given for foreign taxes paid and Bertrand competition prevails, the MNE sets*

    (i) $q > c'$ *in the absence of tariff policy* $(\tau = 0)$, *or*
    (ii) $q < c'$ *if*

$$\tau > \eta \frac{\partial P_2}{\partial P_1} \frac{\partial P_1}{\partial q} \frac{1}{S_1}$$

These conclusions differ from those found under Bertrand competition when a limited tax credit applies, in that the profit-shifting motive always dictates a transfer price below marginal costs. Thus the strategic effect and the profit-shifting effect work in opposite directions, and the optimal transfer price will depend on the relative magnitudes of these two effects.

    For purposes of comparison, Figures 5.1 and 5.2 summarize our findings. It is apparent from these figures that the nature of the competition and the different systems for taxing foreign-source income are of vital importance to the transfer-pricing strategy of the firm. In the absence of tax and tariff rates, Cournot competition leads the MNE to set $q < c'$, whereas under Bertrand competition it sets $q > c'$. The driving force behind both these results is the local rival's response to the more aggressive behavior of the affiliate in country 2. When price is the strategic variable, more aggressive behavior of the affiliate in country 2 will trigger more aggressive behavior by the local rival. In contrast, when quantity is the strategic variable, aggressive behavior by the affiliate in country 2 will lead the competitor to behave less aggressively. Put differently, the rival's optimal response to selection of a large quantity by the MNE's foreign subsidiary is to select for a low quantity (Cournot competition), whereas its optimal response to a low price by the MNE's foreign subsidiary is to set a low price itself (Bertrand competition). We know that a reduction in the transfer price makes the affiliate in country 2 more aggressive. If Cournot competition prevails, such a strategy is beneficial, because it forces the local rival to act less aggressively. If Bertrand competition prevails, however, a low transfer price will indirectly encourage the local rival to set a low output price. Hence the MNE should in that case set a high transfer price and thereby indirectly force the local rival in country 2 to act less aggressively.

5   A Numerical Example

As shown in Figures 5.1 and 5.2, the general results are in some cases ambiguous because the strategic effect and the tax effect may work in opposite directions. In this section we attempt to throw light on how strong the strategic effect is compared with the tax-shifting effect. Could, for example, the strategic effect be almost negligible? To investigate that, we have constructed a simple numerical example based on Figure 5.1.[13]

We assume that the market demand in country 1 is given by the inverse demand function

$$p = a - s \tag{5.22}$$

where a is a constant.

The inverse demand functions for the two producers' products in country 2 are

$$P_1 = A - S_1 - bS_2 \tag{5.23}$$

$$P_2 = A - S_2 - bS_1 \tag{5.24}$$

Assuming $0 < b \leq 1$, the two products are substitutes.

We assume that the two products sold in country 2 are imperfect substitutes. To encompass this, we have set $b = 0.6$. By setting $a = A = 1$, we can make the two markets symmetric in size. The parameter c' denotes

---

[13] Notice that the example is based on equation (5.1), where, in addition, we allow for $T < t$. The example, therefore, must be interpreted as if the source principle of taxation applies. Details concerning the calculus are available from the authors upon request.

the (constant) marginal cost of the MNE, and C' the (constant) marginal costs of the local rival in country 2. Marginal costs are normalized so that $C' = c' = 0$.[14] To simplify, we set $\tau = 0$ and assume that $t = 0.3$. Figure 5.3 compares the optimal transfer prices under Cournot competition and Bertrand competition.

Figure 5.3 confirms the results reported in Sections 3 and 4: In the absence of tax and tariff rates, the MNE should set a transfer price above the marginal costs when Bertrand competition prevails, and a price below the marginal costs under Cournot competition. In particular, $q = -0.08$ under Cournot competition, and $q = +0.06$ under Bertrand competition. The importance of the nature of competition becomes more transparent if we investigate which tax rate in country 2 will lead the MNE to set $q = c'$. Under Bertrand competition, and with $t = 0.3$, the transfer price is set equal to marginal costs if $T = 0.22$. In contrast, for the same pricing policy to occur under Cournot competition, we must have $T = 0.36$.

From Figure 5.3 we also see that for $T > 0.69$, the optimal transfer price is higher under Cournot competition than under Bertrand competition (the result is reversed when $T < 0.69$). This observation (which we cannot infer from our general results) can be explained by the intensity of the competition. As shown by Vives (1985), the competition is more fierce under the terms of Bertrand competition than under the terms of Cournot competition. The intuition is best understood by considering the case in which products are identical. In this case, we know that under Bertrand competition price equals marginal costs; so a transfer price set above marginal costs will imply that the affiliate in country 2 will lose all its sales. In contrast, under Cournot competition, the affiliate in country 2 will have positive sales even if the transfer price exceeds marginal costs. Thus there is greater scope for transfer pricing (above marginal costs) when the competition is Cournot competition.

6   Conclusions

This study has incorporated two features of MNE behavior not found in previous models of MNE behavior and transfer pricing: strategic interaction with other firms in local markets, and delegation of authority to national affiliates to make price (or quantity) decisions. The analysis indi-

---

[14] By normalizing marginal costs to zero, $q < c'$ would imply that the transfer price was negative. Obviously that is unrealistic. However, an example with positive marginal cost could easily be constructed, thereby ensuring that the transfer price would always be positive.

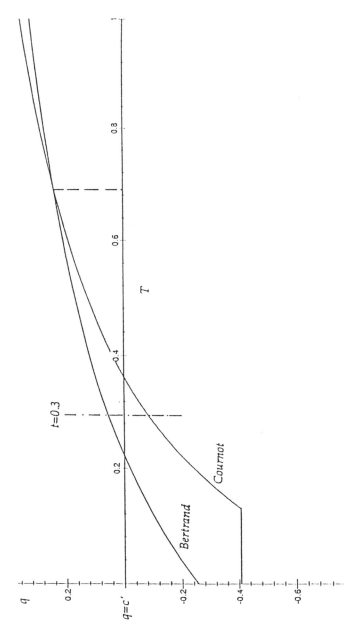

Figure 5.3. Optimal transfer prices under Cournot competition and Bertrand competition.

cates that the existence of a local rival in the importing country implies that the transfer price should deviate from the marginal costs of the exporting division, even in the absence of tax and tariff rates. The optimal transfer price in this framework generally depends on the nature of the competition. It has been shown that in the context of Cournot competition the transfer price should be less than the marginal costs of the exporting affiliate, whereas that is reversed in the context of Bertrand competition. The introduction of tax policy can either reinforce or dampen this pricing strategy. In a numerical example we have shown that the strategic motive for transfer pricing can be quite strong. Indeed, it can dominate the profit-shifting motive, which traditionally has been taken to be the dominant factor in transfer-pricing behavior.

REFERENCES

Basu, K. (1993). *Lectures in Industrial Organization Theory.* London: Blackwell.

Brander, J. A. (1995). Strategic trade policy. In: *The Handbook of International Economics*, vol. 3, ed. G. Grossman and K. Rogoff. Amsterdam: North-Holland, pp. 1395–1455.

Bulow, J., Geanakoplos, J., and Klemperer, P. (1985). Multimarket oligopoly: strategic substitutes and complements. *Journal of Political Economy* 93: 488–511.

Copithorne, L. W. (1971). International corporate transfer prices and government policy. *Canadian Journal of Economics* 4:324–41.

Cordella, T., and Vannini, S. (1993). Tariff policy and MNEs: how to jump tariff jumping. CORE discussion paper 9365. Center for Operations Research and Econometrics, Université Catholique de Louvain.

Eden, L. (1985). The microeconomics of transfer pricing. In: *Multinationals and Transfer Pricing: The Croom Helm Series in International Business*, ed. A. M. Rugman and L. Eden. New York: St. Martin's Press, pp. 13–46.

Elitzur, R., and Mintz, J. (1996). Transfer pricing rules and corporate tax competition. *Journal of Public Economics* 60:401–22.

Fersthman, C., and Judd, K. (1987). Equilibrium incentives in oligopoly. *American Economic Review* 77:927–40.

Hirshleifer, J. (1956). On the economics of transfer pricing. *Journal of Business* 29:172–84.

Hirshleifer, J. (1957). Economics of the divisionalized firm. *Journal of Business* 30:96–108.

Horst, T. (1971). The theory of the MNE: optimal behavior under different tariff and tax rates. *Journal of Political Economy* 79:1059–72.

Horstman, I. J., and Markusen, J. R. (1987). Strategic investments and the development of MNEs. *International Economic Review* 28:109–21.

Horstman, I. J., and Markusen, J. R. (1992). Endogenous market structures in international trade (*natura facit saltum*). *Journal of International Economics* 32:109–29.

Janeba, E. (1996). Foreign direct investment under oligopoly: profit shifting or profit capturing? *Journal of Public Economics* 60:423–45.

Katz, M. L. (1989). Vertical contractual relations. In: *Handbook of Industrial Organization*, ed. R. Schmalensee and R. Willig. Amsterdam: North-Holland, pp. 655–721.

Katz, M. L. (1991). Game-playing agents: unobservable contracts as precommitments. *Rand Journal of Economics* 22:307–28.

Kreps, D., and Scheinkmann, J. (1983). Quantity precommitment and Bertrand competition yield Cournot outcomes. *Bell Journal of Economics* 14:326–37.

Markusen, J. R., and Venables, A. J. (1995). Multinationals and the new trade theory. NBER working paper 5036. Washington, DC: National Bureau of Economic Research.

Motta, M. (1992). MNEs and the tariff-jumping argument: a game theoretic analysis with some unconventional conclusions. *European Economic Review* 36:1557–71.

OECD (1977). *Model Double Taxation Convention on Income and Capital*. Report of the OECD Committee on Fiscal Affairs. Paris: Organization for Economic Cooperation and Development.

Samuelson, L. (1982). The MNE with arm's length transfer price limits. *Journal of International Economics* 13:365–74.

Schelling, T. (1960). *The Strategy of Conflict*. Cambridge, MA: Harvard University Press.

Shapiro, C. (1989). Theories of oligopoly behavior. In: *Handbook of Industrial Organization*, ed. R. Schmalensee and R. Willig, pp. 329–414. Amsterdam: North-Holland.

Sklivas, S. D. (1987). The strategic choice of managerial incentives. *Rand Journal of Economics* 18:452–8.

Tirole, J. (1988). *The Theory of Industrial Organization*. Massachusetts Institute of Technology Press.

Vickers, J. (1985). Delegation and the theory of the firm. *Economic Journal* (Suppl.) 95:138–47.

Vives, X. (1985). On the efficiency of Cournot and Bertrand competition with product differentiation. *Journal of Economic Theory* 36:166–75.

PART IV

Limits to Income Redistribution in Federal Systems

CHAPTER 6

Income Redistribution in an Economic Union: The Trade-off Between International and Intranational Redistributions

Helmuth Cremer and Pierre Pestieau

1   Introduction

Public finance teaches that in a multijurisdiction setting, such as an economic union of nations, there is a strong case for assigning the responsibility for income redistribution to the central, supranational government. The rationale is twofold. First, this makes it possible to avoid the depressive effects of tax competition; in a decentralized setting, national jurisdictions may tend to lower their tax rates in order to attract, say, capital or high-income earners. Second, this is the only way to redistribute income across nations.

Even though this argument sounds strong and rather general, it is not completely clear-cut. It has been argued that decentralized jurisdictions may not be engaging in less income redistribution than central authorities, but rather may be engaging in a different kind of redistribution. This is because they can exploit informational or organizational advantages relative to the central authorities.

If indeed national governments do possess better information or more motivation to effect income redistribution, it does not necessarily follow that the central government ought to abandon all responsibility for income redistribution. Rather, the central government should take advantage of all such information and motivation in designing its optimal policy.

This chapter has been written within the HCM network 921684 on "The Fiscal Implication of European Integration" and with financial support of the SSTC, research program SE/12/042. We are grateful to two referees for excellent comments.

143

That is the viewpoint adopted in this study. We assume that both supranational and national governments attempt to redistribute income within their respective boundaries. Both rich and poor nations join the confederation, and the rich ones know that they are going to lose in the process of redistribution across countries. However, the central government has only imperfect information on individual countries' ability to pay: It observes only the aggregate redistribution effort of each country. There will thus be strong incentive for high-ability-to-pay nations to alter their redistributive efforts. In other words, the optimal redistributive policy of the central government will strike a balance between international and intranational redistributions. Two polar cases can be considered. In the absence of central-authority intervention, there is no redistribution across nations, but redistribution within each is optimal, assuming there is no fiscal competition and no other deadweight losses. In the opposite case of a central government attempting to equalize disposable incomes across countries, national governments will cut their redistributive efforts, and the result will be no redistribution across or within nations. Clearly, the optimal solution derived in this study lies between these two extremes.

Our formal model is as follows: We consider an economic union consisting of two types of countries, each containing a number of poor welfare recipients and a number of rich taxpayers, all with given incomes. The countries differ in the proportion of rich taxpayers among their residents. Mobility is assumed away so as to focus on the issue of between-countries redistribution versus within-countries redistribution without fiscal competition. The two levels of government have a redistributive objective formalized by a utilitarian social-welfare function. However, they do not have the same information. The national governments observe the full structure of incomes and use a tax-transfer policy to maximize their social-welfare function. The central government observes only the redistributive effort of each national government, that is, the aggregate level of taxes or of transfers. The two types of countries differ in their proportions of poor households, which in turn affects their preferences regarding their levels of the redistributive effort. Because of asymmetric information, the central government bases its between-transfer policy on the sole observable variable: the redistributive effort of each country. Consequently the richer countries have to be prevented from mimicking the poorer, and this limits the amount of redistribution that can be effected.

This study follows a growing literature that assumes asymmetric information between centers and regions. Depending on the study, such asymmetry has concerned preferences for or costs of providing a local public good (Boadway, Horiba, and Jha, 1995; Laffont, 1995; Raff and Wilson, 1995; Cornes and Silva, 1996; Bordignon, Manasse, and Tabellini, 1996; Gilbert and Picard, 1996; Cremer, Marchand, and Pestieau, 1996; Lockwood, 1996; Bucovetsky, Marchand, and Pestieau, in press). That literature is quite rich and cannot be easily summarized. Our contribution differs from it in two important respects. First, we focus on the possible conflict between international and intranational redistributions under asymmetric information. In the earlier literature, subcentral governments were not concerned with redistribution. Second, we assume away the moral-hazard problems that can result in productive inefficiency. In our model, the total amount of resources is fixed and is unaffected by redistribution. The novel findings of our study are that asymmetric information can distort the optimum in either direction and that the direction depends on the relative proportions of rich and poor households.

2 Basic Model

We begin with a large number of countries, of two types, indexed by $j = a, b$, and characterized by n_j, the proportion of rich individuals. Rich individuals earn R, and poor individuals $P < R$. Assume that $n_a < n_b$, so that a country of type a is poorer than a country of type b. National governments observe individual incomes and use a tax-transfer policy to redistribute income. They maximize a utilitarian social-welfare function:

$$v_j = n_j u(c_{Rj}) + (1 - n_j)u(c_{Pj}), \tag{6.1}$$

where c_{Rj} and c_{Pj} denote the disposable (after-tax or transfer) incomes of the rich and the poor in country j. This formalization can be justified, for instance, by Pauly's view that income transfers from the rich are undertaken because the utility of the rich depends on the level of income of the poor (Pauly, 1973). In other words, income redistribution is of the nature of a pure public good undertaken collectively by the public sector. In Pauly's argument, these utility interdependences apply only to national (intrajurisdictional) redistribution, not to cross-national redistribution.

We express disposable incomes in terms of fiscal instruments:

$$c_{Rj} = R - b_j/n_j$$
$$c_{Rj} = P + (b_j + T_j)/(1 - n_j) \tag{6.2}$$

where b_j is the redistributive budget of country j, so that b_j/n_j is the tax paid by a rich household, and $b_j/(1 - n_j)$ is the transfer received by each poor household. For the time being we take T_j, the positive or negative transfer from the supranational government, as given.

The inclusion of T_j, the income transfer from the central government, in only the budget constraint for poor households is a pure accounting convention. What matters is that the central government is effectively able to choose the total taxes collected from the rich and the total subsidies provided to the poor in each country subject to an incentive-compatibility constraint and an overall-revenue constraint requiring that the difference between these taxes and subsidies sums to zero across all countries.

Substituting (6.2) into (6.1), we obtain

$$v_j(b_j, T_j) = n_j u(R - b_j/n_j) + (1 - n_j)u[P + (b_j + T_j)/(1 - n_j)] \tag{6.3}$$

We can easily check that

$$\frac{\partial v_j}{\partial T_j} = u'(c_{Pj}) > 0 \tag{6.4}$$

and that the optimal redistributive effort is such that

$$\frac{\partial v_j}{\partial b_j} = -u'(c_{Rj}) + u'(c_{Pj}) = 0 \tag{6.5}$$

Not surprisingly, condition (6.5) implies that given T_j, each national government chooses a redistribution policy that equalizes disposable income: $c_{Rj} = c_{Pj}$. This can be achieved with a redistributive effort equal to

$$b_j^*(T_j) = n_j(1 - n_j)(R - P) - n_j T_j \tag{6.6}$$

This effort decreases with T_j. The total amount received by the poor is given by

$$b_j^*(T_j) + T_j = n_j(1 - n_j)(R - P) + (1 - n_j)T_j \tag{6.7}$$

which is increasing with T_j.

From (6.4) and (6.5), the slope of the indifference curves in the plane (T_j, b_j) is given by

$$\frac{dT_j}{db_j}\bigg|_{v_j} = \frac{u'(c_{Rj}) - u'(c_{Pj})}{u'(c_{Pj})}$$

As shown in Figure 6.1, these curves are U-shaped; their minimum is given by $b_j^*(T_j)$. Note that if $b_j < b_j^*(T_j)$, we have $c_{Rj} > c_{Pj}$, a situation we

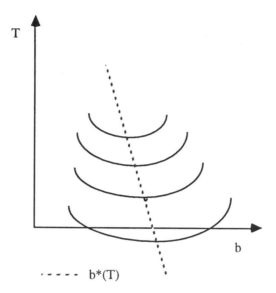

Figure 6.1.

refer to as insufficient redistribution. On the other hand, $b_j > b_j^*(T_j)$ implies $c_{Rj} < c_{Pj}$ and thus excessive redistribution.

Finally, we can analyze the relationship between b_j^* and n_j for a given value of T. We can easily verify that $b_j^*(T)$ is not monotonic in n_j. Given an a country and a b country, when there is a majority of rich households in either country ($n_j > \frac{1}{2}$), the optimal redistributive effort for given identical levels of T is lower in b than in a; when there is a minority of rich ($n_j < \frac{1}{2}$), then the rich households country has a higher optimal redistribution budget than does the poor country. This can be expressed more precisely in the following lemma, which will be needed in Section 4.

Lemma 1

1. If $n_b > n_a > \frac{1}{2}$, then $b_b^*(T) < b_a^*(T)$ for all $T \geq 0$.

2. If $n_a < n_b < \frac{1}{2}$, then $b_b^*(T) > b_a^*(T)$ if $T < (R - P)(n_b - n_a)/2$.

Proof. Part 1 is obvious. The derivative of $b_j^*(T)$ with respect to n_j is unambiguously negative for $n_j > \frac{1}{2}$.

To prove part 2, we first note that the condition on T implies that there is no excessive redistribution. When $T = (R - P)(n_b - n_a)/2$ there is income equality across regions.

$$b_b^*(T) - b_a^*(T) = [n_b(1 - n_b) - n_a(1 - n_a)](R - P) - T(n_b - n_a)$$

Using $T < (R - P)(n_b - n_a)/2$ and $n_j < \frac{1}{2}$, we successively obtain

$$b_b^*(T) - b_a^*(T) > (R - P)\left(n_b(1 - n_b) - n_a(1 - n_a) - \frac{(n_b - n_a)^2}{2} \right)$$

$$= \frac{1}{2}(R - P)(n_b - n_a)(2 - n_a - 3n_b) > 0 \qquad \blacksquare$$

We now turn to the supranational government. It maximizes a utilitarian social-welfare function that depends on the utility of all the residents of the economic union. However, it does not possess the same information as the national governments. It observes neither individual incomes nor the income structure (proportions of rich and poor) in each country; it sees only the redistributive effort b_j. In other words, national governments, particularly those that expect to be burdened by attempts to redistribute incomes across countries, have an incentive not to reveal who pays what and who benefits from what. The only information they cannot hide is the size of the redistributive effort, which is public knowledge.[1] Within this imperfect-information assumption, the redistributive policy of the central government will not be as effective as it would be with full information. As a reference, we first derive the full-information optimum.

This information structure is not meant to be taken literally. One could indeed question the assumption that a supranational government could observe the aggregate redistributive activity and not observe the composition of the population in each country. What we have in mind is not so much a distinction between poor and rich, but distinctions among people who have different needs. Needs are not easily observable and to some extent are quite subjective. With this interpretation, R and P have to be taken as income-adjusted for needs (e.g., through some sort of equivalence scale).

---

[1] The rationale behind this information structure is that national governments are in charge of tax enforcement. Consequently (in combination with the budget b_j), observation of legislated national tax rates is not sufficient to infer the proportions of rich and poor.

3   Full Information Optimum

Assume, for simplicity, that there are just two countries or, to be more precise, that there are equal numbers of both types of countries.[2] They all are of the same size regardless of type. Consequently we can concentrate on two representative countries. Supranational social welfare is then given by $v_1 + v_2$, and its maximization subject to $T_a + T_b = 0$ yields equal consumption levels for all types in all regions:

$$c_{Ra} = c_{Rb} = c_{Pa} = c_{Pb} = (n_a + n_b)(R - P)/2 + P$$

This of course implies that $T_a = -T_b > 0$. In other words, there is a transfer from country b to country a. Under asymmetric information, the former will be tempted to mimic the latter.

4   Optimal Policy Under Asymmetric Information

We now turn to the asymmetric-information case and introduce the following mechanism: A country that declares as type j ($j = a, b$) will be attributed the vector (b_j, T_j), with the constraint

$$T_a + T_b = 0$$

Without loss of generality we restrict our attention to incentive-compatibility mechanisms. We thus state the problem of the central government as maximization with respect to T_j and b_j of the following expression:

$$L = v_a(b_a, T_a) + v_b(b_b, T_b) - \gamma(T_a + T_b) + \lambda[v_b(b_b, T_b) - v_b(b_a, T_a)] \qquad (6.8)$$

where γ and λ are the Lagrange multipliers associated respectively with the budget constraint and the (downward) incentive-compatibility constraint pertaining to country b (the wealthier of the two), being as well off in telling the truth as in mimicking country a.[3]

---

[2] These assumptions simplify notation without affecting any of the results.

[3] Throughout the chapter we shall assume that the upward incentive-compatibility (IC) constraint is not binding. With a utilitarian social-welfare function, the full-information optimum violates the downward incentive constraint; consequently this constraint must be binding at the second-best optimum. When the country's indifference curves satisfy the single-crossing property, this is sufficient to ensure that the upward IC constraint does not bind. However, in our setting, multiple crossings cannot be ruled out for all combinations of n_a and n_b [especially when $n_a < \frac{1}{2} < n_b$; recall that $b^*(T)$ is not monotonic in n]. In the remainder of the chapter we assume away situations where both IC constraints bind at the optimum. It should be pointed out, though, that for the cases on which we concentrate (namely, $n_a < n_b < \frac{1}{2}$ and $\frac{1}{2} < n_a < n_b$), such a solution would be a mere technical curiosity, lacking any economic interest.

Using (6.1), the definition of v, the first-order conditions can be rewritten as follows:

$$\frac{\partial L}{\partial b_a} = -u'(c_{Ra}) + u'(c_{Pa}) + \lambda[u'(\tilde{c}_{Rb}) - u'(\tilde{c}_{Pb})] = 0 \tag{6.9}$$

$$\frac{\partial L}{\partial b_b} = [-u'(c_{Rb}) + u'(c_{Pb})](1 + \lambda) = 0 \tag{6.10}$$

$$\frac{\partial L}{\partial T_a} = u'(c_{Pa}) - \gamma - \lambda u'(\tilde{c}_{Pb}) = 0 \tag{6.11}$$

$$\frac{\partial L}{\partial T_b} = u'(c_{Pb}) - \gamma + \lambda u'(c_{Pb}) = 0 \tag{6.12}$$

where (6.1) is used, and where $\tilde{c}_{Rb} = R - b_a/n_b$ and $\tilde{c}_{Pb} = P + (b_a + T_a)/(1 - n_b)$ denote the consumption levels in the mimicking country. These conditions imply the following results:

First, from (6.10) we obtain $c_{Rb} = c_{Pb}$, so that $b_b = b_b^*(T_b)$. There is optimal redistribution in the rich countries, with complete equalization of after-tax incomes. This is the well-known no-distortion-at-the-top result.

Second, consumption levels in the poor country are *not* equalized ($c_{Ra} \neq c_{Pa}$). However, we cannot be sure of the direction of the inequality. In other words, excessive redistribution cannot be excluded. Specifically, the following two cases have to be considered [see condition (6.9)]. They are represented graphically in Figure 6.2.

Case 1.   When $c_{Ra} > c_{Pa}$ and $\tilde{c}_{Rb} > \tilde{c}_{Pb}$ there is insufficient (relative to full information) redistribution in the poor country as well as in the mimicking country. In Figure 6.2, case 1, we see that the indifference curve of the mimicking country b intersects that of country a to the left of the optimal redistribution. At this point of intersection, the slope of the indifference curve of country a is flatter than that of country b; both are negative. In case 1, $b_b > b_a$ even though there are more poor individuals in country a than in country b.

Case 2.   When $c_{Ra} < c_{Pa}$ and $\tilde{c}_{Rb} < \tilde{c}_{Pb}$ there is excessive redistribution to the benefit of the poor in country a. In Figure 6.2, case 2, we see that the two indifference curves intersect to the left of the optimal redistribution point. They have positive slopes, that of country a being flatter than that of country b.

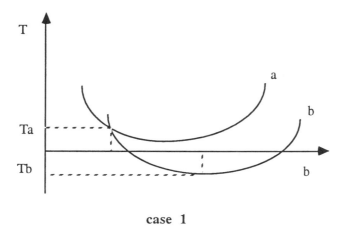

case 1

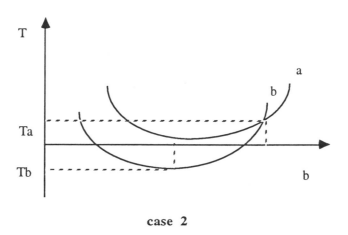

case 2

Figure 6.2.

Before proceeding with the discussion of these cases, let us point out a third result. Combining (6.11) and (6.12), we see that $c_{Pa} < c_{Pb}$; that is, the poor in the poorer country are necessarily worse off than the poor in the richer country. This result holds in both of the foregoing cases, even when there is excessive redistribution in the poorer country. Interestingly, this implies that under asymmetric information, redistribution between countries will result in unequal treatment of the poor (who are initially equal and who would be treated identically under full information).

We now return to the analysis of redistribution within the poor country. Strictly speaking, our earlier discussion shows only that neither of the two cases can be ruled out on the basis of the first-order conditions; that is, it is not sufficient to show that both of them can actually arise. This can be shown most easily through numerical illustration. In Section 5, an example for each case is provided.

Some further analytical treatment is nevertheless useful, as we would like to know under what conditions each case arises. Intuitively, we expect that excessive redistribution is likely to occur (for any given level of T) when the poorer country tends to redistribute more than the richer country, that is, when in each region there is a majority of *rich* taxpayers (see Lemma 1). In this case, the only way to prevent the richer country from mimicking the poorer one (to reduce informational rents) is to offer the poorer country a redistributive package that will reverse the original income distribution. In other words, excessive redistribution is desirable because it "hurts" the mimicking country more than the poorer country. Similarly, if there are majorities of poor taxpayers in both countries, so that poorer countries tend to redistribute less, we can expect insufficient redistribution in the poorer country.

To verify this conjecture, it is convenient to use as a benchmark a policy whereby b_a is set to equalize consumption levels in the poorer country [i.e., $b_a = b_a^*(T_a)$, as defined by (6.6)]. More precisely, we define the policy $\hat{T}_a$, $\hat{T}_b$, $\hat{b}_a$, and $\hat{b}_b$ as the one that maximizes (6.8) subject to the additional constraint that $\hat{b}_a = b_a^*(\hat{T}_a)$. It is easily verified that this policy has the following properties:

1. $\hat{T}_a > 0$
2. the downward incentive-compatibility constraint is binding
3. $\hat{b}_b = b_b^*(\hat{T}_b)$
4. $\hat{T}_a < (R - P)(n_b - n_a)/2$

The first two properties follow directly from the utilitarian objective. Property 3 follows from the fact that the upward incentive constraint cannot be binding [given that $\hat{T}_a > 0$ and $\hat{b}_a = b_a^*(\hat{T}_a)$]. Property 4 implies that the transfer between the two countries is less than the (first-best) level that would equalize total disposable income between countries. This, in turn, is an implication of the binding self-selection constraint. We can then state the following proposition:

Proposition 1. *Starting from an initial policy that maximizes social welfare subject to the self-selection constraint, the revenue constraint, and the constraint that consumption be equalized in the poorer country, excessive (insufficient) redistribution is marginally desirable if the proportion of rich individuals is higher (lower) than 50% in both types of countries.*

Proof. Formally, we can restate this proposition as follows: Let $\hat{T}_a$, $\hat{T}_b$, $\hat{b}_a$, $\hat{b}_b$ be the policy that maximizes (6.8) subject to the additional constraint $\hat{b}_a = b_a^*(\hat{T}_a)$. Consider a variation in b_a starting from $\hat{b}_a$:

1. If $n_b > n_a > \frac{1}{2}$, social welfare can be increased through a marginal *increase* in b_a (resulting in excessive redistribution in *a*).
2. If $n_a < n_b < \frac{1}{2}$, social welfare can be increased through a marginal *reduction* in b_a (resulting in insufficient redistribution in *a*).

The considered policy variation does not affect the resource constraint $(T_a + T_b = 0)$, nor does it change $v_b(b_b, T_b)$. In addition, it has no (first-order) effect on $v_a(b_a, T_a)$, because, by definition, $\partial v_a[b_b^*(T_a), Ta]/\partial b_a = 0$. However, it affects $\tilde{v}_b = v_b(b_a, T_a)$, the utility of the mimicking region. We have

$$\frac{\partial \tilde{v}_b}{\partial b_a} = -u'(\tilde{c}_{Rb}) + u'(\tilde{c}_{Pb}) \tag{6.13}$$

If $n_b > n_a > \frac{1}{2}$, Lemma 1 implies $b_b^*(T_a) < b_a^*(T_a) = b_a$, and thus $\tilde{c}_{Rb} > \tilde{c}_{Pb}$, so that the right-hand side of (6.13) is less than zero.

Hence a marginal increase in b_a will reduce $\tilde{v}_b$ and thus relax the binding self-selection constraint. Welfare will increase; specifically, once the self-selection constraint is relaxed, it will be possible to implement policy changes that will result in a higher degree of redistribution.

If $n_a < n_b < \frac{1}{2}$, Lemma 1 implies $b_b^*(T_a) > b_a^*(T_a) = b_a$, and an exactly symmetric argument will establish that $\partial \tilde{v}_b/\partial b_a > 0$. Hence a reduction in b_a will reduce $\tilde{v}_b$ and will be welfare-improving. ∎

Roughly speaking, this proposition shows that when $n_a < n_b < \frac{1}{2}$, a (marginal) downward distortion in the redistributive effort of the poorer country is welfare-improving. On the other hand, for $n_b > n_a > \frac{1}{2}$, a (marginal) upward distortion is welfare-improving.

These findings are in line with our conjecture, but they fall short of proving it. The proposition provides only local results. Additional regularity (convexity) assumptions would be necessary to ensure that the global maximum would occur along the welfare-improving direction we pointed out.

Note, however, that under some weak continuity assumptions the

Table 6.1. *Numerical example (R = 20, p = 10)*

Case	Solution	n_a	b_b	b_a	b_b	$T_a = -T_b$	c_{Ra}	c_{Pa}	c_{Rb}	c_{Pb}	$\tilde{c}_{Rb}$	$\tilde{c}_{Pb}$
1	First-best	0.2	0.4	1.4	2.8	1	13.00	13.00	13.00	13.00	—	—
	Second-best	0.2	0.4	1.56	2.42	0.05	12.20	12.01	13.95	13.95	16.10	12.68
2	First-best	0.6	0.9	1.5	2.25	1.5	17.5	17.5	17.5	17.5	—	—
	Second-best	0.6	0.9	2.28	1.16	0.29	16.03	16.68	18.7	18.7	17.36	36.70

proposition does allow us to determine the sign of the distortion when n_a and n_b are sufficiently close. In that case, the global optimum is in the neighborhood of $\hat{T}_a$, $\hat{T}_b$, $\hat{b}_a$, $\hat{b}_b$, and the sign of the distortion follows from the local result.[4] Consequently we can also conclude from the proposition that the two cases can indeed arise for some nonempty sets of parameter values. Excessive redistribution is quite surprising. Such a situation, in which the rich consume less than the poor, obviously depends on the assumption of fixed income endowments. If moral-hazard problems, such as labor–leisure distortions, were added to the model, we would expect that excessive redistribution, such as defined here, would disappear.

5   Numerical Example

To illustrate the foregoing and to go beyond the local results provided in Proposition 1, we resort to a simple example with logarithmic utility. The results are presented in Table 6.1. Two cases are distinguished. Case 1 arises when high-income individuals are a minority; as expected, it leads to the "normal" outcome of insufficient redistribution in country *a*. We note that there is even much less redistribution in the mimicking countries. In country *b* there is full redistribution. Compared with the first-best solution, there is much less revenue sharing between countries in the second-best solution.

Case 2 arises when each country has a majority of high-income people; it leads to excessive redistribution in the second-best solution. Again, excessive redistribution is much stronger in the mimicking regions, and the extent of revenue sharing in the second-best solution is lower than in the first-best solution. What this shows is that this kind of excessive interpersonal redistribution (implying a disposable income for

---

[4] This because for $n_a = n_b$, the solution to (8) is simply given by $\hat{T}_a$, $\hat{T}_b$, $\hat{b}_a$, $\hat{b}_b$.

the poor mimicker that will be about four times higher than his original income) is needed to relax the self-selection constraint and allow for some redistribution between countries.

These two cases provide just a sampling of the numerical examples we have considered, all of which have yielded similar results. None of them has allowed us to find a counterexample to our conjecture.

REFERENCES

Boadway, R., Horiba, I., and Jha, R. (1995). The design of conditional grants as a principal–agent problem. Unpublished manuscript, Department of Economics, Queen's University.

Bordignon, M., Manasse, P., and Tabellini, G. (1996). Optimal regional redistribution under asymmetric information. Unpublished manuscript, Department of Economics, University of Bologna.

Bucovetsky, S., Marchand, M., and Pestieau, P. (in press). Tax competition and revelation of preferences for public expenditure. *Journal of Urban Economics*.

Cornes, R., and Silva, E. (1996). Transfers between jurisdictions with private information: the equity/efficiency trade-off. Unpublished manuscript, Department of Economics, University of Keele.

Cremer, H., Marchand, M., and Pestieau, P. (1996). Interregional redistribution through tax surcharge. *International Tax and Public Finance* 3:157–74.

Cremer, H., and Pestieau, P. (1996). Distributive implications of European integration. *European Economic Review* 40:747–58.

Gilbert, G., and Picard, P. (1996). Incentives and the optimal size of local territories. *European Economic Review* 40:19–42.

Laffont, J.-J. (1995). Incentives in China's federal tax system. Unpublished manuscript, IDEI, University of Toulouse.

Lockwood, B. (1996). Interregional insurance with asymmetric information. Unpublished manuscript, Department of Economics, University of Exeter.

Pauly, M. V. (1973). Income redistribution as a local public good. *Journal of Public Economics* 2:35–58.

Raff, H., and Wilson, J. (1995). Income redistribution and well-informed regional government. Unpublished manuscript, Department of Economics, University of Indiana.

Stiglitz, J. E. (1982). Self selection and Pareto-efficient taxation. *Journal of Public Economics* 17:213–40.

CHAPTER 7

Federal Insurance of U.S. States: An Empirical Investigation

Bent E. Sørensen and Oved Yosha

1   Introduction

States participating in a federation can increase their welfare by mutually insuring idiosyncratic output risk. Such insurance can be obtained through transactions on capital markets, through cross-border ownership of productive assets, or via the tax-transfer system of the central government of the federation. Asdrubali, Sørensen, and Yosha (1996) quantified the relative importance of the main channels through which risk sharing occurs among the 50 U.S. states. They found that when the United States is viewed as one integrated market, 39% of shocks to gross state product are insured, on average, by capital markets, and 13% are insured by the federal tax-transfer system. Further consumption smoothing through saving and dis-saving smooths 23% of shocks to output (about half of the uninsured component of income), and 25% of shocks are not smoothed.

In this chapter we investigate in greater detail the channels through which the federal government provides income insurance to U.S. states. In particular, we focus on federal taxes and transfers (e.g., unemployment contributions and benefits) and grants to states. Interest in the insurance role of central fiscal institutions has increased in recent years because of the debate on the European Monetary Union (EMU). In the absence of mechanisms for achieving income insurance and consumption smoothing, countries in recession will have an incentive to leave that union. It is often claimed that cross-country income insurance provided by central fiscal institutions is essential for the stability of a monetary union. Among the first to stress this point were Sala-i-Martin and Sachs

B.E.S. acknowledges the hospitality and financial support of Tel Aviv University. Both authors acknowledge support from the Armand Hammer Fund for Economic Cooperation in the Middle East and from the United States National Science Foundation.

156

(1992), von Hagen (1992), Atkeson and Bayoumi (1993), and Goodhart and Smith (1993).

Market institutions can also provide risk sharing, rendering federal income insurance less essential. Asdrubali et al. (1996) found that interstate income insurance via capital markets has increased considerably in recent decades, rising from 27% of shocks to state output absorbed via capital markets in the 1960s to 48% of shocks absorbed through that channel in the 1980s. The socially optimal amount of federally provided income insurance may depend on the amount of income insurance achieved through capital markets and may therefore have changed over time. We are not able to take a stand on this issue. Our focus here is on documentation of the observed patterns of various forms of federal government income insurance in recent decades.

Asdrubali et al. (1996) took gross state product as given and measured the incremental amounts of income insurance achieved on capital markets and through federal income insurance. Here we take income insurance on capital markets as given and measure to what extent shocks to state income[1] are smoothed via different federal institutions for income insurance.

Like any fiscal system, the federal fiscal system in the United States was not explicitly designed to provide risk sharing. It was designed to raise general revenue and, possibly, to redistribute income. Nevertheless, as emphasized by Sala-i-Martin and Sachs (1992), a progressive tax-transfer system contributes to risk sharing. An interesting question that, to the best of our knowledge, has not previously been addressed is how effective the different institutions of the tax-transfer system are in providing income insurance. For instance, is the social security transfer system less efficient in this respect than the unemployment-insurance system (in which all states contribute to insurance funds every year, and a state receives back significant amounts of benefits only if unemployment in that state is high)?

We seek to evaluate here the relative efficiency of different fiscal mechanisms in providing income insurance by comparing various fiscal institutions on the basis of their "bang for the buck." The "bang" is defined as the fraction of shocks to state income that is smoothed, and the "buck" is the total dollar amount collected (or disbursed, according to the case) as a fraction of aggregate U.S. output.[2]

---

[1] "State income," as defined by Asdrubali et al. (1996), measures the income of a state prior to payment of federal taxes and prior to receipt of federal transfers and grants.

[2] This measure of the cost of federal insurance is somewhat simplistic, because it attributes the same social shadow cost (in terms of misallocation of resources) to every dollar in the federal fiscal system.

Our findings indicate that unemployment benefits are dramatically more efficient in providing income insurance. The fraction of shocks to state income absorbed by unemployment benefits, relative to the total amount of unemployment benefits distributed, is three times larger than the fraction absorbed by any other fiscal institution relative to the total amount received or paid out. This finding has important implications for the debate on the size of the budget for the central fiscal authority in a future EMU, because with an appropriately designed income insurance scheme it may be possible to achieve a considerable degree of risk sharing with a relatively modest budget.

In our analysis we examine whether or not the amounts of income insurance provided by various federal fiscal institutions have remained constant through time, finding, for example, a substantial increase in the amount of income insurance through personal transfers, which is consistent with the rise in recent decades of transfers to individuals as a fraction of aggregate U.S. output. We also examine the impact of federal income insurance on states with different characteristics, finding, for example, that federal transfers contribute more to income insurance in poor states. Finally, we measure the amounts of income insurance through different federal channels over horizons of varying lengths, finding that personal taxes provide substantially more income insurance over a 3-year horizon than over a 1-year horizon.

In Section 2 we present the method of analysis, and in Section 3 we briefly describe the data. Section 4 presents and discusses the results, and Section 5 concludes.

2   Method

We do not distinguish between the residents and the government of a state. Let y_i denote the per-capita state income of state i. State income consists of all forms of income generated within the state, as well as cross-border factor income flows, including wage, dividend, interest, and rental income payments. State income does not include any transfers or grants from the federal government, and it is prior to any federal taxes. In previous work (e.g., Asdrubali et al., 1996) we measured the role of cross-border factor income flows in smoothing shocks to state output. Here we regard income insurance on markets as given, taking state income as exogenous and measuring the role of federal taxes and transfers in providing further income insurance.

Let s_i denote per-capita transfers from the federal government to state i. State i's per-capita disposable (*cum* transfers) income is $y_i + s_i$. To measure the contribution of transfers to income insurance, consider the following identity:

$$y_i = \frac{y_i}{y_i + s_i}(y_i + s_i) \tag{7.1}$$

Income insurance is achieved if $y_i/(y_i + s_i)$ varies positively with y_i; that is, an increase in y_i entails a smaller increase in $y_i + s_i$.

To obtain a simple metric for smoothing from the identity in (7.1), we take logs and time differences, multiply both sides by $\Delta \log y_i$ (minus its mean), and take expectations, obtaining the following decomposition of the cross-sectional variance of state income:

$$\text{var } \Delta \log y = \text{cov}\{\Delta \log y - \Delta \log(y + s), \Delta \log y\}$$
$$+ \text{cov}\{\Delta \log(y + s), \Delta \log y\} \tag{7.2}$$

Our measure of the fraction of shocks to state income smoothed via transfers is

$$\beta^* = \frac{\text{cov}\{\Delta \log y - \Delta \log (y + s), \Delta \log y\}}{\text{var } \Delta \log y} \tag{7.3}$$

where β^* is the ordinary-least-squares (OLS) estimate of the slope in the cross-sectional regression of $\Delta \log y_i - \Delta \log (y_i + s_i)$ on $\Delta \log y_i$. We do not constrain β^* to be positive or less than unity. If federal transfers to states increase more than proportionately with increases in state income, the coefficient β^* will be negative.

Notice that dividing both sides of (7.2) by $\text{var } \Delta \log y$ yields the identity $1 = \beta^* + \beta^u$, where β^u is the OLS estimate of the slope in the cross-sectional regression of $\Delta \log(y_i + s_i)$ on $\Delta \log y_i$ and represents the fraction of shocks to state income not smoothed via federal transfers. This method for measuring income insurance was suggested by Asdrubali et al. (1996), who provided further details.

To estimate β^* from our panel data set, we run the regressions

$$\Delta \log y_{it} - \Delta \log(y_{it} + s_{it}) = v_t + \beta^* \Delta \log y_{it} + u_{it} \tag{7.4}$$

where the v_t parameters are time-fixed effects that capture year-specific aggregate effects. Because we focus on the amount of interstate income insurance that transfers provide, it is essential to control for aggregate income fluctuations. The time-fixed effects capture all aggregate effects including U.S.-wide income shocks, and the panel regression coefficient is therefore a measure of the amount of interstate insurance provided by federal transfers.[3]

---

[3] Asdrubali et al. (1996) demonstrated that the coefficient from such a panel regression with time-fixed effects is a weighted average of the coefficients that would be estimated from year-by-year cross-sectional regressions.

The estimation of income insurance via federal taxes follows an analogous procedure. Letting τ_i denote per-capita federal taxes paid by state i, and $y_i - \tau_i$ state i's per-capita disposable (*cum* tax) income, the fraction of state income insured through federal taxes is obtained by regressing (cross-sectionally) $\Delta \log y_i - \Delta \log(y_i - \tau_i)$ on $\Delta \log y_i$.

We measure the fraction of changes to state income absorbed through different channels of income smoothing. Although we use the phrase "shocks to state income," we do not assume that fluctuations in state income are unpredictable. Our method measures the fraction of shocks to state income, predictable as well as unpredictable, absorbed through various forms of federal insurance.[4]

3   Data

The data, from Asdrubali et al. (1996), cover the period 1963–90 for income levels (and 1964–90 for growth rates). The appendix to that paper contains a detailed presentation of data sources. We provide here a brief description of the data used in this study.

Our measure of state income is an estimate of the income available to the citizens and government of a state before the collection and disbursement of federal taxes and transfers. We start from the Bureau of Economic Analysis (BEA) personal income figures, adding personal and employer Social Security contributions, and subtracting Social Security transfers. We also add state nonpersonal taxes, because we do not distinguish between the state government and the residents of a state – the taxes collected by the government of the state are available for consumption by its residents, possibly in the form of state public goods. Finally, we add the interest revenue on the state's trust funds. The resulting figure, which we denote as state income, is, ceteris paribus, what would have been available for consumption by the residents and the government of the state had there been no fiscal intervention on the part of the federal government.

There is no consensus concerning the incidence of federal nonpersonal taxes (e.g., federal corporate income taxes and federal unemployment taxes). We followed the allocation rules of the Tax Foundation (1974) in constructing weights for the allocation of most federal taxes across individual states.

Because state unemployment trust funds are managed by the Department of the Treasury, and federal legislation has stipulated minimum

---

[4] Asdrubali et al. (1996) found no difference in the amounts of smoothing for the predictable and unpredictable components of gross state product.

contributions and has defined benefits, we regard the unemployment contributions of the state-federal unemployment system as a federal tax, and the unemployment payments as a negative federal tax. Other authors (Sala-i-Martin and Sachs, 1992; von Hagen, 1992) have argued that the system should not be regarded as federal (indeed, many states contribute beyond the minimum requirement). We do not take a stand on this issue. Rather, we isolate the smoothing effects of unemployment contributions and benefits (as well as of other components of federal government smoothing).

4   Results

Table 7.1 shows the fraction of idiosyncratic income shocks insured through subcomponents of federal disbursements and receipts for our full sample period, 1964–90.[5] It is immediately apparent that the major part of federal income insurance, 9.9% of shocks to state income, is obtained via federal direct transfers to individuals. These transfers include Social Security and Medicare payments, which are not primarily intended to provide cross-state income insurance, but because Social Security transfers, for example, do not, in the main, vary with income, they constitute a larger fraction of income in recessions, stabilizing state income and providing insurance. The federal grant system is also very important in providing income insurance, absorbing 4.5% of idiosyncratic shocks. Grants to states include Medicaid and AFDC[6] payments. Implicit insurance, such as disaster relief from the federal government, is also included in federal grants. Unemployment benefits absorb a further 2.2% of income shocks.

The tax system does not provide much income insurance. The personal income tax absorbs only 2.7% of shocks to state income, even though income taxes are progressive. Corporate income taxes dis-smooth income by 1.1%, possibly because of the fact that corporate income taxes are paid with a substantial time lag. We remind the reader that corporate income taxes are imputed, and the results for this series should therefore be interpreted with caution. Excise taxes also dis-smooth shocks, which may reflect the fact that excise taxes tend to be imposed on items such as tobacco and gasoline that exhibit low income elasticities, making such taxes a larger fraction of income in recessions. Our numbers for excise taxes unfortunately also include many imputations. Social Security contributions dis-smooth income, most probably because of the cap on Social Security contributions, which renders these contri-

---

[5] In all the regressions, excluding those in Table 7.7, we use first differenced yearly data.
[6] Aid to Families with Dependent Children.

Table 7.1. *Channels of federal income insurance, 1964–90 (percentage of shocks to state income absorbed)[a]*

Institution	Absorption
Federal disbursements	
Direct transfers	9.9 (0.3)
Grants	4.5 (0.4)
Unemployment benefits	2.2 (0.2)
Federal receipts	
Personal income taxes	2.7 (0.8)
Corporate income taxes	−1.1 (0.1)
Excise taxes	−0.5 (0.0)
Social Security contributions	−2.4 (0.1)
Unemployment contributions	−0.3 (0.1)
Total federal insurance	14.9 (0.9)

[a] Percentages of shocks to state income absorbed through each channel of federal income insurance; standard errors in parentheses. The reported coefficient for a given row is the estimate of the parameter β^* in the panel regression $\Delta \log y_{it} - \Delta \log(y_{it} + x_{it}) = v_t + \beta^* \Delta \log y_{it} + u_{it}$, where x is the federal disbursement or (minus) the federal tax in that row.

butions a smaller fraction of income during booms. Note, however, that Social Security contributions dis-smooth income by nearly as much as personal taxes smooth income, making the net income-insurance effect of federal taxes (including Social Security contributions) near zero. Finally, unemployment contributions dis-smooth state income by a negative 0.3%, probably reflecting the fact that unemployment contributions are experience-rated, with the consequence that a company laying off workers will face higher unemployment taxes.

The total amount of federal income insurance is 14.9%. Asdrubali et al. (1996), using the same data set, reported that the total amount of federal insurance was 13%. They measured the fraction of shocks to gross state product insured by the federal government, whereas we measured the fraction of shocks to state income that is insured. Asdrubali et al. (1996) found that 39% of shocks to gross state product were insured by capital markets. Because state income already incorporates insurance to output shocks via capital markets, the cross-sectional variance of state

Table 7.2. *Total federal disbursements and receipts (percentage of U.S. GDP, by decade)[a]*

Institution	1964–70	1971–80	1981–90
Federal disbursements			
Direct transfers	4.7	7.4	9.1
Grants	1.7	3.1	2.6
Unemployment benefits	0.3	0.6	0.5
Federal receipts			
Personal income taxes	8.5	8.7	8.9
Corporate income taxes	3.8	2.7	1.7
Excise taxes	1.9	1.6	1.4
Social Security contributions	3.2	4.7	6.1
Unemployment contributions	0.4	0.3	0.4

[a] Total per-capita federal disbursements and receipts as percentages of the per-capita GDP of the United States.

income is smaller than the cross-sectional variance of gross state product (i.e., shocks to state income are "smaller" than shocks to gross state product). Therefore, a given dollar magnitude of federal taxes or transfers absorbs a larger fraction of shocks to state income than of shocks to gross state product.

Table 7.2 shows the amount of federal disbursements and receipts as a fraction of U.S. gross domestic product (GDP). We calculated this ratio year by year, and because the U.S. fiscal system changed significantly over the sample period, we took the average over each decade. It is immediate from Table 7.2 that transfers and grants have increased substantially since the 1960s, with grants declining somewhat in the 1980s. Social Security contributions, in contrast, show steady growth for each decade.

Table 7.3 shows the fraction of state income smoothed through each channel by decade. The amount of state income insured via federal direct transfers has grown over time. Insurance through federal grants grew from the 1960s to the 1970s, with no further growth in the 1980s. Social Security contributions show higher dis-smoothing of state income from decade to decade, reflecting the increasing amounts of contributions collected.

The amount of insurance provided through a particular channel may reflect a large budget or high efficiency in providing insurance. To get an

Table 7.3. *Channels of federal income insurance (percentage of shocks to state income absorbed, by decade)*[a]

Institution	1964–70	1971–80	1981–90
Federal disbursements			
Direct transfers	5.2	9.6	12.0
	(0.5)	(0.4)	(0.4)
Grants	1.8	5.4	5.4
	(0.7)	(0.5)	(0.4)
Unemployment benefits	1.4	2.8	1.8
	(0.2)	(0.4)	(0.2)
Federal receipts			
Personal income taxes	2.9	1.7	3.0
	(1.1)	(1.0)	(1.5)
Corporate income taxes	−1.0	−1.5	−0.7
	(0.2)	(0.1)	(0.1)
Excise taxes	−0.6	−0.3	−0.6
	(0.0)	(0.0)	(0.0)
Social Security contributions	−1.4	−2.4	−3.1
	(0.2)	(0.2)	(0.2)
Unemployment contributions	−0.2	−0.2	−0.5
	(0.1)	(0.1)	(0.1)
Total federal insurance	8.0	15.1	17.2
	(1.4)	(1.3)	(1.4)

[a] Percentages of shocks to state income absorbed through each channel of federal income insurance; standard errors in parentheses. The reported coefficient for a given row is the estimate of the parameter β^* in the panel regression $\Delta \log y_{it} - \Delta \log(y_{it} + x_{it}) = v_t + \beta^* \Delta \log y_{it} + u_{it}$, where x is the federal disbursement or (minus) the federal tax in that row.

impression of the efficiency of a particular channel of federal insurance, we compared the fraction of shocks to state income absorbed through a given channel with the amount of money allocated to that channel or collected via that channel, according to the case.[7] Table 7.4 shows the fraction of shocks to state income absorbed relative to the total amount, as a percent age of U.S. GDP, paid out or collected. (These numbers are calculated by dividing each entry in Table 7.3 by the corresponding entry in Table 7.2.)

It is clear from Table 7.4 that unemployment benefits insure state

[7] This attributes the same social shadow cost (in terms of misallocation of resources) to every dollar in the federal fiscal system.

Table 7.4. *Relative efficiency of federal tax-transfer and grant programs in providing income insurance, by decade*[a]

Institution	1964–70	1971–80	1981–90
Federal disbursements			
Direct transfers	1.1	1.3	1.3
Grants	1.1	1.8	2.1
Unemployment benefits	4.1	4.7	3.5
Federal receipts			
Personal income taxes	0.3	0.2	0.3
Corporate income taxes	−0.3	−0.6	−0.4
Excise taxes	−0.3	−0.2	−0.4
Social Security contributions	−0.4	−0.5	−0.5
Unemployment contributions	−0.5	−0.5	−1.3

[a] Ratio of the fraction of shocks to state income smoothed at each level, as displayed in Table 7.2, and the total budget (revenue or expenditure, according to the case), as displayed in Table 7.3.

income very efficiently. This is not surprising, because this channel is explicitly designed to insure income, although the system is not designed to insure state income as such. Table 7.4 also shows that the efficiency of unemployment benefits in providing insurance was lower in the 1980s than in the 1970s. We conjecture that this reflects the relatively idiosyncratic nature of oil-price increases in the 1970s (oil-price shocks affected some states more than others), as compared with the more aggregate (U.S.-wide) and hence less insurable character of income shocks in the 1980s. A more detailed investigation of this issue is left for future research.

We briefly studied whether or not the amounts of federal income insurance were similar across states with different characteristics. We split the sample into two groups: the 25 states with the highest level of per-capita state income and the 25 remaining states. We then examined whether or not high-income states obtained the same amounts of federal insurance as poorer states. The panel regression we ran to answer this question takes the form

$$\Delta \log z_{it} = \nu_t + \beta_1 D \Delta \log y_{it} + \beta_2 (1 - D) \Delta \log y_{it} + u_{it} \qquad (7.5)$$

where $D = 1$ for states in one group, and $D = 0$ for the other states, z is a generic left-hand-side variable [one for each channel, see equation

(7.4)], β_1 is the fraction of shocks smoothed for the first group of states, and β_2 is the fraction of shocks smoothed for the second group of states.

In these regressions we have excluded the 1960s data because of the large changes over time in federal smoothing documented in Table 7.2; the sample period for these regressions is therefore 1971–90. Table 7.5 shows the results for rich states versus poor states. Somewhat more federal insurance is received by the poor states. This is, most likely, a result of the higher direct transfers allocated to these states (however, unemployment benefits provide more smoothing for rich states). Sørensen and Yosha (1997) showed that rich states are much better insured on capital markets against state-specific shocks to gross state product, resulting in "smoother" state income for rich states than for poor states. Thus, although the patterns of federal income insurance relative to state income are roughly similar for rich and poor states, the measured fraction of shocks smoothed relative to state output is larger for poor states.[8]

In Table 7.6 we examined whether or not states receiving large transfers from the federal government (measured as the sum of direct transfers plus grants relative to state income) also obtained large amounts of income insurance from the federal government. The answer is, not surprisingly, affirmative.

If taxes and transfers show a lag in responding to economic conditions (Goodhart and Smith, 1993), then our regressions using 1-year differencing intervals may give an incomplete picture of the relative importance of the various federal channels of income insurance. Hence we examined, in Table 7.7, the amounts of income shocks insured at 1-, 3-, and 5-year differencing frequencies. The fractions of shocks smoothed through transfers, grants, and unemployment benefits did not significantly vary with the differencing frequency. By contrast, the fraction of shocks smoothed by personal income taxes changed dramatically with the differencing interval. At the 1-year differencing frequency, personal taxes provided little income insurance (i.e., they were roughly proportional to state income), but at the 3-year frequency personal income taxes insured 10.9% of income shocks. We do not report the results for other differencing frequencies, but the fractions of shocks absorbed by personal income taxes increased from the 1-year to the 2-year differ-

---

[8] The results in Sørensen and Yosha (1997) have a somewhat different interpretation, because they measured the amount of insurance within, e.g., the group of rich states, rather than the amount of insurance obtained by this group of states within the entire 50 states. Their results, however, are roughly comparable to the results of the regressions we conducted here.

Table 7.5. *Federal income insurance for rich and poor states, 1971–90*[a]

Institution	Rich	Poor
Federal disbursements		
Direct transfers	9.5	11.8
	(0.5)	(0.4)
Grants	5.5	5.2
	(0.5)	(0.5)
Unemployment benefits	2.7	2.0
	(0.4)	(0.3)
Federal receipts		
Personal income taxes	2.5	2.5
	(1.3)	(1.3)
Corporate income taxes	−1.0	−1.3
	(0.1)	(0.1)
Excise taxes	−0.5	−0.4
	(0.0)	(0.0)
Social Security contributions	−2.8	−2.6
	(0.3)	(0.2)
Unemployment contributions	−0.3	−0.4
	(0.2)	(0.1)
Total federal insurance	15.6	16.8
	(1.5)	(1.4)

[a] "Rich" denotes the 25 states with the highest levels of state income, and "Poor" the 25 states with the lowest levels of state income. Percentages of shocks to state income absorbed through each channel of federal income insurance; standard errors in parentheses. The reported coefficients in each row are the estimated parameters β_1 and β_2 in the panel regression $\Delta \log y_{it} - \Delta \log(y_{it} + x_{it}) = v_t + \beta_1 D \Delta \log y_{it} + \beta_2(1 - D)\Delta \log y_{it} + u_{it}$, where x is the federal disbursement or (minus) the federal tax in that row, and D is a dummy variable for "Rich" states.

encing frequency, peaked at the 3-year frequency, and fell gradually as the differencing interval was increased further. Corporate income taxes and Social Security contributions dis-smoothed income more at the 1-year frequency than at longer frequencies. It seems likely that these taxes are close to being proportional to income over longer horizons.

Table 7.6. *Federal income insurance by the amount of transfers received, 1971–90[a]*

Institution	Large	Small
Federal disbursements		
Direct transfers	11.6	9.5
	(0.4)	(0.5)
Grants	5.4	5.3
	(0.6)	(0.5)
Unemployment benefits	2.0	2.6
	(0.3)	(0.4)
Federal receipts		
Personal income taxes	3.0	2.0
	(1.3)	(1.3)
Corporate income taxes	−1.2	−1.1
	(0.1)	(0.1)
Excise taxes	−0.4	−0.5
	(0.0)	(0.0)
Social Security contributions	−2.7	−2.5
	(0.2)	(0.2)
Unemployment contributions	−0.4	−0.2
	(0.1)	(0.1)
Total federal insurance	17.3	15.1
	(1.4)	(1.5)

[a] "Large" denotes the 25 states with the highest levels of federal direct transfers plus grants relative to state income, and "small" the 25 states where these transfers are lowest. Percentages of shocks to state income are absorbed through each channel of federal income insurance; standard errors in parentheses. The reported coefficients in each row are the estimated parameters β_1 and β_2 in the panel regression $\Delta \log y_{it} - \Delta \log(y_{it} + x_{it}) = \nu_t + \beta_1 D \Delta \log y_{it} + \beta_2(1 - D)\Delta \log y_{it} + u_{it}$, where x is the federal disbursement or (minus) the federal tax in that row, and D is a dummy variable for states receiving large amounts of transfers plus grants.

5   Conclusions

We have investigated the channels of federally provided income insurance for U.S. states and have found that a major portion of federal insurance is provided through direct transfers. A comparison of various fiscal institutions in terms of "bang for the buck" reveals that

Table 7.7. *Federal income insurance for various differencing intervals[a]*

Institution	1 year	3 years	5 years
Federal disbursements			
Direct transfers	9.9	10.5	10.8
	(0.3)	(0.5)	(0.6)
Grants	4.5	4.3	3.8
	(0.4)	(0.4)	(0.4)
Unemployment insurance	2.2	2.6	1.9
	(0.2)	(0.3)	(0.3)
Federal receipts			
Personal income taxes	2.7	10.9	5.6
	(0.8)	(0.9)	(0.9)
Corporate income taxes	−1.1	−0.6	−0.5
	(0.1)	(0.1)	(0.1)
Excise taxes	−0.5	−0.5	−0.4
	(0.0)	(0.0)	(0.0)
Social Security contributions	−2.4	−1.1	−1.0
	(0.1)	(0.2)	(0.1)
Unemployment contributions	−0.3	−0.6	−0.5
	(0.1)	(0.1)	(0.1)
Total federal insurance	14.9	25.5	19.6
	(0.9)	(1.2)	(1.3)

[a] Percentages of shocks to state income absorbed through each channel of federal income insurance for various differencing frequencies of the data; standard errors in parentheses. The reported coefficient for a given row is the estimate of the parameter β^* in the panel regression $\Delta \log y_{it} - \Delta \log(y_{it} + x_{it}) = v_t + \beta^* \Delta \log y_{it} + u_{it}$, where x is the federal disbursement or (minus) the federal tax in that row.

unemployment benefits are significantly more efficient in providing income insurance than is any other fiscal institution, which is not surprising in light of the fact that this institution was explicitly designed to insure income. An important implication of this finding is that with an appropriately designed income insurance scheme, it may be possible to achieve considerable risk sharing in a future EMU with a much smaller budget than might be suggested by a comparison of overall federal income smoothing to the overall size of the U.S. budget.

REFERENCES

Asdrubali, P., Sørensen, B. E., and Yosha, O. (1996). Channels of interstate risk sharing: United States 1963–1990. *Quarterly Journal of Economics* 111: 1081–110.

Atkeson, A., and Bayoumi, T. (1993). Do private capital markets insure regional risk? Evidence from the United States and Europe. *Open Economies Review* 4:303–24.

Goodhart, C., and Smith, S. (1993). Stabilization. *European Economy* (*Reports and Studies*) 5:419–55.

Sala-i-Martin, X., and Sachs, J. (1992). Fiscal federalism and optimum currency areas: evidence for Europe from the United States." In: *Establishing a Central Bank: Issues in Europe and Lessons from the U.S.*, ed. M. Canzoneri, P. Masson, and V. Grilli, pp. 195–219. Cambridge University Press.

Sørensen, B. E., and Yosha, O. (1997). Income and consumption smoothing among US states: regions or clubs? Unpublished manuscript, Brown University and Tel Aviv University.

Tax Foundation (1974). *Federal Tax Burdens in States and Metropolitan Areas.* New York: Tax Foundation, Inc.

von Hagen, J. (1992). Fiscal arrangements in a monetary union: evidence from the US. In: *Fiscal Policy, Taxation, and the Financial System in an Increasingly Integrated Europe*, ed. D. Fair and C. de Boissieu, pp. 337–59. Dordrecht: Kluwer.

PART V

Tax Harmonization, Tax Coordination, and the "Disappearing Taxpayer"

CHAPTER 8

Is There a Need for
a World Tax Organization?

Vito Tanzi

1   Introduction

In recent years the world has been enjoying the considerable benefits resulting from progressive integration of the world's economies. Economies that had been autarkic and closed have opened up and are being integrated into a truly world economy. A global capital market has come into existence, allowing huge movements of capital and generating a world interest rate.

The benefits deriving from this process of globalization are many, and some are obvious: (1) World resources are being more efficiently allocated, and thus output and standards of living are on the rise. (2) Because of greater access to foreign goods, individuals are enjoying greater ranges of choices in goods and services. (3) Because the costs of travel have fallen significantly (in terms of time and money), many people are now able to travel to faraway places. (4) The quantity and range of information available to individuals have increased enormously, even as the costs of obtaining information have fallen dramatically.

The significance of these benefits can be easily appreciated. But, as is often the case, these new developments can be associated with some negative aspects. Globalization can create new problems or aggravate existing ones. Therefore it is important to try to control these negative developments so that the problems they entail will not become so serious as to cast a bad light on the entire process of globalization and thus provoke governmental policies aimed at reversing the recent trends. We should mention just a few of these negative developments:

This is a revision of a paper presented at the 52nd Congress of the International Institute of Public Finance, Tel Aviv, Israel, August 26–29, 1996. Comments received from Liam Ebrill, Ludger Schuknecht, Emil Sunley, and Howell Zee are much appreciated. The views expressed are strictly personal and are not official IMF views.

1. Open borders and free trade have generated enormous
    increases in the quantities of goods that are crossing frontiers.
    World trade is growing twice as fast as world income. Countries
    that want to facilitate this trade and reduce costs to exporters
    and importers are finding it difficult to monitor the increasing
    flow of goods and inspect them for unwanted imports such as
    illegal drugs, weapons, and hazardous materials. As a conse-
    quence, it has become easier to smuggle these unwanted items
    into a country, thus creating major difficulties for the battle
    against drugs and for the monitoring of potential terrorist
    threats. Thus, one of the major challenges the world faces is how
    to keep countries democratic and economies open while still
    effectively controlling the flow of illegal drugs and other pro-
    hibited items.
2. Free and growing trade increases the possibility that negative
    externalities may be imposed by one country upon others. Think
    of the potential for export of products that can pose health
    hazards. The problems arising from the export of contaminated
    materials and food provide a case in point.
3. Free movement of individuals and goods, with penetration by
    large numbers of people into remote, almost untouched areas
    (rain forests, etc.), has increased the likelihood that dangerous
    localized viruses and bacteria previously unknown in the wider
    world will move out of those areas and spread to the rest of
    the world. Many health officials are truly worried about this
    problem (Garrett, 1994). Thus the world must face the challenge
    of protecting people from these new disease agents without
    restricting the movements of individuals and materials.
4. In all of its manifestations thus far, the greatest impact of glob-
    alization has been to facilitate the flow of knowledge. Today, a
    person in remote China with access to a computer and a tele-
    phone line can summon up much of the information available
    to anyone living in New York, Paris, or Tokyo. As the literature
    on the "new growth theory" has emphasized, information, ideas,
    and new knowledge are influencing growth as much as, or more
    than, the increases in traditional inputs such as capital and labor.
    Thus, for many countries, efficient use of the newly available
    information and knowledge can lead to rapid rates of growth.
    This is especially true for those countries that have been behind
    in per-capita income and now are able to exploit to their advan-
    tage the available stock of information (China, Korea, Singa-
    pore, etc.). The rates of growth experienced by such countries in

recent decades would not have been possible in the absence of the information revolution and the globalization of markets. Rates of growth that seemed almost normal in some of the countries of eastern Asia would have been considered extraordinary 30 or 40 years ago.

5. In the absence of adequate environmental controls, such rapid growth can create major environmental problems. Some of these problems are purely domestic. Others can spill over national borders and become serious concerns for the entire world community. Furthermore, in the absence of effective environmental policies, rapid growth can generate significant negative international externalities. Just imagine a billion Chinese experiencing 10% real growth in their incomes, and all of them buying automobiles and refrigerators as the citizens of most industrial countries have done! Given China's rate of growth, that development may not be too far in the future! Think of the environmental implications of such economic developments for the ozone layer, especially if the Chinese choose to ignore environmental considerations in their production and use of such goods.

The important point is that globalization contributes to the transformation of national problems into international ones. Such problems can lead to frictions and eventually conflict among countries if they are not addressed and contained in time. In today's world of interlinked markets, even an increase in the discount rate by a major central bank can have international consequences and can give rise to strong reactions by other countries.

The study of economics has taught us that externalities may sometimes justify public-sector intervention. Such intervention would be aimed at reducing negative externalities or at least making those who generate them bear the cost. This is what lies behind the "polluter pays" principle. Public intervention uses instruments such as taxes, subsidies, and regulation to achieve its objective. However, such actions have generally been taken by a government within its own territory. When externalities are international rather than domestic, then in the absence of a world government that could deal with them it is often difficult for independent countries to work out solutions, because free-rider problems make the resolution of such problems difficult. It is easy to foresee conflicts developing over time because of the increasing internationalization of externalities and the lack of a political body with a mandate and the power to deal with such disputes. This problem is likely to intensify in future years.

A keen observer will have noted the increasing roles that international institutions (such as the IMF, the OECD, the WTO, the WHO, the World Bank, the BIS, the UN, and so on) are playing in connection with issues having international ramifications. Such roles are at times controversial, but most observers seem to accept the legitimacy of these institutions, even though they may criticize some of the actions taken and the policies adopted. A keen observer will also have noted that currently there is no international institution responsible for dealing with the cross-border externalities or spillovers created by tax systems.

2   Globalization and Tax Policy[1]

Globalization implies that many national policies will come to have effects that will be felt beyond a country's borders. Globalization thus tends to lead to frictions between the new developments described earlier and the traditional national policies and institutions that to a large extent still reflect the closed-economy environment and thinking that prevailed when they were first developed. These frictions characterize many policy areas and are becoming particularly vehement in the area of taxation. The debate on taxation that has raged within the European Union is evidence of this conflict. However, I shall argue that this is an issue with broader, worldwide implications.

The tax systems of many countries came into existence and evolved when trade among countries was closely controlled and limited, during times when large movements of capital were almost unknown.[2] During those times, trade flows were discouraged by high tariffs or by physical impediments to the movement of goods; capital flows were forbidden or at least tightly controlled. In that environment, enterprises operated largely within the borders of their own countries, and most individuals earned their incomes from activities or investments in the countries in which they were legally resident. Thus trade flows, the profits of enterprises, personal incomes, and consumption could all be taxed by the authorities in a given country without causing any conflicting claims to be made by the authorities in other countries.

In that earlier environment, adherence to the "territoriality principle" (the right of a government to tax all incomes and activities within its territory) caused no conflict or difficulty. The tax policies of any one country

---

[1] For a more detailed discussion of the issues presented in this section, see Tanzi (1996a); there is some overlap between this section and parts of that paper.

[2] For example, views about global income taxes were much influenced by Henry Simons's classic book *Personal Income Taxation*, written in 1938. Value-added taxes were influenced by Maurice Lauré's book, written in 1953.

could be pursued without much concern about how they might affect other countries. Equally, the policy-makers in a given country found the tax policies of other countries of only marginal interest, if any. It should be recalled that until recent years the study of taxation was almost exclusively the study of taxation in a closed economy, as is reflected in most standard textbooks used in recent decades.

Globalization has changed all of that. In the present environment the actions of one government are greatly limited by the actions of other governments, and cross-border spillover effects generated by taxation have become very important. A full treatment of this aspect is beyond the scope of this chapter. However, a few examples will illustrate the point.

2.1 *Sales Taxes*

Some countries try to entice shoppers from other countries by keeping their excise taxes and sales taxes low, especially on easily transportable commodities. In this way they can "export" some of their tax burden, thus reducing other countries' tax revenue. These actions may be particularly advantageous for small countries seeking to attract buyers from larger neighbors. For these smaller countries, the elasticity of tax revenue with respect to changes in the tax rates may be particularly high. Cross-border shopping has been increasing as a result of better information, more international advertising, lower transportation costs, greater mobility of individuals, mail-order shopping, and technological developments such as the use of the internet and of credit cards to pay for cross-border purchases. This process has limited the freedom of some countries to impose the taxes they would like to assess.

2.2 *Taxes on Enterprise Income*

Many enterprises have become multinational, and some have almost lost their original national identity, especially in an economic sense. Some of these enterprises have established integrated production processes in different countries. For example, they may produce raw materials in countries A and B, convert them into intermediate products in countries C and D, and turn them into finished products in country E, from which the finished products will be exported to other countries. Thus the production of a given final product often uses inputs produced by the enterprise's foreign branches or subsidiaries in several countries. The available statistics indicate that a significant part of the growth in world trade is actually trade among the different divisions within the various multinational enterprises. For example, according to the United Nations' 1994 *World Investment Report*, intrafirm trade is estimated to have increased from about 20% of world trade in the early 1970s to around one-third in the early 1990s, excluding trade in services within transnational corporations. This situation poses the problem of how to allocate the income of the enterprise among its various parts located in different countries.

Like all taxpayers, multinational enterprises have an incentive to lower their (worldwide) tax liabilities. They can pursue this objective in various ways. The first is by locating their operations in countries where the statutory tax rates are low or where more generous tax incentives are provided.[3] Tax competition among countries can prompt one country to legislate lower tax rates or more generous tax incentives than other countries in order to attract foreign investment. When capital is mobile and a country is small, the revenue cost of providing tax incentives can be low if capital is attracted from other countries. If these countries have high rates of unemployment, the ensuing employment benefits can be high.

Second, multinational enterprises can manipulate the costs of the inputs that they import from subsidiaries located in other countries ("transfer prices"). These inputs, which can represent a large proportion of the value of the final product, are often made specifically for a given final product, so that there is no genuine market value that can be used in determining their true market cost. Through the manipulation of transfer prices the multinational enterprises can shift profits to subsidiaries located in jurisdictions with low tax rates.[4] These actions reduce the total tax liabilities of the multinational enterprises and cause some reallocation of tax money among the countries involved, with some countries losing revenue and others gaining from these actions. In the views of various tax administrators, this has become a significant problem and has led to an erosion of tax revenue. The technical characteristics of many modern products (airplanes, automobiles, electronics, and intangibles) make the control of transfer prices particularly difficult.[5] Tax jurisdictions are allocating increasing administrative resources to what may be a futile attempt, over the long run, to deal with this problem.[6]

---

[3] For example, Ireland has been a location favored by many enterprises because of its low tax rate.

[4] These shifts do not require specific movements of real capital; only taxable profits move.

[5] A modern airplane can use millions of parts, some of which are made specifically for that model.

[6] The foregoing paragraph has emphasized the manipulation of the prices of real inputs. However, the assignment of costs to trademarks, headquarters expenses, research and development, and loans among different divisions of a multinational enterprise can also create opportunities for manipulations aimed at reducing the total tax burden on the enterprise.

2.3   *Taxes on Individual Incomes*

In recent years there has been explosive growth in the income that individuals have derived from investments made in other countries or from activities carried out in other countries.[7] Because of increased personal mobility and advances in information technology, as well as greater freedom to invest savings abroad, the total incomes of many individuals now contain large and growing components of foreign-earned income. These individuals are likely to underreport (or often not report) their income earned abroad, assuming, often correctly, that the tax authorities in their country of residence will be unable to discover or determine the true value of these foreign-earned incomes.[8] Exchanges of information among tax authorities often are unable to prevent the nonreporting of these incomes and the consequent tax evasions. In fact, conflicting objectives among the tax authorities in various countries, especially tax-haven countries, ensure that in many cases such information will not be provided (Tanzi, 1995; OECD, 1994). As a consequence, official statistics do not fully reflect such incomes, and some countries benefit at the expense of others. That leads to losses in total revenues and to changes in the incidence of the tax burden. It also leads to changes in the statutory tax systems when policy-makers attempt to compensate for such losses by increasing the rates for other taxes.

Obviously the existence of tax-haven countries facilitates tax evasion. In recent years there has been a proliferation of the practice whereby countries and territories allow individuals and enterprises to use them to establish tax addresses through which incomes earned in other countries can be channeled (Doggard, 1993). The tax-haven countries benefit either by the fees they charge or by the low taxes they impose on capital that would not have been channeled through them in the absence of tax considerations. The other countries suffer losses of revenue and decreased control over their tax systems.

Finally, new capital-market instruments (derivatives and other exotic manipulations) are creating complex problems for tax authorities. Tax administrators are having increasing difficulties in identifying incomes, in allocating them to particular countries, and in taxing them, especially

---

[7] One indicator of this can be seen in the sharp increase in portfolio investment income derived from overseas investments. IMF statistics indicate that for the world as a whole, this investment increased from $447 billion in 1988 to $768 billion in 1994. Another indicator of the surge in transnational financial transactions is that cross-border security transactions expanded from less than 10% of major industrial countries' GDP in 1980 to well in excess of 100% of GDP in 1992 (IMF, 1995).

[8] For example, tens of billions of dollars (U.S.) of Latin American capital escaped taxation in the country of origin by being deposited abroad, especially in the United States, in nonresidents' accounts, which were tax-free.

when the firms that handle these transactions operate from tax-haven locations. This is a problem that can only increase with time, because policy-makers are lagging behind the recent technological developments in the financial markets. As capital markets become more integrated and more complex, and as capital movements intensify,[9] the ability of the national tax authorities to deal with these issues is unlikely to be adequate.

Clearly, these developments, as well as others not discussed here, are having adverse impacts on the tax systems and tax revenues of all countries. However, those impacts are not yet fully understood, and it is difficult to assess them quantitatively. Recent reports have indicated that tax revenues in certain countries have been lower than forecast, even when other factors (such as cyclical developments) were taken into account. Some finance ministers have expressed concern over these losses, which certainly are not welcome at a time when reductions in fiscal deficits remain important objectives of economic policy in many countries. Additionally, some countries have experienced sudden capital outflows when they have attempted to introduce certain changes in tax policy, such as tax withholding for particular kinds of capital income.

Fear of tax-base migration has made some countries hesitant to adjust the rates of their taxes or even to tax dividend and interest incomes, thus reducing the margin for maneuver by policy-makers.[10] Concerns have also been expressed about the impact of globalization on the incidence of the tax system and hence its equity, as well as its impact on fiscal deficits if it forces countries to reduce tax rates, especially tax rates on capital incomes, in order to remain internationally competitive.[11] Tax competition has become a fact of life for many countries, and the net effect of such competition is or will be reduced tax revenues and forced changes in the structures of their tax systems.

Those economists, and there are many of them, who believe that tax reduction is always a good thing because governments are inherently wasteful will welcome the downward pressure that the competitive forces mentioned earlier are having or will have on both tax rates and tax revenue. Those who worry about fiscal deficits and those who believe

---

[9] It is estimated that daily capital movements exceed $1 trillion (U.S.). It must be extremely difficult to determine the (taxable) incomes, if any, associated with these movements and to allocate them to specific countries.

[10] For example, there are now several Latin American countries that no longer tax dividend and interest incomes, on the assumption that taxation of those incomes would encourage capital flight.

[11] I have argued elsewhere (Tanzi, 1994) that progressive global income taxes cannot survive in this environment.

that the downward pressure on tax revenue will reduce the ability of governments to finance necessary or inflexible spending will not see this as a welcome development. In either case, the important result is that spillovers across national borders are being created. Alleviation of this situation will be difficult, given that at present there is no official worldwide body, neither a world government nor an international institution, with a clear mandate to deal with the new tax developments that have international implications.

3   An International Tax Organization?

In the preceding two sections I have argued that recent trends in the world's economies (integration of real economies and globalization of capital markets) are contributing to the creation of or the growth in importance of externalities or spillovers that transcend national borders, and that there is no world government to deal with these externalities. In the absence of such a world government, there are three possible ways of dealing with these issues: (1) Rely on spontaneous market solutions. (2) Seek solutions through international agreements. (3) Create international institutions charged with the responsibility of dealing with the consequences of the developments described earlier.

Spontaneous market solutions work in some areas, but not in others. In the presence of "commons problems," for example, when access to a given resource (such as air, or fish in the ocean, or the world tax base) is (relatively) free, the market solution is unlikely to be successful. The incentives for some countries to take advantage of the situation or to impose their views on others are simply too strong. That would also occur with tax competition.

Solutions through international agreements have worked well in some areas (especially when the costs associated with the problem and the benefits associated with the solution have been broadly distributed), but not in others. These solutions are particularly difficult to achieve when free riding on the part of some countries can give them significant advantages and when there are no simple and effective ways of forcing them to join the agreement.[12]

The approach of creating an international institution with a mandate to propose solutions and in some cases to enforce solutions to given problems has been a popular one over the years since World War II. As a consequence, international organizations have proliferated. Some of

[12] For a proposal that would rely on international agreements *cum* sanctions to solve the problem of international money laundering, see Tanzi (1996b).

these institutions are, of course, more efficient than others at carrying out their mandates and contributing to solutions for particular problems.[13] The inefficiency of some has at times led to criticisms of them all. In some cases the problems with these institutions have been that their mandates have not been clear and their resources have been inadequate.

Section 2 of this chapter focused on the impacts of globalization and economic integration on the tax systems of countries. It was argued that in the current circumstances (and probably the future circumstances), some countries will try to exploit to their advantage the "commons," which in our case is the world tax base. It was also argued that as countries' economies become more integrated, and as capital markets become more globalized, these problems are bound to become more pronounced. Given the current tax structures and methods of imposing taxes, it is almost inevitable that tax competition will play a substantial and increasing role, as some countries will face strong incentives to export some of their tax burden by attracting consumers, real capital, or taxable income from other countries. They will do so by imposing lower statutory tax rates or through the use of incentives that will reduce the tax base.

Tax competition may be seen as an attractive development by some, but it is likely to lead to friction and conflict among countries. It may also lead to macroeconomic problems by reducing tax revenue. The spontaneous market solution, wherein countries would compete rather than cooperate, will lead to downward adjustments of tax rates, especially those applicable to mobile tax bases such as capital and highly specialized labor, and to lower rates for consumption taxes, especially those applicable to easily transportable and relatively valuable goods. In regard to reduction of tax rates on sales and on capital incomes, small countries may become the pacesetters, because they are the ones that can gain the most from attracting buyers and investors from abroad.[14] Other likely developments could be increases in source-based taxation for taxes on capital and therefore a progressive abandonment of the concept of global income taxation. For corporate income, formula-based taxation may eventually replace account-based taxation as a method for dealing with the problem of transfer prices, as mentioned earlier.

The option of pursuing international agreements in tax matters is unlikely to be productive, as shown by the experience of the European Community over the past two decades. Countries are not apt to abandon

---

[13] Various observers have had different views of the effectiveness of such institutions. For example, while I was writing this section, Steve Forbes, former U.S. presidential candidate, was reported by Reuter's to have called for the "junking" of the IMF.

[14] Some of these changes will be in a direction favored by theoretical economists.

their national objectives and agree to arrangements that they may see as less beneficial to them than the alternative of going it alone. Also, countries with different political agenda will find it difficult to agree on a given tax structure. Even in the limited area of the European Community, progress toward tax harmonization has been limited. The history of tax-treaty negotiations indicates that tax agreements, even between only two countries, can be difficult to reach and are very demanding of time and effort. In any case, no institutional framework has been established to facilitate discussion of issues and negotiation of agreements on a world-wide basis.

This leaves only the option of creating an international organization that can systematically deal with tax matters or, alternatively, issuing a specific mandate to an existing institution. There is currently a world organization that deals with trade matters (WTO), one that deals with macroeconomic stability and balance-of-payments equilibrium (IMF), one that deals with economic development (IBRD), and many more that deal with other objectives. The IMF, in particular, focuses on the trans-national implications of domestic macroeconomic policies. Yet there is no organization at the world level that supervises or attempts to influence tax developments that have transnational implications. This situation can be considered unusual, because countries are competing less frequently through the use of tariffs, quantitative restrictions on trade, and adjustments in exchange rates, but much more frequently by means of tax incentives, adjustments in tax rates, changes in administrative treatment of some incomes, and so forth. This is the process that in the view of many tax experts is leading to "tax degradation." As trade is liberalized further, and as capital becomes freer to move, the advantages to some countries of engaging in tax competition, and the temptation to do so, will increase. The world tax base will thus become one of the "commons" to be exploited.

Therefore a case can perhaps be made for the establishment of a "World Tax Organization." What would be the mandate for such an organization? There are many possibilities, and this overview can mention only some of them. Of course, its mandate would depend on how much power the member countries would be willing to give it. It would also depend on how representative it would be of the whole world community. Because the levying of taxes is one of the most political of all governmental actions, it is unlikely that at this juncture in time the countries' governments would want to grant a world tax organization the outright power to tax. There has never been an example of a supranational organization that has been given this power. Even the European Commission does not have such a power. However, as I wrote some years ago, "it is conceivable that the day may come when the countries [of the world] create an 'International Revenue Services' to collect taxes that could not be collected by separate governments and to allocate them either to the provision of international public goods or back to the countries" (Tanzi, 1988, p. 277).

Recently, James Tobin's idea of an international tax on cross-border financial transactions (Tobin, 1978) has been adopted by other writers who have proposed international taxes on airline tickets, financial transactions, or other items in order to finance the United Nations (e.g., Spahn, 1995; Shome and Stotsky, 1995). The collection of such a tax or some version of it could be assigned to the proposed "World Tax Organization." However, it is unlikely that the countries of the world are ready for such a step or for similar steps, even though such taxes could provide financing for the activities of some of the international organizations and would remove the decision whether or not to finance established institutions such as the United Nations from the ongoing political debates within countries. Such debate creates uncertainty and sometimes causes major problems for those international organizations.

Rather, the "World Tax Organization" could be given responsibilities other than tax collection. In brief, some of the main activities of the proposed organization could be the following:

1. Identification of major tax trends and problems at the international level. For the OECD countries, the Committee on Fiscal Affairs of the OECD has been doing valuable work aimed at identifying these trends. However, a majority of the countries of the world are not members of the OECD.
2. Compilation and/or generation of relevant tax statistics and tax-related information for as many countries as possible. Much of this information may already be available, but there is no institution that is compiling it for the whole world. Here the work of the OECD and the IMF would provide particularly helpful input.
3. Preparation of periodic (yearly?) "World Tax Development Reports" on the basis of the foregoing information, presenting statistics, describing main trends (both statistically and in terms of policy developments), identifying problems, and perhaps pointing toward feasible solutions for those problems. Emerging problems could also be highlighted, and possible solutions could be studied. Countries' best practices could be identified and made known to other countries.
4. Provision of some technical assistance to countries regarding

tax policy and tax administration, always keeping in mind that the changes recommended should make the tax system of the country receiving the assistance better coordinated or harmonized with the systems of other countries. Technical assistance is already provided by several institutions, including the IMF. However, many needs are not being met, because of limited resources. Furthermore, the goal of the technical assistance provided by the new organization would be to make the tax systems more compatible.

5. Development of basic norms for tax policy and tax administration. This is an area where little progress has been made.[15]

6. Initiation of an international forum in which policy-makers and experts could exchange ideas on tax matters.

7. Establishment of an international forum for tax arbitration when frictions or conflict between countries or among groups of countries arises. Once again, no such forum currently exists.

8. Surveillance of tax developments in the same way that the IMF maintains surveillance of macroeconomic developments. Such monitoring could be conducted at the country level, at the regional level, and at the world level. The modus operandi of the IMF could provide useful guidelines for the new organization.

The "World Tax Organization" would identify tax developments that create cross-border spillover effects and would bring these to the attention of a board of directors representing all the member countries. The board would then recommend changes in those areas where the tax behavior of a country was having negative effects on other countries. For example, it could recommend changes in countries that are obviously raiding the world tax base. The organization would not, however, become involved in tax issues that do not have significant cross-border spillovers. And, of course, it would only recommend changes, not force them.

Broadly speaking, this list represents the major activities to be undertaken by such an organization. Of course, more detailed and specific terms of reference might include other activities.[16]

4 Conclusions

In this brief chapter, I have tried to transmit a sense of the worldwide developments that are having a significant impact on tax systems. These

---

[15] For a recent attempt along these lines, see Hussey and Lubick (1996).

[16] A companion IMF working paper (Tanzi, 1996a) provides additional and complementary information and analysis.

developments are cumulative, so that their impact on tax systems can only grow. Only a sampling of the areas in which globalization and the growing integration of world economies are affecting existing tax systems has been provided.

The essay has concluded that the time may have come to create a world institution that would supervise these developments, encourage countries to coordinate their tax actions, and suggest solutions. The role of this institution would be one of surveillance, distribution of information, and provision of a forum for discussion. It is unlikely that in the foreseeable future such an institution would be given the direct responsibility to collect taxes.

REFERENCES

Doggard, C. (1993). *Tax Havens and Their Uses*. London: *The Economist* Intelligence Unit.

Garrett, L. (1994). *The Coming Plague*. New York: Farrar, Strauss & Giroux.

Hussey, W. M., and Lubick, D. C. (1996). *Basic World Tax Code*. Arlington, VA: Tax Analysts.

IMF (1995). *World Economic Outlook* (May). Washington, DC: International Monetary Fund.

Lauré, M. (1953). *La taxe sur la valeur ajoutee*, 2nd ed. Paris: Librarie Sivey.

OECD (1994). *Tax Information Exchange between OECD Member Countries: A Survey of Current Practices*. Paris: Organization for Economic Cooperation and Development.

Shome, P., and Stotsky, J. (1995). *Financial Transactions Taxes*. IMF working paper WP/95/77. Washington, DC: International Monetary Fund.

Simons, H. (1938). *Personal Income Taxation*. University of Chicago Press.

Spahn, B. (1995). *International Financial Flows and Transactions Taxes: Survey and Options*. IMF working paper WP/95/60. Washington, DC: International Monetary Fund.

Tanzi, V. (1988). Forces that shape tax policy. In: *Tax Policy in the Twenty-first Century*, ed. H. Stein, pp. 266–77. New York: Wiley.

Tanzi, V. (1994). Review of *Tax Policy in OECD Countries: Choices and Conflict*, by K. Messere. *National Tax Journal* 47:447–50.

Tanzi, V. (1995). *Taxation in an Integrating World*. Washington, DC: Brookings Institution.

Tanzi, V. (1996a). *Globalization of Tax Competition and the Future of Tax Systems*. IMF working paper. Washington, DC: International Monetary Fund.

Tanzi, V. (1996b). *Money Laundering and the International Financial System*. IMF working paper WP/96/55. Washington, DC: International Monetary Fund.

Tobin, J. (1978). A proposal for international monetary reform. *Eastern Economic Journal* 4:153–9.

CHAPTER 9

Taxation, Financial Innovation, and Integrated Financial Markets: Some Implications for Tax Coordination in the European Union

Julian S. Alworth

1   Introduction

The past decade has witnessed major changes in the volume, composition, and direction of international capital flows, as well as a wave of deregulation and financial innovation. For the most part, public-finance economists have concentrated their attention on the opportunities this new climate has created for tax evasion and tax competition (Mintz, 1992; Gordon 1995; Tanzi, 1995). By contrast, tax practitioners and financial-market participants have tended to stress the inconsistencies of existing tax systems, the tax impediments to the smooth working of markets, and the inefficiencies of the established anti-tax-avoidance mechanisms (Scholes and Wolfson, 1992; Plambeck, Rosenbloom, and Ring, 1996). Not surprisingly, these different perspectives suggest vastly different policy recommendations.

This study has three objectives. The first is to illustrate that, contrary to a view common among public-finance specialists, the contraction in source-based taxes on portfolio capital flows (i.e., withholding taxes) owes much less to tax competition for "hot-money flows" than to a number of other factors:[1] (1) the increase in the number of institutional investors who benefit from a special tax status in their home countries that they wish to maintain abroad, (2) the expansion of international transactions in securities and the inefficiencies of withholding-tax

I am grateful to Fabio Bassi for assistance in the preparation of this chapter.

[1] The same cannot be said for corporation tax, where tax competition by offshore centers is particularly important. Discussion of this topic is beyond the purview of this study.

187

regimes, and (3) the difficulty, if not impossibility, of applying gross-basis withholding taxes to a number of new financial instruments.

The second objective is to examine the complications involved in operating a full-fledged global income tax based on the residence principle in light of the changes that have occurred in the financial system. These problems concern the definition of income, particularly in the case of sophisticated institutional investors, as well as enforcement and exchange of information in the case of individuals. The third objective is to describe other possible paths for tax reform. Whereas our attention will be concentrated on passive income, this distinction is, to a great extent, increasingly obsolete; indeed, many of the new financial instruments used to manage passive investments are identical with those used for active foreign investments.

The organization of this chapter is as follows: Section 2 describes the principal changes in international capital flows over the past two decades, focusing on the growth of institutional investments. Section 3 provides a brief overview of the changing role assigned to withholding taxes. Section 4 examines several types of transactions that cannot be easily dealt with by withholding taxes, such that income tax rules have to be amended considerably in order to be applicable to the new financial instruments. (An Appendix discusses one example of these issues in somewhat greater analytical detail.) Section 5 examines in detail the various approaches to defining taxable passive income and weighs the pros and cons of various solutions. It discusses several reasons why taxation of income on a global basis is seen as the only way of taxing various income flows. Section 6 summarizes the principal conclusions.

2   The Evolution of Capital Flows and Financial Markets: How Well Do the Stylized Beliefs Fit the Facts?

During the past two decades the surge in capital movement has been accompanied by a shift from direct investment to portfolio flows (Table 9.1). Whereas the tax treatment of multinationals has continued to attract the greatest attention in the United States, increasingly the focus of policy debate (at least in Europe) has moved toward passive investments.

It is widely held that because of recent technological changes, the residence principle is increasingly becoming doomed to failure, owing to the difficulties of preventing tax evasion in residence countries and the ineffectiveness of the existing exchange-of-information arrangements between tax authorities. In other words, cross-border passive investments escape taxation because of the difficulty of monitoring income in the

Table 9.1. *Changes in the composition of gross capital flows (1975–92)*
(annual averages in billions of U.S. dollars)

Sector	1975–79	1980–84	1985–89	1990	1991	1992
Total outflows						
Direct investment	35.3	42.4	134.9	226.0	182.2	158.5
Industrial countries	34.7	41.0	128.4	213.0	171.1	147.1
Developing countries	0.6	1.4	6.5	13.0	11.1	11.4
Portfolio investment						
Industrial countries	12.4	41.8	176.8	152.8	274.0	238.0
Total inflows						
Direct investment	26.9	52.6	117.6	186.0	143.3	133.6
Industrial countries	19.9	36.2	98.1	156.2	101.8	83.9
Developing countries	7.0	16.4	19.5	29.8	41.5	49.7
Portfolio investment						
Industrial countries	25.0	57.8	186.0	154.9	374.6	308.5

Sources: IMF and my own calculations.

countries of residence of the beneficiaries. That, in turn, has encouraged tax evasion. The logical consequence of this view is stated very clearly by Tanzi: "Over the long run there may be no alternative to the policy of imposing minimum withholding taxes on incomes paid abroad that are derived from financial instruments. In this instance the major issue will be the level of the rate at which the withholding tax will be imposed. This rate would have to be agreed upon internationally" (Tanzi, 1995, p. 132).

Although much circumstantial evidence can be mustered to support the belief that substantial sums of passive cross-border investments escape taxation and are motivated by tax considerations (witness the growth in size of offshore centers, the active marketing of tax-advisory services, etc.), that view overlooks several very fundamental trans-formations that have taken place in the past decade. It is those trans-formations that render certain recently proposed tax changes, at least in their most blunt form, somewhat misguided. In order to understand why great care must be taken in guiding the direction of future tax policy, it is important to focus on four major and closely interrelated developments that have affected the operation of financial markets during the past decade: (1) the expansion of the securities markets, (2) the increase in institutional savings, (3) the internationalization of institutional savings, and (4) the development of broad markets for derivative financial instruments. Each of these developments is having important repercussions for international tax policy as well as domestic tax policy.

2.1 The Increasing Importance of Transactions in Securities

Fundamental shifts have taken place in the structure of cross-border portfolio investments during the past decade. These involve movement away from investments primarily in bank deposits (managed separately for high-net-worth individuals) to investments in securities (managed by professional institutional investors, who often make use of derivative financial instruments).

Table 9.2 provides a picture of the structural changes in financial-capital flows in terms of the nature of the instruments involved and the

Table 9.2. *Structure of cross-border portfolio flows (stocks at end of period, billions of U.S. dollars)*

Instrument	1983	1993	1995
International markets	350	2,045	2,800
Short-term notes	0	110	130
Medium-term notes	0	150	460
Bonds	350	1,785	2,210
Domestic markets	690	3,500	3,800
Securities	340	2,200	2,100
Equities	350	1,300	1,700
Cross-border deposits	2,496	6,270	7,810[a]
Non-banks	554	1,370	1,720
Central banks	143	259	310
Banks	1,799	4,641	5,780
Total	3,536	11,810	14,410

[a] Including $325 billion of securities issued by banks.
Sources: BIS (1995, 1996), Barings-ING, and my own calculations.

types of investors. Apart from the explosion in outstanding cross-border financial assets during the past decade, the most striking feature seen in the table is the shift from bank lending to transactions in securities, mostly in the form of debt instruments, but also in equity. Most of the expansion in securities transactions has occurred in international markets (e.g., Eurobond and other Euro-securities), but since the early 1990s, with the lifting of foreign-exchange controls in virtually all major countries and the attempt to standardize trading practices, there has been an increasing presence of foreign investors in domestic markets, typically in the markets for government fixed-income bonds.[2]

The reasons for the shift away from bank intermediation to securities-market transactions can be ascribed to a number of developments, largely of a structural nature: (1) the decline in the credit rating of banks following the Latin American debt crisis, (2) the tightening of bank capital requirements, with the resulting decrease in on-balance-sheet positions and increase in off-balance-sheet exposures, (3) the improvements in clearing and settlement mechanisms for securities, and (4) the growth of public-sector deficits in the industrial countries. These developments have been accompanied and stimulated by an increase in the number of institutional investors with a marked preference for securities over bank-intermediated assets.

Table 9.3 illustrates these developments for the narrower category of non-bank investors (individuals, insurance companies, pension funds, mutual funds, etc.). Among cross-border flows, investments in securities by non-banks recorded the most dramatic increase, accompanied by a sharp decline in the importance of deposits relative to investments in securities. It is also important to note that non-banks accounted for the bulk of business in equity.

---

[2] There is, for example, evidence to suggest that foreign investors in domestic government-securities markets have at times accounted for well over 30% of transactions. In some instances, such as Spain, the foreign presence has been as large as 70% (BIS, 1995). Moreover, an interpretation of the numbers must take account of the fact that the economic distinctions among many individual balance-of-payments items has become blurred: (1) Banks' increasing participation in the securities market, as investors and issuers and users of bonds for collateral (repo transactions), has made it more difficult to distinguish between bank lending and bond financing. (2) The distinction between long- and short-term portfolio capital movements is no longer meaningful, because long-term securities tend to be traded over short horizons. (3) The actual volume of cross-border transactions is many times greater than the changes in assets and liabilities: according to the latest (April 1995) aggregate data available, daily turnover in the foreign-exchange market exceeded $1,260 billion, up from $880 billion only 3 years earlier, with a substantial volume taking place cross-border.

Table 9.3. *International investments by non-banks*
(stocks at end of period, billions of U.S. dollars)

Instrument	1983	1993	1995
International markets	300	1,710	2,520
Short-term notes	0	100	120
Medium-term notes	0	110	400
Bonds	300	1,500	2,000
Domestic markets	471	2,105	2,440
Securities	136	880	840
Equities	335	1,225	160
Cross-border deposits	554	1,370	1,720
Total	1,325	5,185	7,080

Sources: BIS (1995, 1996), Barings-ING, and my own
calculations.

2.2   *The Growth of Institutional Savings*

The growth of institutional investing can be estimated in only a very
rough and indirect fashion. Overall household savings accounted for
as institutional investments in the G7 countries can be estimated at
over $10,000 billion. This number does not, however, provide a complete
picture of the size of institutional investments, because other holders of
financial assets (corporations, charities, endowments, etc.) channel part
of their savings through these intermediaries. For example, in the United
States alone, institutionally managed funds, excluding insurance companies (mutual funds, traditional defined-benefit plans, endowments and
charities, and 401K assets), have been estimated to amount to well over
7,000 billion (Hurley et al., 1995).

The escalation in institutional investing is a relatively recent phenomenon, with the bulk of the expansion having occurred at a breath-
taking rate since the early 1980s. Table 9.4 describes the changing
composition of household savings that are accounted for by institutions.
Mutual funds, for example, have existed for several decades in the United
States, but did not really take off until money-market mutual funds were
launched in the early 1980s to circumvent the limitations imposed by regulation Q and other restrictive practices. The growth of mutual funds in
Europe has lagged that in the United States, owing to the slow process
of financial deregulation in the major continental countries (in mid-1995,
total assets were estimated at $1,300 billion, compared with $2,300 billion

Table 9.4. *Growth of institutional investing (financial assets as percentage of household financial assets)*

Country	Pension funds and life-assurance companies			Collective-investment institutions			Total		
	1980	1990	1995	1980	1990	1995	1980	1990	1995
United States	17.8	23.5	28.9	2.2	7.7	12.3	20.0	31.2	41.2
Japan	13.8	20.8	26.2	1.8	5.6	4.0	15.6	26.4	30.2
Germany	19.4	27.1	28.7	3.2	8.1	12.2	22.6	35.1	40.8
France	8.0	14.7	18.5	2.7	21.7	21.6	10.6	36.3	40.1
Italy	1.6	3.2	5.2	n.a.	2.9	3.6	n.a.	6.1	8.7
United Kingdom	39.9	53.7	46.5	1.6	4.9	5.8	41.5	58.6	52.1
Canada	19.4	26.7	30.9	1.0	3.0	8.4	20.4	29.7	40.3

Sources: BIS (1995, 1996) and national sources.

in the United States). However, the same driving forces have been at work in contributing to the proliferation of these institutions: the opportunity to obtain market-related returns (money-market funds), the benefits of portfolio diversification (domestic and international funds), and cost considerations (relative to individual accounts).

Pension-fund wealth has also expanded very rapidly over the past decade, as has insurance. The growth here has been driven mainly by the increasing pressures on public pension schemes and is likely to accelerate in coming years, as countries such as France, Italy, and Germany set up the appropriate institutional frameworks for such schemes.[3]

Each of these institutions – although not necessarily the ultimate beneficiary – generally enjoys special tax status domestically. In the United States, for example, mutual funds, which do not normally have a corporate or individual tax status, pass yearly income (cash receipts plus realized capital gains) to their beneficiaries for tax purposes. They generally operate, however, as if they were tax-exempt, because the tax status of the beneficiaries of the income can vary from being exempt (in the case of pension funds and 401K plans) to being taxed at corporate rates.[4]

[3] Pension-fund assets in Europe amounted to about $1,850 billion at the end of 1994, compared with $3,750 billion in the United States (Hurley et al., 1995). About half of European pension assets were accounted for by the United Kingdom and The Netherlands.

[4] The U.S. tax code mandates that mutual funds distribute all income, convert short-term gains into income, and defer the recognition of unrealized gains. This creates wide

In the international arena there do not appear to be see-through provisions for taxes withheld at source. Indeed, in many instances mutual funds are subject to special tax treatment under double-tax treaties. Pension funds generally are able to roll up income tax-free, and insurance companies also enjoy tax-privileged positions, in many cases through tax deductions for premium payments and tax deferral for the income earned on reserves.

Foreign diversification of investments has been increasing rapidly, at least in part driven by the numerous studies that have described at length the benefits of international investment in terms of risk and return, facilitated by the closer integration of financial markets during the past decade. Whereas tax considerations may have mattered in terms of specific types of foreign investments, there is little evidence to suggest that tax factors have been major determinants in the overall increase in foreign investment. On the contrary, until quite recently it was common to argue that one factor that may have contributed to the segmentation of markets was precisely the tax treatment abroad accorded to institutional investors, who, unlike individuals, had no reason to evade domestic tax, owing to their privileged status.[5]

Data on foreign assets held abroad by institutional investors are unfortunately not available on a consistent basis, but there is considerable evidence to suggest that the bulk of the expansion in non-bank investments that has taken place over the past decade has largely been due to these entities. There has been a remarkable increase in the share of foreign investments in the total assets of U.S. pension funds (which can be estimated to have grown from less than 2% to around 10% since the beginning of the decade); at present, they can be estimated at about $500 billion. U.S. residents hold $380 billion in bank deposits overseas, and the bulk of that is accounted for by money-market mutual funds and money-market deposit accounts at banks. About 15% of the net inflows to mutual funds in the United States in recent years have been into foreign investments.

The internationalization of institutional holdings has proceeded much further in Europe and Japan. In the United Kingdom, The Netherlands, and Belgium the portions of pension-fund assets invested in foreign shares and bonds amount to 30%, 27%, and 50%, respectively. Many of the French money-market SICAVs also operate in the Euromarket,

disparity in the relative performances of mutual funds on pre-tax and post-tax bases. Few managers, however, consider tax issues when managing their portfolios, because they are judged and hence compensated on the basis of pre-tax returns.
[5] See, for example, Solnik (1988) and Cooper and Kaplanis (1986) for discussion and quantification of the barriers to foreign investment.

similar to their U.S. counterparts, by investing their liquid assets in Euro-French-franc accounts. All in all, the outstanding assets of institutional investors can be estimated to have reached $2,500 billion, or well one-third of total cross-border assets held by non-bank entities.

The expansion of the securities business has been closely connected to the growth of these institutional investors, who by internal regulation or statute are unable to hold nonnegotiable banking assets beyond certain low percentages. It should also be noted that in recent years the growth of government deficits has had the effect of feeding the growth of the securities markets. Derivatives have permitted financial-market participants to tailor the assets they have purchased to the time horizons of their investments.[6]

2.3   *The Growth of the Derivatives Markets*

As already mentioned, the 1980s witnessed explosive growth in the trading of derivative instruments (Tables 9.5 and 9.6). In late March 1995 the outstanding notional value of over-the-counter contracts amounted to a staggering $40,700 billion, and at the end of December 1996 the notional value of exchange-trade contracts was a further $9,200 billion.

These instruments serve the purpose of transferring risk, and the actual marking to market value of the position at $1,750 billion (for over-the-counter transactions) is less than 4% of the notional value of the con-tracts. These transactions, however, have become commonplace and are intimately intertwined with the growth in securities transactions and the expansion in professional management and cross-border transactions.

2.4   *Implications*

These data have a variety of implications. The first concerns the scale of the phenomena. The growth in financial markets has been unprece-

---

[6] Although the topic is beyond the scope of this study, it is important to understand that derivatives have focused attention on financial mathematics and on the arbitrage equiv-alence between primary and synthetic instruments. The techniques of understanding and evaluating complex cash flows, contingencies, and risks have profound implications for our understanding of the tax system. The different tax treatments offered by equivalent cash flows can be considered as "tax options" that might be mispriced in favor of the tax authorities or of taxpayers. A similar approach arises from discontinuities in tax sched-ules, which can give rise to opportunities for "trading" of the tax-status assignment. Examples of the latter abound (leasing mergers, etc.), but the precise general conceptual framework for thinking of the operation of the tax system in these terms owes much to the approaches taken in valuing derivatives.

Table 9.5. *Outstanding DFIs traded on organized exchanges worldwide, at end of year, by market risk category and instrument*

	Contracts (in millions of U.S. dollars)		Notional amounts (in billions of U.S. dollars)	
Instrument	1990	1995	1990	1995
Currencies				
Futures	0.2	0.9	17.0	37.9
Options	0.9	2.7	56.5	43.2
Long-term interest rates				
Futures	0.9	2.0	183.4	388.1
Options	1.2	2.1	148.3	271.8
Short-term interest rates				
Futures	1.4	6.8	1,271.1	5,475.2
Options	0.5	8.2	451.2	2,469.8
Stock-market indices				
Futures	0.5	1.8	69.1	172.2
Options	2.4	7.4	93.7	326.9
Total	7.9	31.8	2,290.4	9,185.3

Source: BIS (1996).

dented, and the international dimension has become important even for households, either directly or (as is more likely to be the case) through specialized financial intermediaries. These institutions tend to invest in securities and are very sensitive to differences in domestic-market practices. They are, for example, behind the push for common standards in accounting, corporate governance, and trading practices that is slowly changing the character of financial markets in Europe. This also makes it increasingly difficult for many professional operators in the market to draw the line between foreign and domestic transactions.

A second observation is that these developments have not been driven primarily by tax motivations. To be sure, there are many examples of tax-driven business: The explosive growth in the market for medium-term notes is due in part to the possibility of structuring returns so as to minimize taxes; derivatives are often employed to avoid taxes, and their uncertain tax status also encourages their use; pension funds and insurance companies have grown because of their tax-privileged status. Nevertheless, tax considerations have been of secondary importance relative to the broader deregulatory trends and have played an

Table 9.6. *Over-the-counter derivatives market at end of March 1995*[a]

Market risk category and instrument type	Notional amount outstanding		Gross market value		Gross market value (as percentage of notional amount outstanding)
	Amount	Percentage share[b]	Amount	Percentage share[b]	
Foreign exchange[c]	13,153	100	1,021	100	8
Forwards and forex swaps[d]	8,742	72	602	70	7
Currency swaps[e]	1,974	11	345	22	17
Options[f]	2,375	16	69	7	3
Single-currency interest rates[c]	26,645	100	646	100	2
Forward rate agreements	4,597	17	18	3	0
Swaps	18,283	69	560	87	3
Options	3,548	13	60	9	2
Equity and stock indices	599	100	50	100	8
Forwards and swaps	52	9	7	14	13
Options	547	91	43	86	8
Commodities	317	100	28	100	9
Forwards and swaps	208	66	21	78	10
Options	109	34	6	22	6

[a] Adjusted for local and cross-border double counting.

[b] To put the shares accounted for by different foreign-exchange instruments on a comparable basis, percentages have been calculated on data that exclude figures for currency swaps and options reported by dealers in the United Kingdom.

[c] The difference between the subcomponent and the total represents transactions classified as "other products."

[d] Data are incomplete because they do not include outstanding forwards and foreign-exchange swap positions of market participants in the United Kingdom.

[e] Notional amounts, excluding data from reported dealings in the United Kingdom, amounted to $1,324 billion.

[f] Notional amounts, excluding data from reported dealings in the United Kingdom, amounted to $1,991 billion.

almost insignificant role in the internationalization of institutional investments.

3   Why Do Withholding Taxes Play Such a Major Role?

3.1   *The Design and Purposes of Withholding Taxes*

Withholding taxes provide a means for collecting tax revenue at the source on interest, dividends, royalties, and other investment income. It is common for withholding taxes to be levied at a fixed rate for a specific category of payment flow; however, most countries adopt various rates, depending on the type of financial instrument and investor. In some countries, withholding taxes are used as devices for anticipating final payment of the taxes on domestic income (Switzerland and the United Kingdom), or as flat (final) levies in lieu of payment of personal income taxes (Belgium, France, and Italy). In nearly all OECD countries, withholding taxes apply to income flowing abroad, although rates vary markedly across countries (reflecting the complex network of double-taxation treaties) and with the type of recipient of the income flow (e.g., individual, unrelated entity, related company).

Withholding taxes can be designed in three ways. The first and simplest is to collect the tax at the time of payment of dividends or interest. As we shall see in the next section, owing to the nonlinearities of tax schedules, this gives rise to various forms of tax-avoidance mechanisms, such as "wash sales," which consist in sale-and-repurchase transactions around payment dates. As far as interest is concerned, because the actual payment is known with certainty between coupon dates, this problem can be avoided if tax is paid on accrual rather than on realization. This implies that purchases and sales in secondary markets are based on dirty prices net of tax that has accrued to date ("net-payments" mechanism). As we shall see in the next section, this can hamper the functioning of certain types of market transactions. Finally, in recent years there has been a shift toward eliminating withholding taxes on securities and shifting the burden of withholding to the paying agents (depository institutions), which discriminate between the beneficiaries of the income flow and withheld tax only in specific cases ("gross payment"). This raises compliance costs for the financial industry, but it avoids the allocative distortions associated with net payments.

Withholding taxes serve several purposes. First, they provide an efficient administrative device for raising revenue, particularly where securities are in bearer form. Collection of withholding taxes tends to be immediate, without any action required on the part of taxpayers or the tax authority, and it occurs during the ordinary course of business for the payer, often a financial institution that is accustomed to making large numbers of payments each day. In addition to this simple machinery for payment, withholding taxes can create an incentive for compliance, because they can be claimed as an expense or deduction in computing other taxable incomes. Second, when in the form of an advance payment they can operate as a backstop for other taxes. In particular, if set at a sufficiently high level, they may motivate individuals to declare their personal income voluntarily. Third, in the international sphere they provide a simple means for source countries to levy taxes on income flowing abroad. Finally, withholding taxes on income flows to nonresidents can help to safeguard the tax bases of third countries that adopt the territorial principle but are unable to administer a residence-based tax system or cannot prevent tax-induced outflows (McLure, 1989).

The unilateral character of withholding taxes nevertheless raises several issues. One problem concerns financial intermediaries. They are assessed in the capital-importing country on gross interest outflows, whereas tax credits for foreign taxes paid are generally based on net foreign-source income after deduction of expenses (Huizinga, in press). Consequently, when withholding taxes exceed offsetting credits, the actual tax borne by foreign investors will depend on the withholding taxes. Moreover, this often can result in the total tax burden on interest coming from abroad being considerably higher than that from domestic sources, where financial institutions are generally exempt from withholding. It is not surprising that banks tend to book their international loans in countries with double-taxation treaties that specify low withholding taxes in borrowing countries. More generally, the wide varieties of rates and conditions attaching to withholding taxes tend to encourage "treaty-shopping" activity.

A similar problem arises where foreign tax credits cannot be used by investors. As already noted, large volumes of portfolio capital represent the investments of such tax-exempt institutions as pension funds, trusts, and foundations for which foreign tax credits are useless insofar as there is no tax liability in the residence country. It is also difficult, as we shall see in the next section, to apply withholding taxes to many of the new financial instruments.

In addition, there are other forms of exemptions that tend to limit the general character of withholding taxes. For example, residents of treaty-partner counties often tend to be exempt. Moreover, as we shall see in the next section, a number of the "payments" that are not defined as interest, dividends, or royalties are not subject to withholding taxes. Both of these exemptions give rise to the various forms of arbitrage that are increasingly being used by market participants (Ross, 1987).

Finally, the withholding-tax mechanism does not appear appropriate where the recipient of income is a collective investment institution, the beneficial owners of which may be resident in various countries; it is not usual for the tax in the country of source to depend on the tax treatment of the ultimate beneficiaries.

3.2   *Selected Country Experiences*

Withholding taxes on income from cross-border financial investments can have markedly different effects, depending on their characteristics, their scope of application, and the provisions of double-taxation treaties. There have been two general trends with respect to withholding taxes, since the mid-1980s. On the one hand, in countries that have traditionally employed withholding taxes as substitutes for personal income taxes rate differentials between financial instruments have been reduced. On the other hand, following the lifting of the U.S. withholding tax on interest payments to nonresidents, several other countries have de facto unilaterally abolished their withholding taxes or set up special procedures to facilitate the reclaiming of the taxes under double-taxation treaties.[7] In the late 1980s, however, the Commission of the European Community (EC) issued a proposal for a common system of withholding taxes that was later abandoned. More recently the EC has been considering a revised version of that proposal. Those proposals have been motivated by the abolition of capital controls following the completion of the Internal Market of the European Union and by the growing volume of cross-border capital flows to countries that do not levy withholding taxes. As far as dividend and royalty payments to nonresidents are concerned, there have been no significant changes in rates since the early 1980s.[8]

Examples of the responsiveness of international capital flows to withholding taxes and the structure of financial intermediation are provided by the experiences of the United States, Germany, and Italy.

---

[7] In the United Kingdom, for example, issues by U.K. companies are considered Eurobonds and hence exempt from withholding tax if (1) the beneficial owner entitled to interest is not a U.K. resident or (2) the security is deposited with a recognized clearing institution (such as Euroclear or CEDEL). The reform of the gilt-edged market presently under way has involved the virtual lifting of withholding taxes on all fixed-income securities.

[8] The dividend directive in the European Union involves intracompany flows.

United States. Before 1984, the United States levied a 30% withholding tax on interest payments to nonresidents, but a number of tax treaties reduced the tax rate considerably (now ranging from 16% to zero). In order to benefit from the lower rates envisaged by the tax treaties, investors had to provide information on their countries of residence and their tax status. Moreover, in the case of bearer bonds, such information had to be provided at each interest-payment date. In order to ensure anonymity to investors, U.S. companies set up conduit companies in The Netherlands Antilles, whose double-taxation treaty with the United States provided for a zero rate, with the sole purpose of issuing Eurobonds. As a result, in 1983 the interest payments to The Netherlands Antilles accounted for more than 33% of all interest payments by U.S. residents to the rest of the world. The fact that most interest payments to foreigners became exempt from withholding taxes had the effect of sharply raising the sales of U.S. domestic bonds to foreigners and reducing the issuance of bonds through The Netherlands Antilles.[9]

Germany. The second example is provided by the announcement of the German Ministry of Finance, in October 1987, that a 10% withholding tax on interest payments to German residents would be levied as of January 1, 1989. The levy was subsequently abolished (April 1989). Between the announcement and the abolition of the withholding tax there were major changes in the composition of international capital flows involving Germany and in the structure of bond issuances in Germany. There was a sharp increase in long-term capital outflows, followed by a pronounced turnaround after abolition of the levy. Moreover, because deutsche-mark bond offerings issued by nonresidents (including the foreign subsidiaries of German companies) were exempt from the withholding tax, foreign issuers increased their share of total deutsche-mark bonds. The withholding tax also resulted in some highly rated foreign issuers being able to raise funds at interest rates below those paid by the German government (Nörbass and Raab, 1990).

More recently, the introduction of a new withholding tax on interest payments to German residents has led to an even higher volume of capital outflows. The German Ministry of Finance, in a submission to the

---

[9] Net of tax benefits, the issuance of Eurobonds was often a more costly means of financing. In addition to requiring the establishment of special-purpose vehicles and incurring the legal costs necessary to ensure that parent guarantees were in place, underwriting fees tended to be higher than in the United States. The importance of the tax benefit was reflected in the stock-price effect following the announcement of Eurobond issues (Kim and Stulz, 1988).

Finance Committee of the Bundestag, estimated that between July 1991 and November 1992, out of the purchases of foreign securities by German residents totaling DM 68.7 billion, more than 80% took the form of acquisitions of Luxembourg "investment funds." Most of those funds flowed back into Germany through the acquisition of deutsche-mark-denominated bonds.

Italy.   Different aspects of the Italian experience are also noteworthy.[10] First, securities are presently negotiated on a "net-payments" basis. The final withholding tax of 12.5% levied on government bonds can be fully or partly recovered under most double-taxation agreements. Prior to April 1991, however, such refunds were subject to very long delays owing to administrative difficulties, and that led some governments to invite their investors to abstain from investing in Italian bonds. Even following an acceleration in repayments, interest-rate swap rates (i.e., the Euro-market interest-rate equivalent of government bonds) tended to lie in a band between the gross and net tax returns on government bonds. That anomalous situation, whereby private-sector borrowers paid less than the Italian government, has commonly been attributed to the delays in reclaiming tax. Indeed, following the announcement that refunds would be accelerated, the swap rate rose temporarily to the top of the band; more recently, the announcement, on May 18, 1993, of a shortening of the delay in reimbursing withholding tax to only two weeks was followed by a sharp rise in the price of government bonds. As of January 1, 1997, securities were to be negotiated on a "gross basis," and tax was to be withheld only for interest payments to countries that did not have tax treaties with Italy or had not agreed to exchanges of information with the Italian authorities (e.g., Switzerland).

Second, prior to September 1992, the Italian government had treated bonds issued by certain international organizations as exempt from with-holding tax. As a result, Italian investors became major purchasers of such bonds and are said to have determined the choices or borrowing instruments used by some of those institutions. Finally, interest payments on loans by foreign-owned banks abroad are subject to withholding tax, whereas the foreign branches of Italian banks are exempt. As a result, in the late 1980s it was common for Italian banks to act as conduits for loans by foreign banks.[11]

---

[10] The withholding tax in Italy has also tended to distort the operation of domestic financial markets. Prior to the lifting of withholding taxes on interbank transactions in February 1992, the interest rates on interbank transactions were widely out of line with other market rates.

[11] "Conduit operations" have recently been subjected to a penal rate of withholding tax.

3.3   *Implications*

Those experiences concerning withholding taxes suggest various undesirable effects arising from the manner in which withholding taxes have
been conceived to date. First, in most instances there have been numerous possibilities for avoiding withholding taxes. Typically, certain types
of securities issues have been exempt from payment. That tends to discriminate against those issuers that cannot structure their transactions
so as to take advantage of the favorable treatment and to provide subsidies in the form of lower tax revenues ("implicit taxes") to tax-
privileged borrowers. For example, issuance of bonds through foreign
subsidiaries is in most circumstances possible only for large companies.
Second, many large investors, particularly tax-exempt institutions,
are especially sensitive to withholding taxes because they are unable
to reclaim the taxes or because recovery depends on double-taxation
treaties or at times is very costly. Furthermore, the absence of some
foreign market participants can result in partial segmentation of
markets and in higher interest rates for borrowers. Third, to the extent
that withholding taxes are impounded in higher interest rates, there are
losses of corporate tax revenues.[12] Fourth, the inefficiencies involved in
applying the withholding tax may result in an increase in the cost of funds
for governments. The unusual behavior of the swap rate in Italy is one
possible indication that this may have been occurring. In Germany,
Nörbass and Raab (1990) found that even after repeal of the withholding tax in April 1989, German interest rates appear not to have returned
to their level prior to the announcement of the levy. They interpreted
this finding as an indication of a loss of credibility for the German
government's tax policy.[13] Finally, the mechanics of applying the
withholding tax in terms of gross or net payments can be of considerable importance. As we shall see in the following section, a net-
payments withholding tax is incompatible with a number of financial
transactions.

[12] This is apparently the reason that Finland and Norway have traditionally had no withholding taxes on interest payments.

[13] The high sensitivity to taxes on capital income in Germany and other European countries can be attributed in part to the rather ambiguous and often extremely contradic-
tory attitudes that have characterized the taxation of capital. Extraordinary capital
levies, inflation taxes, currency reforms, and sudden changes in the structures of withholding taxes have not been uncommon. At the same time, during normal periods governments have been extremely lenient and often have exempted, de facto, wide portions
of capital income, especially interest from government bonds.

4 On the (Almost) Impossible Application of a Source (Gross-Basis) Tax on Passive Income: The Tax Treatment of New Financial Instruments

Financial instruments relating to passive portfolio investments have traditionally been taxed at source by means of schedular, gross-basis withholding taxes. As mentioned earlier, many economists consider widening the scope of these taxes to be necessary to stem the flow of footloose tax-free capital movements. If this is taken as an item deserving of serious consideration in the policy agenda, as it appears many economists increasingly believe, it is necessary to investigate closely what this will entail for the wide variety of financial instruments currently being utilized in financial markets, not merely what it will entail for "plain vanilla" loans/deposits, where the currencies of the borrower and lender coincide. Before turning to several examples that will illustrate specific issues involving a wide number of financial instruments, it is important to highlight some of the general features that make withholding taxes noncomparable to income taxes. These general issues, as well the specific issues discussed later, underscore the extent to which most contemporary comparisons of source-based and residence-based taxes are, in practice, wide of the mark and exceedingly misleading.

First, source-based taxes on financial transactions are founded on a disaggregated approach: Every single contract (interest, dividends, royalties, etc.) is viewed as standing on its own, regardless of any economic connection with other financial transactions.[14] Only the connections that are established in the contract are relevant for fiscal purposes. This means that, typically, withholding taxes are based on schedular systems; that is, they are not based on any comprehensive notion of income. Second, withholding taxes tend to operate asymmetrically: They apply only to positive out-payments on a contract, whereas increasing numbers of new financial instruments envisage both positive and negative cash flows. Third, because withholding taxes tend to apply to well-identified streams of payment, it is difficult to adapt them to new forms of cash flows. As a result, unless it is possible to redefine the payment stream in terms of identifiable income categories that are subject to withholding taxes, the outflows from the source country will be exempt. In addition, there may

---

[14] Tax treaties have generally complicated this situation, because they were framed before nontraditional instruments were introduced. The OECD commentary on the "model double-taxation agreement" has recently been changed to allow exclusion of certain forms of payment where there is no underlying debt from withholding taxes, unless a loan is considered to exist under a "substance-over-form" rule or "abuse-of-rights" principle.

be overlaps between instruments subject to different types of withholding taxes. In this context it is important to underscore that, with a few notable exceptions, derivative financial instruments (DFIs) are not subject to withholding taxes, because the income from DFIs is not considered income from capital, in the same sense as dividends and interest, unless the foreign beneficiary is a permanent establishment in the source country.

4.1   *Coupon Bonds and Strips*

In this section we consider two examples that illustrate the difficulty of applying withholding taxes in a consistent fashion across a wide spectrum of financial instruments. The first example consists in comparing a coupon-bearing instrument with a so-called strip. A strip consists of the decomposed coupon and the principal elements of a bond, treated as separate components. Consider a two-period bond with coupon payments of 10%, issued at par (= $100). In the absence of taxes, and assuming that the term structure is flat at issue, the present value of the two coupon payments and the principal will be approximately $9.10, $8.26, and $82.64. If the security were stripped (and in the absence of any market imperfection), each of the three components could be sold as separate securities, with values as just described. The principle of conservation of value ensures that as time elapses, the value of the coupon-bearing security and the value of the sum of the strips will always be equal.

Uniform withholding taxes distort the conservation-of-value principle. Strips cannot be taxed in the same fashion as coupon payments; income must be taxed on the difference between price at maturity and the price at issue of the particular segment of the strip.[15] In other words, the tax base is not the gross coupon payment or principal; rather, by analogy with a deposit, it is the income that is accrued between the purchasing of the component to the strip and the date when it matures. In terms of our earlier example, the incomes subject to withholding taxes for the three components, if taxation is deferred until realization, are $0.91, $1.74, and $17.36, respectively. The taxable-income streams for the components of the original bond are instead $10, $10, and zero. In present-value terms, revenues from the two streams of cash flows would be equal only if the discount factor were nil.

One way of solving this problem is to adopt a constant-yield approach to taxation of the accrued interest in each period. This consists in apply-

---

[15] This example abstracts from the problem of defining the manner in which taxes should accrue over time.

ing the yield to maturity at issuance of the unstripped bond (10% in this example) to the values of the stripped components in each time period.[16] In our example, the income on the sum of the stripped components would be simply 10 [= (9.10 + 8.26 + 82.64)(0.1)] in the first time period and 10 [= (8.26 + 82.64)(1.1)(0.1)] in the second, thereby reconstituting the value of the taxable coupon payments in the bond.[17] This method, which could be easily applied to a withholding tax, would remove the distortion arising from the application of tax only to the discounted elements defining the stream of tax payments in each period.

One important assumption that allows this result to follow without any problem is that the term structure of interest rates is flat (i.e., the reinvestment rate is constant, or, in other words, the yield to maturity is equal to the interest rate at each time horizon). If the term structure were upward-rising, but still with a 10% yield to maturity (i.e., if the interest rate on 1-year and 2-year zero-coupon bonds were 6.15% and 10.2%, respectively, with an implicit 1-year forward rate of 14.4%), applying the constant-maturity rule (i.e., of setting the tax on the basis of the accrued income obtained from capitalizing the present value of each component of the strip by the yield at issue) would introduce distortions. But taxing coupons only, without taking account of changes in the value of bonds, would also produce distortions.

To see what the correct procedure would be, it is best to begin with the strip payments. At the end of the first year, the portfolio of two coupons and cover will have earned interest at 6.15%. Hence the present value of taxes paid in the first period should be 0.579 = [10%(6.15/1.0616)]. In the second period, interest accrues at 14.4%. This means that if interest accruals are recorded correctly, the taxes in the two periods will not be identical as they would have been in the case of a flat yield curve. This occurs because the term structure of interest rates implies that the price of the bond must fall between the first period and second period. If this capital loss (from 100 to 96.15) is not allowed as an offset against earnings from coupons, the present values of tax payments on the strips and on the bond will not be equal.

Withholding taxes on interest payments, unless coupled with a capital-gains tax, will give rise to distortions. The reason for that is not difficult to understand. Withholding taxes do not apply to income inclusive of accrued capital gains and losses. Neither allowing for coupon payments

---

[16] The method actually adopted in the Untied States is somewhat more general, because it allows for coupon payments on deep-discount bonds.

[17] It should be noted that the actual cash amount of tax payments on the principal component of the stripped security tends to rise over time.

to be adjusted for discounts at issue nor computing tax payments on a synthetic interest derived from an arbitrary yield assumption based on a constant curve would be sufficient to eliminate the distortion. What this means is that for a source country to apply a uniform withholding tax on securities, it would be necessary to introduce a complex implicit accrued-capital-gains tax based on the underlying term structure. This is, in theory, feasible, although it has not been implemented.

As we have just seen, the deferral of taxes until income is realized is the crucial element behind the distortion that arises if single cash-flow elements are traded at a discount and taxed separately. This is true whether tax is levied on a withholding basis or as an income tax. The difference, then, between a withholding tax and an income tax is that the latter can cope with capital gains and losses.

4.2   *High- and Low-Yielding Currencies*

Another interesting case is that of foreign currency. Covered interest parity implies that the interest-rate differential between two currencies is approximately equal to the difference between the forward and the spot exchange rates.[18] The interest-parity relationship means that it is possible to view the hedging of a foreign-currency position as equivalent to borrowing in one currency to invest in another. If the two types of transactions are not equivalent for tax purposes, there will be an incentive to restructure operations in order to minimize the fiscal consequences. Because foreign-exchange gains or losses tend to be considered as capital gains, rather than interest, for purposes of gross-basis withholding taxes, their treatment is generally more favorable. Hence it will be in the interest of lenders to provide funds in low-yielding currencies and hedge the position in the forward market.[19]

There are three ways in which a gross-basis withholding tax could be constructed to be neutral. The first would be to apply a substance-over-form test whereby the diverse components of the transactions would be reconstituted (i.e., a swapped borrowing in foreign currency would be considered as a domestic-currency transaction). The second would be to treat spot/forward transactions (i.e., the swap rate) as interest and hence subject to the same treatment given interest flows under the withholding tax – this amounts in actual fact to the aggregation of transactions.

---

[18] It is exactly equal with continuous compounding.

[19] As noted by Levi (1977), if these transactions are significant, there may be significant deviations from interest parity or cross-hauling of finance between countries merely to exploit the tax-arbitrage possibility.

Finally, capital gains on currencies could become subject to withholding taxes. It should be noted, however, that each of these measures entails abandonment of the gross-basis criterion underlying withholding taxes, in favor of a net basis.

Interbank transactions tend to be exempt from withholding taxes because they involve a large volume of two-way flows and because crediting of gross withholding taxes against net margins tends to result in the generation of excess tax credits for the lender. To be sure, anti-tax-avoidance mechanisms are in place, so that interest payments to an offshore center or a country that does not benefit from a double-taxation treaty may well entail the levying of withholding taxes.

4.3   *Swaps and Other Streams of Payment*

Traditional financial instruments entail the concept that payments result from the underlying principal. In the simplest case interest is the return on a loan. The newer vintages of DFIs have been devised essentially for risk-management purposes. There is no exchange of principal; rather, contracts are established on the basis of a notional underlying capital amount. At inception, the value of the instrument may well be nil, as in the case of a futures contract; only movements in prices give rise to cash flows and hence to positive or negative values. In these instances the taxable amount for a gross-basis withholding tax is not very clear, because payments do not constitute a return on capital invested. At the same time, these financial instruments are derivatives, and hence are connected to underlying securities; they can be used to create synthetic positions that in actual practice will yield cash flows identical with interest or dividend payments. These problems are well appreciated by the tax authorities:

It would be difficult in practical terms, if not impossible, to apply withholding tax to a net payment flow, particularly if there was a mismatch in timing of the swap payments and at the date a payment was made by one party it was not known what subsequent payments might be made or received by that party. It might also be difficult in more sophisticated swaps to relate a swap to a particular borrowing. If a company entered a swap to hedge a mismatch between its global assets and liabilities, it would also be difficult to say whether the swap primarily modified the interest cost of the liabilities or the interest yield of the assets and it would also be difficult to determine to what extent the swap should be linked to a particular cross-border borrowing. [OECD, 1994]

To clarify this type of complication, consider the case of a simple interest-rate swap in which two counterparties agree to exchange fixed- and floating-rate payments. Assume that initially the borrower A has taken out a 5-year loan at a fixed interest rate of 10% in order to fund an asset with a 5-year payback period. If these assets turn out to vary considerably with the interest-rate cycle, the borrower may decide to connect the liabilities to a floating index in order to hedge the exposure that has been created. In this instance, A will enter into a swap to pay B a floating rate, such as a sixth-month LIBOR, against fixed-rate receipts of 10%. Every sixth month, A will pay to or receive from B the net amount (LIBOR−10%). If withholding taxes were levied on the gross interest payment, taxes would be levied on both the 10% and the LIBOR. If the two rates happened to be equal and swap payments were nil, then under a tax system based on gross payments the taxes would be positive despite no net income transfers. Indeed, the margin for an intermediary arranging the swap would be nil. If the swap were to apply to net payments (i.e., apply only to the interest, not to the swap), the borrower would be prejudiced if the LIBOR turned out to be less than 10%, but would be advantaged if the opposite occurred. Naturally, if the various transactions could be aggregated, this problem would not arise, because payments would be based on the LIBOR. Alternatively, swaps could be subject to positive and negative withholding taxes.

4.4   *Options*

Another form of recombination of income streams is offered by options (Cox and Rubinstein, 1985). The purchaser of an option has the right, but not the obligation, to buy (a "call" option) or sell (a "put" option) a specific quantity of an underlying financial instrument at a specific price (the "strike price" − K) on a specified future date. Conversely, the seller of the option (the "writer") acquires the obligation to sell or to buy in the case of a call or a put, respectively.[20] Options can be written on almost any type of financial instrument. The counterparty, who has the obligation to perform under the contract if requested to do so by the holder, is said to "write" the option. The price of the option is called a "premium." At maturity, the payoff and hence the value of the call option C for an underlying financial instrument with a price S will be given by

$$C = \max(S - K, 0)$$

Similarly, the value of the put option, P, at expiration will be equal to

---

[20] It is interesting to note that the acts of purchasing a call and simultaneously selling a put are equivalent to acquiring both the right to and the obligation of the underlying asset, i.e., holding the assets or having the full characteristics associated with property. The acts of buying a put and selling a call are exactly the same as forgoing property.

Table 9.7. *Put–call parity relationships*

	Present date	Expiration date $S* \leq K$	$S* \geq K$
Write call	C	—	$K - S*$
Buy put	$-P$	$K - S*$	—
Buy underlying	$-S$	$S*$	$S*$
Borrow	$K(1 + r)^{-T}$	$-K$	$-K$
Total		—	—

$$P = \max(K - S, 0)$$

Consider the following simultaneous positions in a call option and put option on the same underlying security with the same strike price, which can be exercised only at expiration (European option) at time T: Write one call (receive the premium), purchase one put (pay the premium), buy one unit of the underlying, and borrow $K(1 + r)^{-T}$ by selling zero-coupon bonds with a maturity of T at an interest rate r. Table 9.7 illustrates the payoffs to this strategy, which gives an amount $C - P - S + K(1 + r)^T$ at time zero. If the share price at expiration, $S*$, is less than K, the put option will be worth $K - S*$, and the call option will expire worthless. By contrast, if $S* \geq K$, the call option will be worth $S* - K$, and the put option will expire worthless. In both cases the stock will be owned, and the loan principal K will be paid back. The overall value of this portfolio will be zero. The reverse position (selling a put, buying a call, selling the underlying, and investing at the riskless zero-coupon rate with a maturity of T) will have the same value. Consequently the initial investment must be nil on both counts:

$$C - P + S - K(1 + r)^T = 0$$

The implications of this parity relationship are very wide-ranging. First, through the put–call parity it is possible to decompose transactions into an even greater number of constituent parts and recompose them into other financial instruments. Unless the tax system is designed to harmonize the various components, it will be difficult to obtain neutrality. Second, options can be used very effectively to restructure ownership rights and hence reduce taxes, as is the case with other types of derivatives.

As we saw in Sections 4.3 and 4.4, the existence of no-arbitrage relationships linking financial instruments is essential to understanding the difficulties that arise with taxes that apply to only one leg of a financial transaction.

5   Applying the Residence Principle

In the preceding sections we examined the practical problems involved in operating a source-based, schedular, gross-basis withholding-tax system. In particular, we highlighted the near impossibility of applying a source-based gross withholding tax to many DFIs (as has been recognized by legislation in most countries) (Plambeck et al., 1996) and the possibility that taxpayers may seek to disguise otherwise-taxable transactions as DFIs for the purpose of avoiding tax at source.[21]

We now turn to the difficulties that arise in implementing a residence-based system. Whereas some of the issues arising from the new financial instruments are analogous to those for source-based taxes, we show that they can be solved, at least conceptually. Even in the case of DFIs, under certain circumstances it is possible for tax authorities in each country to define a residence-based tax on all income.

On the other hand, the approach based on residence has three major drawbacks that have drawn increasing criticism (Tanzi, 1995): (1) Taxes tend to be deferred until realized.[22] (2) The shifting of residence by individuals or by recipients of income other than natural persons (i.e., funds) cannot be easily accommodated. (3) The tax administration of the country of residence is not always capable of acquiring information on income from foreign sources. We shall concentrate attention here on the third criticism.

5.1   *Defining Income*

Innovative financial instruments raise a number of problems for defining income, in addition to the traditional issues of character and timing. In particular, as noted earlier, DFIs are difficult to classify into the well-established categories common to most tax systems and recognized by double-taxation treaties. Three approaches have been taken to define the

---

[21] The tax treatment of branches raises very specific issues with respect to source rules and to the dual nature of branches – as separate taxable entities and as part of a larger (single) taxable entity. The topic is especially important for financial institutions that have highly integrated activities in which offsetting positions may be booked in different centers.

[22] Increasing attention has been paid to limiting the benefits of the deferral provision for passive income. For example, under subpart F legislation in the United States, passive investment income accumulated abroad is assumed to have been fully repatriated.

tax base in these circumstances: independent instrument, bifurcation, and general (Table 9.8).

The independent-instrument approach is the traditional position away from which most countries are trying to move. In accordance with most tax systems that share elements of source (separate schedules) and comprehensive income, that approach maintains the artificial differences in the character of income flows that lie at the origin of the distortions mentioned in the preceding section. Each transaction is defined and treated separately before aggregating the overall liability. This approach largely overlooks the similarities between cash flows, forces taxpayers to define the purpose for which each transaction has been entered, and largely ignores overriding financial strategies or methods for managing risk exposures. The distinctions among the various types of categories also entail increasingly complex legislation meant, on the one hand, to

Table 9.8. *Problems associated with the definition of income under various approaches*

Independent instrument	General	Bifurcation
A. Difficult assignment to specific categories: 1. Debt/equity 2. Capital/income 3. Asset/liability 4. Gains/losses 5. Interest/foreign exchange 6. Ordinary/ investment 7. Active/passive 8. Two-way (net) payments B. Difficult assignment of source C. Complex anti-avoidance rulings; difficult to apply "substance over form" D. Requires classification of new financial instruments each time they appear	A. In the absence of accruals, taxation "baskets" for anti-avoidance purposes B. Source-based gross-basis withholding taxes inapplicable C. Requires full consolidation of accounts across jurisdictions D. Application limited to institutions because of need to mark to market	A. There is no unique way of subdividing the components of instruments B. Decomposition difficult, especially for individual taxpayers C. Arbitrary in many circumstances (comparability problems) D. Valuation of single segments may not account for co-movements of prices

pigeonhole each new instrument into a specific category and, on the other, to establish anti-tax-avoidance provisions.

Where rights and obligations are taxed differently according to whether they are combined or issued separately, it is arguable that taxes are not neutral. One approach considered by tax authorities in an attempt to circumvent the problems raised by instruments that have different characteristics is to "bifurcate" or "unbundle" the component parts of individual transactions and subject each part separately to appropriate tax rules. A typical example that is often cited is a convertible bond that carries the right of conversion into shares at a specified price. Economically, the instrument consists of a discount bond and an equity option, each of which can be taxed separately.

Bifurcation has the attractive feature that it permits the individual-transaction approach (if it is considered still viable) to be applied in a wide range of circumstances once the various categories of each transaction have been identified. In practice, however, it runs into a number of problems of implementation. First, there are always several different ways of subdividing a transaction into its component parts, owing to the multiplicity of equilibrium relationships that exist between various financial instruments. Second, valuation of the segments may not always be possible if the prices for the individual components or comparable instruments are not available. Finally, there may be synergism between the individual components of unbundled financial instruments, so that the sum of the parts is more difficult to price or is greater than the price of the whole.

The final approach that has been used is that of aggregating together the various individual transactions. One general method that has been adopted in several countries is hedge accounting, where offsets of various kinds are allowed between different positions.[23] A simple example of such a hedge is that consisting of a long position in a portfolio of shares against which a futures contract has been sold: The decline in the value of the portfolio will be offset by the increase in the value of the position in futures. Where tax systems have moved toward hedge accounting, this trend has tended to be selective; the possibility of adopting these accounting practices has been limited to only certain parts of the portfolio. That has given rise to the twofold problem that a number of transactions are not considered legitimate hedges, and at the same time differences between realization and accrual can be used to minimize taxes. Moreover, limiting tax recognition of hedges to only parts of a portfolio may have the effect of reducing the micro-risks and increasing the macro-risks.

---

[23] Broadly speaking, "hedging" is any action taken to reduce or eliminate risk.

Table 9.9. *Problems associated with various approaches to the definition of timing of income*

Realization	Marking to market	Accruals
A. Deferral B. Timing options	A. Illiquidity and false price B. Cash flow for unrealized gains C. High compliance costs for positions nonprofessionals	A. Correct only on ex-ante basis B. Limited number of instruments C. Incorrectly hedged

A more comprehensive general approach is that of "marking to market," or valuing portfolios every year on an accruals basis. The distinctions and classifications that we have discussed earlier become meaningless in these circumstances: Each transaction is treated as having been disposed at market value at year's end and repurchased at that value at the opening of the subsequent accounting period. Conceptually, marking to market is the closest approximation to a measure of income over a particular period, and it is increasingly being adopted by those financial-market participants whose portfolios are frequently turned over.

However, marking to market suffers from three types of problems: (1) Not all market participants (especially households) are in a position to mark their portfolios to market. (2) Nontraded assets (or instruments that are traded infrequently) are not easy to mark to market if the prices of comparable assets are not available. (3) Unrealized gains may pose cash-flow problems. Some of these problems can be partially solved. The marking to market of positions held by households should not be difficult if intermediaries can produce accounts on this basis. Similarly, if tax rates are proportional, accrued gains (losses) can be carried forward, held in tax-suspension accounts that are charged a market rate of interest, and liquidated (including interest accruals) either when actual realizations take place or at discrete time intervals. Similarly, taxes on accrued income of illiquid instruments may be recognized at a particular period and carried forward at a market rate of interest until the position is sold. Various options could be used for the timing of tax payments that would guarantee neutrality (Table 9.9).

5.2   *Enforcing the Residence Principle*

Arriving at a definition of income, particularly with respect to sophisticated financial transactions, is basically a problem for institutional investors and corporate entities. In the case of individual investors, most of the complications arising from the new financial instruments will remain of secondary importance for the tax authorities, compared with the problems of identifying income and enforcing payment of taxes.[24]

Although it has been argued that the pressure for lowering withholding taxes has been coming from institutional investors, this does not mean that the pool of assets invested abroad and escaping taxation is insignificant. In Switzerland alone, assets under management have been estimated to amount to around \$2,000 billion, of which a very substantial share is accounted for by foreigners.

One way to facilitate collection of residence-based taxes is through more efficient exchange of information, which will involve several factors: (1) identification, (2) fulfillment of the obligation of third-party reporting, (3) cross-border exchanges of information, and (4) matching. *Identification* of the recipients of the flows is important for the source country because it allows treaty benefits to be extended to the recipients. It depends crucially, however, on the quality of information received by the payer in the source country. For example, if two countries agree to exchange information, that may not extend to flows of payments to third countries. Hence, if a tax evader decided to channel investments through a third country with which his country of residence did not have a double-taxation treaty, it would be possible to avoid taxes in his country of residence. Another problem with respect to identification of the beneficiary arises when the "source" and payer are not in the same jurisdiction, as is often the case with paying agents for securities.

At present, the *obligation* to report tax information varies markedly across countries: It will generally apply to banks and other paying agents, but these entities do not necessarily report tax-related information automatically to their own authorities. These differences reflect different approaches across countries to the taxation of capital income, variations in banks' secrecy laws, and the varying abilities of tax authorities to process the information they receive. In addition, some countries appear reticent to impose excessive compliance burdens on financial intermediaries, though technological improvements appear to be reducing that worry to some extent.

Routine *exchanges of information* across borders are envisaged by a

---

[24] To be sure, complex tax shelters that make use of DFIs can be devised by individuals to escape or defer tax. Independent of that issue, which a combination of marking to market and anti-avoidance provisions should be able to curb, enforcement is much more difficult in the case of individuals, because they do not have appropriate accounts.

number of international agreements,[25] but in practice these have been limited by many laws and rules operative in countries that are being asked to supply the information. Such limitations include, as already mentioned, the fact that the source-country tax authorities often do not have the information being requested. In addition, efficient exchange of information is hampered by technical difficulties (reliability of data, administrative costs, etc.). It is also not clear to what extent controls should be implemented and how automatic they should be: Does a residence country single out taxpayers suspected of evading taxes, or does it automatically receive data on all its residents? It has also been argued that many existing exchange-of-information agreements do not protect the confidentiality of information; abuse of tax information is not uncommon in many countries. Finally, as noted by Tanzi (1995), it should be recalled that even in the United States, tax audits cover less than 1% of returns each year.

Finally, it is necessary to establish mechanisms for automatic and efficient matching of taxpayers in the source and residence countries. Here, too, a number of technical problems arise, particularly with respect to the use of taxpayer identification numbers across countries.

Another complementary approach to enforcement would be to couple a withholding-tax regime with exchange of information as an incentive for compliance. That would achieve higher voluntary compliance if the withholding tax were significantly higher than that available under a double-taxation treaty, and in other cases it would guarantee that some revenue would be raised. Such a two-pronged approach appears to have considerable following in official circles. It is, however, subject to two types of criticism. The first is that such a measure would require quite high withholding taxes among tax-treaty countries (at least as high as the final taxes) in order to avoid round-tripping through third countries (Gordon, 1995). The second is that it would not prevent capital from flowing abroad to nontreaty countries.[26]

Exchanges of information have slowly but surely been improving as new technological developments, increasing international cooperation, the lifting of bank secrecy in some areas (e.g., money laundering), and

---

[25] The EC Directive on Mutual Assistance between the Competent Authorities of Member States in the Field of Direct Taxation (1977); the Council of Europe/OECD Multilateral Convention on Mutual Administrative Assistance in Tax Matters; the Nordic Convention on Mutual Assistance in Tax Matters; many bilateral "executive agreements" specific to exchange of information concluded by the United States.

[26] This would result in further differentiation in the structure of interest rates in the form of implicit taxes. The problem would then become one of capturing the benefits accruing to the issuers of securities in the offshore center.

"reputation" considerations have tended to decrease the grip of confidentiality. However, information sharing will remain a very imperfect aid for ensuring enforcement so long as it is not universal. Even the linking of withholding taxes to exchanges of information will not succeed in eliminating tax evasion fully, although if large countries were to take part in such an agreement it would have a much greater chance of success.

6   Conclusions

This study has focused on several interrelated developments: the growth of international transactions involving financial intermediaries that enjoy special tax status; the reasons for the contraction of source-based withholding taxes; the expansion of business in DFIs, which render traditional tax categories irrelevant and require a shift in the focus on the definition of income; the enforcement of residence-based taxes.

The first important conclusion of this study is that the pressure for lowering taxes on financial investments is coming from institutional investors who are unwilling to bear source taxes because they have no way of achieving recovery, particularly if the potential underlying tax credits cannot be transferred to the ultimate beneficiaries of the investments. Moreover, these same institutions often benefit from special domestic tax regimes (exemption from taxes or deferral until benefits are paid out), while at the same time they are absorbing a growing share of savings.

The pressure on aggregate savings in industrial countries and the public-pension crisis, for which privately funded systems are widely viewed as a solution, probably will – if anything – accentuate that trend. The growth of these institutions has wider implications that, although not discussed in this study, deserve some mention. Ultimately, taxation of capital income for most households will largely be concentrated during retirement, when paid-out benefits will be supplied by pension funds. In other words, the tax system will operate in practice as if it were based on consumption. Their growth also means that capital-income taxation for those parts of savings that are not channeled through institutional investors will be concentrated even more than at present on the upper-income brackets.

The second conclusion is that traditional schedular gross-basis withholding taxes are incompatible with the operation of modern financial markets. The changes in financial markets that have taken place in recent years should give us pause to consider how our tax systems actually operate and the types of incentives to which they give rise. Simplistic approaches to international capital mobility, such as those calling for a uniform gross-basis withholding tax at source, are doomed to failure under the inevitably complex and burdensome procedures that will need to be implemented in order to guarantee minimally correct treatment of passive-income flows. As correctly noted by Plambeck et al. (1996), "a paradox of DFI (and perhaps taxation in general) is that the more complex a system becomes in order to curb avoidance, the more the possibilities for avoidance appear."

It is not surprising in this context to observe a general opposition to proposals such as those of the commission for a uniform minimum withholding tax. In the face of major exemptions on domestic capital income, far from helping to complete the Internal Market, a uniform withholding tax would result in further discriminations between countries and reverse tax competition if not levied appropriately. Harmonization would occur for the benefit of "domestic" investments, but with vast misallocations of capital.

Such proposals need to be articulated much more carefully, distinguishing between the types of investors to which they would be addressed (i.e., individuals, but not corporations and institutions) and the manner in which they would be levied (from paying agents, not from securities), all the while considering that sufficient offsets must be available in the country of residence of the investor to account for the issues raised by DFIs.

The final conclusion is that movement toward a full residence principle is not currently feasible in many countries, because enforcement is hampered by legal, political, and technical difficulties regarding exchanges of information. This is, nevertheless, the direction in which many countries are slowly moving, making it increasingly difficult for income flows from blacklisted countries to be allowed access to domestic markets.

APPENDIX: TAXATION OF OPTIONS: ARBITRAGE CONDITIONS

In order to illustrate the tax treatment of options, it is useful to compare two identical arbitrage portfolios (1) in the spot-forward market and (2) in the options market (put–call parity). For this purpose, consider the case in which the strike price is given by the forward price of an underlying asset (commodity, stock-price index, etc.). By interest arbitrage,

$$F = S_0(1 + r)^T$$

In the absence of tax, this condition implies that a forward sale of a spot position financed by borrowing should yield zero profit; hence taxes should also be nil. At expiration, the taxes on the forward sale of a spot purchase financed by borrowing can be divided into the following:

A1, tax on capital gains/losses on underlying (t_K^S): $S_1 - S_0$
A2, tax on capital gains/losses on forward contract (t_K^F): $F - S_1$
A3, tax deduction for interest-rate payment (t_R):
$-S_0[(1 + r)^T - 1]$

If these components can be offset against one another and the tax rates are identical, there will be no taxes. It should be noted that earnings on the forward contract, $F - S_0$, are known with certainty ex ante. It is therefore possible to apply constant-yield formulas to the income accruals over time instead of applying a capital-gains-tax regime.

It is easy to show that in the case of an option where the strike price is equal to the forward price, the put–call parity becomes $c = p$.

From Table 9.7, and substituting F for K, it is interesting to decompose the various components that may be taxed separately at expiration of the contract and compare these elements to the taxes on the forward contract shown earlier. In general, with the option contract there will be four sources of gain or loss (in the case $S_1 < F$):

B1, tax on capital gains/losses on underlying (t_K^S): $S_1 - S_0$
B2, tax on the short (call) option position (t_K^0): 0
B3, tax on the long (put) option position (t_K^0): $F - S_1$
B4, tax deduction for interest-rate payment (t_R):

$$-\left(F - \frac{F}{(1+r)^T}\right) = -S_0\left[(1+r)^T - 1\right]$$

In this particular instance, in order to replicate the forward contract with calls and puts, only the differentials between tax liability (A2) and tax liabilities (B2) and (B3) matter. An important distinction between (1) the purchase of a call and the sale of a put and (2) the forward contract is that the values of the individual legs of the option contracts are unknown ex ante: Neither the amount nor the direction of a price change is known, although the value of the portfolio is certain. Consequently it is impossible to apply ex-ante rules such as the constant-yield formula to these sources of income.

The examples of covered interest arbitrage and option pricing illustrate the three general conditions that must be satisfied in order for taxes to leave economic decisions unaffected:

1. Capital gains, interest, and dividends are all taxed at the same constant rate.

2. Taxes are collected on an accruals basis.
3. Full loss offsets are allowed at the same rate of tax (capital losses, interest on borrowing, and short sales are treated in the same fashion).

REFERENCES

BIS (1995). *Annual Report*. Basel: Bank for International Settlements.
BIS (1996). *International Banking and Financial Market Development* (various issues). Basel: Bank for International Settlements.
Cooper, I., and Kaplanis, E. (1986). Costs to cross-border investment and international equity market equilibrium. In: *Recent Developments in Corporate Finance*, ed. J. Edwards, J. Franks, C. Mayer, and M. Bray, pp. 209–40. Cambridge University Press.
Cox, J., and Rubinstein, M. (1985). *Options Markets*. Englewood Cliffs, NJ: Prentice-Hall.
Gordon, R. (1992). Can capital income taxes survive in open economies? *Journal of Finance* 47:1159–80.
Gordon, R. (1995). Tax evasion on international financial investments: What can be done? Unpublished manuscript.
Huizinga, H. (1994). International interest withholding taxation: Prospects for a common European policy. *International Tax and Public Finance* 1:277–91.
Huizinga, H. (in press). The incidence of interest withholding taxes: evidence from the LDC loan market. *Journal of Public Economics*.
Hurley, M. P., Meers, S., Bornstein, B. J., and Strumingher, N. R. (1995). *The Coming Evolution of the Investment Management Industry: Opportunities and Strategies*. New York: Goldman Sachs.
Kim, Y. C., and Stulz, R. M. (1988). The Eurobond market and corporate financial policy: a test of the clientele hypothesis. *Journal of Financial Economics* 22:189–205.
Levi, M. (1977). Taxation and "abnormal" capital flows. *Journal of Political Economy* 85:635–46.
McLure, C. E. (1989). US tax laws and capital flight from Latin America. NBER working paper 2687. Washington, DC: National Bureau of Economic Research.
Mintz, J. (1992). Is there a future for capital income taxation? Economics working paper 108. Paris: Organization for Economic Cooperation and Development.
Nörbass, K. H., and Raab, M. (1990). Tax arbitrage and the German withholding tax experiment. Discussion paper 419, Department of Economics, University of Mannheim.
OECD (1994). *Taxation of New Financial Instruments*. Paris: Organization for Economic Cooperation and Development.
Plambeck, C. T., Rosenbloom, H. D., and Ring, D. M. (1996). Tax aspects of derivative financial instruments: general report. *Cahiers de Droit Fiscal International* 81:653–90.
Ross, S. (1987). Arbitrage and martingales with taxation. *Journal of Political Economy* 95:371–93.

Scholes, M., and Wolfson, M. (1992). *Taxes and Business Strategy*. Englewood Cliffs, NJ: Prentice-Hall.

Solnik, B. (1988). *International Investments*. Reading, MA: Addison-Wesley.

Tanzi, V. (1995). *Taxation in an Integrating World*. Washington, DC: Brookings Institution.

CHAPTER 10

Can International Commodity-Tax Harmonization Be Pareto-Improving When Governments Supply Public Goods?

Ben Lockwood

1   Introduction

Coordination of commodity taxes among the member countries of the European Union (EU) has been a policy issue since the mid-1980s. In 1987 the European Commission proposed that rates for value-added taxes (VATs) and excise taxes be harmonized to lie within certain bands.[1] Those proposals were eventually implemented in modified form in 1993 as directives on minimum rates for VATs and excise taxes, but it is believed that harmonization remains a long-term policy objective of the commission (Bovenberg and Horne, 1992). The harmonization proposals were aimed primarily at restricting the amount of cross-border shopping in the post-1992 "single market," which the commission believed would reach unacceptable levels if tax-induced price differentials proved to be greater than 5% (Smith, 1992). However (especially as the extent of tax-induced cross-border shopping in the EU seems, in practice, to be rather small) (Fitzgerald, Johnston, and Williams, 1994), it is worth asking under what conditions harmonization can also yield benefits in a setting

This study was completed while I was visiting the Economic Policy Research Unit (EPRU) at Copenhagen Business School. I would like to thank the members of the EPRU, especially Pascalis Raimondos, Søren Bo Nielsen, and Peter Birch Sørensen, for their hospitality and their helpful comments on an earlier version of the manuscript. Comments from Mick Keen, Sajal Lahiri, Anca Porojan, and seminar participants at the EPRU, the University of Essex, and the University of Warwick, as well as three referees, are also gratefully acknowledged. Any remaining mistakes are my own.
[1] For example, the initial 1987 proposals included a VAT standard-rate band of 14–20% and a reduced band of 4–9% to be applied to "basic" goods and services, such as food. The minimum standard and reduced rates now in force are 15% and 5%, respectively. For more details, see Smith (1992).

of commodity taxation that is fully destination-based[2] (i.e., without tax-induced cross-border shopping).

In two influential papers, Keen (1987, 1989) addressed this question. Assuming two countries in a customs union, and assuming that the countries had no tax-revenue requirements, he derived conditions under which a certain class of "harmonizing" commodity-tax reforms could either make both countries better off (an actual Pareto improvement) or at least allow the gainer to compensate the loser (a potential Pareto improvement). A harmonizing reform, in Keen's sense, moves both tax vectors in the direction of a common tax vector; this common tax vector is constructed so as to leave world producer prices unchanged and to be a weighted average of the initial tax vectors for the two countries. Keen showed that in that setting the conditions required for potential Pareto improvements were relatively weak; all that was required was that the initial tax vector be suboptimal (i.e., nonzero) and that there be a condition[3] ruling out the transfer paradox (Keen, 1987). Sufficient conditions for actual Pareto-improvements are stronger.[4]

It was recognized by Keen himself that the major limitation of his analysis was that the countries in his model faced zero-tax-revenue requirements, or, alternatively, there was no public expenditure in his model (Keen, 1993b, p. 24). The purpose of this study is to investigate how (if at all) those findings about the desirability of commodity-tax harmonization extend to the more realistic setting in which governments supply public goods and thus have revenue requirements.[5] Our point of departure is the observation that a straightforward attempt to extend Keen's findings to this case is likely to fail.[6] The reason is simple: With a

---

[2] For analysis of the welfare effects of hamonization in models with origin-based taxation, see Kanbur and Keen (1993) and Lopez-Garcia (1996).

[3] The condition is that an increase in the home country's endowment of the numeraire must make it better off.

[4] In particular, sufficient conditions are that there be no income effects in the demand for all taxed goods and that one of the following set of conditions hold: (1) There are two goods, and each country initially taxes its importables. (2) There are two goods, and initial taxes are Nash-equilibrium taxes. (3) There are n goods, the initial taxes are Nash-equilibrium taxes, and either (a) there are no cross-price effects between taxed goods in consumption or production or (b) the representative countries have identical Slutsky matrices at the initial taxes.

[5] For simplicity, we assume that the revenue is used only to provide a public good, but all of our arguments can be generalized to the case in which the government provides a private good or service (as long as the level of supply does not affect demands for traded goods).

[6] Lahiri and Raimondos (1995) also considered harmonizing tax reforms with public goods, but in a model similar to that of Keen (i.e., with m fixed factors, and general production technologies). The cost of working with such a general model was that Lahiri

revenue requirement, the optimal tax structure for each country, taking world producer prices as given, will be determined by the preferences of its residents for public and private goods (ignoring distributional issues). If the preferences in the two countries of the customs union are very different, their optimal tax structures will be different, and harmonization will be undesirable for most initial tax vectors.

In this study we shall develop this argument using a two-country model with an arbitrary number of goods, a single factor of production (labor) in elastic supply, and constant returns to scale in production. We focus on the case in which the initial taxes are Nash-equilibrium taxes. In this setting there are externalities, or spillover effects, associated with endogenous terms of trade (the terms of trade being simply the ratio of wages in the two countries) that are not internalized at the Nash equilibrium. For example, with two goods, each country will tax its imported good more heavily than it would if it were to take the terms of trade as fixed,[7] in order to improve its own terms of trade – the *tariff effect*. So the general principle for evaluating tax reforms is as follows: *Tax reforms that reinforce (offset) the effects of these terms-of-trade externalities will tend to decrease (increase) welfare in both countries.* All of our results follow from this general principle.

The first result will be a simple and general characterization of Pareto-improving tax reforms (Proposition 1, as stated later). We shall show that under weak conditions a tax reform will be Pareto-improving if and only if the reform will increase the value of each country's (compensated) demand for imports. Such reforms will offset the terms-of-trade externality by raising the demand for imports in both countries. It will follow from this general result that Pareto-improving harmonizing reforms may not be possible. For example, in the two-good case, a harmonizing tax reform will always make both countries worse off if the importer of either good taxes it less than the exporter of the good and the two goods are substitutes [Proposition 2(*i*)]. The reason is that in this case, harmonization implies that importers of both goods must raise the tax on the

and Raimondos were obliged to focus almost exclusively on three special cases to get results: fixed producer prices; uniform commodity taxation within countries; only one non-numeraire good. However, all of those assumptions are strong, as the first rules out tax externalities, and the last two do not allow for analysis of the crucial role that the pattern of initial taxes across goods and countries plays in determining the existence of Pareto-improving reforms.

[7] In this study, we call the taxes that are optimal for a country taking the terms of trade as fixed *Ramsey taxes* (relative to those terms of trade). So this sentence could be rephrased thusly: At Nash equilibrium, each country will tax its imported good at a greater rate than the Ramsey tax (at those terms of trade) in order to improve its own terms of trade.

relevant good, thus decreasing rather than increasing the value of their imports.

Next we shall present a two-good example that identifies conditions under which the country importing each good will tax it less heavily than the exporter at the Nash equilibrium – that is, if the revenue requirement is large enough and the demand for the imported good is sufficiently price-elastic in relation to the exported good in both countries (Proposition 3). The intuition behind this example is that without a revenue requirement, the usual optimal-tariff argument implies that the imported good will be taxed at a positive rate and that the exported good will be untaxed. If the imported good is sufficiently price-elastic relative to the exported good, however, then, as the revenue requirement rises, it will eventually be taxed less than the exported good. Propositions 2(*i*) and 3, taken together, establish that Keen's result – that a potentially Pareto-improving reform can always be found – fails to generalize to the case of a positive revenue requirement (Keen, 1987).

The question then arises as to what positive results regarding harmonization are possible. We shall establish conditions on the initial taxes and on the responses of import demands to prices that will guarantee that Pareto-improving harmonizing reforms can exist in both the two-good and *n*-good cases [Propositions 2(*ii*), 2(*iii*), and 4]. These results will imply that we are unlikely to find highly general conditions under which Pareto-improving harmonizing reforms are possible. As remarked earlier, this is ultimately due to preference diversity across countries; different countries may prefer different levels and structures of commodity taxation. This study, therefore, will conclude by briefly suggesting an alternative notion of tax harmonization – difference harmonization – that is intended to control for such diversity.

A second contribution[8] of this study is that the analysis will be done using a model somewhat different from that of Keen's; it will incorporate variable rather than fixed factor supply and constant rather than decreasing returns to scale. There are two reasons for this. First, one of the objectives of this study is to relate the analysis closely to the optimal-commodity-tax literature, and it is usual in that literature to

---

[8] This study can also be interpreted as contributing to the literature on tax design in a large, open economy. Boadway, Maital, and Prachowny (1973) studied optimal use of trade and commodity taxes to raise revenue for a single country that may face endogenous terms of trade; see also Yang and Tsai (1992) and Fehan (1988). Diewert, Turunen, and Woodland (1989) and Abe (1992) studied tax and tariff reforms in an open economy with a revenue requirement. However, unlike this study, that literature was concerned only with a policy leading to welfare improvement in a single open economy, not with Pareto improvements in a customs union or a free-trade area as a whole.

work with variable factor supply and constant returns to scale (e.g., Atkinson and Stiglitz, 1980; Auerbach, 1985). Second, if there were fixed factors, revenue could be raised in a nondistortionary way by taxing those factors first, which would complicate the analysis.

The remainder of this chapter is arranged as follows: Section 2 describes the model. Section 3 establishes some useful comparative-statics results. In Section 4, Nash equilibrium in taxes is defined and characterized. Sections 5 and 6 investigate Pareto-improving and harmonizing reforms, respectively. Section 7 concludes the study.

2   The Model

There are two countries, a and b, that produce, trade, and consume n goods $j = 1, 2, \ldots, n$. In each country there is only one factor of production, labor, which is internationally immobile. Taxation is on a destination basis, so there is a world producer price for good j, denoted p_j, $j = 1, \ldots, n$. The consumer price for good j in country i is $q_j^i = p_j(1 + t_j^i)$, where t_j^i is the corresponding ad-valorem rate of taxation.[9] The wage rate in country i is w^i, $i = a, b$.

For simplicity, we assume complete specialization at all producer prices. In particular, we assume that country a can produce only goods $j = 1, \ldots, m$, and country b only goods $m + 1, \ldots, n$. Moreover, one unit of labor will produce one unit of either good in the relevant country. These assumptions are strong, but they allow us to model terms-of-trade effects in a very simple way. Finally, all firms are price-takers. Under these assumptions, producer prices are determined by the wages in each country:

$$p_j = w^a \qquad (j = 1, \ldots, m) \tag{10.1a}$$

$$p_j = w^b \qquad (j = m + 1, \ldots, n) \tag{10.1b}$$

Within each country there is a representative consumer, with preferences defined over the traded goods, a public good, and leisure, who faces a budget constraint where "full" expenditure on goods and leisure equals "full" income. As there are no pure profits, full income is simply the wage times the labor-time endowment, assumed to be unity. Thus, we can represent consumer equilibrium by the following equation:

---

[9] Keen used specific taxes. Here we use ad-valorem taxes, as the tax rates in Nash tax equilibrium can be shown to depend on the choice of numeraire when taxes are specific, but are independent of the choice of numeraire when taxes are ad-valorem; see Lockwood (1996a) for details.

$$e^i(q^i, w^i, u^i \, g^i) = w^i \qquad (i = a, b) \tag{10.2}$$

where $q^i = (q^i_1, q^i_2, \ldots, q^i_n)$. Here, w^i is full income, and e^i is the full-expenditure function, which depends on the prices of goods and leisure, on utility u^i, and on public-good provision g^i. Note that u^i depends only on g^i, not g^j, so there are no spillover effects between countries through public-good provision. We denote the derivatives of e^i by the following shorthand: $\partial e^i/\partial q^i_j = e^i_j$, $\partial e^i/\partial w^i = e^i_w$, $\partial e^i/\partial u^i = e^i_u$, and $\partial e^i/\partial g^i = e^i_g$. Second and higher derivatives are denoted similarly.

Finally, the tax revenue raised by the government of country i finances the provision of g^i. We suppose that public goods are not traded and, for simplicity, that in both countries the production of one unit of the public good requires one unit of labor. Then the government budget constraints are

$$\sum_{j=1}^{n} t^a_j p_j e^a_j = w^a g^a \tag{10.3a}$$

$$\sum_{j=1}^{n} t^b_j p_j e^b_j = w^b g^b \tag{10.3b}$$

That is, tax revenue must equal the cost of providing the public good in each country.

Now $-e^i_g$ is the reduction in expenditure on other goods that can be sustained following a unit increase in g^i while keeping u^i constant. So $\mu^i = -e^i_g > 0$ can be interpreted as the marginal willingness to pay for the public good. It will be useful to compare our results to those of Keen in what follows, using μ^i. To do this, we consider an alternative specification of the model in which there is no public good, and revenue is returned in a lump sum to the representative consumer. Let g^i then be interpreted as the size of this lump-sum transfer in country i. In this case, clearly, $-e^i_g = \mu^i \equiv 1$, as one dollar transferred to the household allows it to achieve the same utility with an expenditure of a dollar less out of its own pocket. In what follows, we refer to this alternative specification as *the case without a revenue requirement*.

Finally, we state our assumptions regarding the structure of demand. First, we assume that levels of public-good provision have no effect on commodity demands in either country (i.e., $e^i_{jg} = 0, i = a, b, j = 1, \ldots, n$). This is quite a weak assumption, requiring only that direct utility be separable in goods and leisure on the one hand, and the public good on the other. Second, we assume that all goods are normal (i.e., $e^i_{ju} \geq 0, i = a, b, j = 1, \ldots, n$).

3   World Equilibrium and Comparative Statics

The equilibrium conditions of the model are as follows: First, equations (10.2) and (10.3) must hold. Second, we require labor-market clearing in each country:

$$1 - e_w^a = \sum_{j=1}^{m}(e_j^a + e_j^b) + g^a \tag{10.4a}$$

$$1 - e_w^b = \sum_{j=m+1}^{n}(e_j^a + e_j^b) + g^b \tag{10.4b}$$

The left-hand side of equation (10.4a) gives the labor supply by the representative consumer in country a (i.e., the time endowment, 1, minus the leisure demand, e_w^a); the right-hand side gives the total labor demand, composed of demand from the private sector, $\sum_{j=1}^{m}(e_j^a + e_j^b)$, and the labor required to produce the public good, g^a. Equation (10.4b) has a similar interpretation.

Equations (10.1)–(10.4) are $n + 6$ equations in $n + 6$ unknowns $p_1, \ldots, p_n, w^a, w^b, u^a, u^b, g^a, g^b$. Note that all the equations are homogeneous of degree zero in the price variables $p_1, \ldots, p_n, w^a, w^b$. Following Keen, we normalize by setting the wage in country a equal to unity ($w^a = 1$), and so set $w^b = w$. The variable w has a nice interpretation; it is the terms of trade – the price of exports relative to that of imports – for country b, and $1/w$ is the terms of trade for country a.

By Walras's law, we can drop either equation (10.4a) or (10.4b). Moreover, the price–cost equations (10.1a) and (10.1b) determine the p_j once w is known, so that the remaining five equations, (10.2), (10.3a), (10.3b), and (10.4a) or (10.4b), determine w, u^a, u^b, g^a, and g^b. It turns out that for the following analysis we can focus on the trade-balance condition derived from these five equations. This says that the value of country a's imports (at producer prices) is equal to the value of its exports. Using (10.1), the normalization rule $w^a = 1$, $w^b = w$, and $e_{jg}^i = 0$, and the homogeneity of degree zero of e_j^b in (q^b, w), we can write the trade-balance condition as

$$\sum_{j=1}^{m} e_j^b(q^b w^{-1}, 1, u^b) = \sum_{j=m+1}^{n} we_j^a(q^a, 1, u^a) \tag{10.5}$$

where $q^b w^{-1} = (q_1^b/w, \ldots, q_n^b/w)$.

Now consider a tax reform (dt^a, dt^b), where $dt^i = (dt_1^i, \ldots, dt_n^i)$. This reform will, of course, affect all the endogenous variables in the model. It turns out that for our analysis, we need to keep track of only the effects of the reform on w, the terms of trade. From (10.5), these effects can straightforwardly be calculated as follows: Let $m^a(t^a, u^a, w) = \sum_{j=m+1}^{n} we_j^a(q^a, 1, u^a)$ be the value at producer prices of a's imports, and similarly $m^b(t^b, u^b, w) = \sum_{j=1}^{m} e_j^b(q^b w^{-1}, 1, u^b)$. Then the trade-balance condition can be written $m^b - m^a = 0$. It follows directly from implicit differentiation of $m^b - m^a = 0$ that

$$\frac{dw}{dt_j^a} = \frac{1}{D}[m_j^a + m_u^a u_j^a], \qquad \frac{dw}{dt_j^b} = \frac{1}{D}[m_j^b + m_u^b u_j^b] \qquad (10.6)$$

where

$$m_j^i = \frac{\partial m^i}{\partial t_j^i}, \qquad m_u^i = \frac{\partial m^i}{\partial u^i}, \qquad u_j^i = \left.\frac{\partial u^i}{\partial t_j^i}\right|_{w \text{ const.}}, \qquad D = m_w^b - m_w^a$$

Now $D > 0$, under the assumption that the equilibrium is stable under the usual adjustment process, and so we assume $D > 0$ in what follows. Note that

$$u_j^i = \left.\frac{\partial u^i}{\partial t_j^i}\right|_{w \text{ const.}}$$

is the change in endogenous utility u^i induced by the change in t_j^i, assuming that g_i changes through the government budget constraint. Thus the first term in either expression in (10.6) – for example, m_j^a/D – is the *substitution effect* (i.e., holding utility constant) of a change[10] in the relevant tax rate on w. The second term can be thought of as an *income effect* of a change in the relevant tax rate on w (i.e., the effect of a change in t_j^i on w induced[11] through a change in u^i). In what follows, explicit expressions for the u_j^i are not needed.

4 Tax Equilibrium

Throughout, we assume that initial taxes are Nash-equilibrium taxes. A *Nash tax equilibrium* is formally defined as a pair of tax vectors $\hat{t}^a = (\hat{t}_1^a, \ldots, \hat{t}_n^a)$ and $\hat{t}^b = (\hat{t}_1^b, \ldots, \hat{t}_n^b)$ such that $\hat{t}^a$ maximizes u^a, given $\hat{t}^b$ fixed, and vice versa. In general, a variation in t_j^i will have both a direct effect on u^i,

---

[10] It is easy to verify that if $n = 2$, the substitution effects on w of the taxes on imported goods t_2^a and t_1^b are negative and positive, respectively, indicating that absent income effects, an increase in the tax on imported goods will improve the terms of trade for each country.

[11] It is clear from inspection of equations (10.1)–(10.4) that a change in t_j^i, holding w fixed, will have no effect on $u^j, j \neq i$.

holding the terms of trade fixed, and an indirect effect through the terms of trade. At a Nash equilibrium, the sum of these effects must be zero for any country and tax:

$$\frac{du^i}{dt^i_j} = u^i_j + \frac{\partial u^i}{\partial w}\frac{dw}{dt^i_j} = 0 \qquad (i = a, b, j = 1,...,n) \tag{10.7}$$

where dw/dt^i_j is defined in (10.6), and

$$u^i_j = \frac{\partial u^i}{\partial t^i_j}\bigg|_{w\ const.}$$

is as before. It is useful to call the direct effect the Ramsey effect, and the indirect effect the tariff effect. If country i ignored the tariff effect, its optimal tax structure would be given implicitly by $u^i_j = 0$, which would reduce to the usual Ramsey tax conditions (e.g., Atkinson and Stiglitz, 1980, p. 372), given the producer prices prevailing at Nash equilibrium. If, on the other hand, there were no revenue-raising requirement ($\mu^i \equiv 1$), then the optimal taxes would be determined by the tariff effect only. In the two-good case, with $\mu^i \equiv 1$, $i = a, b$, it is easy to show that at the Nash equilibrium in each country the exported good would be untaxed, and tax on the imported good would be given by a variant of the usual optimal-tariff formula.[12]

Returning to (10.7), which of the two effects will dominate in the determination of taxes? Consider the two-good case, where each country imports one good and exports one good. It should be intuitively clear that if the demand for the imported good is more elastic than that for the exported good, then the Ramsey effect might work in the direction opposite to the tariff effect (abstracting from cross-price effects). It is equally clear that if, in addition, the government revenue requirement is high enough, the Ramsey effect might dominate, causing the exported good to be taxed more heavily than the imported good. The following example with two goods makes this point. Later, the example will also serve to show that some of Keen's results do not generalize to the case in which a revenue requirement is present ($\mu^i > 1$, $i = a, b$).

---

[12] A general proof of this result can be found in an earlier version of this study, available from the author on request. This result is similar to standard results in the trade literature (e.g., Boadway et al., 1973). The intuition for an untaxed exportable is that the tax on the exportable is imposed on both exports and domestic consumption. Thus, from the point of view of country a, it is a second-best instrument for manipulating the terms of trade; it is dominated by the import tax, and so is set to zero.

Example

1. Preferences in the two countries are symmetric over private goods and identical over labor and the public good; that is, $e^a(p, q, w, g, u) \equiv e^b(q, p, w, g, u)$ for all $p, q, w, g,$ and u.
2. There are zero cross-price effects and income effects for traded goods: $e^i_{jk} = 0,\ e^i_{ju} = 0,\ i = a, b, j, k = 1, 2$.
3. There are constant own-price elasticities of demand; the (absolute values of) the elasticities of demand for goods 1 and 2 are ε and σ, respectively, in country a and σ and ε, respectively, in country b.
4. The marginal willingness to pay for the public good is constant and is the same in both countries (i.e., $\mu^a = \mu^b = \mu > 1$).

There certainly exist utility functions satisfying conditions 1–4 simultaneously. For example,

$$u^a = \frac{\left(x_1^a\right)^{1-1/\varepsilon}}{(1 - 1/\varepsilon)} + \frac{\left(x_2^a\right)^{1-1/\sigma}}{(1 - 1/\sigma)} + \ell^a + \mu g^a$$

(and symmetrically for b). Because of the symmetry of the example, we can focus on a symmetric Nash equilibrium where $\hat{t}_1^a = \hat{t}_2^b = t^*$ and $\hat{t}_2^a = \hat{t}_1^b = t^{**}$. After some computation, the general first-order conditions (10.7) reduce to

$$\frac{\mu - 1}{\mu} - \varepsilon \frac{t^*}{1 + t^*} = 0 \tag{10.8}$$

$$\frac{\mu - 1}{\mu} - \sigma \frac{t^{**}}{1 + t^{**}} + \gamma \left[(\sigma - 1) \frac{t^{**}}{1 + t^{**}} + \frac{1}{\mu} \right] = 0 \tag{10.9}$$

(Ramsey effect)   (tariff effect)

where $\gamma = \sigma/(2\sigma - 1)$. Stability of world equilibrium requires that $2\sigma - 1 > 0$, so $\gamma > 0$. Solving (10.8) and (10.9), we get

$$\frac{t^*}{1 + t^*} = \frac{\mu - 1}{\mu \varepsilon}, \qquad \frac{t^{**}}{1 + t^{**}} = \frac{\mu - 1 + \gamma}{\mu[\sigma + (1 - \sigma)\gamma]} \tag{10.10}$$

Note that there is no revenue requirement if $\mu = 1$. In this case, from (10.10), $t^* = 0$ and $t^{**}/(1 + t^{**}) = 1/\sigma$. Hence the exported good is untaxed, and $1/\sigma$ is the optimal import tariff. On the other hand, if σ is large relative to ε, then we can have $t^* > t^{**}$, so that the Ramsey effect dominates (a precise statement of the conditions required will be given later with Proposition 3).

5   Pareto-Improving Tax Reforms

We can now characterize Pareto-improving tax reforms, starting from a Nash equilibrium, in a simple and intuitive way. To avoid tedious discussion of borderline cases, we focus on reforms that are strictly Pareto-improving (i.e., reforms that induce $du^a > 0$, $du^b > 0$). We then have the following:

Proposition 1. *Assume that the initial taxes are Nash, that an improvement in the terms of trade for each country increases welfare, holding taxes fixed (i.e., $\partial u^a/\partial w < 0$, $\partial u^b/\partial w > 0$), and that income effects are not too large ($m_u^i < D/|\partial u^i/\partial w|$, $i = a$, b). Then a reform (dt^a, dt^b) is Pareto-improving if and only if*

$$\sum_{j=1}^{n} m_j^a \, dt_j^a > 0, \qquad \sum_{j=1}^{n} m_j^b \, dt_j^b > 0 \qquad (10.11)$$

that is, if the value of compensated (i.e., utility-constant) demand for imports in both countries rises as a result of the reform.

Proof.   From (10.7), $du^a/d_j^a = 0$ at Nash equilibrium, so the effect of a tax reform on country a's welfare is

$$du^a = \frac{\partial u^a}{\partial w} \sum_{j=1}^{n} \frac{dw}{dt_j^b} \, dt_j^b \qquad (10.12)$$

But from (10.6), using the fact that from the Nash-equilibrium condition (10.7) $u_j^b = -(\partial u^b/\partial w)(dw/dt_j^b)$, we see that

$$\frac{dw}{dt_j^b} = -\frac{1}{D}(m_j^b + m_u^b u_j^b) = -\frac{1}{D}\left(m_j^b - m_u^b \frac{\partial u^b}{\partial w} \frac{dw}{dt_j^b}\right) \qquad (10.13)$$

Rearranging (10.13), we get $dw/dt_j^b = -m_j^b/E$, where $E = D - m_u^b (\partial u^b/\partial w)$. Note that $E > 0$, by the assumption that m_u^b is not too large. Substituting this into (10.12), we get

$$du^a = c^a \sum_{j=1}^{n} m_j^b \, dt_j^b \qquad (10.14)$$

where $c^a = -(\partial u^a/\partial w)E^{-1}$. Now $\partial u^a/\partial w < 0$ by assumption, and $E > 0$, as argued earlier. So $c^a > 0$, and therefore $du^a > 0$ if and only if (iff) $\sum_{j=1}^{n} m_j^b \, dt_j^b > 0$. A similar argument will show that $du^b > 0$ iff $\sum_{j=1}^{n} m_j^a \, dt_j^a > 0$. ∎

The conditions in (10.11) for a Pareto improvement are remarkably simple compared with similar conditions in the literature.[13] This simplicity derives from (1) the envelope property of Nash equilibrium (a change in t^i does not affect u^i, as t^i is chosen optimally from country i's point of view) and (2) the simple structure of production.

The intuition for Proposition 1 is as follows. Any tax reform can affect country a's welfare only through changes in country b's taxes, as country a's taxes are already chosen optimally from its point of view. So, given $\partial u^a / \partial w < 0$, b's tax reform must improve a's terms of trade (reduce w) if it is to be welfare-improving for a. This means, from (10.6), that dt^b must increase the value of b's imports.

The result is illustrated in Figure 10.1 for country a in the case $n = 2$. Let $\Delta m^i = (m_1^i, m_2^i)$; then any reform that raises u^a must have a positive inner product with Δm^b. Then, by definition, $m^b = e_1^b$, so $\Delta m^b = (e_{11}^b w^{-1}, e_{12}^b)$; if the two goods are substitutes ($e_{12}^b > 0$), Δm^b must point northwest, as shown.

One important implication of Proposition 1 is that there are several simple rules of thumb for tax reform that will ensure Pareto improvements. One such rule is to reduce t_j^i only if $m_j^i < 0$ (i.e., if an increase in q_j^i causes the value of i's imports to fall). In the special case $n = 2$, this rule of thumb reduces to the very simple rule that taxes on imports, t_1^b and t_2^a, should always be reduced, because $m_2^a = w^2 e_{22}^a < 0$ and $m_1^b = w^{-1} e_{11}^b < 0$. As there is complete specialization in production, these two taxes t_1^b and t_2^a are simply import tariffs, and so this last rule is just a variant of the well-known rule in the tariff literature to the effect that "both countries gain from small mutual reductions of tariffs below their Nash equilibrium values" (McMillan, 1986).

6 Harmonizing Tax Reforms

In this section we study harmonizing tax reforms. Given that, as argued earlier, there are several simple reforms that will deliver Pareto improvements, it is worth emphasizing why this is of interest. First and foremost, whatever the intellectual justification (or lack of it) for harmonization, the European Commission has been committed to such a policy for both VAT and excise taxes, at least since the mid-1980s, and this policy is embedded in legislation now binding on member states of the European Union, as described in the Introduction. For that reason alone, the welfare properties of harmonization are worth investigating. Second, as

---

[13] See, for example, Abe (1992), who developed conditions for welfare-improving tariff reform in a small open economy with public production. Also see Lahiri and Raimondos (1995).

tax on
good 1

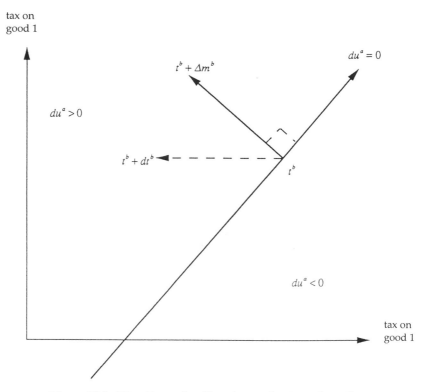

Figure 10.1. Directions of welfare-improving tax reform for country a.

remarked in the Introduction, a body of academic literature has already studied the welfare properties of harmonizing reforms.

We begin by defining the concept of harmonizing tax reforms. A *harmonizing tax reform* is a tax reform (dt^a, dt^b) that moves each country's tax vector toward a common vector $h = (h_1, \ldots, h_n)$, where h_j is a weighted combination of t_j^a and t_j^b. Consequently, we require the reform to satisfy

$$dt_j^i = \beta^i(h_j - t_j^i) \qquad (\beta^i > 0, i = a, b, j = 1,...,n) \qquad (10.15)$$

$$h_j = \lambda_j t_j^a + (1 - \lambda_j)t_j^b \qquad (\lambda_j \in (0, 1), j = 1,...,n) \qquad (10.16)$$

This definition of harmonization is more general than that of Keen in that it does not require producer prices to be left unchanged. Tax-harmonizing reforms are illustrated in Figure 10.2 for $n = 2$. The initial

tax on
good 2

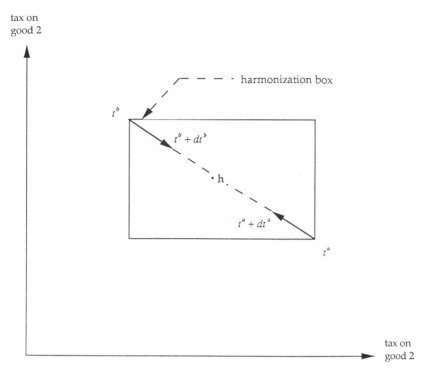

Figure 10.2. A harmonizing tax reform (dt^a, dt^b).

tax vectors are t^a and t^b. A harmonizing reform (dt^a, dt^b) must have the property that dt^i points into the "harmonization box" in the diagram for each $i = a, b$.

Using Proposition 1, we can now investigate whether or not Pareto-improving harmonizing reforms can be found for given initial taxes. Our first results are for the case of two goods. For easy comparison between our results and those of Keen, we assume that the two goods are substitutes in both countries ($e_{12}^i > 0$, $i = a, b$) or that the goods are independent ($e_{12}^i = 0$, $i = a, b$).

Proposition 2. *Assume that the initial taxes are Nash and that an improvement in country i's terms of trade improves its welfare, given that taxes are fixed ($\partial u^a/\partial w < 0$, $\partial u^b/\partial w > 0$) and that income effects are not too large ($m_u^i < D/|\partial u^i/\partial w|$, $i = a, b$). Then*

(i) *If the importer of either good taxes it less than the exporter (i.e.,*
    $\hat{t}_2^a < \hat{t}_2^b$, $\hat{t}_1^b < \hat{t}_1^a$*), then any tax-harmonizing reform will cause
    welfare in both countries to fall* (du^a, $du^b < 0$*), so that there
    does not exist even a potentially Pareto-improving harmoniz-
    ing tax reform.*

(ii) *If the importer of either good taxes it more than the exporter
    (i.e.,* $\hat{t}_2^a > \hat{t}_2^b$, $\hat{t}_1^b > \hat{t}_1^a$*), then any harmonizing reform will be
    Pareto-improving.*

(iii) *If both taxes in one country are higher than those in the other
    country (i.e.,* $\hat{t}_j^i > \hat{t}_j^k$, i, $k = a, b, j = 1, 2$*) and the two traded
    goods are substitutes, then at least one Pareto-improving har-
    monizing tax reform can be found if and only if at least one of
    the following holds:* $\Delta t'_a \Delta m^a < 0$, $\Delta t'_b \Delta m^b < 0$*, where* $\Delta t_i = \hat{t}^i$
    $- \hat{t}^k$*. If the two traded goods are independent, then no Pareto-
    improving harmonizing reform can exist.*

Proof.   First, from (10.5), $m^a = we_2^a$ and $m^b = e_1^b$. Using this and equations (10.14)–(10.16), we have

$$du^a = c^a \beta^b \left[e_{11}^b w^{-1} \lambda_1 (\hat{t}_1^a - \hat{t}_1^b) + e_{12}^b \lambda_2 (\hat{t}_2^a - \hat{t}_2^b) \right] \tag{10.17}$$

$$du^b = c^b \beta^a \left[we_{21}^a (1 - \lambda_1)(\hat{t}_1^b - \hat{t}_1^a) + w^2 e_{22}^a (1 - \lambda_2)(\hat{t}_2^b - \hat{t}_2^a) \right] \tag{10.18}$$

Then parts (i) and (ii) follow directly from inspection of equations
(10.17) and (10.18), given the inequalities satisfied by the taxes in each
case, and recalling that e_{11}^a, $e_{22}^b < 0$ and e_{12}^b, $e_{21}^a \geq 0$. Part (iii) is proved in
the Appendix.   ∎

Note that Proposition 2 gives a complete characterization of Pareto-
improving harmonizing tax reforms with two traded goods for any possible configuration of initial taxes (ignoring borderline cases where $\hat{t}_j^i =$
$\hat{t}_j^k i, k = a, b, j = 1, 2$). The necessary and sufficient condition for the existence of Pareto-improving harmonizing tax reforms with high- and low-
tax countries is illustrated in Figure 10.3, where $\Delta t'_b \Delta m^b < 0$. In general,
what is required is that for *some* country, the differences between home
and foreign taxes on the two goods be negatively correlated with the
responses of the value of home imports to the two prices.

Also, the intuition for parts (i) and (ii) of Proposition 2 should be clear
from Figure 10.4, which has been constructed by combining Figures 10.1
and 10.2. Proposition 2(i) hypothesizes that the importer of each good
initially taxes it less heavily than the exporter. This is shown in Figure
10.4, where a's initial tax vector, $\hat{t}^a$, is to the southeast of b's vector, $\hat{t}^b$.
So harmonizing tax reforms (i.e., vectors pointing into the harmoniza-
tion box for both countries, as shown) must involve raising (lowering)

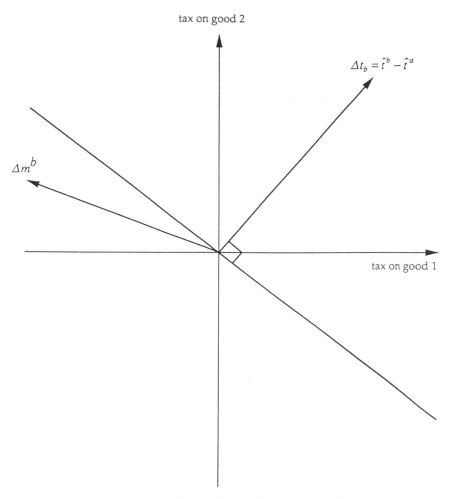

Figure 10.3. A case involving a high-tax country (*b*) and a low-tax country (*a*) in which Pareto-improving harmonizing tax reforms are carried out.

the tax on the imported (exported) good in both countries. In these conditions, harmonizing tax reforms must necessarily point in directions different from those for Pareto-improving tax reforms. By contrast, Proposition 2(*ii*) hypothesizes that the importer of either good taxes it more highly than the exporter. So here, harmonizing tax reforms must involve lowering the tax on the imported good in both countries,

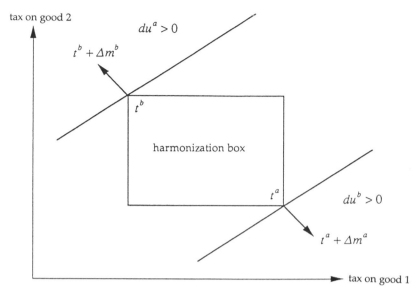

Figure 10.4. The case in which Pareto-improving harmonization is impossible.

implying that harmonizing tax reforms must necessarily be Pareto-improving, as shown in Figure 10.5.

The tax configuration described in part (*iii*) of Proposition 2 is an interesting one in practice. For example, the tax-revenue–GDP ratio varies considerably across the European Union, and indirect taxes on most commodities tend to be higher in countries where this ratio is higher.[14] However, the kind of harmonizing reform considered in practice (e.g., by the European Commission) is a move toward a simple average of the taxes (i.e., where $\lambda_j = \frac{1}{2}, j = 1, 2$). It is clear from the proof of Proposition 2(*iii*) that this type of harmonization may not lead to a Pareto improvement.

We can now relate the results from Proposition 2 to those in the existing literature. As mentioned earlier, the main result proven by Keen (1987) is that a potentially Pareto-improving reform can exist on the basis of arbitrary initial taxes, under a very weak condition (no transfer paradox), which is automatically satisfied in our model by imposing no

[14] For example, the highest and lowest tax-revenue–GDP ratios in 1990 were 49% (Denmark) and 34% (Spain). In Denmark, the standard rate for the VAT was 25%, with no reduced rate; in Spain, the standard rate was 13%, with a reduced rate of 6% (Keen, 1993a).

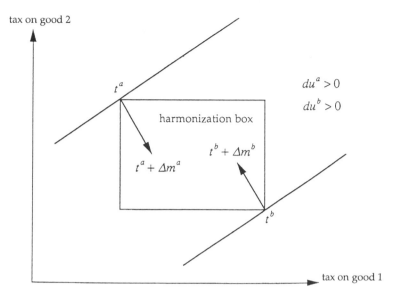

tax on good 2

t^a

$du^a > 0$

$du^b > 0$

harmonization box

$t^b + \Delta m^b$

$t^a + \Delta m^a$

t^b

tax on good 1

Figure 10.5. The case in which every harmonizing tax reform is Pareto-improving.

income effects. His Proposition 3 (Keen, 1989) states that if there are only two goods and each country is initially taxing its imported good (but initial taxes are otherwise arbitrary), then harmonization is also actually Pareto-improving. Proposition 2(*i*) herein shows that neither of these results need hold in the case of a positive revenue requirement as long as it is possible that at the Nash equilibrium both goods will be taxed more heavily by the exporter than by the importer.

It is not entirely obvious that this configuration of taxes can occur, as elasticities of demand help determine both the Ramsey- and optimal-tariff effects [e.g., equation (10.10)]. However, we can show the following:

Proposition 3. *If, in the example given earlier, the elasticity of demand for the imported good is high enough relative to the elasticity of demand for the exported good ($\sigma > 1 > \varepsilon$), and if the revenue requirement is high enough ($\mu > 2$), then there exists no potentially Pareto-improving harmonizing tax reform, starting from Nash-equilibrium taxes.*

Proof. First, note that the configuration of taxes described in Proposition 2(*i*) occurs if $\sigma > 1 > \varepsilon$ and $\mu > 2$. To see this, it suffices to show that

$\hat{t}_2^a = \hat{t}_1^b = t^{**} < t^* = \hat{t}_1^a = \hat{t}_2^b$. Now, from (10.10), we see that $t^{**} < t^*$ if $\sigma > [\varepsilon + (\sigma - 1)\ \gamma]/(\mu - 1)$. As $\sigma > 1$, $\gamma = \sigma/(2\sigma - 1) < 1$, so $\sigma > [\varepsilon + (\sigma - 1)]/(\mu - 1)$ or $\sigma\ (\mu - 2) > \varepsilon - 1$ is sufficient for $t^{**} < t^*$. But $\sigma(\mu - 2) > \varepsilon - 1$ certainly holds as $\sigma > 1 > \varepsilon$ and $\mu > 2$ by assumption.

So, Proposition 3 will follow from Proposition 2(i) if we can show that the assumptions of Proposition 2 all hold in the example. First, there are, by assumption, no income effects in the demand for traded goods (property 2 of the example), so $m_u^i = 0$, $i = a, b$, implying that the condition on m_u^i in Proposition 2 is certainly satisfied. Second, by the envelope theorem, and because of the assumptions of no income effects and no cross-price effects and the government budget constraint, it is possible to show that $\partial u^a/\partial w < 0$ and $\partial u^b/\partial w > 0$ (details provided on request). Therefore the assumptions of Proposition 2 all hold in the example, as required. ∎

We now turn to the issue of generalizing Proposition 2 to the case of $n > 2$ goods. At first sight, this appears to be extremely difficult, as the number of possible tax configurations and the number of possible sign patterns in $\Delta m^i = (m_1^i, \ldots, m_n^i)$, $i = a, b$, all rise geometrically with n. However, an obvious case to be examined is that in which all traded goods are *independent* (i.e., neither substitutes nor complements, $e_{jk}^i = 0$, $i = a, b, j, k = 1, \ldots, n, k \neq j$): In this case, Keen (1989) has shown that without a revenue requirement, a class of Pareto-improving harmonizing reforms from Nash-equilibrium taxes does exist.[15] We can show that with a revenue requirement, Keen's result can be generalized only with an additional condition on the initial taxes. Moreover, the condition required is a generalization of that in Proposition 2(ii).

Proposition 4. *Assume that all traded goods are independent. Then a Pareto-improving harmonizing reform can exist if and only if there is some good exported by each country that is taxed more highly by the importing country than by the exporting country; that is, $\hat{t}_k^b > \hat{t}_k^a$ for some $k \in \{1, \ldots, m\}$, and $\hat{t}_l^a > \hat{t}_l^b$ for some $l \in \{m + 1, \ldots, n\}$.*

Proof. With $e_{jk}^i = 0$, $i = a, b, j, k = 1, \ldots, n, k \neq j$, it is easy to verify that $m_j^a = 0$, $j = 1, \ldots, m$, and $m_j^a = w^2 e_{jj}^a$, $j = m + 1, \ldots, n$. Similarly, $m_j^b = w^{-1}\ e_{jj}^b$, $j = 1, \ldots, m$, $m_j^b = 0$, $j = m + 1, \ldots, n$. So, substituting

---

[15] Keen [1989, prop. 4(i)]. Keen's model allows for a general production technology in each country and also requires a condition on that technology, namely, that there be no cross-price effects in profit-maximizing supplies in each country. That condition is automatically satisfied by the assumptions on technology in this study, and so it is only Keen's condition on demand that is relevant.

these formulas for m_j^i and equations (10.15) and (10.16) into the formula for du^a in (10.14), and the corresponding formula for du^b, we get

$$du^a = c^a \beta^b \sum_{j=1}^{m} w^{-1} e_{jj}^b \lambda_j (\hat{t}_j^a - \hat{t}_j^b),$$

$$du^b = c^b \beta^a \sum_{j=m+1}^{n} w^2 e_{jj}^a (1 - \lambda_j)(\hat{t}_j^b - \hat{t}_j^a) \tag{10.19}$$

To prove sufficiency, recall that $\lambda_j > 0$ and $e_{jj}^i < 0$ and that $\hat{t}_k^b > \hat{t}_k^a$ for some $k \in \{1, \ldots, m\}$ is assumed. Set $\hat{\lambda}_k = 1 - \varepsilon$ and $\hat{\lambda}_j = \varepsilon, j = 1, \ldots, m, j \neq k$. Then for ε small enough, from (10.19), $du^a = c^a \beta^b w^{-1} e_{kk}^b \lambda_k (\hat{t}_k^a - \hat{t}_k^b) > 0$. As $\hat{t}_l^a > \hat{t}_l^b$ for some $l \in \{m + 1, \ldots, n\}$ is also assumed, a similar argument shows that setting $\hat{\lambda}_l = \delta, \hat{\lambda}_j = 1 - \delta, j = m + 1, \ldots, n, j \neq l$, and choosing δ small enough implies $du^b > 0$. So $\hat{\lambda} = (\hat{\lambda}_1, \ldots, \hat{\lambda}_n)$ is the required reform. To prove necessity, note that if the condition in Proposition 4 does not hold, then $\hat{t}_k^b \leq \hat{t}_k^a$ for all $k \in \{1, \ldots, m\}$, and $\hat{t}_l^a \leq \hat{t}_l^b$ for all $l \in \{m + 1, \ldots, n\}$. It then follows immediately from (10.19) that $du^a, du^b \leq 0$ for all $\lambda_1, \ldots, \lambda_n$. ∎

The relationship of Proposition 4 to Keen's result is that the condition in Proposition 4 is satisfied automatically in the case with no revenue requirement (i.e., where $\mu^i = 1, i = a, b$). Proposition 4 can be interpreted as a generalization of Proposition 2(ii) to the case of n goods under the assumption of no cross-price effects.

7   Extensions and Conclusions

Propositions 2(i), 3, and 4 indicate that it is fruitless to search for very general conditions under which harmonizing reforms, in the obvious sense, can be Pareto-improving, the underlying reason being that heterogeneity in preferences implies that optimal tax structures will, in general, be different between countries. One response to this is to reject the idea of harmonization altogether and concentrate on simple tax reforms guaranteed to deliver Pareto improvements, as discussed earlier. However, the idea of harmonization seems to have political appeal. So one might ask if there is another way of formulating harmonizing tax reforms in such a way as to yield Pareto improvements under more general conditions.

In an earlier version of this chapter, such an alternative formulation was proposed. The trick is to "factor out" tax differences due to heterogeneity of preferences when defining harmonizing tax reforms and concentrate on harmonizing the "remainder" of the tax vector. This works as follows: Fix the Nash-equilibrium producer-price vector $\hat{p}$. Define the

Ramsey taxes for country i as those taxes $t_{1,r}^i, \ldots, t_{n,r}^i$ that will maximize u^i, taking producer prices as fixed at $\hat{p}$ (these taxes will, in general, be different from the Nash-equilibrium taxes). Also, define the tax difference $z_j^i = t_j^i - t_{j,r}^i$ to be the difference between the actual taxes and Ramsey taxes, and define a *difference-harmonizing tax reform* as a reform dz_j^i that will satisfy the analogues of (10.15) and (10.16). That is, starting from the Nash-equilibrium tax difference $z_{j,n}^i = t_{j,n}^i - t_{j,r}^i$, the reforms must satisfy $dz_j^i = \beta^i(h_j - z_{j,n}^i)$, $\beta^i > 0$, $i = a, b$, $j = 1, \ldots, n$, and $h_j = \lambda_j z_{j,n}^a + (1 - \lambda_j)z_{j,n}^b$, $j = 1, \ldots, n$.

We then might expect that a difference-harmonizing reform from a Nash equilibrium will lead to a Pareto improvement, very generally, that is, (1) without imposing any conditions on the configuration of the taxes at the initial Nash equilibrium and (2) for a general class of preferences. In fact, the result obtainable (Lockwood, 1996b, prop. 6) states that any difference-harmonizing reform will lead to a Pareto improvement, given (1), but for a rather restricted class of preferences. In particular, the result requires that utility be linear in leisure and the public good, that there be no cross-price effects in compensated demands, and finally that there be a fairly weak condition on the second derivative of compensated demand. The reason that such strong conditions are required is that to establish the result, Ramsey taxes and Nash-equilibrium taxes need to be compared; in optimal-tax models, such "global" comparisons are always difficult.

The model presented in this chapter has several obvious limitations: The production technology in each country is rather special (one factor of production, traded goods produced under constant returns to scale, and no intermediate goods), the initial taxes are assumed to be Nash, and the goods markets are assumed to be perfectly competitive. Of these, the assumption of competitive markets is probably the easiest to relax. Given the importance, in practice, of intraindustry trade between EU members, analysis of the imperfectly competitive case would also be rather interesting. So study of the welfare effects of harmonization with imperfect competition is a topic for future work.

APPENDIX: PROOF OF PROPOSITION 2(iii)

Assume, without loss of generality, that $\hat{t}_j^b > \hat{t}_j^a$, $j = 1, 2$, so that country b is the high-tax country. First, let $(\lambda_1, \lambda_2) \in (0, 1)^2$ be such that $du^a = 0$. Then, from (10.17), this requires

$$\lambda_2 = \varkappa\lambda_1, \qquad \varkappa = -e_{11}^b w^{-1}(\hat{t}_1^a - \hat{t}_1^b)/[e_{12}^b(\hat{t}_2^a - \hat{t}_2^b)] > 0 \qquad (10.\text{A}1)$$

From (10.A1), $\lambda_2 \in (0, 1)$ requires $\lambda_1 \in (0, \gamma)$, $\gamma = \min\{1, 1/\varkappa\}$. We then have two cases.

Case 1. In the case $\varkappa > 1$, a Pareto-improving reform always exists. Set $\lambda_1 = 1/\varkappa$, $\lambda_2 = \varkappa\lambda_1 - \varepsilon$, $\varepsilon > 0$. Then, from (10.17) and (10.18), we have

$$du^a = \varepsilon c^a \beta^b e_{12}^b (\hat{t}_2^b - \hat{t}_2^a),$$

$$du^b = c^b \beta^a \left[we_{21}^a \left(1 - \frac{1}{\varkappa}\right)(\hat{t}_1^b - \hat{t}_1^a) + \varepsilon w^2 e_{22}^a (\hat{t}_2^b - \hat{t}_2^a) \right] \qquad (10.\text{A}2)$$

As β^i, $c^i > 0$, $i = a, b$, it is clear from (10.A2) that $du^a > 0$ as $\varepsilon > 0$ and that for ε small enough, $du^b > 0$ as $\varkappa > 1$. ∎

Case 2. In the case $\varkappa \leq 1$, any reform can be expressed as $(\lambda_1, \varkappa\lambda_1 - \varepsilon)$ $\in (0, 1)^2$, $\varkappa\lambda_1 > \varepsilon > \varkappa\lambda_1 - 1$. Then, from (10.17) and (10.18), we have

$$du^a = \varepsilon c^a \beta^b e_{12}^b (\hat{t}_2^b - \hat{t}_2^a) \qquad (10.\text{A}3)$$

$$\frac{du^b}{c^b \beta^a} = (1 - \lambda_1)we_{21}^a(\hat{t}_2^b - \hat{t}_2^a) + (1 - \varkappa\lambda_1)w^2 e_{22}^a(\hat{t}_2^b - \hat{t}_2^a) + \varepsilon w^2 e_{22}^a(\hat{t}_2^b - \hat{t}_2^a)$$

$$= f(\lambda_1) + \varepsilon w^2 e_{22}^a(\hat{t}_2^b - \hat{t}_2^a) \qquad (10.\text{A}4)$$

From (10.A3), $du^a > 0 \leftrightarrow \varepsilon > 0$. Moreover, if $f(\lambda_1) > 0$, ε can be chosen small enough so that $du^b > 0$. So a necessary and sufficient condition for a Pareto-improving harmonizing reform is that there be a $\lambda_1^* \in (0, 1)$ such that $f(\lambda_1^*) > 0$. As $f(\ )$ is linear in λ_1, such a λ_1^* exists iff either $f(0) > 0$ or $f(1) > 0$ or both. Now,

$$f(0) = we_{21}^a(\hat{t}_2^b - \hat{t}_2^a) + w^2 e_{22}^a(\hat{t}_2^b - \hat{t}_2^a) = \Delta t_b' \Delta m^a \qquad (10.\text{A}5)$$

$$f(1) = (1 - \varkappa)w^2 e_{22}^a(\hat{t}_2^b - \hat{t}_2^a) \qquad (10.\text{A}6)$$

From (10.A6) and $w^2 e_{22}^a < 0$, $f(1) > 0$ implies $\varkappa > 1$, contradicting the definition of case 2. Thus there exists a Pareto-improving harmonizing reform in case 2 iff $\Delta t_b' \Delta m^a > 0$. Finally, $\Delta t_b' \Delta m^a > 0 \leftrightarrow \Delta t_a' \Delta m^a < 0$.

So we conclude that strictly Pareto-improving reform can exist iff either $\Delta t_a' \Delta m^a < 0$ or $\varkappa > 1$ or both. From (10.A1), $\varkappa > 1 \leftrightarrow e_{11}^b w^{-1} (\hat{t}_1^b - \hat{t}_1^a) + e_{12}^b(\hat{t}_2^b - \hat{t}_2^a) = \Delta t_b' \Delta m^b < 0$. So if the two goods are substitutes in both countries, we conclude that there exists a Pareto-improving harmonizing reform iff $\Delta t_i' \Delta m^i < 0$, with some $i = a, b$, as claimed.

To prove the last part of Proposition 2(*iii*), note that if $e_{12}^i = 0$, (10.17) and (10.18) reduce to $du^a = c^a \beta^b e_{11}^b w^{-1} \lambda_1(\hat{t}_1^a - \hat{t}_1^b)$ and $du^b =$

244   **Lockwood**

$c^b\beta^a w^2 e_{22}^a(1 - \lambda_2)(\hat{t}_2^b - \hat{t}_2^a)$; as one of $\hat{t}_1^a - \hat{t}_1^b$ and $\hat{t}_2^b - \hat{t}_2^a$ must be positive, so one of du^a and du^b must be negative for all $\lambda_1, \lambda_2 \in (0, 1)^2$. ∎

REFERENCES

Abe, K. (1992). Tariff reform in a small open economy with public production. *International Economic Review* 33:209–22.
Atkinson, A. B., and Stiglitz, J. (1980). *Lectures on Public Economics*. New York: McGraw-Hill.
Auerbach, A. J. (1985). The theory of excess burden and optimal taxation. In: *Handbook of Public Economics*, ed. A. J. Auerbach and M. Feldstein. Amsterdam: North Holland.
Boadway, R., Maital, S., and Prachowny, M. (1973). Optimal tariffs and public goods. *Journal of Public Economics* 2:391–403.
Bovenberg, L., and Horne, J. (1992). Taxes on commodities: a survey. In: *Tax Harmonisation in the European Community: Policy Issues and Analysis*, ed. G. Kopits. Occasional paper 94. Washington, DC: International Monetary Fund.
Diewert, E., Turunen, A. H., and Woodland, A. D. (1989). Productivity and Pareto-improving changes in taxes and tariffs. *Review of Economic Studies* 56:199–216.
Fehan, J. P. (1988). Efficient tariff financing of public goods. *Journal of International Economics* 24:155–64.
Fitzgerald, J., Johnston, J., and Williams, J. (1994). Indirect tax distortions in a nation of shopkeepers. Unpublished paper, The Economic and Social Research Institute, Dublin.
Kanbur, R., and Keen, M. (1993). Jeux sans frontiers: tax competition and tax coordination when countries differ in size. *American Economic Review* 83:877–92.
Keen, M. (1987). Welfare effects of commodity tax harmonisation. *Journal of Public Economics* 33:107–14.
Keen, M. (1989). Pareto-improving indirect tax harmonisation. *European Economic Review* 33:1–12.
Keen, M. (1993a). The structure of the fiscal and social charges according to their degree of mobility. Report prepared for the European Commission.
Keen, M. (1993b). The welfare economics of tax co-ordination in the European Community: a survey. *Fiscal Studies* 14:15–36.
Lahiri, S., and Raimondos, P. (1995). Public good provision and the welfare effects of indirect tax harmonisation. Unpublished manuscript, Department of Economics, University of Essex.
Lockwood, B. (1996a). Choice of numeraire and Nash equilibrium in tax and tariff policy games. Unpublished manuscript, Department of Economics, University of Exeter.
Lockwood, B. (1996b). Commodity tax harmonisation with public goods – an alternative perspective. CEPR discussion paper 1304, Centre for Economic Policy Research, London.
Lopez-Garcia, M. (1996). The origin principle and the welfare gains from indirect tax harmonisation. *International Tax and Public Finance* 3:83–96.

McMillan, J. (1986). *Game Theory in International Economics*. Reading: Harwood.

Smith, S. (1992). "Subsidiarity" and the coordination of indirect taxes in the European Community. *Oxford Review of Economic Policy* 9:67–94.

Yang, C., and Tsai, T. R. (1992). Optimum tariffs – north–south. *Journal of International Economics* 32:369–77.

CHAPTER 11

Fiscal Separation
with Economic Integration:
Israel and the Palestinian Authority

Ephraim Kleiman

1   Introduction

The Israeli-Palestinian accord of 1994 led to the establishment of the Palestinian National Authority (PNA), with economic responsibilities and its own fiscal jurisdiction in the Gaza Strip and parts of the West Bank. Political separation, in that case, was to be accompanied by a common external tariff and by removal of some existing obstacles to fuller economic integration of the Palestinian and Israeli economies. But the establishment of a separate fiscal jurisdiction meant that the need to coordinate fiscal policies, inherent in a customs-union framework, would have to be accommodated and that mechanisms would have to be found for the apportioning of tax revenues. Those problems and the solutions offered to them are the subjects of this study.

After providing a brief historical perspective and surveying the evolution of the situation that existed when the new regime was being negotiated, the fiscal problems raised by a common customs envelope will be analyzed. The arrangements ultimately made to deal with those problems are then discussed, with special emphasis on the questions of decision-sharing and of the tax-clearance mechanism.

The few years that have passed since the establishment of the PNA have been too short a period to allow complete evaluation of the workings of the system as it has functioned in practice, the more so because political and security developments have overshadowed and disrupted the economic scene for most of the period. However, some matters of

This chapter was written while I was Senior Fellow at the U.S. Institute of Peace, Washington, D.C., in 1996. Its contents and conclusions are to be considered only within the framework of that time period.

246

principle to which the system has given rise are discussed briefly in the concluding section.[1]

2 Historical Background

The Palestinian territories, where the fiscal jurisdiction of the PNA now applies, came under Israel's rule in the wake of the 1967 Six-Day War. They are roughly the same areas that, according to the 1947 United Nations resolution, were to constitute the Palestinian Arab state to be established alongside of Israel. But in the intervening two decades, the West Bank came to be incorporated into the Hashemite Kingdom of Jordan, and the Gaza Strip was occupied by Egypt. During that period there were no economic contacts whatsoever between either of those territories and Israel.

The removal, shortly after the 1967 war, of most of the barriers to movements of people and goods between the Palestinian territories and Israel provides a textbook example of the effects of economic integration. The integration was not perfect: Israel tried to prevent the growing and importation of farm produce that would compete with its own highly protected agriculture, and it used administrative means to hamper the establishment of industrial plants that could compete with Israeli firms. But the negligible costs of transporting goods and the ease with which Palestinian workers could commute daily to work in Israel more than offset the remaining barriers. In fact, although it may come as a surprise to some in view of later developments, for over two decades there was practically complete free movement of people and goods between the Palestinian territories and Israel. The overall results were what economic theory would lead us to expect: Despite a Palestinian population increase of nearly 80% between 1968 and 1992, GNP per capita grew, on average, by 5.7% annually, in real terms, over those 24 years. Much of that growth represented income from work in Israel, which came to account for employment of more than one-third of the entire labor force of the West Bank and Gaza. But the GDP figures, which do not include income earned outside the economy, also registered a respectable 4.2% annual growth during that period, about 50% higher than that for Israel itself.

Part of that growth was due to expansion of exports to the newly accessible and relatively very large Israeli market. Israel came to absorb nearly three-quarters of all Palestinian merchandise exports, some of

---

[1] The actual developments were surveyed at the 52nd Congress of the International Institute of Public Finance by the Palestinian Vice Minister of Finance, Dr. Atef Alawneh (1996).

which took the form of subcontracting for Israeli firms selling in world markets. The remaining exports were to Jordan and, through Jordan, to the Persion Gulf states as well. But at the same time that it opened Israel's markets to Palestinian exports, Israeli occupation subjected Palestinian imports from abroad to Israeli customs tariffs and virtually restricted their points of entry to Israeli harbors and airports. As a result, as much as 90% of all imports into the West Bank and Gaza used to come either by way of Israel or from Israel itself.

Because the Palestinian territories exported large amounts of labor services, not only to Israel but also, for much of that period, to Jordan and the Gulf states, the Palestinian merchandise trade was in great imbalance. In particular, exports to Israel paid for only about one-third of imports from Israel, the rest being covered by proceeds from the export of labor services. This import surplus amounted to more than 25% of the GNP of the Palestinian territories.

Under Israeli rule, the economic role of government in the Palestinian territories was carried out by the Civil Administration (CivAd), a branch of the Israeli army set up especially for that purpose. The CivAd collected direct taxes and licensing fees according to the Jordanian and British colonial fiscal laws in force in the West Bank and the Gaza Strip, respectively, amended for inflation. It also collected purchase taxes, excises, and the general value-added tax (VAT) as they existed in Israel at the time, as well as customs duties, at Israeli rates, on the minuscule imports entering the West Bank directly through the Jordan bridges.[2] There being no customs boundaries between the Palestinian territories and Israel, customs duties on all other Palestinian imports from abroad were collected at their point of entry into Israel, the revenue from them accruing to the Israeli tax authorities, as did the revenue from all other indirect taxes on Palestinian purchases from Israel.

Abstracting from the question of ultimate tax incidence, fiscal legislation and practice usually regard indirect taxes as falling on the final consumer and assign the tax revenue correspondingly. Adopting the destination principle, rather than the origin principle, as the basis for taxation, most countries tax imports but exempt exports from domestic taxes. Because the CivAd collected all taxes in the Palestinian territories, it also received the revenue from taxes on purchases made there by Israelis. But because of the great trade imbalance vis-à-vis Israel, those sums were

---

[2] A tacit agreement between Jordanian and Israeli authorities, in the wake of the 1967 war, kept the bridges over the Jordan River open to movements of Palestinians from the West Bank and to Palestinian exports, mainly of agricultural produce, despite the official state of hostilities between the two countries that existed until 1994.

greatly outweighed by the revenue from indirect taxes and customs duties on Palestinian purchases from Israel and on their imports entering through it, which went to the Israeli fiscus, rather than to the CivAd fiscus in the Palestinian territories.[3] If we consider, as a first approximation, that the annual import surplus with Israel during the past decade fell in the range of $600–900 million U.S., then at a tax rate of 17%, the VAT revenues alone lost by the CivAd amounted to $100–150 million each year. Compared with a total CivAd annual budget of just over $300 million, that was a very large sum, the lack of which greatly restricted its operations. Not surprisingly, the appropriation of those and similar tax revenues by the Israeli treasury was a sore point not only with the Palestinian public but also with the CivAd, which pressed to obtain them for its own budget but succeeded ultimately in receiving only the taxes paid on Palestinian imports of motor vehicles.[4]

Beyond the issue of the customs and VAT revenues denied to the Palestinian territories, there was also the issue of the taxes on the wages of Palestinians employed in Israel. Those consisted of a levy imposed on both employee and employer, equivalent to the Israeli national-insurance (social-security) payments, and of income taxes deducted at source. The former was originally introduced to reduce the incentive for Israeli employers to prefer Palestinian workers to Israeli workers. But because Palestinian workers were not residents of Israel, they were eligible for only a small fraction of the social-security benefits, so that most of the levy constituted an employment tax.[5] Unlike the proceeds from that levy, the revenues from income taxes deducted at source seem to have been credited to the CivAd's budget, in the form of a subvention from the Israeli treasury. However, in the absence of fiscal transparency

---

[3] It should be emphasized that the "Civil Administration" was an Israeli military organ, entrusted with the role of looking after the needs of the civil population in the Palestinian territories occupied by Israel as a result of the 1967 war, and had a completely independent budget.

[4] For a detailed attempt to estimate the tax revenue thus denied the Palestinian territories, see Hamed and Shaban (1993). Being, however, mainly intent on proving that the Israeli occupation immiserized the West Bank and Gaza, their estimates tended to be very much upward biased. More importantly, perhaps, they failed to realize that the national accounts for these territories being derived from the expenditure side, they already netted out the taxes retained by Israel. Had these taxes been credited to the Palestinian territories, the GNP and GDP estimates there would have been higher than those actually reported. See also World Bank (1993) and Hausman and Karasik (1993).

[5] It could be argued that with the supply of Palestinian labor in Israel in those years being almost infinitely elastic at a wage just above that prevailing in the West Bank and Gaza, any employment tax fell in full on the Israeli employer.

regarding these payments, it has been impossible to ascertain whether or not they were indeed transferred in full.

Because it bears on governmental ability to resort to inflationary financing, it should be pointed out that the Palestinian territories did not have (and still do not have) their own currency (although the issue of a special currency had been briefly considered at the time those territories first came under Israeli rule). Formally, the New Israeli Sheqel (NIS) circulated alongside the Jordanian dinar (JD) in the West Bank and, along with the Egyptian pound (E£), in Gaza. In practice, especially in the wake of the Israeli runaway inflation of the early 1980s, the NIS came to be used as the main medium of exchange, while the JD and (following the JD's collapse in 1988) increasingly the U.S. dollar served as units of account, as stores of value, and as means of deferred payments.

3   The Fiscal Aspects of a Common Customs Envelope

The rules governing the current fiscal relationships between Israel and the PNA are spelled out in the economic protocol signed by Israel and the Palestine Liberation Organization (PLO) in 1994 as part of the agreement setting up the PNA. Formally, the protocol applied only to the 5-year transition period during which a permanent settlement of the issues between the two sides was to be negotiated. However, it was hoped that the arrangements spelled out in the protocol would also provide the basis for an economic relationship that would hold after its termination.[6]

Those arrangements had to accommodate several conflicting demands: On the Palestinian side, there was the wish, only natural under the circumstances, to distance themselves politically and administratively, as much as possible, from Israel; at the same time, they wanted to retain and even widen their access to Israel's markets. On the other hand, Israel, for external and internal political reasons, wanted to avoid giving the PNA a formal territorial frontier that might prejudice a final settlement; but at the same time it sought to prevent undermining thereby its own fiscal regime, which could occur in the absence of borders. The outcome was an agreement on arrangements closely resembling a customs union. It was intended to ensure that there would be no economic obstacles to free movement of goods between the Palestinian territories and Israel, except for a small number of farm products, to which

---

[6] See "Protocol on Economic Relations between the Government of the State of Israel and the P.L.O. Representing the Palestinian People," signed in Paris, April 29, 1994. See State of Israel (1995) and ISEPME (1994).

restrictive quotas (to be gradually relaxed until completely phased out by the end of a 4-year adjustment period) were temporarily to apply.[7]

Most of the other provisions of the economic protocol followed from that basic premise. In evaluating them, it must be remembered that they were intended to provide for a relationship between an established political and administrative entity and an entity that had not yet come into existence. Insofar as fiscal arrangements were concerned, the protocol gave the PNA a completely free hand in determining those parts of its tax regime that could be expected to have little or no direct diversionary effect on the Israeli economy. But it did spell out very close coordination, almost identity, for the two systems in those areas where such effects seemed unavoidable in its absence.[8]

Differences in rates of indirect taxation – customs duties in particular – are inconsistent with the free movement of goods between two tax jurisdictions. An attempt to maintain different customs tariffs will result in imports being rerouted through the jurisdiction with the lower duty, thereby vitiating, in effect, the higher of the two tariffs. Admittedly, separate tariffs can be maintained if free movement is restricted to only domestic production, as is the case in free-trade-area (FTA) agreements. But an FTA arrangement requires that even shipments of exempt goods be inspected at the border, if only to verify their right to pass freely, and therefore it depends crucially on the existence of an economic border. Small economies may also find it difficult to fulfill the local value-added-content condition for goods to qualify as having been produced domestically.

Because of political sensitivities on both sides, no formal customs union could be concluded in the present case. But what was agreed upon did have the main feature of such a union: a common external tariff. Excluded from that common customs envelope were certain goods whose untaxed gravitation from one jurisdiction to the other was believed to be preventable even in the absence of economic borders. They included motor vehicles, for which registration provides a notional border, allowing customs to be collected when ownership, rather than the good itself, passes across jurisdictions. The other exemptions were for

---

[7] Although it was already clear at the time that the provisions of the economic agreement would be subservient to security considerations, no one seems to have envisaged then that the rise in violence against civilians in Israel would lead to the present severe restrictions on the movements of Palestinians and Palestinian vehicles, restrictions that play havoc with the whole economic relationship between the Palestinian territories and Israel.

[8] The following discussion draws on my earlier work (Kleiman, 1994). See also Elmusa and El-Jafari (1995).

limited quantities of certain specified imports from Arab countries that the PNA wished to make available at low cost to its public and which it expected to be willing and able to prevent from finding their way onto the Israeli market. In one case, that of gasoline, the exemption was conditional on the price to consumers in the Palestinian territories not falling short of that in Israel by more than a certain stipulated margin (15%).

For the rest, the tariffs applying in the areas under the PNA's tax jurisdiction were to be the same as those in Israel. Because effective tariffs and thus the protection provided for industries are functions not only of the formal tariff rates but also of the commodity-classification system and the valuation methods used for customs purposes, those as well had to be the same. It may be of historical interest to point out that the various bodies that had considered the establishment of two national states in the area under discussion all recommended similar arrangements, ranging from the "common tariff over the widest possible range of imported articles" of the 1937 British Royal Commission on Palestine to the "customs union with a joint currency system" of the partition plan adopted by the United Nations in 1947.[9] The decision-sharing and revenue-allocation questions that such a system invariably raises will be considered in Sections 4 and 5.

Free passage of goods across fiscal jurisdictions, such as was envisioned in the Israeli-Palestinian economic agreement, makes it possible to circumvent not only the higher customs tariff but also other higher indirect taxes, whether on imports or on domestic production; hence the requirement that taxes be the same in both jurisdictions. The only exception was the VAT. To prevent what would have amounted to double taxation, the VAT paid to either jurisdiction was made deductible from the VAT owed to the other. That also meant that with the VAT being a multistage sales tax, any tax savings achieved by purchasing inputs in the lower-tax jurisdiction would be corrected for by a higher effective tax rate being paid at the following stage.

To illustrate, consider an Israeli firm selling goods at a pre-tax value of NIS 1,000, of which NIS 600 represents the pre-tax value of purchased inputs, and the rest is value added in processing them. At the Israeli VAT rate of 17%, that firm would have paid, inclusive of the tax, NIS 702 for its inputs and would have sold its output at a gross price of NIS 1,170. It would owe the Israeli treasury NIS 68, the difference between the VAT collected (NIS 170) and paid (NIS 102) by it, equal to

---

[9] See RCP (1937) and United Nations Resolution 181 (II) of November 29, 1947 (part D), respectively.

the VAT at that rate on the value added by the firm. But suppose that the VAT rate under the PNA was only 10%. The firm could then save NIS 42 by purchasing its inputs in the West Bank or in Gaza, but it would be able to offset only NIS 60 from the VAT of NIS 170 it would collect on its own sales. Thus it would end up paying a VAT of NIS 128 on a value added of NIS 400 (i.e., at an effective rate of no less than 32%).[10]

But whereas business firms would therefore have no incentive to divert their purchases to a lower-VAT jurisdiction, final consumers certainly would. Worldwide, anecdotal evidence abounds of consumers traveling to purchase heavily taxed goods, such as alcohol, tobacco, and gasoline, in neighboring EU countries or in U.S. states where the rates of the VAT or the sales taxes rates are lower. The savings thus achieved depend on the size of the tax differential and on the amount spent on these items. Aside from the mere wish to get the better of the authorities, the savings must be balanced against the pecuniary and nonpecuniary costs of the extra travel and transportation involved, which usually are prohibitively high, except for residents of border areas.

In the present case, however, the whole country constitutes a border area. Current closures and security checks apart, most consumers in the Palestinian territories and in Israel probably are no more than half an hour's drive away from the nearest shopping center in the other jurisdiction. Even with the same VAT rate applying to both parties, Israeli consumers used to shop in the West Bank and Gaza to take advantage of the lower nontradable component of prices there, a consequence of the lower levels of Palestinian incomes.[11] At the same time, however, considerable price differentials were known to exist within individual Israeli cities, suggesting that for many consumers even minimal travel distances, when combined with social or ethnic divisions and with the costs of information, posed objective or psychic barriers sufficiently high to outweigh the potential price savings. In light of a perhaps unduly conservative assessment of those barriers, the PNA was given with the discretion to set its VAT rate below the Israeli rate, but by no more than 2 percentage points. Because of the presumption that the PNA would wish to

---

[10] By the same token, firms purchasing their inputs in the higher-rate jurisdiction would end up paying VAT on the value added by them at a rate below that applying to their sales. It is tacitly assumed here that the two tax authorities allow the mutual deductions of VAT paid to each other from the firms' tax liabilities. Otherwise, the tax due by the firm in the present example would have been NIS 170, which on a value added of NIS 400 would constitute a tax of 42.5%.

[11] They also shopped for VAT-exempt fruits and vegetables, whose prices in the Palestinian territories were kept artificially low by the restrictions on their commercial importation to Israel.

maintain tax rates lower than those prevailing in Israel, the question of a similar restriction in the opposite case was never raised, that is, of the VAT rate in Israel falling below the Palestinian rate.

Differences in rates and procedures for direct taxes can also affect the location of economic activity, attracting firms to set up business where, for example, corporate taxes are lower. Unlike the case of customs duties and indirect taxes, however, here there exists a notional border in the form of the nationality or residence of the individual recipient or the site of corporate registration. A tax jurisdiction can therefore counteract any diversionary effects of direct taxation by unilateral action aimed at its own citizens or residents. Consequently, the common customs envelope did not restrict either side in its direct taxation.

4   The Decision-Sharing Quandary

An agreement to maintain customs tariffs that were to be overwhelmingly common between the two parties inevitably raised the question of who was to make the decisions regarding changes in those tariffs. In principle, several solutions were possible, most of which, however, would not have been applicable to the present case.

One seemingly reasonable possibility was a bilateral commission or committee. But that would only have shifted the question one stage, becoming a question of how decisions in such a committee were to be reached. Given the potential conflicts of interest resulting from the differences in size and in economic development between the two parties in question, any arrangement that would have given them equal votes in such a committee would have invited a stalement on any substantive issue.

Any non-parity arrangement, on the other hand, would have given the majority party unilateral discretion in its decisions. Such, in fact, had been the case in the 1922 customs union between Belgium and Luxembourg, the forerunner of Benelux, from which the European Union may be said to have ultimately evolved. With the economic size of Luxembourg at the time, relative to that of Belgium (probably similar to the size of the Palestinian economy relative to that of Israel in 1994), all decision-making was left in Belgian hands (Meade, 1956). But the history of Israeli-Palestinian relationships made such an arrangement unacceptable to the Palestinians, unless accompanied by some built-in safeguards against its misuse by Israel.

That, as well as the avoidance of stalemates, could have been resolved by outside arbitration. Israel, however, had always shunned letting any third party have the final say either in its domestic affairs or in its relations with others. It also may have feared that, in view in the disparity in economic sizes, an arbiter would tend to side with the Palestinians, who, for the same reason, tended to favor the arbitration idea. In fact, the Benelux experience suggested that arbitration might be a very cumbersome tool for settling customs-union disputes.[12]

Economic theory seems to provide a neat and elegant solution to those problems, in the form of the compensation principle: If a change desired by one party damages the other, let it compensate the injured party sufficiently to make it worthwhile for the latter to agree to the proposed change; alternatively, let the party to be damaged bribe the other party sufficiently to make it worth its while to desist from making the change (which would lead to the same decisions but to a different distributional outcome). But this again would only have shifted the stage at which the question had to be addressed – in that case of how and by whom such potential damages were to be assessed. In the absence of satisfactory answers to those questions, the issue of compensation remains unresolved, inviting either stalemating or even blackmailing on the part of the potentially injured party.[13]

The existing agreement contains two provisions intended to mitigate the severity of the problem. One is the previously mentioned exemption, whereby limited quantities of certain goods imported from Arab countries are exempt from Israeli customs duties and standards. Looked at obversely, this means that the common tariffs apply to only a part (even though a large part) of Palestinian imports. That makes the arrangement, at least in principle, something of a hybrid between a customs union and an FTA agreement.

The other provision is the assignment to the Palestinians of an exclusive right to set the joint common tariff rates on a number of goods, predominantly machinery and equipment for agriculture and industry. Formally, this pertains only to imports into the areas under the PNA's jurisdiction. But in practice it requires Palestinian assent to any increase in the tariffs on importation of such goods to Israel, and it vests the

---

[12] The Benelux agreement required the arbiter to be fluent in the languages of both countries, but to be a citizen of neither, and to be familiar with the industry or trade to which the case pertained. On the first occasion in which the need for arbitration arose, it took considerable time to find an individual who fulfilled those conditions. Having spent considerable time studying the case, the arbiter then passed away before resolving the case. The Benelux countries never resorted to arbitration again, opting instead for consensual decision-making (Meade et al., 1962).

[13] Although compensation for fiscal loss alone probably could be assessed on the basis of tax-revenue data for the periods before and after the change.

power to unilaterally lower them in the PNA, with Israel being forced to follow suit if it is unwilling to see its imports rerouted through the Palestinian territories.[14]

Thus the agreement between Israel and the PNA does not solve the question of power-sharing in regard to decisions affecting the customs union. However, instead of allocating power over all decisions between the two parties, it divides the decision-making into spheres wherein one side or the other enjoys full discretion. It does so on a limited scale only, but the principle itself might be worth further investigation, and it may well play a role in future regional arrangements between the PNA and Israel, and possibly other partners as well.[15]

5   Revenue Clearance and Revenue Sharing

Under a customs union, customs duties are collected at the point of entry, irrespective of the final destination of the goods within the union. Thus both of the parties to the union may be collecting duties on imports destined for the other party. Unless the customs revenues from such transjurisdictional imports are more or less equal, some mechanism or formula for revenue allocation must be devised if one of the parties is not to end up subsidizing the other. This problem is especially acute in the present case, as most Palestinian imports from the rest of the world reach the Palestinian territories through Israeli harbors and airports, and a large share of them will continue to do so even if a harbor and an airport are constructed in the Gaza Strip.

A similar problem arises with respect to other indirect taxes, in particular, the VAT, if the convention is upheld that these are taxes on the ultimate consumer.[16] In the absence of economic borders, the VAT on transactions across the tax-jurisdiction line is collected, in practice, according to the origin principle, rather than to the more generally accepted destination principle. As described in Section 2, because of the

---

[14] Those were the goods on the so-called list B of the Paris protocol. The quantities of certain goods intended for domestic Palestinian use that could be imported free of Israeli customs duties were specified in lists A1 and A2 there.

[15] A noneconomist friend commented that this principle has long been followed in his household, where the responsibility for furnishing and decorating different rooms was divided by agreement between the spouses. With their preferences differing widely, he said, they would soon have reached a stalemate had they to agree on decorating any or all of them, and the place would have remained unfurnished.

[16] As we well know, this convention is only rarely supported in full by tax-incidence analysis. Furthermore, if the VAT is to be regarded, as its name implies, as a tax on value added in production, then its revenues should fall to the tax jurisdiction in which production takes place, rather than to the one in which the final products are consumed.

large import surplus of the Palestinian territories vis-à-vis Israel, the VAT revenue collected by the Israeli fiscus on Palestinian purchases from Israel greatly exceeds that collected by the Palestinian fiscus on Israeli purchases from the territories under the PNA's tax jurisdiction. Given the expected difficulties of collecting direct taxes in a low-income economy, the importance of those revenues in financing the PNA's budget necessitated some system for their retrieval.

Revenue-sharing or rebate schemes can be constructed on either of two alternative principles: that of some general formula, or that of actual revenue clearance. Whereas the former has the advantage of administrative simplicity, it also raises questions of the formula's derivation and of its adjustment over time. In the case of the VAT, for example, the simple formula for applying the Israeli VAT rate to the Palestinian import surplus (used in Section 2 as a first approximation for estimating the net excess of Palestinian VAT payments to the Israeli exchequer) fails to take into consideration the composition of trade. With VAT-exempt fruits and vegetables constituting a larger share of Palestinian exports to Israel than of imports from Israel, such a formula probably would overestimate the VAT revenue on Israeli purchases accruing to the PNA, consequently underestimating the sum to be rebated to it from Israel. More detailed formulas, on the other hand, would require frequent updating and renegotiations.

Consequently, the general-formula approach has been forgone in favor of what may be called the bookkeeping approach of revenue clearance on the basis of actual payments made. In the case of customs duties and other levies such as purchase taxes collected on imports brought in through Israel, this requires that their ultimate destination be identified. Insofar as imports of goods for final use are concerned, such information should be readily available from the computerized customs-clearance system operated by the Israeli customs authorities. In practice, however, goods destined for the Palestinian territories often are brought in by Israeli importers, making it difficult if not outright impossible to determine their ultimate destination simply by inspecting the relevant shipping documents. This applies, of course, even more strongly to imported raw materials and other inputs used in the production of goods ultimately exported to the Palestinian territories. But with most raw materials not subject to customs duties in Israel, the amount of customs revenue lost to the PNA on this account is probably negligible.

In contrast, the very mechanism of the VAT system lends itself easily to the clearance of revenues from the VAT collected on all Palestinian purchases from Israel (and Israeli purchases from the Palestinian territories), except for those made by final consumers. As mentioned in earlier sections, because the VAT is a multistage sales or purchase tax, it is based on the principle of taxes paid on inputs being rebated from the tax liability of the seller of the product. To prevent double taxation, which would have had an extremely detrimental effect on the trade between them, each of the two parties agreed to recognize for this purpose the VAT payments made to the other's tax authority. The evidence required by each tax authority for this purpose (a VAT invoice issued by the seller under the other tax jurisdiction) also provides the necessary documentation for claiming this sum for itself. Thus the documentation submitted to the Palestinian tax authority by Palestinian firms claiming a rebate for VAT paid on inputs purchased in Israel provides, at the same time, the evidence needed for retrieving that money from the Israeli exchequer, and vice versa.

Such a mechanism allows each side to recoup from the other sums it has allowed firms under its jurisdiction to deduct from their VAT liabilities. It provides each side with an incentive to widen the effective coverage of the tax, even if the resultant net revenue collected domestically is marginal, because by doing so it also increases the sums it retrieves from the other side. A "virtuous cycle" is thereby created, the elasticity of total revenues with respect to domestic VAT collection exceeding unity.

Final consumers, on the other hand, are not eligible for VAT rebates by either tax authority. To obtain the necessary evidence, the respective tax authorities would have to offer some compensation to consumers for them to send in the receipts for the VAT paid on their purchases from vendors under the other's jurisdiction. A trade in such receipts could not, then, be counted out. Unlike the case of inputs, however, where a sheqel of VAT revenue claimed from the other side represents a sheqel of VAT forgone in domestic VAT revenues, in the case of final purchases there is no safeguard against either side trying to submit as many VAT receipts as possible, irrespective of their provenance. Because of this, as well as the fact that VAT payments on purchases by final consumers consist of very many small transactions and probably are roughly balanced, they are not credited to their respective tax authorities.[17]

It should be pointed out that, unlike the case of customs and of purchase taxes on imports, the inherent nature of the VAT and of the VAT clearance system results in the Palestinian tax authorities ultimately receiving all the VAT paid, directly and indirectly, from imported inputs onward, on goods ultimately purchased in Israel by Palestinian firms. A numerical example illustrating this point is provided in the Appendix.

---

[17] With the exception of the VAT paid on purchases in Israel by the PNA itself.

There are also tax-clearance arrangements with respect to payroll taxes on the wages of Palestinians employed in Israel. Insofar as the income taxes deducted at source from those wages are concerned, the question arises whether they should accrue to the tax jurisdiction in which the workers reside or to the tax jurisdiction where the taxed income was earned. The general argument in favor of the latter procedure is as follows: It is the fiscal authority under which the income in question is produced that finances the infrastructure and services that make production possible. It also provides much of the infrastructure used and the social services consumed by workers employed outside their areas of residence. Unlike the case of other "guest workers," however, the overwhelming majority of the Palestinians employed in Israel used to commute to work daily, even in the days when no attempt was made to prevent them from staying overnight in Israel (Kleiman, 1992).

With the services test clearly favoring the tax jurisdiction in which these workers reside, insofar as the social services consumed by them are concerned, the revenues from income taxes on their earnings have to be split in some way between that jurisdiction and the tax jurisdiction in which the income they earned was generated. The actual proportions agreed on (75% to the PNA and 25% to Israel), although arbitrary, reflect recognition of this fact.

Finally, a clearance arrangement also had to be made with respect to the social-security taxes that (as described in Section 2) were levied on the wages of Palestinians employed in Israel, in order to equalize the cost of their employment with that of Israeli workers. Here again the services test was followed. Payments for benefits to which these workers are eligible aside, all the social-security-equalization levies collected from both employers and employees were to be transferred to the PNA to provide social benefits or welfare services to these workers.

6　　Some Remaining Problems

As initially agreed, the relationship between Israel and the Palestinian territories under the PNA was to closely approximate a customs union. In fact, with restrictions on the importation of farm produce from the West Bank and Gaza into Israel relaxed, and soon to be phased out completely, and with the licensing of industrial plants there no longer under Israeli jurisdiction, the economic integration between the Palestinian territories and Israel would hold even at a time when they were becoming politically separated. Political separation, however, also means separately decided and separately managed budgets to serve the two populations.

Thus, economic integration was to be accompanied by fiscal separation, notwithstanding the considerable fiscal coordination required.

The arrangements set up for that purpose combined a high degree of fiscal uniformity (particularly in customs duties and other indirect taxation) with a system of tax rebates and tax clearances intended to apportion revenues to the appropriate tax authority, irrespective of which one collected it.

Although the operation of these arrangements in practice falls outside the scope of this study, it may be worthwhile to point out some of the problems encountered in their implementation.[18] An increase in violence against Israeli civilians led to the imposition of severe restrictions on movements of people, vehicles, and goods from the Palestinian territories into Israel, culminating in the lengthy closure of 1996. A de-facto security border was established between the Gaza Strip and Israel, with a somewhat more porous one in the West Bank. That could not but play havoc with much of the notion of economic integration, although considerably more could have been done to reduce its disruptive effects on economic flows.

The general economic effects of those developments aside, the fiscal arrangements themselves seem to be operating quite satisfactorily. The main exception, probably, is their failure to deal adequately with taxes (other than the VAT) on the foreign-import component of goods purchased from Israel. The original agreement stipulated that revenues from customs and other import duties, collected on goods destined for the area under Palestinian jurisdiction were to be transferred to the PNA. However, brand-name goods are often imported by Israeli firms acting as the sole, exclusive agents of the foreign producers. Such importers enjoy a certain monopoly position in the Israeli market, as well as in the Palestinian market, that they are not keen to relinquish, and their foreign suppliers also prefer to be thus represented.[19] As a result, the customs on many high-duty final consumer goods (as well as on the already mentioned generally exempt or low-duty raw materials) are not credited to the Palestinian tax authority. This led the PNA to try to restrict their entry to goods imported solely by Palestinian importers.

Problems have also arisen regarding rebatement of excise taxes to the PNA. The actual sums of excise and purchase taxes paid by Palestinians

---

[18] For a description and analysis of the actual operation of the fiscal arrangements between the PNA and Israel, see Alawneh (1996).

[19] Besides increasing the costs of communication etc., the simultaneous operation of more than one representative or importer also reduces the readiness of any of them to advertise the product (rather than their own agencies).

on fuel or on other centrally supplied goods are easily identifiable. But attempts to ascribe to the PNA its share of all sales made in Israel for goods such as, say, watches and cosmetics have met with considerable difficulties.

On the other hand, what may have seemed the most complicated part of the revenue-clearance mechanism, that pertaining to the VAT, has turned out to operate most robustly. After some initial difficulties, due in part to delays in passing the Israeli legislation that would allow the rebating of tax revenues collected in Israel, and attempts by some Israeli businesses to claim rebates on the basis of false VAT invoices from phantom suppliers in the Palestinian tax jurisdiction, the system has proved to operate smoothly. At this early stage of the PNA's existence, its financial transactions are not yet clearly accounted for in full. But the figures made public thus far indicate that the tax revenues rebated by Israel amounted to almost two-thirds, if not more, of the total budgetary revenue of the PNA in 1996. Indeed, from the point of view of the PNA, perhaps the greates of advantage of its fiscal arrangements with Israel is the convenience of having much of its tax revenue collected by others, freeing it of the administrative burden and of the social and political opprobrium usually associated with tax collection in a newly established political entity.

APPENDIX: THE VAT-CLEARANCE CALCULATION

Consider a three-stage import-and-production process, involving two firms, I and II, belonging to two separate tax jurisdictions, A and B, respectively, with $100 of value added at each stage. The same rate of 17% is assumed to apply under both jurisdictions. The transactions and the ensuing tax payments are summarized in Table 11.1.

In the first stage, firm I imports $100 worth of inputs from, say, the United States and pays the VAT due on importation: $17 to the treasury of jurisdiction A. Having processed those inputs, it proceeds, in the second stage, to sell its product at double the net, pre-tax cost of the imported inputs to firm II in jurisdiction B. According to the usual VAT procedure, it also collects from Firm II the sum of $34 in VAT, but pays only the difference between the VAT collected and that incurred on its inputs, equaling $17, to A's tax authority. But together with the $17 collected on the imports, the A authority receives the full $34 of VAT on the final sale.

In the third stage, firm II, having processed its purchase from firm I further, sells it to final consumers in its own tax jurisdiction for the net, pre-tax sum of $300, collecting from them another $51 in VAT. But after

Table 11.1. Schematic VAT rebate and remittance system

					Price	Jurisdiction A			Jurisdiction B		
Step	Firm	Jurisdiction	Transaction	From or to	net of tax	Gross tax	Rebate	Net tax	Gross tax	Rebate	Net tax
(1)	I	A	imports	US	100	17	—	17			
(2)	I	A	sells	B	200	34	-17	17			
(2a)[a]	II	B	buys	A	200	34					
(3)	II	B	sells	B	300	—	—	—	51	-34	17
(4)		A	remits	B		—		-34			34
Net revenue	B							0			51

[a]Stage (2a) is the obverse of stage 2, as seen from jurisdiction B.

deducting the VAT it paid on the inputs it bought from I, it passes only $17 to the tax authority of jurisdiction B. Then, B's tax authority presents A's tax authority with the evidence of the VAT invoices presented to it by firm II, and B receives from A $34 under the tax-clearance arrangement.

In the final account, B's tax authority has received revenues of $51, equal to the full VAT paid by its final consumers of these goods. Of this, $17 has been paid by firm II, and $34 has been recouped from jurisdiction A under the tax-clearance arrangements.

REFERENCES

Alawneh, A. (1996). A fiscal system for a new political entity: the case of the Palestinian National Authority. Paper presented at the plenary session of the 52nd Congress of the International Institute of Public Finance, Tel Aviv, August 26–29.

Elmusa, S., and El-Jafari, M. (1995). Power and trade: the Israeli Palestinian economic protocol. *Journal of Palestinian Studies* 24:20–31.

Hamed, O., and Shaban, R. A. (1993). One-sided customs and monetary union: the case of the West Bank and Gaza Strip under Israeli occupation. In: *The Economics of Middle East Peace*, eds. D. Rodrik and E. Tuma, pp. 112–48. Massachusetts Institute of Technology Press.

Hausman, L. J., and Karasik, A. D. (eds.) (1993). *Securing Peace in the Middle East: Project on Economic Transition*. Cambridge, MA: Harvard University Institute for Social and Economic Policy in the Middle East.

ISEPME (1994). *Near East Economic Progress Report*, no. 2. Institute for Social and Economic Policy in the Middle East, Harvard University. Cambridge, MA: Harvard University Press.

Kleiman, E. (1992). The flow of labour services from the West Bank and Gaza to Israel. Department of Economics working paper 260, The Hebrew University of Jerusalem.

Kleiman, E. (1994). The economic provisions of the agreement between Israel and the PLO. *Israel Law Review* 28:347–73.

Meade, J. E. (1956). *The Belgium-Luxembourg Economic Union, 1921–1939*. Essays in International Finance, no. 25, Princeton University Press.

Meade, J. E., Lisner, H. H., and Wells, S. J. (1962). *Case Studies in European Economic Union*. Oxford University Press.

RCP (1937). *Report of the Royal Commission on Palestine*. Cmd. 5479. London: HMSO.

State of Israel (1995). Agreement on the Gaza Strip and the Jericho area. *Rashumot: Kitvei Amana (Official Gazette: Treaties)* (Jerusalem: Government Printer) 32:124–214.

World Bank (1993). *Developing the Occupied Territories: An Investment in Peace. Vol. II: The Economy*. Washington, DC: World Bank.

PART VI

Political-Economy Aspects
of International Tax Competition

CHAPTER 12

Factor Taxation, Income Distribution, and Capital-Market Integration

Andreas Haufler

1   Introduction

Given the ongoing rapid integration of world capital markets and the expected fierce competition for internationally mobile capital, there have been surprisingly few changes in the overall tax treatment of capital income since the 1980s. Although many countries have reduced statutory tax rates on corporate and private capital income, tax bases have simultaneously been broadened, leading to only very moderate decreases in effective capital-tax rates for the Organization for Economic Cooperation and Development (OECD) average. Furthermore, there is no clear evidence that corporate taxes have converged over the years as a result of market forces. For the European Union (EU), the Ruding report (CEC, 1992, p. 12) states that most of the observed convergence has been "attributable to downward convergence of interest and inflation rates rather than deliberate action on the part of tax authorities." Controlling for these factors, the cost of capital has actually risen in a number of EU countries, such as Denmark, Italy, The Netherlands, Spain, and the United Kingdom (CEC, 1992, table 8.19). A recent update that also incorporates other taxes (CEC, 1996) shows a somewhat clearer shift from capital to labor taxation in the EU average, but also reports exceptions to that general trend.

These mixed empirical findings contrast with the strong indication from economic theory that if the residence principle cannot be effec-

An earlier version of this study was published in 1997 in the *Scandinavian Journal of Economics* 99:425–46. I have benefited greatly from comments and suggestions by Noel Edelson (my session chairman at the IIPF conference in Tel Aviv), Harry Huizinga, Martin Kolmar, Sajal Lahiri, Arjan Lejour, Søren Bo Nielsen, Assaf Razin, Guttorm Schjelderup, Günther Schulze, Peter Birch Sørensen, and Ian Wooton. Financial support through the European Union's HCM Network Program and the Ludwig-Boltzmann Institut (Wien) is gratefully acknowledged.

tively enforced worldwide and if capital is perfectly mobile internationally, it is optimal for small countries to completely exempt capital income from taxes (Gordon, 1986; Razin and Sadka, 1991; Bucovetsky and Wilson, 1991). The conflict is only partially resolved by empirical studies indicating relatively low degrees of international capital mobility (Gordon and Bovenberg, 1996). Although that may explain why capital taxes do not fall to zero, one would still expect an unambiguous downward trend in tax rates as market integration proceeds. This applies in particular to Europe, where most obstacles to international capital flows have been removed as part of the internal-market program and where the scheduled monetary union is expected to further lower the extra costs and risks associated with international investments.[1]

Most of the literature on competition over capital taxes has focused on one-consumer models in which the representative agent owns all factors of production. One possible explanation for the observed rigidity of tax rates on capital may therefore be a distributional motive. Persson and Tabellini (1992) used an endowment model in which a positive tax rate on capital was levied for redistributive purposes, with the median voter being in favor of income redistribution via that tax. In their model, the voting majority anticipates a process of downward tax competition and thus elects a more redistributive government to partly offset that effect. Nevertheless, the model still predicts a general reduction in the level of capital taxation as a result of closer capital-market integration and a convergence of tax rates for different countries.

The interaction between efficiency and the distributional aspects of capital taxation has been taken up in recent studies by Lopez, Marchand, and Pestieau (1996), Huizinga and Nielsen (1997b), and Bjerksund and Schjelderup (1997). However, none of those studies analyzed the effects of closer capital-market integration, and thus there is as yet no theoretical model that could explain the divergent developments in capital taxation observed during the past decade.

This study attempts to contribute to this new field of research by analyzing the effects of capital-market integration in a two-country, two-class model of capital-tax competition. Our model differs from the Persson and Tabellini analysis in two main respects. First, production is modeled explicitly, and governments solve a conventional optimal-tax problem, choosing between a wage tax and a source tax on capital in order to meet a fixed revenue constraint. This model allows direct com-

---

[1] Other arguments for positive source taxes on capital have also been advanced in the literature. These include the role of corporate income taxes as a backstop for wage taxation (Gordon and MacKie-Mason, 1995) and as an indirect way of taxing pure profits (Huizinga and Nielsen, 1997a).

parisons of our results and those obtained in representative-agent models when the government has multiple tax instruments at its disposal. Second, and more important for our central result, we employ an alternative model of the political equilibrium by assuming that the government maximizes a political-support function where workers and capitalists are the only two interest groups.

In this model, the effects of capital-market integration on the distribution of factor incomes are exactly opposed for the capital exporter and the capital importer. We show that, in contrast to the findings of Persson and Tabellini, distributional effects can then lead to a capital-tax increase in the exporting country and to diverging rates of capital taxation. Finally, we briefly compare our results to some new findings in the parallel literature on tax-financed social-insurance schemes (Lejour and Verbon, 1996; Gabszewicz and van Ypersele, 1996).

The remainder of this chapter is organized as follows: Section 2 describes the model and the optimal-tax problem faced by each country's government. The properties of the Nash equilibrium in capital-tax rates are analyzed in Section 3. The main results of the study are in Section 4, which derives the effects of capital-market integration on optimal tax policy in each of the trading countries. Section 5 concludes the discussion.

2 The Model

The analysis is based on a static model of capital-tax competition between two countries that produce a homogeneous output using internationally mobile capital and internationally immobile labor. This model is extended to allow for mobility costs, and we distinguish between two income groups, workers and capitalists, in each country. Individuals in each group are homogeneous, and workers supply only labor, whereas capital owners do not work.[2] Countries are endowed with fixed amounts of labor and capital. All endowments are normalized to unity and hence are equal across countries.

Governments have two tax instruments at their disposal: a wage tax and a source tax on capital. The incorporation of residence-based taxes on capital (i.e., taxes on savings) would require a two-period framework

---

[2] Taken literally, this rigid class structure clearly is not justified from an empirical perspective, nor from a life-cycle-savings approach. However, all that is needed in our model is that, for example, a labor tax fall relatively more heavily on one income group ("the poor") than on the other ("the rich"). The assumption that the second group earns no labor income at all is then merely a simplifying device that does not qualitatively affect our results.

and thus is excluded from this analysis. This can be justified by arguing that there is no international cooperation to report foreign earnings to the investor's country of residence. Therefore, residence-based taxes can always be fully evaded, and taxation at source represents the only way of taxing capital income. In the following, we first describe the production relationships and international arbitrage in the capital market and then turn to the optimal-tax problem faced by each country's government.

A standard assumption in the literature on capital-tax competition is that production functions are identical across countries. Furthermore, in the present context there is little to be gained from generalizing with respect to the underlying production structure. Following Bucovetsky (1991), we therefore assume a quadratic technology, which leads to several convenient simplifications and allows us to focus more closely on the issues specific to our two-class model. Denoting countries by subscripted numbers $i \in \{1, 2\}$, these assumptions imply

$$f(k_i, 1) = (a - bk_i)k_i \ \forall \ i \in \{1, 2\} \qquad (a > 0, \ b > 0)$$

where the input of labor is fixed at unity, and k_i is the amount of capital used in each region (and is equal to the capital–labor ratio). Assuming that the technology parameter a is sufficiently large relative to b, the quadratic production function exhibits the usual property of a positive but falling marginal productivity of capital:

$$f' = a - 2bk_i > 0, \qquad f'' = -2b < 0 \qquad (12.1)$$

With the capital endowment of each country normalized to unity, the full-employment condition for this factor is

$$k_1 + k_2 = 2 \qquad (12.2)$$

Capital exports are subject to convex transaction costs that reflect all of the extra complications of foreign operations, such as additional information requirements and differing regulations across countries. These transaction costs are required for our analysis of the effects of capital-market integration, which will be modeled as an exogenous decrease in the extra costs of foreign investment.[3] Again, a convenient and frequently used specification is that transaction costs ϕ are quadratic in the volume of foreign investment:

---

[3] This is a standard procedure in tax-competition models. Note, however, that the costs of foreign investment may themselves be regarded as a policy instrument, as is the case in the literature on capital controls. For analyses of the latter in a political-economy context, see, for example, Alesina and Tabellini (1989) and Schulze (in press).

$$\phi = \frac{1}{2}\beta(1 - k_i)^2 \qquad (\beta > 0) \tag{12.3}$$

where we assume that the transaction-cost function is the same for both countries (because ϕ is not indexed), and where $(1 - k_i)$ are the capital exports of country i. By equating gross and net trade flows, this specification implies that capital flows in only one direction in equilibrium. The derivatives of (12.3) with respect to $(1 - k_i)$ are

$$\phi' = \beta(1 - k_i), \qquad \phi'' = \beta \tag{12.4}$$

Arbitrage by capitalists ensures that international differences in the net-of-tax returns to capital must be equal to the marginal transaction costs incurred in equilibrium. Assuming, for simplicity, that the tax rates on capital, t_i, are unit taxes,[4] the arbitrage condition is

$$f'(k_i) - t_i = f'(k_j) - t_j - \beta(1 - k_i) \; \forall \; i, j \in \{1, 2\} \qquad (i \neq j) \tag{12.5}$$

When country i is the capital exporter, $f'(k_j) - t_j > f'(k_i) - t_i$ must hold in the trade equilibrium. It then follows from the assumptions of equal endowments and technologies and the falling marginal productivity of capital that the country with the higher tax rate on capital must always be the capital exporter in this analysis.

From the capital-market-clearing condition (12.2) and the arbitrage condition (12.5), the capital employment in each region can be determined as a function of the two tax rates, the technology constant b, and the transaction-cost parameter β. Using (12.1) gives, after straightforward manipulations,

$$k_i(t_i, t_j, \beta) = 1 - \frac{(t_i - t_j)}{4b + \beta} \; \forall \; i, j \in \{1, 2\} \qquad (i \neq j) \tag{12.6}$$

with first- and second-order derivatives

$$\frac{\partial k_i}{\partial t_i} = \frac{-1}{4b + \beta} < 0, \quad \frac{\partial k_i}{\partial t_j} = \frac{1}{4b + \beta} > 0, \quad \frac{\partial k_i}{\partial \beta} = \frac{(t_i - t_j)}{(4b + \beta)^2} \gtreqless 0 \quad \text{if } t_i \gtreqless t_j,$$

$$\frac{\partial^2 k_i}{\partial t_i \partial \beta} = \frac{1}{(4b + \beta)^2} > 0, \quad \frac{\partial^2 k_i}{\partial t_j \partial \beta} = \frac{-1}{(4b + \beta)^2} < 0 \tag{12.7}$$

In each country i, an increase in the domestic capital-tax rate t_i causes a capital outflow and reduces the amount of capital employed in this country, whereas an increase in the foreign country's tax rate t_j has the

---

[4] This implies that transactions costs are not deductible from the capital-tax base.

opposite effect. An increase in the transaction-cost parameter β reduces capital flows for any given tax differential; this increases the capital stock in the capital-exporting region and decreases it in the capital-importing region.

We assume that governments in both regions face a fixed, nonnegative revenue constraint $g_i = \bar{g}_i$ and have two tax instruments at their disposal. These are the unit tax on capital (t_i) and a tax on wages (τ_i). Either of the two taxes (but not both) can be negative as long as the overall revenue requirement is met. Because the labor supply in each country is fixed and labor is immobile across countries, the wage tax represents a lump-sum instrument in this model. To determine the optimal mix of tax rates (t_i, τ_i), we first derive the comparative-statics effects of each tax on the consumption levels of workers (denoted by a superscript L) and capitalists (superscript K). Using (12.1), the workers' budget constraint in each country is given by

$$c_i^L = f(k_i, 1) - f'(k_i)k_i - \tau_i = bk_i^2 - \tau_i \; \forall \, i \in \{1, 2\} \qquad (12.8)$$

The income of capitalists must be determined separately for the two countries if mobility costs are present. Capitalists in the exporting state own some assets in both jurisdictions, whereas capitalists in the importing country invest everything at home. Let us assume (exogenously, for the moment) that country 1 is the capital exporter whenever capital flows occur in equilibrium.[5] Thus $1 - k_1 \geq 0$, and $1 - k_2 \leq 0$. We also assume that all transaction costs ϕ [equation (12.3)] must be borne by the capital exporter. Then the net incomes for capitalists in the two countries are

$$\begin{aligned} c_1^K &= k_1[f'(k_1) - t_1] + (1 - k_1)[f'(k_2) - t_2] - \phi = f'(k_1) - t_1 + \phi \\ c_2^K &= f'(k_2) - t_2 \end{aligned} \qquad (12.9)$$

where the second step in the equation for c_1^K has used the arbitrage condition (12.5) and the transaction-cost function (12.3). The effects of the labor tax on the feasible consumption levels for workers and capitalists are determined by differentiating (12.8) and (12.9) with respect to τ_i. This yields

$$\frac{\partial c_i^L}{\partial \tau_i} = -1 \; \forall \, i \in \{1, 2\} \qquad (12.10)$$

---

[5] In Section 3 we shall derive this equilibrium from differences in the political weights of workers in the two countries.

$$\frac{\partial c_i^K}{\partial \tau_i} = 0 \ \forall \ i \in \{1, 2\} \tag{12.11}$$

Because the labor supply is fixed, the wage tax falls exclusively on labor and leads to a one-to-one reduction in the net wage, while capital income remains unaffected.

Similarly, the effects of the capital tax are obtained by differentiating (12.8) and (12.9) with respect to t_i. These effects differ for the capital exporter (country 1) and the capital importer (country 2). Substituting in from (12.1), (12.3), and (12.7), we get

$$\frac{\partial c_i^L}{\partial t_i} = \frac{-2bk_i}{4b + \beta} < 0 \ \forall \ i \in \{1, 2\} \tag{12.12}$$

$$\frac{\partial c_1^K}{\partial t_1} = \frac{-2b - k_1\beta}{4b + \beta} < 0, \qquad \frac{\partial c_2^K}{\partial t_2} = \frac{-2b - \beta}{4b + \beta} < 0 \tag{12.13}$$

In each country, the capital tax is borne jointly by capitalists and workers. The tax reduces wage income by lowering the capital–labor ratio and hence the marginal productivity of labor in the taxing jurisdiction. The net return to capital must also fall in both regions. Note that the two equations (12.13) coincide when the transaction-cost parameter β is zero or when the equilibrium is symmetric and $k_1 = k_2 = 1$.

We can now turn to the constrained-optimization problem faced by the two regions. Each government maximizes a function $\Pi_i[u_i^L(c_i^L), u_i^K(c_i^K)]$ that depends positively on the utilities of both classes, which in turn are exclusively determined by the consumption levels (or net factor incomes) of the two groups. In principle, this function can be viewed either as a social-welfare function or as a political-support function. We adopt the latter approach here, in line with most of the recent literature on redistributive taxation and social insurance under conditions of increasing factor-market integration. This implies the view that the government, in its own self-interest, balances the diverging interests of different groups. Although the political process is not modeled explicitly, the political-support function provides a simple way to describe how policy responds to exogenous shocks in order to maintain a political equilibrium.[6]

[6] As Grossman and Helpman (1994) have recently shown, the political-support function can be seen as the "reduced form" of an explicit political model, where each interest group provides a contribution that depends on the chosen policy vector, and the government maximizes the sum of contributions and general well-being.

Budget balance in each country requires $\bar{g}_i = \tau_i + t_i k_i$, leading to the Lagrangians

$$\mathcal{L}_i = \Pi_i[u_i^L(c_i^L), u_i^K(c_i^K)] + \lambda_i(\tau_i + t_i k_i - \bar{g}_i) \; \forall \; i \in \{1, 2\} \quad (12.14)$$

Differentiating with respect to τ_i and substituting in from (12.10) and (12.11) gives the first-order condition for the wage tax:

$$\frac{\partial \mathcal{L}_i}{\partial \tau_i} = -\frac{\partial \Pi_i}{\partial u_i^L}\frac{du_i^L}{dc_i^L} + \lambda_i = 0 \; \forall \; i \in \{1, 2\} \quad (12.15)$$

Thus the Lagrange parameter λ_i is simply the marginal political support that policy-makers derive from an increase in labor income. This is intuitive, because the Lagrange parameter gives the shadow price of public revenues, and the wage tax offers an instrument to transfer one unit of income from workers to the government.

The first-order condition for optimal use of the capital tax is derived analogously. Differentiating (12.14) with respect to t_i gives

$$\frac{\partial \mathcal{L}_i}{\partial t_i} = \frac{\partial \Pi_i}{\partial u_i^L}\frac{du_i^L}{dc_i^L}\frac{\partial c_i^L}{\partial t_i} + \frac{\partial \Pi_i}{\partial u_i^K}\frac{du_i^K}{dc_i^K}\frac{\partial c_i^K}{\partial t_i} + \lambda_i\left(k_i + t_i\frac{\partial k_i}{\partial t_i}\right) = 0 \; \forall \; i \in \{1, 2\}$$

$$(12.16)$$

In the following analysis, it will be useful to specify the political-support function Π_i in more detail. A frequently used formulation is that political support is a weighted average of the utility levels attained by different income groups, and the utility of each group is a concave function of its own level of income (cf. Peltzman, 1976; Hillman, 1982). In our model this implies $\partial \Pi_i/\partial u_i^L = s_i^L$ and $\partial \Pi_i/\partial u_i^K = s_i^K$, where s_i^L and s_i^K represent the exogenous political weights of workers and capitalists, which may, for example, indicate the sizes of the two groups. A nonincreasing marginal utility of income is represented by a constant-elasticity-of-substitution (CES) function of the form

$$\Pi_i = \frac{1}{\rho}\left[s_i^L \cdot \left(c_i^L\right)^\rho + s_i^K \cdot \left(c_i^K\right)^\rho\right] \forall \; i \in \{1, 2\} \quad (1 \geq \rho > -\infty) \quad (12.17)$$

This specification allows us to clearly distinguish between the political weights s_i^L and s_i^K and the elasticity parameter ρ, which is assumed to be the same across countries. The lower is ρ, the more concave is the utility function of each group, and the more difficult it is to substitute workers' political support for capitalists' political support, and vice versa. The marginal political impact of any income group is thus determined jointly by that group's exogenous political weight, its income level, and the elasticity ρ.

Next we introduce the government's marginal rate of substitution between the support from workers and that from capitalists. Differentiating (12.17) with respect to the consumption levels of both income groups, this is given by

$$m_i(c_i^L, c_i^K) \equiv \frac{\partial \Pi_i / \partial c_i^K}{\partial \Pi_i / \partial c_i^L} = \frac{s_i^K}{s_i^L} \left(\frac{c_i^K}{c_i^L} \right)^{\rho-1} \quad \forall\, i \in \{1, 2\} \qquad (12.18)$$

Country-specific first-order conditions for the capital tax are obtained by inserting the partial derivatives from (12.7), (12.12), and (12.13) into (12.16). Furthermore, we can substitute out for λ_i using (12.15) and multiply through by $(4b + \beta)/(\partial \Pi_i / \partial c_i^L)$. The resulting modified first-order conditions are denoted by F_i. Using (12.18), these are given by

$$F_1(t_1, t_2, \beta) = (2b + \beta)k_1 - t_1 - m_1(2b + \beta k_1) = 0 \qquad (12.19)$$

$$F_2(t_1, t_2, \beta) = (2b + \beta)k_2 - t_2 - m_2(2b + \beta) = 0 \qquad (12.20)$$

The functions F_i in (12.19) and (12.20) depend on the capital-tax rate of region j through the terms k_i [cf. equation (12.6)] and represent best-response functions for the capital exporter and the capital importer, respectively. Incorporated in each country's best response for the capital tax rate is the optimal adjustment of wage taxes in the political equilibrium.

3   Nash Equilibrium

We first derive the properties of the symmetric Nash equilibrium, where the political-support functions for the two countries are identical. In the symmetric equilibrium, $k_1 = k_2 = 1$, and (12.19) and (12.20) simultaneously reduce to

$$F_i = (2b + \beta)(1 - m_i) - t_i = 0 \Leftrightarrow (1 - m_i) = \frac{t_i}{2b + \beta} \quad \forall\, i \in \{1, 2\} \qquad (12.21)$$

Equation (12.21) shows that the two countries' best-response functions coincide for $t_1 = t_2$; hence reaction functions will be continuous at that point, and a symmetric Nash equilibrium will exist.[7]

---

[7] This is not a trivial result in models with transactions costs; cf. the commodity-tax model of Mintz and Tulkens (1986), where reaction functions are generally not continuous. However, it was shown by Haufler (1996) that a symmetric Nash equilibrium exists in

In the symmetric case, each country will choose a positive tax rate on capital if and only if the policy-maker's marginal rate of substituting labor income for capital income is less than unity. In the second formulation of equation (12.21), the left-hand side gives the marginal gains from using the capital-tax instrument (i.e., the increase in political support when one dollar of tax revenue is raised from capitalists, as opposed to workers). On the right-hand side are the marginal revenue losses to the economy incurred by levying a tax on internationally mobile capital, as opposed to internationally immobile labor. In the optimum, each government balances the marginal political gains and the marginal efficiency losses of using the capital-tax instrument, as opposed to exclusive reliance on wage taxation.

To link the condition for a positive capital-tax rate to the values of exogenous model parameters, we substitute (12.1), (12.8), (12.9), and (12.18) into (12.21) and note that $k_1 = k_2 = 1$ in the symmetric equilibrium. Furthermore, we assume as a benchmark that the government revenue requirement is financed exclusively by the wage tax ($g_i = \tau_i$) and consider the value of m_i at this point. The results are summarized as follows:

Proposition 1. *Capital-tax rates in the symmetric Nash equilibrium are determined by*

$$t_i \underset{<}{\overset{>}{=}} 0 \Leftrightarrow \frac{s_i^L}{s_i^K}\left(\frac{a-2b}{b-g_i}\right)^{1-\rho} \underset{<}{\overset{>}{=}} 1$$

From Proposition 1 it is straightforward to identify the conditions for positive tax rates on capital in the noncooperative equilibrium. Consider first the special case $\rho = 1$, which implies a constant marginal utility of income for each group. This isolates the roles of the exogenous political weights s_i^L and s_i^K, and the tax rate on capital will be positive if and only if workers have the higher weight in each country's political-support function. In the special case where the weights of the two income groups are just equal (and $\rho = 1$ still holds), the politician will simply maximize national income, and the optimal source tax on capital will be zero. This result is well known for representative-agent models of small open economies under conditions of perfect capital mobility (Gordon, 1986; Razin and Sadka, 1991; Bucovetsky and Wilson, 1991). In our model, the

this model if the marginal transactions costs are zero for a zero level of cross-border shopping and the slopes of the two countries' marginal-transaction-cost functions are equal at this point. These assumptions are implied by the identical and quadratic transaction-cost functions in our analysis.

result holds even for "large" countries and imperfect capital mobility because of our simplifying assumption that the labor supply is fixed and the wage tax is a lump-sum instrument.

In the more general case $\rho < 1$, additional factors enter the analysis. A high marginal productivity of capital [a high value of $(a - 2b)$ in equation (12.1)] lowers the marginal utility of income for capitalists and tends to increase the optimal tax rate on capital. Furthermore, a high government revenue requirement g_i also tends to imply positive tax rates on capital, because exclusive financing by wage taxes reduces labor income and thus increases the marginal political impact of this group. This last factor is not present in models in which the revenue from the capital tax is directly redistributed to workers (Persson and Tabellini, 1992; Lopez et al., 1996). Instead, in the model of Huizinga and Nielsen (1997b), exogenous changes in public spending play a similar role in determining the sign of individual tax rates. Their median-voter model, however, focuses on the structure of capital taxation (profit tax, residence- and source-based capital taxes), rather than on a mix of wage taxation and (source-based) capital taxation.

In the following, we assume that exogenous model parameters are chosen such that capital-tax rates are positive in the symmetric Nash equilibrium. The next step is to introduce an asymmetry between the trading countries. We focus on the case where the exogenous political weight of workers is higher in country 1 than in country 2. Starting from the symmetric equilibrium, this is modeled by a small increase in s_1^L holding s_2^L constant. From (12.18) we have $\partial m_1 / \partial s_1^L < 0$. From (12.21) it then follows that the impact effect of this shock is to raise the capital-tax rate in country 1. However, the tax rate in country 2 may also rise in the new Nash equilibrium. Establishing that the tax increase in country 1 must dominate in the neighborhood of a symmetric initial equilibrium requires either a stability argument or the assumption that the Nash equilibrium is unique. This is discussed in the Appendix, and the result is stated in the following:

Proposition 2.   *For small differences between the two countries, there exists a Nash equilibrium in which the country with the higher political weight of workers (country 1) levies the higher tax rate on capital.*

Proof.   See the Appendix.   ∎

Using Proposition 2 in the arbitrage condition (12.5) shows that the high-tax country must be the capital exporter when endowments and production functions are identical across countries. In this asymmetric Nash equilibrium, country 1 thus exports capital to the low-tax region 2, and the pattern of trade flows postulated exogenously in our earlier discussion is now motivated by cross-country differences in the relative political influences of the two income groups.

4   Capital-Market Integration

Capital-market integration is modeled as an exogenous reduction in the transaction-cost parameter β. Because this change increases the elasticity of the capital-tax base, it tends to raise the costs of capital taxation in both countries relative to the nondistortive wage tax. A complication arises from terms-of-trade effects, which tend to increase the tax rate in the capital-importing region and thus counteract the tax-base externality in that country. It will be seen, however, that the quadratic specification of the production and mobility cost functions in our model ensures that tax-base effects will dominate terms-of-trade effects in both countries. In representative-consumer models, the outcome of capital-market integration will then be an unambiguous shift away from capital taxation and toward wage taxation.[8] The issue here is whether or not and how this result will be modified when the effects on the distribution of income within each country are also taken into account.

The importance of distributional effects for tax policy depends crucially on the elasticity parameter ρ in the political-support function (12.17). A low level for this parameter ($\rho \to -\infty$) leads to a rigid ratio of net labor income to net capital income. This implies that losers from capital-market liberalization will vigorously oppose the income loss suffered, and the distributional effects of market integration will have strong repercussions on optimal tax policy. On the other hand, if ρ is high ($\rho \to 1$), then a given change in the distribution of income will have only minor effects on the policy-maker's marginal rate of substitution between the support from different income groups.

We shall first analyze the effects on workers' consumption and capitalists' consumption in each country induced by changes in the foreign tax rate and the transaction-cost parameter, respectively. With one exception, these effects are unambiguous and follow directly from the

---

[8] Bucovetsky and Wilson (1991, sec. 3) have shown, for example, that any increase in the number of (identical) countries engaged in tax competition will reduce the level of capital taxation at source, relative to the level of wage taxation. A related result was derived by Hoyt (1991). Increasing the number of regions in a model without mobility costs will raise the elasticity of capital supply in a way very similar to the reduction of mobility costs in our two-country framework.

private budget constraints (12.8) and (12.9), the set of partial derivatives (12.7), and Proposition 2 (which implies $t_1 > t_2$):[9]

$$\frac{\partial c_1^L}{\partial t_2} > 0, \qquad \frac{\partial c_1^K}{\partial t_2} < 0, \qquad \frac{\partial c_2^L}{\partial t_1} > 0, \qquad \frac{\partial c_2^K}{\partial t_1} < 0 \qquad (12.22)$$

$$\frac{\partial c_1^L}{\partial \beta} > 0, \qquad \frac{\partial c_1^K}{\partial \beta} < 0, \qquad \frac{\partial c_2^L}{\partial \beta} < 0, \qquad \frac{\partial c_2^K}{\partial \beta} > 0 \qquad (12.23)$$

Turning first to the terms collected in (12.22), we see that the effects of a foreign tax change are symmetric in the two countries. An increase in country j's capital-tax rate causes capital to flow to region i and benefits workers in region i, while making capitalists worse off. On the other hand, it is seen from (12.23) that the direct effects of a *reduction* in β on the incomes of the two classes are directly opposed in the capital-exporting region and the capital-importing region. At unchanged tax rates, liberalization increases country 1's capital exports to country 2. This hurts workers in country 1 and benefits workers in country 2. Also, capitalists in country 2 are hurt by the capital inflow, whereas capitalists in country 1 gain from the increased investment opportunities.

In both countries, the change in the optimal domestic tax rate on capital in response to the exogenous variation in the transaction-cost parameter β is given by the following equation, which is derived in the Appendix:

$$\frac{dt_i}{d\beta} = \frac{1}{|J|} \left[-\frac{\partial F_j}{\partial t_j} \frac{\partial F_i}{\partial \beta} + \frac{\partial F_i}{\partial t_j} \frac{\partial F_j}{\partial \beta} \right] \forall \, i, j \in \{1, 2\} \qquad (i \neq j) \qquad (12.24)$$

It is also argued in the Appendix [equation (12.A3)] that the determinant of the Jacobian matrix J must be positive. For each country i, there are two effects in equation (12.24): The first term gives the direct response of country i's optimal capital-tax rate to the change in the

---

[9] Signing the effects in (12.22) and (12.23) is straightforward, except for the derivative $\partial c_1^K / \partial \beta$. Differentiating (12.9) and substituting in for k_1 using (12.6) gives, after straightforward manipulations,

$$\frac{\partial c_1^K}{\partial \beta} = -[2b + \beta(1 - k_1)] \frac{(t_1 - t_2)}{(4b + \beta)^2} + \frac{1}{2}(1 - k_1)^2$$

$$= \frac{-(t_1 - t_2)}{2(4b + \beta)^3} \{4b[(4b + \beta) - (t_1 - t_2)] + \beta(t_1 - t_2)\} < 0$$

which is negative, because (12.6) requires $(4b + \beta) \geq (t_1 - t_2)$ for a nonnegative capital stock in country 1.

transaction-cost parameter, whereas the second effect describes country i's best response to the induced change in the capital-tax rate of country j.

From the second-order condition of each country's optimal-tax problem we know that $\partial F_j/\partial t_j < 0 \, \forall j \in \{1,2\}$. In the following, we determine the signs of the other partial derivatives in (12.24) in order to evaluate the overall effects. We first turn to the direct effect of the parameter change on the tax rate of the capital-exporting country 1. Differentiating (12.19) with respect to β and using (12.18) gives[10]

$$
\frac{\partial F_1}{\partial \beta} = \underbrace{(1 - m_1)k_1 + [2b + (1 - m_1)\beta]\frac{\partial k_1}{\partial \beta}}_{(+)}
$$

$$
+ \underbrace{(2b + \beta k_1)(1 - \rho)m_1 \frac{c_1^L}{c_1^K}\frac{\partial(c_1^K/c_1^L)}{\partial \beta}}_{(-,\,0)} \tag{12.25}
$$

where the first effect is signed with the help of Proposition 1 ($m_1 < 1$) and (12.7), whereas the signing of the last effect has used (12.23). From our discussion of the optimal-tax condition in the symmetric Nash equilibrium [equation (12.21)], the interpretation of (12.25) is straightforward. The first effect gives the increase in the efficiency costs of capital taxation as capital exports increase because of the lower mobility-cost parameter. With a lower tax base, less revenue can be collected by the use of the capital tax, and this effect tends to reduce the optimal level of t_1. On the other hand, a reduction in β also increases the political gains from capital taxation from the perspective of country 1's government by lowering labor income and raising the income of capitalists. This increases the marginal political impact of workers, relative to capitalists, and tends to push the capital-tax rate upward. Note that this effect is absent (and the second term equals zero) when the marginal utility of income is constant for each group ($\rho = 1$).

Next we consider the direct effect of the reduction in β on the optimal tax rate in the capital-importing country 2. Differentiating (12.20) gives[11]

[10] At this point, the main reason for our use of quadratic production functions becomes clear, because this assumption eliminates third derivatives of the production function with respect to k_i.

[11] To obtain the first effect in (12.26) we expand the initial derivative by adding and subtracting 1 and then substituting in for k_2 and $\partial k_2/\partial \beta$ using (12.6) and (12.7).

$$\frac{\partial F_2}{\partial \beta} = \underbrace{(1 - m_2) - 2b\frac{\partial k_2}{\partial \beta}}_{(+)} + \underbrace{(2b + \beta)(1 - \rho)m_2 \frac{c_2^L}{c_2^K} \frac{\partial(c_2^K/c_2^L)}{\partial \beta}}_{(+,\,0)} > 0 \tag{12.26}$$

As before, the signing of individual effects has used (12.7) and (12.23), and $m_2 < 1$ must hold in the neighborhood of a symmetric equilibrium. A lower level of β leads to increased efficiency costs of capital taxation for the capital importer, despite the fact that a source tax on capital improves country 2's terms of trade by reducing its net import demand for capital.[12] However, under a quadratic specification of the production and mobility cost functions this terms-of-trade gain is dominated by the higher tax-base loss incurred from capital taxation; see Haufler (1996, prop. 3) for a similar result. In contrast to the capital exporter, a reduction in β also lowers the political benefits of capital taxation in country 2 (for $\rho < 1$), because capital-market integration causes a redistribution of income from capitalists to workers. Hence, economic and political forces work in the same direction for the capital importer, and the direct effect of a reduction in β unambiguously leads to a lower tax rate on capital.

Whether the positive sign of $\partial F_2/\partial \beta$ tends to increase or reduce country 1's optimal capital-tax rate through the indirect (second) effect in (12.24) depends on the slope of country 1's reaction function. This is given by the derivative

$$\frac{\partial F_1}{\partial t_2} = \underbrace{\frac{2b + (1 - m_1)\beta}{4b + \beta}}_{(+)} + \underbrace{(2b + \beta k_1)(1 - \rho)m_1 \frac{c_1^L}{c_1^K} \frac{\partial(c_1^K/c_1^L)}{\partial t_2}}_{(-,\,0)} \tag{12.27}$$

where the second effect is signed from (12.22). The slope of country 1's reaction function exhibits ambiguity similar to the direct effect of a reduction in the mobility-cost parameter [equation (12.25)]. The decrease in the tax rate of country 2 increases the capital outflow from country 1 and reduces that country's tax base. Thus the efficiency costs of capital taxation are increased for country 1 as a result of the initial tax response in the low-tax region. However,

---

[12] From the perspective of the capital-importing country, the terms of trade are given by the net return, $f'(k_j) - t_j$, that must be paid to foreign investors. Hence any reduction in this net interest rate represents a terms-of-trade improvement. This gives an incentive to the capital importer (country 2) to increase the source tax t_2 and thus reduce its import demand for capital.

the capital outflow from country 1 also causes a redistribution of income from workers to capitalists, and this increases the political benefits of capital taxation.

Finally, we turn to the slope of country 2's reaction function, which is given by

$$\frac{\partial F_2}{\partial t_1} = \underbrace{\frac{2b+\beta}{4b+\beta}}_{(+)} + \underbrace{(2b+\beta)(1-p)m_2 \frac{c_2^L}{c_2^K} \frac{\partial(c_2^K/c_2^L)}{\partial t_1}}_{(-,0)} \tag{12.28}$$

This partial derivative is also ambiguous: An increase in t_1 raises country 2's tax base and increases the economic incentive for capital taxation by the first effect. On the other hand, an increase in country 1's capital-tax rate also redistributes income in country 2 from capitalists to workers, and that reduces the political incentive to raise t_2.

Summarizing the effects that capital-market integration has on optimal capital-tax rates in both countries, it is obvious that the parameter p plays a crucial role. The value of this parameter, which measures the degree of "income stickiness" inherent in the political process, determines the sizes of the second terms in all partial effects (12.25)–(12.28). In the following, we consider the two benchmark cases where p is either at the upper end or at the lower end of its permitted range. In both instances this leads to unambiguous changes in optimal capital-tax rates as a result of capital-market integration. The results are summarized in the following:

Proposition 3. *(a) When the political support from workers and that from capitalists are close substitutes from the government's perspective ($p \to 1$), then capital-market integration will reduce optimal tax rates on capital in both countries. (b) When it is very difficult for policy-makers to substitute between the political support from workers and that from capitalists ($p \to -\infty$), then capital-market integration will reduce the optimal tax rate on capital in the capital-importing country, but increase the capital-tax rate in the exporting country.*

Proof. As $p \to 1$, the second effects in (12.25)–(12.28) approach zero, and $\partial F_i/\partial \beta > 0$, $\partial F_i/\partial t_j > 0 \; \forall \; i \in \{1, 2\}$, $i \neq j$. Substituting these partial effects into (12.24) demonstrates part (*a*) of the proposition. For $p \to -\infty$, the second effects in (12.25)–(12.28) become arbitrarily large and dominate the first effects. This gives $\partial F_1/\partial \beta < 0$, $\partial F_2/\partial \beta > 0$, $\partial F_1/\partial t_2 < 0$, $F_2/\partial t_1 < 0$. Substituting these partial effects in (12.24) gives part (*b*) of the proposition. ∎

Table 12.1. *Effects of capital-market integration ($\beta\downarrow$) on optimal tax rates on capital*

Case	Capital exporter (country 1)	Capital importer (country 2)
Case (a): $\rho \to 1$		
Direct effect: $(\partial F_j/\partial t_j) \times (\partial F_i/\partial \beta)$	$t_1\downarrow$	$t_2\downarrow$
Indirect effect: $(\partial F_i/\partial t_j) \times (\partial F_j/\partial \beta)$	$t_1\downarrow$	$t_2\downarrow$
Case (b): $\rho \to -\infty$		
Direct effect: $(\partial F_j/\partial t_j) \times (\partial F_i/\partial \beta)$	$t_1\uparrow$	$t_2\downarrow$
Indirect effect: $(\partial F_i/\partial t_j) \times (\partial F_j/\partial \beta)$	$t_1\uparrow$	$t_2\downarrow$

To explain these results in more detail, Table 12.1 summarizes the partial effects (12.25)–(12.28) for each of the two cases. In case (a), ($\rho \to 1$), distributional effects of capital-market integration do not effectively feed back into the policy-makers' optimal-tax problems, and the increased efficiency costs of capital taxation dominate in both countries. The direct effect of a reduction in mobility costs is to intensify the competition for the internationally mobile capital-tax base, and this lowers capital-tax rates in both countries. In addition, both reaction functions are upward-sloping in this case: Other things being equal, the initial reduction in each country's tax rate reduces the capital-tax base in the other region, and this further weakens the incentive to employ source taxes on capital. Therefore, direct and indirect effects work in the same direction, and both countries will unambiguously reduce the level of capital taxation.

In case (b), ($\rho \to -\infty$), distributional effects are central to policy-makers' optimal-tax problems, because resistance to income changes caused by capital-market integration is very high in both countries. In this case, political considerations dominate the effects of increased efficiency costs of capital taxation. The initial response to a reduction in mobility costs is then a tax reduction in the capital-importing country 2 [where, from (12.23), workers gain from the additional capital inflow, while capitalists lose] and a tax increase in country 1 (where the capital outflow hurts labor and benefits capital). Also, both reaction functions are downward-sloping in this case, and indirect effects again reinforce the direct effects in both countries. The additional capital inflow to country 2 resulting from the initial tax increase in country 1 benefits workers and hurts capitalists in the capital-importing region. To counteract these income changes, the tax rate on capital must decrease further in country 2. On the other hand, the initial tax reduction in country 2 attracts capital to this region, and this hurts workers and benefits capitalists in country 1. Therefore, country 1's capital-tax rate must increase further (and the wage tax can accordingly decrease) in order to shield workers from the income loss.

As it stands, Proposition 3 describes the effects of capital-market integration only for the special cases where either efficiency or distributional effects are central for tax policy. However, a more general result is also implicit in our analysis, if we are willing to assume that the direct effect of capital-market integration dominates the indirect effect in both countries [cf. equation (12.24)]. With this assumption we can state that the lower the elasticity parameter ρ, and thus the more important the distributional considerations, the more the capital-tax rates in the two countries will diverge as a result of capital-market integration. Formally, we have to show that $(dt_1/d\beta - dt_2/d\beta)$ must be monotonously rising in ρ. From (12.24) and the foregoing assumption, this in turn requires that $\partial F_1/\partial\beta$ must be monotonously rising in ρ, whereas $\partial F_2/\partial\beta$ must be monotonously falling. But it is directly seen from (12.25) and (12.26) that this condition is fulfilled. Hence, as the political resistance to income changes in increased (ρ falls), the downward adjustment of tax rates is reinforced in the low-tax country 2, but is slowed down and eventually turned around in the high-tax country 1.

It remains to link our results to related findings in the literature. Proposition 3(a) corresponds to the conventional notion that increased capital mobility will lead to a general reduction in the level of capital taxation. This result is typical for one-consumer models of capital-tax competition (Bucovetsky and Wilson, 1991; Hoyt, 1991) and is reproduced in our more general framework when policy-makers can easily substitute increased political support from one income group for the reduced support from the other.

In contrast, Proposition 3(b) shows that when distributional concerns are predominant, the optimal tax rate on capital increases in the capital-exporting country. Because the capital exporter is the high-tax country in our analysis, this result also implies a divergence of tax rates as a result of capital-market liberalization. This finding differs not only from the findings in one-consumer analyses but also from the results obtained by Persson and Tabellini (1992). In their analysis, changes in the political equilibrium mitigate the economic effects of capital-market integration, but the net effect in both countries is a reduction in the rate of capital taxation. Also, Persson and Tabellini argue that capital-market integration induces a larger reduction in tax rates in the high-tax country, thus implying a convergence of capital-tax rates across countries.

These differences in results can be traced back to different assumptions regarding the political process. Persson and Tabellini modeled a median voter who anticipates the noncooperative tax setting by national governments and delegates tax policy to a more "left-wing" (i.e., redistributive) government in order to (partly) offset the effects of capital-tax competition. Stability conditions then dictate that this "political effect" cannot dominate the "economic effect" of increased tax competition, a constraint that is not present in our framework. To put it differently, voter behavior in the model of Persson and Tabellini is directed at overcoming the economic inefficiencies of capital-tax competition, and this effect is clearly symmetric in the trading countries.[13] In contrast, the interest groups modeled in our analysis respond solely to the distributional effects of capital-market integration, and these effects are directly opposed in the capital-importing and capital-exporting regions. This comparison shows that the median-voter approach and the interest-group approach may lead to rather different conclusions, even if the underlying economic models are largely comparable.

Finally, we shall briefly compare our results to some recent findings in the related literature on tax-financed social-insurance schemes. Gabszewicz and van Ypersele (1996) showed in a median-voter model that the level of social protection (which takes the form of a minimum wage in their model) always falls when capital mobility is introduced, even if the median voter receives wage income only. This result is, however, derived for the case of symmetric countries, and the focus is on what we have labeled here the "efficiency effect" of capital-market integration. Closer to our approach is that of Lejour and Verbon (1996), who modeled two asymmetric countries providing unemployment insurance to risk-averse agents in the presence of imperfect capital mobility. Capital mobility matters because social-security payments are partly shifted to firms in the process of wage bargaining. In that model the degree of risk aversion plays a role similar to that of the elasticity parameter ρ in our framework, and hence the "distributional effects" are similar to ours: If risk aversion is sufficiently high, then capital-market integration will reduce the level of social insurance in the capital-importing country and increases it in the capital-exporting country (Lejour and Verbon, 1996, p. 506). However, there are no "efficiency effects" of capital-market integration in the model of Lejour and Verbon, so that the effects of capital-market integration on social-insurance

---

[13] As Persson and Tabellini (1992, p. 698) explicitly noted, the "delegation game" played by the median voter is welfare-improving for a majority of agents, because it partially relaxes an ex-post incentive constraint.

policy are always exactly opposed in the capital-exporting and capital-importing countries.

5   Conclusions

This study has employed a two-country, two-class model of tax competition to discuss the effects that capital-market integration has on the optimal mix of factor taxes. In this framework, policy-makers have to weigh the increased efficiency costs of capital taxation in a world with higher capital mobility against the distributional effects that arise when interest groups try to reverse in the political arena the income changes brought about by market forces. The analysis has shown that the trade pattern introduces a systematic asymmetry to the effects that capital-market integration has in the two countries, with distributional and efficiency implications working in the same direction for the capital-importing country, but in opposite directions for the capital exporter. Therefore we would generally expect that capital-exporting countries would exhibit a less pronounced shift to labor taxation in response to liberalized capital markets and might possibly even increase the taxation of capital.

A first look at the data (IMF, 1987, 1994) shows that there may be some support for this proposition, but there are also counterexamples. Among the countries that have raised their effective tax rates on capital since the 1980s, The Netherlands and the United Kingdom have been exporters of long-term capital in most years. It is also interesting to note that Germany has significantly reduced the tax burden on capital in the 1990s, while at the same time turning to a large capital importer as a consequence of German unification. Counterexamples to the predicted pattern are Italy and Spain, both typical capital importers with rising effective tax rates on capital. However, in both of those countries the general level of taxation has increased markedly in the past decade, so that the capital-tax increase does not represent a structural shift away from labor taxation. This last example already shows that a careful econometric analysis is needed to isolate changes in the level versus the structure of factor taxation in different countries. Moreover, our analysis has isolated the shocks to the distribution of income as a result of capital-market integration. In practice, these shocks will overlap with other exogenous disturbances to either wages or capital incomes, and possibly also with exogenous policy shifts as a result of changes in the political balance of power.

The limitations of our theoretical analysis also have to be pointed out. In line with most of the related work, including Persson and Tabellini

(1992), it has been assumed here that capital flows are exclusively determined by tax differentials. This assumption is particularly relevant for the question of tax-rate convergence. If the high-tax country is also the capital exporter, then distributional effects tend to cause diverging rates of capital taxation in our model as a result of capital-market integration. The same need not be the case, however, if production-related differences across countries are the main reasons for international trade. Finally, our model has oversimplified the government's equity–efficiency trade-off by assuming that the wage tax is a lump-sum instrument and that there is only one (distortive) instrument of capital taxation. A more general analysis of the efficiency-versus-distributional effects of capital-market integration would have to endogenize the labor-supply decision and allow for different forms of capital-income taxation.

To summarize, the simple model used here clearly does not claim to "explain" why the empirical evidence for falling and converging rates of capital taxation has been relatively weak since the 1980s. However, it may nevertheless indicate one possible route through which distributional effects counteract the clear-cut predictions derived from conventional one-consumer models of capital-tax competition.

APPENDIX

The general form of the best-response functions (12.19) and (12.20) is

$$F_1(t_1, t_2, \theta_1) = 0, \qquad F_2(t_1, t_2, \theta_2) = 0 \tag{12.A1}$$

where θ_i are exogenous shift parameters. Totally differentiating (12.A1) and inverting gives

$$
\begin{bmatrix} dt_1 \\ dt_2 \end{bmatrix} = \frac{1}{|J|} \begin{bmatrix} -\dfrac{\partial F_2}{\partial t_2} & \dfrac{\partial F_1}{\partial t_2} \\ \dfrac{\partial F_2}{\partial t_1} & -\dfrac{\partial F_1}{\partial t_1} \end{bmatrix} \begin{bmatrix} \dfrac{\partial F_1}{\partial \theta_1} \, d\theta_1 \\ \dfrac{\partial F_2}{\partial \theta_2} \, d\theta_2 \end{bmatrix} \tag{12.A2}
$$

where the Jacobian is

$$
J = \begin{bmatrix} \partial F_1/\partial t_1 & \partial F_1/\partial t_2 \\ \partial F_2/\partial t_1 & \partial F_2/\partial t_2 \end{bmatrix}
$$

The determinant of the Jacobi matrix can be signed as

$$|J| = \frac{\partial F_1}{\partial t_1} \frac{\partial F_2}{\partial t_2} - \frac{\partial F_1}{\partial t_2} \frac{\partial F_2}{\partial t_1} > 0 \tag{12.A3}$$

either by assuming that the Nash equilibrium is unique, and using the index theorem (Mas-Colell, 1985, pp. 201–4), or by interpreting (12.A3) as a stability condition (Dixit, 1986, p. 110). For a symmetric initial equilibrium this stability requirement is equivalent to the familiar condition that the slopes of best-response functions must be less than unity in absolute value.

Proof of Proposition 2. To analyze the effects of an increase in the political weight of workers in country 1, we substitute $d\theta_1 = ds_1^L$ and $d\theta_2 = 0$ in (12.A2). Because the initial equilibrium is symmetric, (12.21) and (12.18) can be used to obtain

$$\frac{\partial F_1}{\partial s_1^L} = -(2b + \beta)\frac{\partial m_1}{\partial s_1^L} = (2b + \beta)\frac{m_1}{s_1^L} > 0 \qquad (12.A4)$$

Using (12.A3) and (12.A4) and the second-order conditions $\partial F_i/\partial t_i < 0$ $\forall i \in \{1, 2\}$ in the first line of (12.A2) gives $dt_1/ds_1^L > 0$. Combining this with the change in t_2 [the second line in (12.A2)] gives

$$\frac{\partial F_2}{\partial t_1}\frac{dt_1}{ds_1^L} = -\frac{\partial F_2}{\partial t_2}\frac{dt_2}{ds_1^L} \qquad (12.A5)$$

From the symmetry of the initial equilibrium ($\partial F_1/\partial t_1 = \partial F_2/\partial t_2$ and $\partial F_1/\partial t_2 = \partial F_2/\partial t_1$) and the stability condition $|J| > 0$ in (12.A3), it follows that $dt_1/ds_1^L > dt_2/ds_1^L$, whether or not dt_2/ds_1^L is positive. Because tax rates are equal initially, this demonstrates Proposition 2 for small deviations from the symmetric equilibrium. ∎

Derivation of Equation (12.24). Equation set (12.A2) simultaneously includes the solution for the more general case in which the best responses in both countries are altered by shift parameters. Setting $d\theta_1 = d\theta_2 = d\beta$ yields equation (12.24).

REFERENCES

Alesina, A., and Tabellini, G. (1989). External debt, capital flight, and political risk. *Journal of International Economics* 27:199–220.

Bjerksund, P., and Schjelderup, G. (1997). Capital flight and the efficiency–equity trade-off. Revised version of discussion paper 1/96, Norwegian School of Economics and Business Administration, Bergen.

Bucovetsky, S. (1991). Asymmetric tax competition. *Journal of Urban Economics* 30:167–81.

Bucovetsky, S., and Wilson, J. D. (1991). Tax competition with two tax instruments. *Regional Science and Urban Economics* 21:333–50.

CEC (1992). *Report of the Committee of Independent Experts on Company Taxation* (Ruding report). Brussels: Commission of the European Communities.

CEC (1996). *Tableaux de bord prélèvements obligatoires* (Task Force on Statutory Contributions and Charges XXI-02). Brussels: Commission of the European Communities.

Dixit, A. (1986). Comparative statics for oligopoly. *International Economic Review* 27:107–22.

Gabszewicz, J., and van Ypersele, T. (1996). Social protection and political competition. *Journal of Public Economics* 61:193–208.

Gordon, R. H. (1986). Taxation of investment and savings in a world economy. *American Economic Review* 76:1086–102.

Gordon, R. H., and Bovenberg, A. L. (1996). Why is capital so immobile internationally? Possible explanations and implications for capital income taxation. *American Economic Review* 86:1057–75.

Gordon, R. H., and MacKie-Mason, J. K. (1995). Why is there corporate taxation in a small open economy? The role of transfer pricing and income shifting. In: *The Effects of Taxation on Multinational Corporations*, ed. M. Feldstein, pp. 67–91. University of Chicago Press.

Grossman, G. M., and Helpman, E. (1994). Protection for sale. *American Economic Review* 84:833–50.

Haufler, A. (1996). Tax coordination with different preferences for public goods: conflict or harmony of interest? *International Tax and Public Finance* 3:5–28.

Hillman, A. (1982). Declining industries and political-support protectionist motives. *American Economic Review* 72:1180–7.

Hoyt, W. H. (1991). Property taxation, Nash equilibrium, and market power. *Journal of Urban Economics* 30:123–31.

Huizinga, H., and Nielsen, S. B. (1997a). Capital income and profits taxation with foreign ownership of firms. *Journal of International Economics* 42:149–65.

Huizinga, H., and Nielsen, S. B. (1997b). The political economy of capital income and profit taxation in a small open economy. EPRU working paper 1997-01, Economic Policy Research Unit, Copenhagen Business School.

IMF (1987). *Balance of Payments Statistics Yearbook*, Part 2. Washington, DC: International Monetary Fund.

IMF (1994). *Balance of Payments Statistics Yearbook*, Part 2. Washington, DC: International Monetary Fund.

Lejour, A., and Verbon, H. (1996). Capital mobility, wage bargaining and social insurance policies in an economic union. *International Tax and Public Finance* 3:495–514.

Lopez, S., Marchand, M., and Pestieau, P. (1996). A simple two-country model of redistributive capital income taxation. CORE discussion paper 9625, Université Catholique de Louvain.

Mas-Colell, A. (1985). *The Theory of General Economic Equilibrium*. Cambridge University Press.

Mintz, J., and Tulkens, H. (1986). Commodity tax competition between member states of a federation: equilibrium and efficiency. *Journal of Public Economics* 29:133–72.

Peltzman, S. (1976). Toward a more general theory of regulation. *Journal of Law and Economics* 19:211–40.

Persson, T., and Tabellini, G. (1992). The politics of 1992: fiscal policy and European integration. *Review of Economic Studies* 59:689–701.

Razin, A., and Sadka, E. (1991). International tax competition and gains from tax harmonization. *Economics Letters* 37:69–76.

Schulze, G. (in press). *The Political Economy of Capital Controls*. Cambridge University Press.

Wilson, J. D. (1991). Tax competition with interregional differences in factor endowments. *Regional Science and Urban Economics* 21:423–51.

CHAPTER 13

Interjurisdictional Tax Competition:
A Political-Economy Perspective

Carlo Perroni and Kimberley A. Scharf

1   Introduction

The academic literature on tax competition has shed light on the fiscal externalities that can arise if sovereign jurisdictions select their fiscal policies in an uncoordinated fashion in situations in which their economies are linked by commodity or factor trade flows. From a welfare-economics perspective, those externalities could have undesirable effects. With respect to commodity taxation, welfare-maximizing governments could choose to depart from second-best optimal rate structures in an attempt to manipulate the terms of trade in their favor (Mintz and Tulkens, 1986). When factor taxes are involved, jurisdictional governments could be induced to choose suboptimal source-based taxes in order to prevent the tax base and the associated rents from moving outside their jurisdictions' borders (Gordon and Wilson, 1986; Zodrow and Mieszkowski, 1986).

The majority of this literature has examined tax competition in an institutional vacuum. Typically it has been assumed that fiscal choices are made by some fictional jurisdictional authority that aims to maximize a well-defined objective such as national welfare. This type of approach finds its roots in the welfare-based tradition of public economics, combining the central-planning paradigm of the literature on optimal tax design with the insight, borrowed from the theory of noncooperative games, that uncoordinated responses typically lead to inefficient equilibria – two paradigms that seem rather at odds with each other.

Arguably, tax and spending choices are not the result of welfare maximization by benevolent central planners; this simple observation has fueled the research on public choice for the past 30 years. At best, in a direct democracy, fiscal choices are made through majority voting; more often, they are made by elected officials – individuals who belong to political parties, who are subject to pressures from producers' lobbies

291

and other interest groups, who base their decisions on imperfect information, and who rely on bureaucrats for policy implementation. These political aspects of decision-making have been moved to the forefront in recent analyses of international trade-policy formation (Mayer, 1984; Grossman and Helpman, 1994; 1995a,b), but there has been comparatively less research on the political-economy foundations of fiscal choices, with even less specific attention devoted to tax competition.

Drawing on that limited but growing literature, this chapter examines the linkages between tax competition and the political economy of fiscal choices and argues that a correct characterization of the processes leading to fiscal choices is crucial for understanding interjurisdictional tax competition. Not only can the objectives of tax-setting authorities diverge from welfare maximization (either because policy-makers are self-interested or because they face institutional constraints), but also, when tax policies are part of the outcome in a political-economy equilibrium, it may not even be possible to approximate decision-making by way of an optimization mechanism. Furthermore, tax competition can affect the very nature of the institutional structure within which fiscal choices are made.

The need to account for political mechanisms when studying tax competition thus goes beyond a concern for realistic modeling; the predictions and conclusions that are reached concerning the economic implications of tax competition can in fact be centrally affected. For example, the tax-competition literature stresses the welfare costs of policy-coordination failure and comes to the conclusion that cooperation among jurisdictions is desirable on efficiency grounds. That conclusion could be overturned if fiscal choices arise as part of a political-economy equilibrium, one stemming from imperfect public-choice mechanisms and exhibiting varying degrees of coherence with social objectives such as welfare. Conversely, as we shall see, tax competition can have implications for political and constitutional equilibria and can affect some of the conclusions derived from analyses of political processes that have abstracted from fiscal competition. Finally, political-economy mechanisms can affect the viability of tax-coordination agreements between jurisdictions.

The remainder of this chapter is structured as follows: Section 2 discusses the implications of tax competition in the presence of nonbenevolent policy-makers. Section 3 focuses on voting and political equilibria in representative democracies, and Section 4 delineates some possible implications of lobbying activities for tax-competition outcomes. Section 5 discusses how tax competition can affect constitutional choices. Section 6 draws on the preceding discussion to examine the question of the desirability of interjurisdictional fiscal-policy coordination, and Section 7 examines how the political-economy dimensions of tax competition might affect prospects for coordination. Section 8 summarizes and concludes the chapter.

2　　Nonbenevolent Policy-Makers

The study of tax competition is firmly rooted in the planning tradition of public economics, a tradition that has removed policy-makers from the process to be explained and has treated them as abstract entities in charge of pursuing social objectives. Clearly, that assumption was never proposed as a realistic characterization of behavior; rather, it reflected a normative thrust in tax-policy analysis, which traditionally has been thought of as being aimed at dispensing enlightenment for the benefit of policy-makers. In recent years, however, there has been some fundamental rethinking of the role of economic analysis, and policy-makers have more and more become actors in economists' models, rather than simply providing an audience for economists' prescriptions.

Social scientists have described the behavior of policy-makers in various terms, usually as being motivated by ambition and the pursuit of personal wealth and power. An economist's translation of that view of policy-makers' behavior can readily be fitted into the paradigm of constrained maximization of a self-interested objective, a foundation upon which economists have built the rest of their models. The difference here is that whereas decentralized decision-making by self-motivated consumers and firms can foster efficiency, that generally is not the case with respect to policy-makers, who are entrusted with the responsibility of making choices that will directly affect other individuals. And when policy-makers' objectives depart from welfare maximization, predictions about the effects of tax competition can be drastically affected.

Consider, for example, capital-tax competition. With source-based taxes on capital income and in the presence of welfare-maximizing governments, if all jurisdictions had identical endowments, technologies, and preferences, then a coordinated policy could attain a first-best outcome, whereas uncoordinated choices would lead to suboptimal levels of taxation and spending. As a simple departure from that scenario, suppose that the fiscal authority maximized revenues; then a coordinated equilibrium would feature a 100% rate of taxation, whereas taxes would be lower in a noncooperative solution. Furthermore, in principle, the noncooperative-equilibrium taxes might happen to coincide with those required for a first-best allocation.

In essence, that is the nature of the argument put forward by Edwards and Keen (1996). Those authors examined how tax competition would affect noncooperative equilibria when fiscal choices were made by "Leviathans" (i.e., nonbenevolent policy-makers who were not concerned exclusively with social welfare, but also with personal power and wealth).

Their model features a number of independent jurisdictions that trade goods and factors with each other. In each jurisdiction, the preferences of a representative citizen are defined over a private good and a public good, and taxes are levied on a mobile factor. Both the consumption good and the public good are produced using the immobile and the mobile factors. Policy-makers are assumed to be partly benevolent and partly self-serving. This assumption is modeled by specifying the objective as a function of both the representative consumer's welfare and wasteful public consumption. The latter competes with public-good spending for resources from the government's budget.

Edwards and Keen show that, as in standard welfare-based analyses of capital-tax competition, noncooperative equilibria are characterized by lower taxes than would be seen in a coordinated solution. Also, starting from a noncooperative equilibrium, an increase in the tax rate will, as expected, unambiguously raise the decision-maker's welfare; but the effect of a tax increase on the welfare of the representative consumer will be positive only if the elasticity of the tax base with respect to changes in the tax rate (or, equivalently, the marginal excess burden associated with capital taxation) is large relative to the policy-makers' marginal propensity to waste tax revenues.

Their analysis thus suggests that, in contrast with the welfare-maximization view of tax competition, allowing jurisdictions to compete with one another for the same tax base could bring discipline to fiscal choices: In a war between Leviathans, the citizenry could emerge as the winners.

3   Voting and Representative Democracy

The Edwards and Keen analysis remains close to the notion that fiscal choices derive from a well-defined maximization calculation carried out by a policy-maker. There may be a more fundamental reason why fiscal choices veer from welfare maximization: Simply stated, fiscal choices are, in reality, the result of political-economy equilibria, which can be incongruous with welfare maximization.

Real-world political mechanisms are complex, and they result from the interaction of individually rational choices by a large number of agents. Under certain very stringent assumptions it may be possible to represent the political process by means of a political-support function (Long and Vousden, 1991; Grossman and Helpman, 1994), but in general, the mapping from the institutional structure to policy choices cannot be approximated by means of an optimization metaphor. In such cases, political mechanisms need to be modeled explicitly, taking into account the individual behavior of the various political actors.

There have been very few studies examining the effects of tax competition on political equilibria. Persson and Tabellini (1992) developed a two-country, two-period model in which policy-makers were elected by majority voting. They described a political-economy equilibrium as the outcome of a three-stage game: In the first stage, voters, who have identical preferences but differ in terms of their endowments, elect representatives; in the second stage, the representatives in each country select source-based tax rates as a best response to the other country's choice; in the last stage, investors make their capital-location decisions.

In such an equilibrium, it is shown that the representative elected by the median voter is not the one who has the median endowment. This is because the median voter, accounting for the simultaneous setting of tax policies by the two policy-makers in the second stage of the game, will find it optimal to delegate fiscal choices to an individual who ex post will select a higher capital-tax rate (i.e., a policy-maker whose policy preferences lie to the "left" of the median voter's; in their specification, this is an individual with a below-median endowment).

Persson and Tabellini show that an increase in capital mobility will lower the equilibrium tax rates selected by policy-makers, but it will also tend to increase the difference between the median voter's ex-ante and ex-post policy preferences, which in turn will induce voters to elect a policy-maker whose preferences lie further to the left of their own; this effect will partly offset the downward pressure on taxes generated by increased capital mobility.

According to their argument, political-economy mechanisms interact with tax competition and can serve as a partial remedy for it. Thus, political competition within jurisdictions is a surrogate for coordination. Relative to a world in which tax policies are aimed at welfare maximization, the prediction of their analysis is for convergence of policies.

Voting models can also be used to address certain unresolved puzzles in the real-world choices of tax instruments in open economies. In a recent study, Huizinga and Nielsen (1996) examined the political economy of capital-income taxation in a small open economy to explain why distortionary capital taxes may be chosen instead of nondistortionary profit taxes. In their two-period model, first-period endowment income can be used for first-period consumption and for savings/investment, which in turn can be used to produce output through a concave production function in the second period. The agents differ in their endowments and profit income (associated with second-period production); capital-income taxes consist of taxes on savings/investment and profit taxes.

They showed that in a representative-agent framework, limited profit taxation can be rationalized only if domestic firms are foreign-owned; but in a political-economy setting, if the median voter's share of profits is relatively large, an equilibrium may feature limited profit taxation alongside negative savings or investment taxes, even if firms are fully domestically owned.

The analysis of voting equilibria can thus shed light on aspects of tax competition that otherwise would remain unexplained. Nevertheless, voting is a very stylized description of the political process in modern democracies. Party politics are intertwined with a number of other important dimensions of political competition, such as lobbying by industry and other interest groups and pressure from self-motivated administrators. In the next section we shall attempt to draw some implications of lobbying activities for tax competition.

4   Lobbying and Pressure Groups

Lobbying by domestic industries and other interest groups has received much attention in recent analyses of endogenous trade protection. Magee, Brock, and Young (1989) have articulated a theory of political competition that features lobbying and in which the outcomes of elections involving parties that have precommitted to certain trade-policy platforms are affected by campaign contributions by industry lobbyists. More recently, Grossman and Helpman (1994, 1995a,b) have proposed a different specification of lobbying behavior based on the assumption that elected policy-makers can actively modify their policies in response to lobbying pressure, effectively "selling" protection to domestic lobbies in exchange for financial contributions.

Whatever the characterization of the lobbying game through which lobbyists can affect policy choices, it is clear that the presence of lobbying could be important for the outcome of interjurisdictional tax competition. How this outcome will be affected by lobbying will generally depend on how taxation affects individual industries.

As in the case of trade barriers, lobbying could affect the choice of indirect taxes. A high tax on a certain commodity would negatively affect final demand for that commodity and thus profits and returns to the primary factors employed in its production, while positively affecting other sectors. Although on welfare-maximization grounds the reason for deviating from a second-best choice of commodity taxes is (as for trade barriers) to manipulate the terms of trade in a region's favor, there is a fundamental difference between a tariff and a commodity tax: Whereas a tariff affords protection to import-competing industries, a tax will have negative impacts on such industries, accompanied by positive, albeit less concentrated, impacts on other sectors. Whether or not lobbying will reinforce or offset the effects of commodity-tax competition thus will depend on the relative lobbying strength of import-competing industries relative to other producers.

With respect to factor taxes, lobbying by domestic firms and labor unions could help explain why even small countries tax foreign-owned capital and, more generally, why distortionary source-based taxation is often preferred to residence-based income taxation. Lobbies representing domestic investors may be able to exploit the lower "political visibility" of their offshore investments to pressure policy-makers into taxing foreign-owned capital, while granting comparative relief to foreign-source income.

Lobbying could also have implications stemming from the spending side of the government's budget. If government spending is directed toward goods produced by industries that are effective lobbyists, the political equilibrium could involve overspending. Similarly, bureaucrats endowed with private information about the costs of public-good provision may also manage to pressure policy-makers into funding larger budgets. In either case, if tax competition generates downward pressure on tax revenues, it could play a positive disciplinary role, much as it would with nonbenevolent policy-makers. And, vice versa, lobbying for larger budgets could partly offset the pressure that tax competition places on tax rates.

In addition, lobbying by foreign firms could act as a mitigating influence on tax competition. For example, multinational enterprises might be able to benefit from harmonized tax treatment of their various activities across the jurisdictions where they operate; a parent company might then lobby a foreign government, either directly or through a subsidiary, to adopt tax rules that would be consistent with the tax treatment received at home. But it is also conceivable that in the pursuit of favorable tax treatment, multinationals might instead pressure foreign governments into a more aggressive tax-competition stance.

The matter of the linkages between lobbying and tax competition promises to provide a rich research agenda, but just how productive that line of investigation will be remains to be seen.

5   Constitutional Choices

Our discussion thus far has focused on the interaction between tax competition and political equilibria. But tax competition can have implications that go beyond political equilibria: It can also shape the framework within which the political game takes place, affecting constitutional rules and constitutional choices at the stage where jurisdictions are created.

In a recent study (Perroni and Scharf, 1997) we examined the linkage between capital-tax competition and jurisdiction formation using a locational model in which jurisdictions are endogenously formed as groupings of individuals having similar preferences for different varieties of local public goods, and where fiscal choices within jurisdictions are made by majority voting.

We can formalize this preference structure by assuming that there exists a continuum of individuals uniformly distributed along the real line. Each point on the real line also represents a different variety of a local public good that is consumed in conjunction with private goods. The key idea here is that each individual prefers the variety of public good that corresponds to her location over any other variety available. In this formulation, location reflects only preferences and is exogenous.

Each individual is endowed with a certain amount of an immobile factor that is situated in the jurisdiction to which the individual belongs, as well as with one unit of capital, which is interjurisdictionally mobile. Output is produced using both factors and can be used either for private consumption or for providing local public goods. The latter are financed by a source-based tax on the capital employed within a jurisdiction's borders. Forming larger jurisdictions will thus result in cost and tax savings with respect to public-good provision; on the other hand, larger jurisdictions will also result in some individuals being "too far" from their preferred variety, which places an upper bound on jurisdictional enlargement.

Jurisdiction formation in the presence of tax competition is characterized as a three-stage game: In the first stage, individuals arrange themselves into jurisdictions, reaching an equilibrium when individuals located on the boundary between two jurisdictions are indifferent between staying in the jurisdiction to which they belong and moving to an adjacent one. In the second stage, public-good provision is determined by majority voting within jurisdictions, with individuals voting on public-good varieties, taxes, and levels of public-good provision. In the final stage, the owners of the mobile factor make their capital-location decisions, arbitraging across domestic- and foreign-investment opportunities. This sequencing, first proposed by Westhoff (1977), can be interpreted as reflecting a situation in which the costs of changing jurisdictional affiliation are negligible over the long term, whereas the short-term costs of gaining access to public goods provided in other jurisdictions are prohibitive.

Because this model has a large number of jurisdictions, individual jurisdictions are price-takers for the net-of-tax price of capital. With respect to the third stage of the game, this implies that in the absence of a public-good requirement, the optimal capital levy will be zero. With reference to the second stage of the game, the large-numbers assumption implies that individual voters will take taxes in other jurisdictions as given; hence, in a representative system, individuals cannot affect the tax-competition outcome by strategically voting for a candidate whose preferences differ from their own [as in the Persson and Tabellini model (1992, 1994)]; here the median voter simply votes for the median candidate.

Tax competition affects the third stage of the game by raising the marginal cost of public funds (because of the capital-flight effect of source-based taxation), thus lowering the tax rate favored by all individuals in a given jurisdiction. We also show that in the voting stage of the game, an enlargement of a jurisdiction will cause the level of public-good provision chosen by the median voter to change in a direction that will have an adverse effect on consumers whose preferences lie farther away from the median preferences in the jurisdiction. That, in turn, will discourage peripheral consumers from joining the jurisdiction in the first stage of the game, resulting in a suboptimal equilibrium size for all jurisdictions.

Interjurisdictional tax competition affects the jurisdiction-formation game in the following way: Not only does it lower the tax rate preferred by each individual within a jurisdiction, but it also reduces the gap between the rate favored by the median voter and that favored by peripheral individuals, dampening the adverse effect that the median voter's reaction has on membership decisions. This results in a larger equilibrium jurisdiction size and a smaller number of varieties of the local public good. (A more detailed account of the model and results is given in the Appendix.) Thus, international integration of factor markets could exert upward pressure on the sizes of local jurisdictions, making local governments less viable in relation to the central taxing and spending authorities.

Our analysis ignores the incentives for enlargement associated with becoming a larger player. If jurisdictions are small open economies (an assumption we maintain throughout our analysis), then enlargement will have no effect on market power. If, on the other hand, jurisdictions are large economies, then enlargement could bring more power in capital markets, which from the point of view of individual jurisdictions would ensure a more favorable outcome in a noncooperative tax equilibrium. With large jurisdictions, however, simultaneous enlargements by competing jurisdictions could result in global welfare losses, a point that was first made by Krugman (1991) with reference to customs unions. If regions compete for a mobile base, on the other hand, forming larger jurisdictions would result in larger best-response tax rates and hence a more efficient outcome.

6   Competition or Coordination?

The usual prescription from analyses of tax competition is that coordination of tax policies across jurisdictions is necessary in order internalize cross-border fiscal externalities (Sinn, 1994). That view has spawned a copious academic literature on tax harmonization (Keen, 1987, 1989; Turunen-Red and Woodland, 1990; de Crombrugghe and Tulkens, 1990) and has gained much currency in policy circles. In the European Union, the pursuit of tax coordination across member states is increasingly being regarded as a priority, as can be seen, for example, from the *Report on the Development of Tax Systems* (Commission of the European Communities, 1996), following an informal meeting of European finance ministers in Dublin earlier the same year.

Even abstracting from any political-economy dimensions of tax competition, one can find a number of reasons why coordination may not be desirable. Fiscal federations do not exist in isolation from each other, but interact with the rest of the world; as already discussed in Section 5, coordination, if limited to a subset of all concerned jurisdictions, could make things worse. Also, policy choices by well-meaning policy-makers may be constrained by credibility considerations. Kehoe (1989) has shown that when benevolent policy-makers are faced with a time-inconsistency problem in setting their capital-tax rates, the downward pressure on taxes associated with tax competition can act as a commitment mechanism; in such an environment, tax coordination may lead to decreased efficiency. Finally, coordination is not costless:

Implementation of tax coordination within a fiscal federation, if pursued through a definition of rules rather than through a delegation of discretionary power, could be seriously hampered by incentive problems (Dhillon, Perroni, and Scharf, 1998).

Yet political-economy-based objections can deal an even more fundamental blow to the coordination argument – an argument that is squarely built on the premise that tax policies result from constrained maximization and that the objective of the tax authority is citizens' welfare.

In the Edwards and Keen model of competition among Leviathan governments, tax competition can act as a beneficial antidote to wasteful fiscal choices by nonbenevolent policy-makers. This conclusion is consistent with a market-oriented approach to public choices, an approach that has had increasing influence on economists' views of government activities, particularly in North America. Although markets may be unable to function properly when public goods are involved, there is still a role to be played by market-like competition mechanisms in the public sector. Thus, for example, as first suggested by Tiebout (1956), competition among jurisdictions seeking new members can induce revelation of preferences for public goods and lead to the selection of efficient tax-expenditure combinations. The analysis by Edwards and Keen suggests that tax competition among jurisdictions for a given tax base, if unimpeded, can also play an efficiency-enhancing role.

Similarly, in our analysis of jurisdiction formation under capital-tax competition (Perroni and Scharf, 1997) we have shown that through an expansion of jurisdictional boundaries and a reduction in the number of public-good varieties, an increase in interjurisdictional capital mobility can lead to rationalization in the provision of local public goods. Tax competition can thus offset the efficiency costs of political-coordination failure that arise because of the lack of a credible political-commitment mechanism vis-à-vis prospective members. Indeed, we cannot exclude the possibility that this positive efficiency effect could dominate the direct welfare costs of tax competition. In the Appendix we present examples in which this effect is so strong that it leads to a Pareto improvement within a given jurisdiction, even in the absence of compensation: Not only do peripheral voters gain, but the median voter herself can be made better off by an increase in tax competition.

In conclusion, it seems clear that positing tax coordination as a desirable objective is unwarranted without a positive theory of fiscal choices. Yet this simple point seems to have gone largely unnoticed in the policy debate on fiscal harmonization that is currently taking place in Europe.

7   Sustaining Cooperation

Assuming that it is desirable, how can fiscal coordination among independent jurisdictions be sustained? In the absence of a preexisting central authority, tax-coordination agreements – negotiated through bargaining or through some other means – may not be easily enforceable.

Again, we can draw on the recent literature on trade agreements, which has resorted to tacit-collusion arguments formalized by means of infinitely repeated game constructions. In those models, cooperation can be sustained noncooperatively by an appropriate supporting penalty structure (Dixit, 1987). This explanation of how cooperation is maintained relies on a well-known property of infinitely repeated games – namely, that provided the discount rates applied to future payoffs are sufficiently low, any outcome that is Pareto-superior to the disagreement payoffs can be supported by suitable strategies as a subgame perfect Nash equilibrium of the repeated game (Folk Theorem).

This type of argument has several drawbacks. First, it offers limited predictive power as to what form of global cooperation will actually take place. Second, it does not explain how formal agreements actually materialize; because tacit collusion need not be embodied in formal rules, according to this explanation trade agreements would be devoid of any normative force. This problem of interpretation is particularly serious with reference to taxation, where cooperation involves harmonization of often complex tax rules. Nevertheless, tacit collusion represents the most compelling paradigm available for explaining international cooperation.

Political-economy dimensions can impact on the viability of tax coordination agreements supported in this way. By affecting the form and arguments of the payoff functions of the players concerned, they can affect the relative sizes of the gains from cooperation and unilateral defection, as well as the severity of retaliation costs. This, in turn, may make it possible to maintain cooperation even between relatively impatient players; conversely, it might make cooperation more problematic if, for example, players were relatively myopic (hence impatient) elected politicians, rather than benevolent, farsighted social planners.

When policy-makers are subject to lobbying pressures, there can also be implications for the form that tax coordination takes. Politically sensitive industries may need to be granted some form of preferential treatment in a tax-coordination agreement if it is to be politically viable; Grossman and Helpman (1995b) make this point with respect to the formation of free-trade agreements. On the other hand, coordination of lobbying activities across regions by firms belonging to a collusive industry and operating in different jurisdictions, or by multinationals, could improve the prospects for coordination.

Finally, some recent international-trade literature has examined how the enlargement of trading blocs can affect the viability of cooperation at a broader level (Krugman, 1991). If we apply those ideas to tax coordination, then we might conclude that larger blocs pose a threat to cooperation. But taking political-economy considerations into account might yet again change our conclusions. Richardson (1993) has shown that when trade policies reflect a political-economy equilibrium, the formation of preferential trading areas can lead to lower external tariffs as individual interest groups see their influence diluted.

Research on the positive foundations of tax coordination is still in its infancy, but political-economy dimensions are sure to become an integral part of the research agenda.

8   Conclusions

This chapter has presented arguments relating interjurisdictional tax competition to the political economy of fiscal choices. We have argued that tax competition is an important factor in the determination of political equilibria and that, conversely, accounting for political-economy mechanisms is essential for a correct understanding of the implications of tax competition.

Tax competition can act as a restraint on wasteful policy-makers; it can influence voting outcomes in a representative democracy and lead to lobbying by affected interest groups. Tax competition can also have an impact on jurisdictional-affiliation decisions and thereby on jurisdiction size, in addition to reducing the costs of political-coordination failure within jurisdictions. In turn, tax competition can be mitigated by induced changes in political equilibria, and it can be better explained if political-economy considerations are invoked. Finally, both the desirability and sustainability of tax-coordination arrangements depend crucially on the political-economy determinants of tax competition.

The foregoing listing is likely to be incomplete. As research on these issues is only now beginning, future work undoubtedly will uncover other dimensions of the interaction between political-economy equilibria and tax competition that we have neglected here. Our partial account nevertheless gives a clear indication that political-economy mechanisms are bound to become an essential ingredient of any future studies of interjurisdictional tax competition.

APPENDIX: CAPITAL-TAX COMPETITION AND
JURISDICTION FORMATION

This Appendix describes the jurisdiction-formation model discussed in
Section 5. For further details, see Perroni and Scharf (1997).

Consider a continuum of individuals uniformly distributed along the
real line. Each point j on the real line represents a different variety of
a local public good, and an individual's location on the line reflects her
preferred variety. Each individual $i \in (-\infty, \infty)$ consumes the local public
good together with private goods. The idea that an individual prefers the
variety of local public good that coincides with her location is captured
by assuming that the effective amount of local-public-good consumption
l that consumer i obtains from g units of variety j decreases with the dis-
tance $s \equiv |i - j|$ between i and j (we shall use a circumflex and an inverted
circumflex to denote functions, and subscripts to denote partial
derivatives):

$$\hat{l}[g, s] \equiv \hat{y}[s]g \tag{13.A1}$$

where $\hat{y}[0] = 1, \hat{y}' < 0$, and $\hat{y}'' < 0$. Preferences over private consumption
c and public-good consumption l are described by a quasi-linear utility
function

$$\hat{u}[c, l] \equiv c + \hat{h}(l) \tag{13.A2}$$

with $\hat{h}' > 0, \hat{h}'' < 0$, that is the same across consumers. For notational simplicity we shall use the shorthand $\hat{v}[g, s] \equiv h[\hat{y}[s]g]$.

Individuals are partitioned into jurisdictions (i.e., groupings of contiguous consumers) and they consume only the public goods provided in
the jurisdiction to which they belong. The marginal rate of transformation between public goods and private goods in production is constant
and equal to unity. Each individual is endowed with z units of an immobile factor that is situated in the jurisdiction to which the individual
belongs, as well as one unit of a mobile factor. Output is produced using
both factors, according to constant-returns-to-scale technologies that are
summarized by a quasi-concave production function; per-capita output
is $\hat{q}[z, k]$, where $k = 1 + m$ is the per-capita input of the mobile factor,
with m denoting the per-capita net flow of the mobile factor from and
to other jurisdictions. To simplify notation, we shall represent production
by means of a concave production function $\hat{f}[k] \equiv \hat{q}[z, k]$, with $\hat{f}' > 0$,
$\hat{f}'' < 0$.

Jurisdictions are assumed to be small open economies (price-takers)
that levy a source-based tax at rate t on the capital employed within their

borders. Arbitraging of investment opportunities across jurisdictions implies

$$(1-t)\hat{f}'[1+m] = r \tag{13.A3}$$

where r is the world net-of-tax rental. This condition defines an implicit function $\hat{m}[t, r]$ linking factor inflows to the tax rate in the jurisdiction and to the world net-of-tax rate of return. By differentiating (13.A3), we obtain

$$\hat{m}_t = \frac{\hat{f}'}{(1-t)\hat{f}''} = \eta \frac{1+\hat{m}}{1-t} < 0 \tag{13.A4}$$

where $\eta = \hat{f}'/((1+\hat{m})\hat{f}'')$ is the elasticity of demand for the mobile factor with respect to its gross-of-tax rental price. If the jurisdiction size is n, public-good provision will be equal to

$$g = nt\frac{r}{1-t}(1+\hat{m}[t, r]) \equiv \hat{g}[n, t, r] \tag{13.A5}$$

Private per-capita consumption (which equals net-of-tax income) is

$$c = \hat{f}(1+\hat{m}[t, r]) - \frac{r}{1-t}(t+\hat{m}[t, r]) \equiv \hat{c}[t, r] \tag{13.A6}$$

where $r/(1 - t)$ represents the gross-of-tax rate of return.

In a voting equilibrium (the second stage of the game), the median voter will select the median variety of the local public good (i.e., the variety that is located at a distance $n/2$ from the boundaries of the jurisdiction). Given this choice of variety, the level of tax preferred by an individual located at a distance $s \in [0, n/2]$ from the center will be given by the condition

$$\hat{v}_g[\hat{g}, s] = -\frac{\hat{c}_t}{\hat{g}_t} \tag{13.A7}$$

This defines an implicit function $\check{t}[n, s, r]$ giving the preferred tax rate for individual s. If we totally differentiate (13.A7), we find that $\check{t}[n, s, r]$ is increasing or decreasing in s depending on how easy it is for an individual to substitute private goods for public goods. If the inverse elasticity of the marginal valuation of the public good with respect to public-good provision, $\varepsilon \equiv \hat{h}'/(\hat{t}\hat{h}'') < 0$, is greater than unity in absolute value, then peripheral consumers prefer lower taxes; otherwise they prefer higher taxes.

The median voter here will be represented by an individual located at a distance $n/4$ from the center of the jurisdiction, and thus the tax rate selected in a political equilibrium will be $\hat{t}[n, r] \equiv \check{t}[n, n/4, r]$. This equilibrium rate is increasing or decreasing in n depending on whether the absolute value of ε is greater than or less than unity. Thus, following an enlargement of the jurisdiction, the tax rate changes in a direction that goes counter to the direction favored by peripheral individuals.

In the first stage of the game, the boundaries of jurisdictions are determined endogenously by the free movement of individuals. For such an equilibrium we require that it must not be possible for alternative jurisdictions to form and achieve an outcome that Pareto-dominates the given outcome for all individuals belonging to the new jurisdiction; and there must not exist any incentive for individuals to unilaterally move from one jurisdiction to another (Wooders, 1988; Greenberg and Weber, 1993). If we define the utility of a border individual (i.e., an individual who is located at a distance $n/2$ from the center) as

$$\hat{b}[n, r] \equiv \hat{c}(\hat{t}[n, r], r) + \hat{v}[\hat{g}(n, \hat{t}\{n, r\}, r), n/2] \tag{13.A8}$$

then the foregoing equilibrium conditions can be stated as

$$\hat{b}_n[n, r] = 0 \tag{13.A9}$$

and the second-order curvature condition is

$$\hat{b}_{nn}[n, r] < 0 \tag{13.A10}$$

Condition (13.A9) can be interpreted as stating that the border individual ($s = n/2$) must be indifferent between staying in her current jurisdiction and moving to a contiguous identical jurisdiction, and condition (13.A10) states that (13.A9) must identify a maximum for $\hat{b}[n, r]$.

The boundary indifference condition (13.A9) identifies an implicit function $\hat{n}[r]$ linking jurisdiction size n with the world net-of-tax return to the mobile factor:

$$n = \hat{n}[r] \tag{13.A11}$$

In a symmetric equilibrium, the tax rate will be the same across jurisdictions:

$$t = \hat{t}[n, r] \tag{13.A12}$$

and interjurisdictional flows of the mobile factor will be zero, implying $k = 1$ and therefore

$$r = (1 - t)\hat{f}'[1] \tag{13.A13}$$

Conditions (13.A11)–(13.A13) together define a noncooperative equilibrium characterized by an endogenous jurisdiction size n^*, a tax rate t^*, and a world net-of-tax rental r^*. It can be shown that such an equilibrium will feature an excessive number of jurisdictions, each of suboptimal size. The intuition for this result is simply that, as previously shown, the median voter's reaction to a jurisdiction's enlargement will be to change taxes in a direction that will hurt peripheral consumers; that, in turn, will discourage peripheral consumers from joining the jurisdiction.

Capital mobility and tax competition affect this outcome as follows. Higher capital mobility, which we represent by an increase in the absolute value of the elasticity of demand for capital, $\mu = |\eta|$, raises the marginal cost of public funds on the right-hand side of (13.A7), thus lowering the tax rate preferred by all individuals in a given jurisdiction. That effect, however, will reduce the gap between the rates preferred by peripheral individuals and that preferred by the median voter and will dampen the adverse effect that the median voter's reaction has on membership, which in turn will result in larger jurisdictions. This can be seen by totally differentiating (13.A11)–(13.A13) with respect to n^*, t^*, r^*, and μ, which yields

$$\frac{\partial n^*}{\partial \mu} > 0 \tag{13.A14}$$

Thus, tax competition imposes discipline on the fiscal choices of the median voter, and that in turn encourages membership. It is indeed possible for the political-coordination gains brought about by an increase in tax competition to more than offset the direct efficiency losses associated with tax competition, resulting in a Pareto improvement for all members of a given jurisdiction, even in the absence of interpersonal transfers.

REFERENCES

Commission of the European Communities (1996). *Taxation in the European Union: Report on the Development of Tax Systems*. Brussels: Commission of the European Communities.

de Crombrugghe, A., and Tulkens, H. (1990). On Pareto-improving tax changes under fiscal competition. *Journal of Public Economics* 41:335–50.

Dhillon, A., Perroni, C., and Scharf, K. A. (1998). Implementing tax coordination. Forthcoming, *Journal of Public Economics*.

Dixit, A. (1987). Strategic aspects of trade policy. In: *Advances in Economic Theory: Fifth World Congress*, ed. T. Bewley, pp. 329–62. Cambridge University Press.

Edwards, J., and Keen, M. (1996). Tax competition and Leviathan. *European Economic Review* 40:113–34.

Gordon, R., and Wilson, J. D. (1986). An examination of multijurisdictional corporate income taxation under formula apportionment. *Econometrica* 54:1357–73.

Greenberg, J., and Weber, S. (1993). Stable coalition structures with a unidimensional set of alternatives. *Journal of Economic Theory* 60:62–82.

Grossman, G. M., and Helpman, E. (1994). Protection for sale. *American Economic Review* 84:833–50.

Grossman, G. M., and Helpman, E. (1995a). Trade wars and trade talks. *Journal of Political Economy* 103:675–708.

Grossman, G. M., and Helpman, E. (1995b). The politics of free trade agreements. *American Economic Review* 85:667–90.

Huizinga, H., and Nielsen, S. B. (1996). The political economy of capital income and profit taxation in a small open economy. Unpublished manuscript, Tilburg University and EPRU, Copenhagen Business School.

Keen, M. (1987). Welfare effects of commodity tax harmonisation. *Journal of Public Economics* 33:107–14.

Keen, M. (1989). Pareto-improving indirect tax harmonization. *European Economic Review* 33:1–12.

Kehoe, P. J. (1989). Policy cooperation among benevolent governments may be undesirable. *Review of Economic Studies* 56:289–96.

Krugman, P. R. (1991). Is bilateralism bad? In: *International Trade and Trade Policy*, ed. E. Helpman and A. Razin, pp. 9–23. Massachusetts Institute of Technology Press.

Long, N. V., and Vousden, N. (1991). Protectionist responses and declining industries. *Journal of International Economics* 30:87–103.

Magee, S. P., Brock, W. A., and Young, L. (1989). *Black Hole Tariffs and Endogenous Policy Theory: Political Economy in General Equilibrium*. Massachusetts Institute of Technology Press.

Mintz, J., and Tulkens, H. (1986). Commodity tax competition between member states of a federation: equilibrium and efficiency. *Journal of Public Economics* 29:133–72.

Perroni, C., and Scharf, K. (1997). Tiebout with politics: capital tax competition and jurisdictional boundaries. Working paper, Institute for Fiscal Studies, London.

Persson, T., and Tabellini, G. (1992). The politics of 1992: fiscal policy and European integration. *Review of Economic Studies* 59:689–701.

Persson, T., and Tabellini, G. (1994). Representative democracy and capital taxation. *Journal of Public Economics* 55:53–70.

Richardson, M. (1993). Endogenous protection and trade diversion. *Journal of International Economics* 34:309–24.

Sinn, H. W. (1994). How much Europe? Subsidiarity, centralization, and fiscal competition. *Scottish Journal of Political Economy* 41:85–107.

Tiebout, C. M. (1956). A pure theory of local expenditures. *Journal of Political Economy* 64:416–24.

Turunen-Red, A. H., and Woodland, A. D. (1990). Multilateral reform of domestic taxes. *Oxford Economic Papers* 42:160–86.

Westhoff, F. (1977). Existence of equilibria in economies with a local public good. *Journal of Economic Theory* 14:84–112.

Wooders, M. H. (1988). Stability of jurisdiction structures in economies with local public goods. *Mathematical Social Sciences* 15:29–49.

Zodrow, R. G., and Mieszkowski, P. (1986). Pigou, Tiebout, property taxation and the underprovision of local public goods. *Journal of Urban Economics* 19:356–70.

PART VII

Migration of Skilled and Unskilled Labor

CHAPTER 14

Economic Integration, Factor Mobility, and Wage Convergence

Gilles Saint-Paul

1   Introduction

When several regions get integrated into a single political entity, many issues arise because of asymmetries across those regions: One region may be richer than another, or better endowed in skills or physical capital. Regions also are of different sizes and exert different political weights in common decision-making.

A paradigmatic example of that process is provided by German reunification: One region was poorer and smaller than the other, and its political decomposition implied that most of the relevant decisions would be made by West Germany. Another example is Italy, where the north's larger industrial base makes it dominant in several respects.

An issue that may be particularly relevant for the integration of European countries or regions is wage determination: In many countries, wages are set by collective bargaining at the sectoral level, and the associated agreements apply to every region. When there are large political and economic asymmetries across regions, wage rates at the national level are likely to be determined by the interests of the dominant region. Thus, in Italy, where the north's unemployment rate is much lower than that in the south, it has been found that national wages are much more reactive to northern unemployment rates than to southern rates (e.g., Di Monte, 1992). In Germany, a very rapid pace of wage convergence between the two regions had been agreed upon after unification, thus generating excess unemployment in the east. See Sinn and Sinn (1992) for a description of many aspects of the German reunification process, including the evolution of unemployment and how eastern wages were negotiated; see also Dornbusch and Wolf (1992).

This study was presented at the 52nd Congress of the International Institute of Public Finance, Tel Aviv, August 1996.

In this study we seek to analyze the effects of the pace of wage convergence on economic activity in two integrated, initially asymmetrical regions: There are two factors, raw labor and human capital, and one region (the west) has a higher relative endowment of human capital. Both factors are mobile across the two regions, but at a cost. The production function is the same in the two regions and has constant returns to scale, implying that over the long term, wages and relative factor endowments will be equalized across the two regions and that the allocation of production will be determined by initial conditions. We shall then analyze the impacts of an exogenously imposed faster pace of wage convergence for raw labor and show that it generates a hump-shaped curve for unemployment in the poorer region and hastens the migration of raw labor toward the west, while slowing the movement of human capital toward the east.

An important aspect of our analysis is the political economy of wage convergence. We assume that the rate of wage convergence is set by the "insiders" of the western region so that it will maximize the present discounted value of raw labor's wages in the west. We shall show that although in the long term their welfare will be unaffected by the pace of wage convergence, over the transition period the western insiders will gain from more rapid wage convergence because it will retain human capital in the west, but they will lose to the extent that more raw labor will migrate westward. As a result, the larger the migration cost of raw labor relative to human capital, the greater the incentives for western unions to increase the pace of wage convergence. This condition of excess wage convergence arising in the presence of political equilibrium is consistent with the findings in the empirical literature indicating that skilled workers are more regionally mobile than unskilled workers (e.g., Antolin and Bover, 1993).

Although we have not discovered any studies dealing with this particular issue, our study is related to several strands in the literature dealing with migration of skilled and unskilled workers, interactions between unemployment and immigration,[1] and the effects of integration

---

[1] There is an abundant literature on the effects of unemployment and wage differentials on migration, and the converse. Studies concerned with unemployment include Gabriel, Shack-Marquez, and Wascher (1993), Pissarides and McMaster (1990), Schmidt, Stilz, and Zimmermann (1994), Hughes and McCormick (1994), Decressin and Fatas (1995). For example, Pissarides and McMaster (1990) found that migration eventually eliminated disequilibrium unemployment differentials, but at a slow rate. Hughes and McCormick (1994) found little impact of unemployment differentials on migration for manual workers, but a standard response for nonmanual workers. However, Keil and Newell

on wage determination.[2] The analysis of migration in the context of unemployment clearly goes back to the famous paper by Harris and Todaro (1970), but here the logic is quite different: Whereas in Harris and Todaro's work unemployment prevailed in the rich (host) region, which nevertheless attracted people because wages were high (and rigid downward), here unemployment is created by centralized wage-setting institutions in the poor (migration) region, thus hastening the migration of raw labor toward the host region.

Among more closely related studies, Razin and Sadka (1995) analyzed the impact of wage rigidity in the destination region on the welfare effects of immigration for natives of the destination region; that topic is related to our study, but they had a different focus. Burda and Funke (1991) addressed the same issue we shall address here, namely, the effect of economic integration on wage determination. In their model, the elasticities of labor demand differed across the two regions and unions set wages as perfectly discriminating monopolists. They then analyzed the impact of migration on the union's optimal wage structure. Hence, they focused on how a discriminating union's preferred wage differential was affected by immigration, whereas our study will focus on how unions can be led to impose a pace of wage convergence more rapid than that in equilibrium in order to manipulate relative factor endowments in ways that will be favorable to them. In another related study, Burda and Wyplosz (1991) analyzed the welfare economics of migrations of human capital and physical capital, with no discussion of unemployment and wage rigidity.

This chapter is organized as follows: In the next section we set up the basic model for migrations of raw labor and human capital. We then study equilibrium determination in the full-employment case. Wage rigidity, captured by an exogenous pace of wage convergence, is then

---

(1994), using data on migration between Ireland and England, found a strong response of migration to unemployment and wages.

For the causality among migration, wages, and unemployment, the reader may refer to Friedberg and Hunt (1995), who found small effects. Hatzius (1994) studied the impact of migration on unemployment and wages in western Germany.

[2] Similar issues have been discussed in the context of international trade theory. Brecher and Choudhri (1987) introduced unemployment (induced by a minimum wage) in the capital-abundant country in the standard model of international trade. Danthine and Hunt (1994) argued that greater integration makes wage determination less sensitive to the degree of centralization. Zimmermann (1995) argued that immigration is likely to make wage determinations more competitive. For an overview of the interactions between integration and labor markets, see Ehrenberg (1994).

introduced. We then conclude with an analysis of how the pace of wage convergence affects the welfare of unions in the dominant region.

2   The Basic Model

There are two regions, east (E) and west (W), and two factors of production, raw labor (L) and human capital (H), which can be interpreted as "technology," "skilled labor," and so forth. What is crucial is that there is some limit to the supply of human capital, so that raw labor has an interest in attracting human capital to its own region at the expense of the other region.

Together, the two regions are made up of a mass L of individuals, each endowed with one unit of raw labor, of which L_E is located in the east, and L_W in the west:

$$L_E + L_W = L$$

Similarly, there is a mass H of individuals, each endowed with one unit of human capital: H_E are in the east, and H_W are in the west. $H_E + H_W = H$. The production function within region i is Cobb-Douglas, with constant returns:

$$Y_i = A H_i^{\alpha} L_i^{1-\alpha}$$

Each production factor is paid its marginal product, implying

$$w_{H_i} = \alpha A H_i^{\alpha-1} L_i^{1-\alpha}$$
$$w_{L_i} = (1-\alpha) A H_i^{\alpha} L_i^{-\alpha}$$

For simplicity we assume the same production function for both regions. The utility function of an agent is then given by

$$E_0 \int_0^{+\infty} \log[w_{jit}(1 - u_{jit})] e^{-\rho t}\, dt \tag{14.1}$$

where w_{jit} is the wage of an agent endowed with one unit of factor $j \in \{H, L\}$ and working in region $i \in \{E, W\}$ at date t, and u_{jit} is the corresponding unemployment rate. Note that for simplicity we have assumed a perfect redistribution between the employed and the unemployed of a given region, so that an owner of factor j in region i earns and consumes $w_{jit}(1 - u_{jit})$ whether employed or not. Alternatively, we could allow the employed to have an instantaneous utility greater than that of the unemployed, in which case we would have to specify how mobility between unemployment and employment takes place, with a potential difference appearing between natives and immigrants.

Each individual can migrate between the two regions, provided he pays a fixed cost. The fixed cost is equal to

$$\frac{c_L L}{L_E L_W} \left| \frac{dL_E}{dt} \right|$$

for factor L, and

$$\frac{c_H H}{H_E H_W} \left| \frac{dH_E}{dt} \right|$$

for factor H. The derivative term captures a congestion effect: The migration cost per individual is higher when more people migrate. The migration cost is also inversely related to $L_E L_W$, primarily for computational convenience.

3   Migration and Equilibrium in the Full-Employment Case

Up until date $t = 0$ each region is a closed economy, with initial factor endowments L_{W0}, H_{W0} for the west and L_{E0}, H_{E0} for the east. At time $t = 0$ the frontiers are opened and migration proceeds, provided that the relative factor endowments differ across the two regions.

In this section we compute the evolution dynamics for the two regions under the assumption of full employment. We assume that the initial conditions are such that the west is richer in human capital:

$$\frac{H_{W0}}{L_{W0}} > \frac{H_{E0}}{L_{E0}}$$

Consequently, human capital will migrate eastward, and raw labor westward. At each instant of time the migration cost must equal the present discounted utility differential between the host and home regions, or

$$\frac{c_L L}{L_E L_W} \frac{dL_E}{dt} = \int_t^{+\infty} (\log w_{L_E} - \log w_{L_W}) e^{-\rho(u-t)} \, du < 0$$

$$\frac{c_H H}{H_E H_W} \frac{dH_E}{dt} = \int_t^{+\infty} (\log w_{H_E} - \log w_{H_W}) e^{-\rho(u-t)} \, du > 0 \qquad (14.2)$$

Let l be the fraction of total raw labor located in the west, and h the fraction of human capital located in the west. Let $\lambda = \log l - \log(1 - l)$, and $\eta = \log h - \log(1 - h)$. Then, using the marginal-product conditions, the foregoing equations can be rewritten as

$$-c_L \dot{\lambda} = \int_t^{+\infty} a(\lambda - \eta)e^{-\rho(u-t)}\, du$$

$$-c_H \dot{\eta} = \int_t^{+\infty} (1-a)(\eta - \lambda)e^{-\rho(u-t)}\, du$$

The solution to this problem is given by[3]

$$\lambda = \frac{a(\lambda_0 - \eta_0)}{a + (1-a)c_L/c_H}(e^{-z_1 t} - 1) + \lambda_0$$

$$= \lambda_\infty + \frac{ac_H(\lambda_0 - \eta_0)}{ac_H + (1-a)c_L}e^{-z_1 t} \qquad (14.3)$$

and

$$\eta = \eta_\infty + \frac{(1-a)c_L(\eta_0 - \lambda_0)}{ac_H + (1-a)c_L}e^{-z_1 t} \qquad (14.4)$$

where λ_0 and η_0 are the initial values of λ and η at $t = 0$,

$$z_1 = \frac{\{\rho^2 + 4[ac_H + (1-a)c_L]/c_L c_H\}^{1/2} - \rho}{2}$$

and $\lambda_\infty = \eta_\infty$ are the asymptotic values of λ and η, given by

$$\lambda_\infty = \eta_\infty = \frac{(1-a)c_L\lambda_0 + ac_H\eta_0}{ac_H + (1-a)c_L}$$

This formula is explained as follows. Because of constant returns to scale, the allocation of production across the two regions would, in the absence of adjustment costs, be indeterminate. Because of adjustment costs, it is determined by history, that is, by the initial allocation of factors of production across the two regions. The preceding formula tells us that it is the factor with the largest adjustment cost, weighted by its share in production, that tends to attract the other factor in its region. If, say, c_L is very large relative to c_H, then most of the adjustment will come from migration of human capital, implying that in the long run the share of either of the two factors located in the west will be very close to the initial share of raw labor located in the west, or, equivalently, that λ_∞ and η_∞ will be very close to λ_0; λ and η have to be the same asymptotically,

---

[3] These equations can be differentiated with respect to t, and they then collapse to a system of two linear second-order differential equations given by

$$c_L\ddot{\lambda} = \rho c_L\dot{\lambda} + a(\lambda - \eta)$$
$$c_H\ddot{\eta} = \rho c_H\dot{\eta} + (1-a)(\eta - \lambda)$$

Eliminating explosive solutions, we obtain (14.3) and (14.4).

because relative factor endowments must eventually be equalized. The factor shares appear in the calculation because, for instance, the higher the share of raw labor, the lower the wage differential generated by a given discrepancy in relative factor endowments, and the lower the incentive for raw labor to migrate. Note that there would be full hysteresis for raw labor ($\lambda_\infty = \lambda_0$) if it were the single factor of production ($a = 0$), if human capital were perfectly mobile ($c_H = 0$), or if the initial relative endowments were the same ($\lambda_0 = \eta_0$), in which case no adjustment would be needed.

The foregoing model implies a rate of adjustment of relative endowments equal to z_1. It is decreasing with adjustment costs and with the rate of time preference ρ: More impatient people are less willing to incur the up-front cost of migration. Similarly, the wage differential between the two regions vanishes at rate z_1; to see this, note that

$$\log w_{L_W} - \log w_{L_E} = a(\eta - \lambda) = a(\eta_0 - \lambda_0)e^{-z_1 t}$$

4   Wage Rigidity and Unemployment

We shall now compute the solution under the assumption that the western unions determine the wage rates in both regions. We assume that the market for human capital remains in equilibrium and that the interregional mobility for both factors is still described by the specification given in the preceding section.

The first step is to show that wages and unemployment rates have to be equalized between the two regions over the long run. To see this, first note that mobility of human capital implies that incomes must be equalized. This, in turn, implies equal relative factor endowments, and thus equal marginal products of raw labor. Thus the wages of raw labor have to be equal over the long run. Last, mobility of raw labor implies that, given equal wages, unemployment rates must be the same over the long run. The unions' wage policy must therefore be compatible with these constraints.

Next we show that the western unions will maintain full employment in the west. Note first that the unemployment rate for raw labor in region i is given by

$$1 - u_i = \left(\frac{w_{L_i}}{A(1-\alpha)}\right)^{-1/\alpha} \frac{H_i}{L_i}$$

or, in logarithms,

$$\log(1 - u_W) = -\frac{1}{\alpha}\log w_{L_W} + \log h - \log l + k_0 \tag{14.5}$$

$$\log(1 - u_E) = -\frac{1}{\alpha}\log w_{L_E} + \log(1 - h) - \log(1 - l) + k_0 \qquad (14.6)$$

with $k = \log[(1 - \alpha)A]/\alpha + \log H - \log L$.

Because of (14.5), (14.6), and the factor-price frontier, we can write evolution equations for η and λ entirely driven by the wage differential $\log w_{L_W} - \log w_{L_E} = x.$[4]

$$-c_H\dot{\eta} = \int_t^{+\infty} \frac{\alpha - 1}{\alpha}(\log w_{L_E} - \log w_{L_W})e^{-\rho(u-t)}\,du \qquad (14.7)$$

$$-c_L\dot{\lambda} = \int_t^{+\infty}\left[\frac{\alpha - 1}{\alpha}(\log w_{L_E} - \log w_{L_W}) + \lambda - \eta\right]e^{-\rho(u-t)}\,du \qquad (14.8)$$

Now the utility function for western employees is given by (14.1), which can be rewritten, using (14.5), as

$$\int_0^{+\infty}\left(\frac{\alpha - 1}{\alpha}\log w_{L_W} + \log h - \log l\right)e^{-\rho t}\,dt$$

For any given paths of h and l, workers in the west therefore will have an interest in setting wages at the lowest level, that is, at the full-employment level. This is because the full-unemployment insurance scheme makes their consumption essentially dependent on the total wage bill, which, because the elasticity of employment is $-1/\alpha < -1$, falls with w_{L_W}. Because western unions have two instruments, x and w_{L_W}, and because the paths for h and l depend only on x, w_{L_W} will be set so as to achieve full employment in the west.

The only variable that remains to be determined by western unions is the path of x, the wage differential between the two regions. To preserve the analytical tractability of the system, we shall restrict ourselves to the

---

[4] The factor-price frontier implies a one-to-one correspondence between the wage rate and the return to human capital, given by

$$\log w_{H_i} = \frac{\alpha - 1}{\alpha}\log w_{L_i} + k_1$$

with $k_1 = \log \alpha + (1 - \alpha)\log(1 - \alpha)/\alpha + (\log A)/\alpha$. As a result the arbitrage condition for the migration of human capital, (14.2) can now be written in terms of the wage differential for raw labor, yielding (14.7).

As for the migration of raw labor, we have to reintroduce unemployment into the arbitrage condition, which yields

$$-c_L\dot{\lambda} = \int_t^{+\infty}[\log w_{L_E} - \log w_{L_W} + \log(1 - u_E) - \log(1 - u_W)]e^{-\rho(u-t)}\,du$$

Using (14.5) and (14.6) and the definitions of λ and η, we get (14.8).

case in which the unions determine a single parameter: the convergence rate γ. Wages are therefore determined by the full-employment condition in the west and by the requirement that at any time t the wage gap be equal to

$$x_t = x_0 e^{-\gamma t}$$

We restrict γ to be such that there cannot be excess demand for raw labor in the east; that is, the rate of wage convergence imposed by unions exceeds the rate that naturally prevails in competitive equilibrium:

$$\gamma > z_1$$

We assume that the two regions were in equilibrium before unification; therefore the initial wage gap was simply $x_0 = \alpha (\eta_0 - \lambda_0)$.

Given γ, the rate of wage convergence chosen by the unions, we can readily compute the dynamics of η and λ and of the unemployment rate in the east. The solution to (14.7) is equal to

$$\eta = \frac{(1-\alpha)(\eta_0 - \lambda_0)(e^{-\gamma t} - 1)}{c_H \gamma (\gamma + \rho)} + \eta_0 \tag{14.9}$$

Once the path for η has been computed, we can compute the dynamics of λ using (14.8). The solution is given by

$$\lambda = (\eta_0 - \lambda_0)\left[\frac{(1-\alpha)(c_L - c_H)}{c_H[c_L\gamma(\gamma + \rho) - 1]} - 1 \right]e^{-z_2 t}$$

$$+ \frac{(1-\alpha)(\eta_0 - \lambda_0)}{c_H\gamma(\gamma + \rho)} \frac{c_H\gamma(\gamma + \rho) - 1}{c_L\gamma(\gamma + \rho) - 1} e^{-\gamma t} + \eta_0 - \frac{(1-\alpha)(\eta_0 - \lambda_0)}{c_H\gamma(\gamma + \rho)} \tag{14.10}$$

In this equation, z_2 is the characteristic root of the dynamic equation associated with λ; that is, $z_2 = [(\rho^2 + 4/c_L)^{1/2} - \rho]/2$.

5   How Would Western Employees Set γ?

The main question we are interested in is this: Under what conditions will western employees want eastern wages to converge rapidly to western levels? To answer this question, we have to analyze the impact of γ on the welfare of western workers. Given that full employment prevails in the west, this welfare is given by the present discounted value of log real wages; that is,

$$\alpha \int_0^{+\infty} (\log h - \log l)e^{-\rho t}\, dt + \log A + \log(1 - \alpha)$$

Western insiders will therefore choose the value of γ that will maximize the integral, which can be rewritten as

$$\int_0^{+\infty} [u(\eta) - u(\lambda)]e^{-\rho t}\, dt \tag{14.11}$$

where $u(x) = e^x/(1 + e^x)$. Note that u is concave. Therefore western insiders will want to design γ so as to maintain a high value of η and a low value of λ.

Our main result is that more rapid wage convergence will slow the eastward migration of human capital, while hastening the westward migration of raw labor.

Proposition 1.   *Assume $\eta_0 > \lambda_0$. Then at any date t,*

$$\partial \eta_t / \partial \gamma \geq 0$$
$$\partial \lambda_t / \partial \gamma > 0$$

Furthermore, in the long run, η and λ will converge to the same value, which is equal to

$$\lambda_\infty = \eta_\infty = \eta_0 - \frac{(1-\alpha)(\eta_0 - \lambda_0)}{c_H \gamma(\gamma + \rho)} \tag{14.12}$$

This is increasing in γ and is equal to the initial value of η, η_0, when γ goes to infinity.

Proof.   See the Appendix.   ∎

Therefore, higher wages in the east will reduce the return to human capital there, thus reducing the incentives for eastward mobility of H. At the same time, they will create unemployment in the east, so that despite higher wages there the incentives for migration will increase. Last, γ will have a long-term impact on the allocation of output across the two regions. The higher the value of γ, the closer η and λ will be to the initial value of human capital in the West, η_0. In our model, this locational effect is irrelevant. But it could positively or negatively affect the welfare of those living in the west if we were to add production externalities or congestion externalities. Another interesting property of (14.12) is that the long-term allocation of production no longer depends on the adjustment cost for raw labor, c_L. This is because the migration of human capital is entirely determined by the exogenously fixed wage differential and thus is unresponsive to the relative supply of raw labor. By contrast, the migration of raw labor is sensitive to the relative supply of human capital because it affects unemployment levels in the east.

Insiders in the west therefore face a trade-off: More rapid wage convergence will prevent human capital from leaving the west, but at the same time it will hasten the migration of raw labor from east to west, which will push down their wages. How this trade-off is resolved clearly will depend on relative migration costs: The higher the migration cost of raw labor relative to human capital, the more sluggish the response of raw labor to a given increase in the pace of wage convergence, and the more the western wage will increase along the transition path. Conversely, if the migration cost of raw labor is low relative to human capital, an increase in the pace of convergence will have an adverse effect on wages in the west as eastern workers rapidly flow in to escape high unemployment in their home region.

This principle can be illustrated by some special cases. Assume first that migration costs are the same: $c_H = c_L = c$. Then we can show the following:

Proposition 2. *Assume $c_H = c_L = c$. Then the optimal value of γ for eastern insiders will be the smallest possible value, that is, the one that will maintain full employment in the east: $\gamma = z_1$.*

Proof. Then λ becomes

$$\lambda = -(\eta_0 - \lambda_0)e^{-z_2 t} + \frac{(1-\alpha)(\eta_0 - \lambda_0)}{c\gamma(\gamma + \rho)}e^{-\gamma t} + \eta_0 - \frac{(1-\alpha)(\eta_0 - \lambda_0)}{c_H\gamma(\gamma + \rho)}$$

Subtracting from (14.7), we find

$$\eta - \lambda = (\eta_0 - \lambda_0)e^{-z_2 t}$$

Thus we note that the differential in relative factor endowments decreases exponentially at a rate that is independent of γ. This rate is the one that would obtain under perfect competition, because we can confirm that in this case $z_2 = z_1$. The evolution of $\eta - \lambda$ is therefore independent of γ; an increase in γ will raise η and λ by the same amount $d\eta$. Now the effect of the western employees' instantaneous utility is

$$d[u(\eta) - u(\lambda)] = u'(\eta)\,d\eta - u'(\lambda)\,d\lambda = [u'(\eta) - u'(\lambda)]\,d\eta$$

which is negative if $d\eta > 0$ and $\eta > \lambda$, because u is concave. Thus western employees will choose the lowest possible value for η at every period, which is achieved with the lowest possible value of γ: $\gamma = z_1 = z_2$. ∎

Let us now consider the case in which c_L is infinite. Then we have the following:

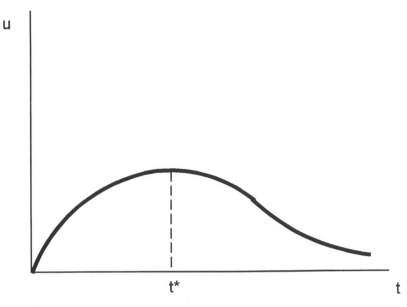

Figure 14.1.

Proposition 3.   *Assume $c_L = +\infty$. Then the optimal value of γ for western insiders is $\gamma = +\infty$ (i.e., instantaneous wage equalization).*

In this case, λ stays constant and is equal to its initial value λ_0, so that maximizing western wages amounts to maximizing η. Because η is increasing in γ, this amounts to choosing $\eta = +\infty$. Because eastern raw labor is totally immobile, instantaneous wage convergence allows us to have the highest value of wages in the west along the convergence path.

The foregoing results suggest that convergence of wages at a more rapid rate than that at market equilibrium will be valuable to western employees only if raw labor faces a migration cost that is substantially higher than the migration cost for human capital.

It is also possible to characterize the evolution of the unemployment rate in the east.

Proposition 4.   *For all $\gamma > z_1$, unemployment first goes up and then down (Figure 14.1). If $c_L > c_H$, $\partial u_{E_t}/\partial \gamma > 0$ for all $\gamma > 0$. Furthermore, $\partial t^*/\partial \gamma < 0$, where t^* is the time at which unemployment in the east reaches its maximum.*

Table 14.1.

c_H	z_1	$\lambda_\infty(z_1)$	γ_{max}	$\lambda_\infty(\gamma_{max})$	u_E^*
1	0.975	−0.4	0.975	−0.4	0
0.8	1.059	−0.49	1.059	−0.49	0
0.6	1.186	−0.59	1.186	−0.59	0
0.4	1.407	−0.71	1.75	−0.12	0.195
0.2	1.924	−0.842	3.46	0.42	0.48
0.05	3.757	−0.96	11.48	0.79	0.73
0.001	26.43	−0.999	120	0.9	0.84

Note: $c_L = 1$; $\alpha = 0.3$; $\rho = 0.05$; $\eta_0 = 1$; $\lambda_0 = -1$.

Table 14.2.

c_L	z_1	$\lambda_\infty(z_1)$	γ_{max}	$\lambda_\infty(\gamma_{max})$	u_E^*
2	0.897	−0.647	0.897	−0.647	0
3	0.870	−0.75	1.23	0.11	0.3
4	0.855	−0.81	1.41	0.32	0.42
10	0.829	−0.92	2.04	0.672	0.65
50	0.815	−0.983	4.49	0.931	0.82

Note: $c_H = 1$; $\alpha = 0.3$; $\rho = 0.05$; $\eta_0 = 1$; $\lambda_0 = -1$.

Proof. See the Appendix. ∎

Note that more rapid wage convergence unambiguously increases unemployment only when $c_L > c_H$. When $c_L < c_H$, migration from the east is so responsive to wage convergence that unemployment can actually fall.

We have also numerically computed (14.11) for different parameter values, which allows us to compute the optimal value for γ. These numerical simulations (Tables 14.1 and 14.2) confirm the intuition that the larger the migration cost for raw labor relative to that for human capital, the more rapid will be the wage convergence that western insiders will impose. In Table 14.1, the migration cost for human capital is gradually decreased, while that for raw labor is held constant. For c_H greater than 0.6, eastern insiders will not alter the functioning of the market. As c_H falls further below 0.6, they will impose increasingly more rapid wage convergence, thus generating larger unemployment rates in the east and increasingly biasing the long-term allocation of resources in favor of the west, whereas the market would increasingly favor the east. Similar conclusions emerge from Table 14.2, where c_H has been held constant and c_L increased: As c_L increases, the insiders' most desired value for γ increases.

A graphic illustration of this study's main result is provided in Figures 14.2–14.4, where the economy's paths for η and λ are depicted for $\gamma > z_1$ and for the full-employment case. We have also drawn isochrons that match points in the two trajectories corresponding to the same instants of time, as well as the indifference curves for the instantaneous utility function $u(\eta) - u(\lambda)$. Utility increases when one moves to the southeast of this diagram. Increasing γ generates a clockwise rotation on the equilibrium path, thus generating higher values for λ and η along the whole path (Proposition 1); therefore the full-employment trajectory (which has $\gamma = z_1$) is to the left of the underemployment trajectory. Both trajectories end up on the 45° line, because $\eta = \lambda$ in the long run. In Figure 14.2 we have assumed $c_H \ll c_L$, so that η moves much faster than λ. Consequently, the isochrons are flat, implying that any point A' on the underemployment trajectory typically yields a higher utility than its isochron match A on the full-employment trajectory. Figure 14.3 depicts the case where $c_H = c_L$. In this case the isochrons are parallel to the 45° line: An increase in γ affects λ_t and γ_t by the same amount. Because $u(\ )$ is concave, with a slope lower than unity, points along the underemployment path have lower utility than their matches on the Walrasian path. Last, Figure 14.4 depicts the case where $c_L \ll c_H$, with steep isochrons and A' clearly yielding lower utility than A. Figures 14.2–14.4 therefore illustrate that western insiders are more likely to benefit from rapid wage convergence the lower c_H is relative to c_L.

6   Conclusions

This study has established the conditions under which the more advanced economic region's employees may have an interest in setting a fast pace of wage convergence, thus generating unemployment in the other region. We have seen that this is more likely if the migration cost for raw labor is large relative to the migration cost for human capital. This seems a plausible condition: We typically think of skilled workers as more mobile than unskilled workers.

The model also highlights a number of effects that deserve closer investigation. Most notably, more rapid wage convergence biases the long-run allocation of production in favor of the most advanced region. Although this is immaterial in our model, the welfare consequences

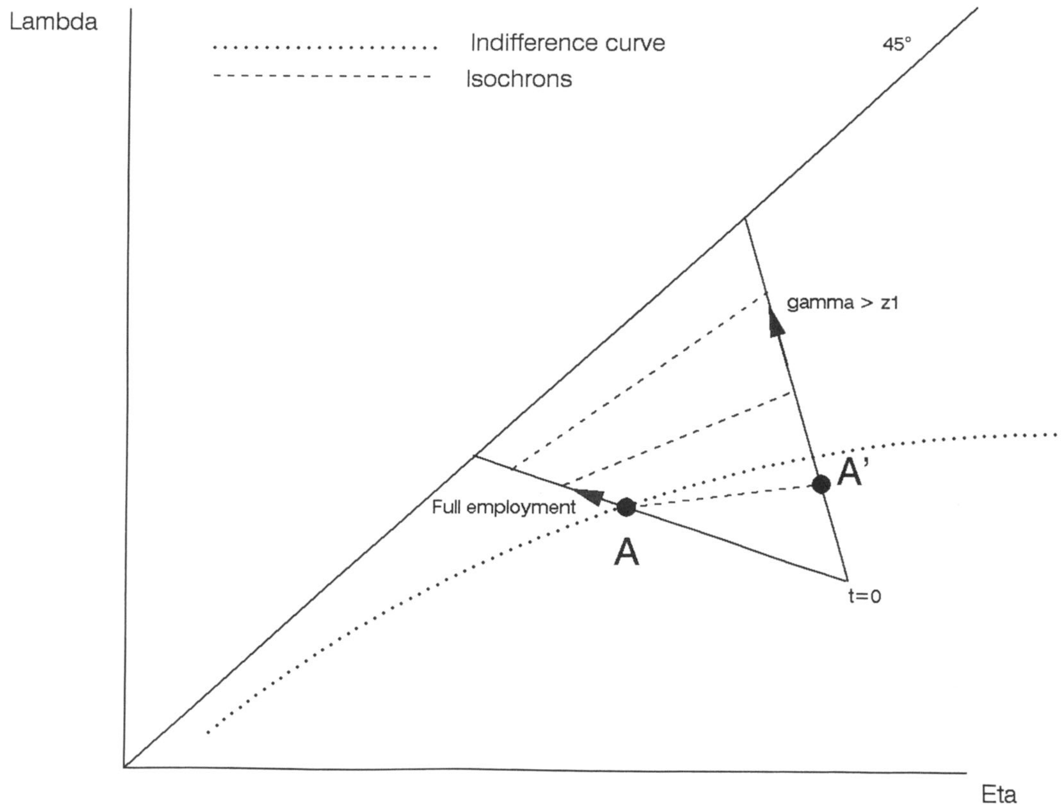

Figure 14.2.

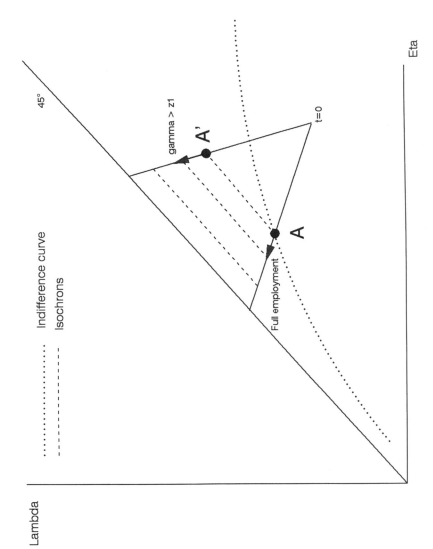

Lambda

45°

gamma > z1

Indifference curve
Isochrons

A'

Full employment

A

t=0

Eta

Figure 14.3.

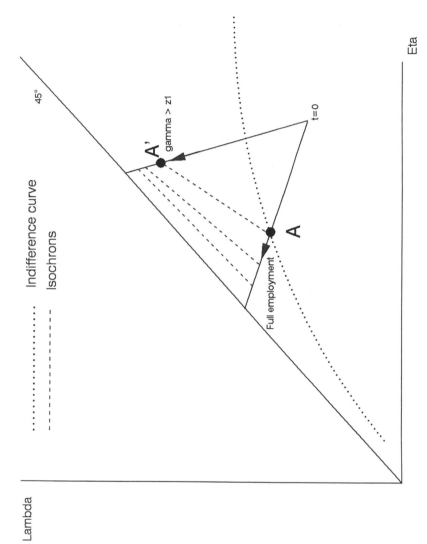

Lambda

45°

Indifference curve
Isochrons

A'
gamma > z1

Full employment

A

t=0

Eta

Figure 14.4.

of this mezzogiorno problem may be of concern if we introduce local externalities.

The model potentially could be extended to take into account a richer structure of the labor market, in particular by introducing imperfect unemployment insurance and explicit unemployment dynamics and by analyzing the implications of differential job-finding rates between natives and immigrants.

APPENDIX

Proof of Proposition 1. The proof of (14.12) is straightforward. To prove that $\partial \eta_t / \partial \gamma \geq 0$, note that up to a positive multiplicative constant it is equal to $(1 - e^{-\gamma t})(2\gamma + \rho) - \gamma(\rho + \gamma)te^{-\gamma t}$, which is positive, because the left-hand side is increasing in t and is equal to zero for $t = 0$.

We shall now prove that $\partial \lambda_t / \partial \gamma > 0$. We already know that for all t, η_t increases with γ, and x_t decreases, provided $\eta_0 > \lambda_0$. Taking the difference of (14.8) with respect to two values of γ, we have

$$c_L \Delta \dot{\lambda} = \int_t^{+\infty} [\phi(u) - \Delta \lambda_u] e^{-\rho(u-t)} \, du \qquad (14.\mathrm{A}1)$$

where $\phi(u) = (\alpha - 1)\Delta x_u / \alpha + \Delta \eta_u$. Now $\phi > 0$, provided that $\Delta \gamma > 0$. This implies that $\Delta \lambda > 0$ for all t.

To see this, assume that there exists $u_1 > 0$ such that $\Delta \lambda(u_1) < 0$. Then, because $\Delta \lambda(0) = 0$, there must exist $u_2 < u_1$ such that $\Delta \lambda(u_2) = 0$ and $\Delta \dot{\lambda}(u_2) < 0$. Now, we cannot have $\lambda < 0$ for all $u > u_2$; otherwise, by (14.A1), we would have $\Delta \dot{\lambda} > 0$ over this range (because $\phi > 0$), implying $\Delta \lambda(u) \geq 0$ for all $u > u_2$ [because $\Delta \lambda(u_2) = 0$]. Thus, $\Delta \lambda(u) > 0$ for some $u > u_2$, so that there must exist $u_3 > u_2$ such that $\Delta \lambda(u_3) = 0$ and $\Delta \dot{\lambda}(u_3) > 0$. Let us take the smallest possible value of u_3, so that $\Delta \lambda(u) < 0$ for $u \in]u_2, u_3[$. Then there exists $u_4 \in]u_2, u_3[$ such that $\Delta \dot{\lambda}(u_4) = 0$. Now, we have

$$0 = c_L \Delta \dot{\lambda}(u_4) = \int_{u_4}^{+\infty} [\phi(u) - \Delta \lambda_u] e^{-\rho(u-u_4)} \, du$$

$$= \int_{u_4}^{u_3} [\phi(u) - \Delta \lambda_u] e^{-\rho(u-u_4)} \, du + \int_{u_3}^{+\infty} [\phi(u) - \Delta \lambda_u] e^{-\rho(u-u_4)} \, du$$

$$= \int_{u_4}^{u_3} [\phi(u) - \Delta \lambda_u] e^{-\rho(u-u_4)} \, du + e^{-\rho(u_3-u_4)} c_L \Delta \dot{\lambda}(u_4) > 0$$

The first integral is always positive, because $\Delta \lambda(u) < 0$ for $u \in]u_2, u_3[$. We clearly have a contradiction, and therefore we cannot have $\Delta \lambda(u_1) < 0$. ∎

Proof of Proposition 4. Using equations (14.5) and (14.6), the definitions of x, λ, and η, and the full-employment condition for the west, we get

$$\log(1 - u_E) = x/a + \lambda - \eta \qquad (14.\text{A2})$$

Plugging (14.9) and (14.10) into (14.A2), we get

$$\log(1 - u_{E_t}) = (\eta_0 - \lambda_0)\left[\frac{(1-a)(c_L - c_H)}{c_H[c_L\gamma(\gamma + \rho) - 1]} - 1\right]\left(e^{-z_2 t} - e^{-\gamma t}\right)$$

This formula implies that for all $\gamma > z_1$, unemployment goes up and then down, as illustrated in Figure 14.1. It reaches its maximum at $t = t^* = \log(\gamma/z_2)/(\gamma - z_2)$, and this maximum is equal to

$$u_E^* = (\eta_0 - \lambda_0)\left[\frac{(1-a)(c_L - c_H)}{c_H[c_L\gamma(\gamma + \rho) - 1]} - 1\right](z_2 - \gamma)\gamma^{-\gamma/(\gamma - z_2)}z_2^{z_2/(\gamma - z_2)}$$

Differentiating this expression, we can show that $\partial t^*/\partial\gamma$ has the same sign as $\log(z_2/\gamma) + 1 - z_2/\gamma$, which is always negative.

To prove that unemployment increases with γ for $c_L > c_H$, note that we then have $z_1 > z_2$, implying $\gamma > z_2$. That $\gamma > z_1$ implies

$$\frac{(1-a)(c_L - c_H)}{c_H[c_L\gamma(\gamma + \rho) - 1]} - 1 < 0$$

and $\gamma > z_2$, implies $(e^{-z_2 t} - e^{-\gamma t}) > 0$. Thus $\log(1 - u_{E_t})$ is the product of a negative factor that falls with γ and a positive factor that rises with γ; therefore it falls with γ, implying that u_{E_t} increases with γ. By contrast, these two factors' absolute values move in opposite directions whenever $c_L < c_H$, so that the net effect of u_{E_t} is ambiguous. ∎

REFERENCES

Antolin, P., and Bover, O. (1993). Regional migration in Spain. Working paper, Bank of Spain, Madrid.

Brecher, R. A., and Choudhri, E. U. (1987). International migration versus foreign investment in the presence of unemployment. *Journal of International Economics* 23:329–42.

Burda, M., and Funke, M. (1991). German trade unions after unification: third-degree wage discriminating monopolists? CEPR working paper 573, Centre for Economic Policy Research, London.

Burda, M., and Wyplosz, C. (1991). Human capital, investment and migration in an integrated Europe. CEPR working paper 614, Centre for Economic Policy Research, London.

Danthine, J.-P., and Hunt, J. (1994). Wage bargaining structure, employment and economic integration. *Economic Journal* 104:528–41.

Decressin, J., and Fatas, A. (1995). Regional labor market dynamics in Europe. *European Economic Review* 39:1627–55.

Di Monte, P. (1992). La disoccupazione in Italia e la natura dei divari territoriali. *Economia e Lavoro* 26:29–45.

Dornbusch, R., and Wolf, H. (1992). Economic transition in Eastern Germany. *Brookings Papers on Economic Activity*.

Ehrenberg, R. G. (1994). *Labor Markets and Integrating National Economies.* Washington, DC: Brookings Institution.

Friedberg, R., and Hunt, J. (1995). The impact of immigrants on host country wages, employment and growth. *Journal of Economic Perspectives* 9:23–44.

Gabriel, S. A., Shack-Marquez, J., and Wascher, W. L. (1993). Does migration arbitrage regional labor market differentials? *Regional Science and Urban Economics* 23:211–33.

Harris, J. R., and Todaro, M. P. (1970). Migration, unemployment, and development: a two-sector analysis. *American Economic Review* 60:126–42.

Hatzius, J. (1994). The unemployment and earnings effect of German immigration. Unpublished manuscript, Department of Economics, Oxford University.

Hughes, G., and McCormick, B. (1994). Did migration in the 1980s narrow the North–South divide? *Economica* 61:509–27.

Keil, M., and Newell, A. (1994). International migration and unemployment in Germany: an Anglo-Irish perspective. CEP working paper 201, London School of Economics.

Pissarides, C., and McMaster, I. (1990). Regional migration, wages, and unemployment: empirical evidence and implications for policy. *Oxford Economic Papers* 12:812–31.

Razin, A., and Sadka, E. (1995). Immigration and wage rigidity. *American Economic Review* 85:312–16.

Schmidt, C. M., Stilz, A., and Zimmermann, K. (1994). Mass migration, unions, and government intervention. *Journal of Public Economics* 55:185–201.

Sinn, G., and Sinn, H.-W. (1992). *Jumpstart: The Economic Unification of Germany.* Massachusetts Institute of Technology Press.

Zimmermann, K. (1995). Tackling the European migration problems. *Journal of Economic Perspectives* 9:45–62.

CHAPTER 15

Human-Capital Formation, Asymmetric Information, and the Dynamics of International Migration

Nancy H. Chau and Oded Stark

1   Introduction

Whatever workers may take with them when they migrate, they cannot possibly transfer their home country's information structure. Consequently, foreign-country employers are not as well informed about home-country workers as are home-country employers. Typically, migration runs across cultures as well as countries. Foreign-country employers who do not share the culture, background, and language of migrants as do home-country employers lack a common framework for assessing the quality and individual merits of migrant workers. For these reasons, the skills of migrant workers cannot be easily discerned, and screening is likely to be imprecise and expensive. In mainstream migration research, incorporation of the natural assumption that migration is inherently associated with a heterogeneous information structure (as opposed to the homogeneous information structure that characterizes nonmigrant employment relationships) has, somewhat surprisingly, been an exception rather than the rule (Kwok and Leland, 1982; Katz and Stark, 1987, 1989; Stark, 1991, 1995). The relative ignorance of foreign employers should not be taken as a constant, however. Exposure breeds familiarity, and increased experience with employing migrants is bound to reduce information asymmetries. Such a change can entail interesting dynamics. For example, the accumulation of information erodes both the pooling of low-skill migrant workers with high-skill migrant workers and the associated wage-determination rule (viz., paying all migrants the same wage, based on the average productivity of the entire cohort of migrants). Absent

We thank Yoram Weiss and Ilyse Zable for helpful suggestions. Partial financial support from the Austrian Science Foundation under contract number P10967-SOZ is gratefully acknowledged.

pooling, however, low-skill migrant workers may find it advantageous to return-migrate (Stark, 1995).

There is little doubt that, in general, migration gives rise to human-capital depletion in the home country. The standard argument holds that, absent migration, the home country would have had available to it a more skilled workforce and concomitantly would have enjoyed higher per-capita output. Indeed, the "drain-of-brains" view has influenced migration research for at least three decades now (Grubel and Scott, 1966), with the associated literature concentrating largely on how to mitigate this adverse consequence (Bhagwati and Wilson, 1989). However, that migration induces skill *formation* has essentially escaped analysis. Obviously, workers are not endowed with marketable skills at birth. Skills are acquired, and their level is determined by optimizing workers who, given their innate learning ability (efficiency in skill formation), weigh the prospective market rewards for enhanced skills, both at home *and* abroad, in addition to the cost of acquiring those skills.

The possibility of migration thus changes the opportunities set, the incentive structure, and the information environment. Herein, study these simultaneous changes and trace their implications. Specifically, we depart from earlier approaches by dropping the strong simplifying assumptions that the distribution of migrants' abilities and the monitoring capabilities of migrants' employers are exogenously given. We endogenize the human-capital formation decisions of migrant workers and allow the monitoring capabilities of employers to improve over time as their experience with employing migrants accumulates. This allows us to explore the intertemporal interactions among the decision to migrate, the choice to undertake education, and the monitoring capabilities of migrants' employers.

Our framework explains a number of pertinent characteristics of the migration of skilled workers (the brain drain). For example, as the experience of employing migrants accumulates, the resulting intertemporal adjustments in the probability of deciphering true skill levels lead to a sequence of migratory moves that progressively selects higher skilled workers. We argue that by raising the likelihood of discovering the true qualities of workers, accumulation of experience with migrant employment enhances the incentive for brighter brains to migrate permanently, while it reduces the incentive for low-ability workers to pursue migration. As the probability of discovery of abilities rises, the ability composition of subsequent migrant cohorts shifts rightward. Whenever the average quality of a migrant cohort exceeds that of a previous cohort, wage offers are bid upward, prompting a subsequent wave of migration involving workers who are even more able. However, this is just a first-round effect. The accumulation of experience in employing migrants also implies that both high- and low-ability workers are more likely to be discovered. Accordingly, the probability of permanent migration by high-ability workers and the extent of return migration by low-ability workers rise simultaneously. The result is continuing improvement in the average ability of migrant workers remaining in a country. Until the steady-state equilibrium probability of discovery is reached, a virtual cycle of migration of the more able ensues as wage offers are adjusted over time favoring migration of higher ability workers. Meanwhile, the wages of the migrants who stay increase, though not because of an increase in their human capital.

Our model extends earlier work by Katz and Stark (1987). We introduce endogenous human-capital formation and examine the dynamics of human-capital formation as well as the corresponding intertemporal pattern of migration and return migration. We derive several dynamic predictions that are consistent with a considerable body of empirical literature, as reviewed and synthesized by LaLonde and Topel (1997) and Razin and Sadka (1997). Migration is a process, not an event. It is phased, and it is sequential: Not all workers who migrate will move at the same time. Each cohort of migrants includes workers who will stay and workers who, with a well-defined probability, will return-migrate. Ravenstein's century-old "law of migration" (1885, p. 199), which predicts that "each main current of migration produces a compensating countercurrent" (often quoted, but not demonstrated analytically), turns out to be an implication of our model. Within cohorts, migration is positively selective (Stark, 1995).[1] Cohort by cohort, the average quality of migrants rises.[2] The "cost of migration" is a decreasing function of the stock of previous migrants for some workers, but it is an *increasing* function of that stock for others, contrary to the findings of Carrington, Detragiache, and Vishwanath (1996): Migration of low-skill workers pulls down the average of the marginal product of the contemporaneous group of migrant workers, thereby lowering the wage of high-skill workers. Conversely, the presence of high-skill migrant workers in a pool of low-skill and high-skill workers enables low-skill workers to enjoy a wage higher than their marginal product. As migration proceeds and the cumulative stock of migrants rises, the probability of discovery rises. This favors high-skill would-be migrants but dissuades low-skill would-

---

[1] Returnees tend to be less well educated than the migrants who stay (DaVanzo, 1983; Reilly, 1994).

[2] Borjas (1987) provided evidence that the quality of migrant workers from western Europe to the United States was increasing over the period 1955—1979. However, his measures of quality were different from those we use.

be migrants. Thus an increase in the stock of migrant workers confers a positive externality on subsequent migration of high-skill workers, but a negative externality on the migration of low-skill workers.

We pay particular attention to the change in the welfare of the home-country population in the wake of international migration. In contrast to the received welfare-theoretic analysis of the brain drain,[3] we show that when potential migrant workers incorporate the feasibility of migration in their education decisions, not only does the level of education acquisition in the home country rise, but national welfare may rise as well, if the contribution to national income by educated workers increases. We show that a gain in national welfare generated by migration of educated workers is possible given a positive probability of return migration by educated workers once their true productivities are deciphered.

The remainder of this chapter is organized as follows: In Section 2 we model a home economy not open to migration and determine the extent of education acquisition and the per-capita output as benchmarks for subsequent comparisons. In Section 3 we present a two-country framework. The information asymmetry between foreign employers and home-country workers is introduced, and the effect of migrant employment experience on the probability of deciphering the true ability of individual migrant workers is incorporated. In addition, we study the education and migration decisions of home-country workers in the presence of asymmetric information. We also compare the resulting level of education with that obtained in the absence of the possibility of migration. Section 4 analyzes the relationship between the dynamic process of skilled-worker migration and the probability of discovery, as well as the associated steady-state equilibrium probability of discovery. We trace the circumstances under which migration progressively selects higher-ability workers. In section 5 we conduct a welfare analysis and define conditions under which national welfare improves when free migration of skilled workers is permitted. Section 6 summarizes the analysis.

2   An Economy without Migration

2.1   *Production*

During each time period t the home economy h produces a single composite good in two sectors: An unskilled sector u and a skilled sector

---

[3] The primary conclusion of Grubel and Scott (1966) and Berry and Soligo (1969) was that whereas very low levels of migration have no impact on the welfare of those who stay behind, finite levels of migration unambiguously reduce welfare.

s. Output in the unskilled sector during time t is generated through a simple constant-returns-to-scale production function $X_t^u = a_u^h L_t$, where L_t denotes the number of workers employed in sector u. Similarly, output in the skilled sector is given by a constant-returns-to-scale production function $X_t^s = a_s^h E_t$, where E_t is the input of skilled labor measured in efficiency units. Thus, a_u^h is the marginal and average product of a worker in sector u, and a_s^h is the marginal and average product of an efficiency unit of labor in the skilled sector. Without loss of generality, the price of a unit of output is assumed to be unity. There is perfect competition in both output and factor markets. Therefore, the wage paid by profit-maximizing employers to a worker in the unskilled sector is $w_u^h = a_u^h$, and the wage paid for an efficiency unit of work in the skilled sector is $w_s^h = a_s^h$.

2.2   Individuals and the Population

In each period, N individuals are born. Individuals live for two periods. Thus, the population size during any time period is $2N$. Individuals are characterized by endowments and preferences. Each individual is endowed with one unit of physical labor (a pair of hands) and with innate ability (talent) $\theta \in [0, \infty]$. The distribution of θ over the population is summarized by a cumulative distribution function $F(\theta)$, where $F(\theta)$ is continuously differentiable and is associated with a strictly positive density function $f(\theta)$. Assume, in addition, that the expectation of θ [$\int_0^\infty \theta f(\theta) \, d\theta$] is finite. Denote by y_t the income of the individual in period t. The individual's preferences are summarized by a utility function $u(y_t, y_{t+1})$. To simplify, we take $u(y_t, y_{t+1}) = y_t + \beta y_{t+1}$, where $0 < \beta < 1$ is the time discount rate.

An individual born during any time period t faces the following choice: remain uneducated and work in the u sector for the two periods of his life, or spend the first time period acquiring education and work in the s sector in the second period of his life. Acquiring education involves a direct cost c that is incurred at the beginning of period t. Having no funds, the individual borrows c in a perfectly competitive credit market where the interest rate is assumed to be zero. The educated individual, whose innate ability is θ, supplies θ efficiency units of labor to the skilled sector. The supply of efficiency units of labor by an uneducated individual in the s sector is zero, irrespective of his level of innate ability. The labor input supplied by a worker in the unskilled sector is independent of his innate abilities and is equal to his physical-labor endowment (one unit).

It follows that the discounted lifetime utility of an educated worker is equal to his discounted second-period income, net of education costs:

$$Y_t^s(\theta) \equiv \beta(w_s^h\theta - c)$$

The discounted lifetime utility of an uneducated worker is:

$$Y_t^u \equiv (1+\beta)w_u^h$$

Thus, an individual whose innate ability is θ will decide to acquire education if $Y_t^s(\theta) \geq Y_t^u$, but will choose to remain uneducated otherwise. We thus have

$$Y_t^s(\theta) \geq Y_t^u \Leftrightarrow \beta(w_s^h\theta - c) \geq (1+\beta)w_u^h$$

or,

$$\theta \geq \frac{1}{w_s^h}\left[\frac{(1+\beta)w_u^h}{\beta} + c\right] \equiv \theta*$$

That is, individuals whose $\theta \geq \theta*$ will become skilled workers, and individuals whose $\theta < \theta*$ will remain unskilled.

Therefore, the $2N$ individuals from the "young" and the "old" generations are distributed across three activities: work in the u sector, work in the s sector, and acquisition of education. Because the fraction of uneducated workers per generation is $F(\theta*)$, the number of uneducated workers in the population is $2NF(\theta*)$. The fraction of the old generation employed in the s sector is $1 - F(\theta*)$. The number of individuals employed in the s sector is thus $N[1 - F(\theta*)]$. Finally, because a fraction $1 - F(\theta*)$ of the young generation pursues education, the number of individuals being educated during any time period is $N[1 - F(\theta*)]$. Of course, $2NF(\theta*) + N[1 - F(\theta*)] + N[1 - F(\theta*)] = 2N$. From our previous analysis it can be confirmed that $\theta*$ is decreasing in w_s^h: The higher the rewards to education, given θ, the larger the fraction of individuals who will invest in education, $[1 - F(\theta*)]$, and the larger the number of individuals who will do so, $N[1 - F(\theta*)]$.

2.3   *Production and Equilibrium*

An equilibrium in the economy, at any time, is fully characterized by the parameter $\theta*$. Once $\theta*$ is known, the allocation of labor across the two employment options and the associated outputs of the two sectors are given. The output of the u sector is $X_t^u = w_u^h 2NF(\theta*)$. In addition, total labor input (measured in efficiency units) in the skilled sector is

$E_t = N\int_{\theta*}^{\infty}\theta f(\theta)d\theta.$[4] The resulting s-sector output is therefore $X_t^s = N\int_{\theta*}^{\infty}w_s^h\theta f(\theta)\,d\theta.$

We can now calculate the value of national output, net of education expenditures, and investigate the dependence of national output on $\theta*$. We denote by $V(\theta*)$ the time-invariant value of national output, net of the cost of education. We have

$$V(\theta*) = N\left\{2w_u^h F(\theta*) + \int_{\theta*}^{\infty}w_s^h\theta f(\theta)\,d\theta - c[1 - F(\theta*)]\right\}$$

Output per capita is thus

$$v(\theta*) = \frac{1}{2}\left\{2w_u^h F(\theta*) + \int_{\theta*}^{\infty}w_s^h\theta f(\theta)\,d\theta - c[1 - F(\theta*)]\right\} \qquad (15.1)$$

It follows that[5]

$$\frac{\partial v(\theta*)}{\partial\theta*} = \frac{1}{2}[-w_s^h\theta* f(\theta*) + 2w_u^h f(\theta*) + cf(\theta*)]$$

$$= -\frac{1}{2}f(\theta*)(w_s^h\theta* - 2w_u^h - c)$$

$$= -\frac{1}{2}f(\theta*)w_u^h\frac{1-\beta}{\beta}$$

$$< 0$$

The value of per-capita output is decreasing in $\theta*$. Recall that an increase in $\theta*$ is equivalent to a reduction in the fraction of the educated workforce. It follows that per-capita output increases as the share of educated workers increases. Starting from an equilibrium in which there is no governmental interference in individuals' decisions to acquire education, it follows that per-capita output increases as the share of educated workers increases. Note that if in the far-right-hand side of $\partial v(\theta*)/\partial\theta*$ we have $\beta = 1$, then $\partial v(\theta*)/\partial\theta* = 0$. In other words, if individuals do not discount future income, the invisible hand is nicely at work: The level of $\theta*$ chosen by individuals who maximize expected lifetime utility is exactly the same level of $\theta*$ that a social planner will choose to maximize per-capita output.

---

[4] The average number of efficiency units of labor supplied by a skilled worker is $\int_{\theta*}^{\infty}\theta f(\theta)\,d\theta/\int_{\theta*}^{\infty}f(\theta)\,d\theta$. Because there are $N[1 - F(\theta*)]$ skilled workers, their total supply of skilled work is $[\int_{\theta*}^{\infty}\theta f(\theta)d\theta/\int_{\theta*}^{\infty}f(\theta)d\theta]N[1 - F(\theta*)] = N\int_{\theta*}^{\infty}\theta f(\theta)d\theta$.

[5] To derive the last equality, note that from the definition of $\theta*$, $w_s^h\theta* - c = (1 + \beta)w_u^h/\beta$. Hence, $w_s^h\theta* - 2w_u^h - c = (1 - \beta)w_u^h/\beta$.

3   A Two-Country World with Migration

3.1   *The Foreign Economy*

The foreign economy f also consists of a u sector and an s sector. We denote by $\tilde{L}_t$ and L_t^m the numbers of foreign workers and migrant workers employed in the u sector, respectively. The output of the u sector is $\tilde{X}_t^u = a_u^f(\tilde{L}_t + L_t^m)$. The output of the s sector, $\tilde{X}_t^s$, is governed by the production function $\tilde{X}_t^s = a_s^f(\tilde{E}_t + E_t^m)$, where $\tilde{E}_t$ denotes the foreign workforce (measured in efficiency units) employed in the s sector and E_t^m is the input of the migrant workforce, also measured in efficiency units. We assume that the foreign country uses superior technologies relative to economy h in both its u and s sectors, so that $a_i^f > a_i^h$, $i = u, s$. Perfect competition in both output and factor markets guarantees that the wage paid by profit-maximizing employers to a worker in the unskilled sector is $w_u^f = a_u^f > a_u^h = w_u^h$, and the wage paid to an efficiency unit of work in the skilled sector is $w_s^f = a_s^f > a_s^h = w_s^h$.

Foreign employers are assumed to be perfectly aware of the true abilities of indigenous workers. However, the true abilities of individual migrant workers are unknown. Each migrant worker can nevertheless be distinguished as belonging to one of two identifiable groups of workers: educated or uneducated. Following our specification in Section 2, wage payments to uneducated migrant workers by profit-maximizing employers depend only on the sector of employment, not on individual abilities. In particular, an uneducated migrant worker receives zero wages in the s sector, because the efficiency labor input of such a worker in this sector is zero. Similarly, an uneducated migrant worker in the u sector receives w_u^f as a wage payment because the physical labor input of such a worker in the u sector is one. The same wage-determination procedure no longer applies to educated migrant workers, however, when the educated migrant workforce consists of individuals with heterogeneous abilities.

At any time t, let the wage offer to an educated migrant worker whose true ability is unknown to foreign employers be $w_s^f\theta_t^a$, where θ_t^a denotes the average supply of efficiency labor inputs by the migrant population having unknown individual abilities. In addition, let the total number of migrants at any time τ be $\mathcal{M}_\tau$, and let the cumulative number of migrants until time $t - 1$ be $M_{t-1} = \Sigma_{\tau=0}^{t-1}\mathcal{M}_\tau$. We assume that with probability $m_t = m(M_{t-1})$ the actual productivity of a worker who supplies $\theta \neq \theta_t^a$ amount of skilled labor will be discovered. The probability of discovery, m_t, is taken to be strictly positive, increasing in migrant hiring experience, $m'(M_{t-1}) > 0$,[6] and bounded from above with $\lim_{M_{t-1} \to \infty} m(M_{t-1}) = \hat{m} < 1$. Once the true ability of a worker is discovered by one foreign employer, the same information becomes instantly available to all foreign employers (this follows from our assumption of perfect competition in factor markets); hence the wage payment for such a worker in the s sector of the foreign country is determined by his true ability θ.

3.2   The Individuals Revisited

Migration entails a per-period cost k that can be perceived as the cost of separation from home. We take this cost to be independent of the level of education acquired and of the stock of migrants. Accordingly, under symmetric information, the per-period income, net of the separation cost for an educated worker who migrates to the foreign country, is just $w_s^f \theta - k$. Figure 15.1 illustrates the income schedules for an educated worker in the home country and in the foreign country. The value of θ corresponding to the point of intersection, $\bar{\theta} = k/(w_s^f - w_s^h)$, denotes a critical level of innate ability such that any educated home-country worker with an innate ability $\theta \geq \bar{\theta}$ enjoys a higher income in the foreign country, net of the migration cost, than at home. In the absence of asymmetric information, the most talented will migrate, whereas skilled workers endowed with ability less than $\bar{\theta}$ will remain in the home country because the per-period foreign wage, net of the cost of migration, $(w_s^f \theta - k)$, is less than the corresponding home-country wage $(w_s^h \theta)$.

Once the prevalence of asymmetric information and the possibility of migration are incorporated into the decision-making calculus of the home-country workers, the problem of a worker born at any time t spans two consecutive periods. In the first period, an individual may acquire education and incur its cost c. Otherwise, the individual finds employment in the unskilled sector of the home country or the foreign country. In the second period, the uneducated individual reviews his migration decision and chooses to work either in the home country or in the foreign country. For an educated worker, there are four possible, more elaborate second-period employment options:

1. An educated worker of ability θ chooses to migrate. With probability m_t the true ability of the worker is discovered, and the worker return-migrates. With the complementary probability $1 - m_t$ the true ability of the worker is not discovered, and he

---

[6] A prime denotes the first derivative with respect to M_{t-1}.

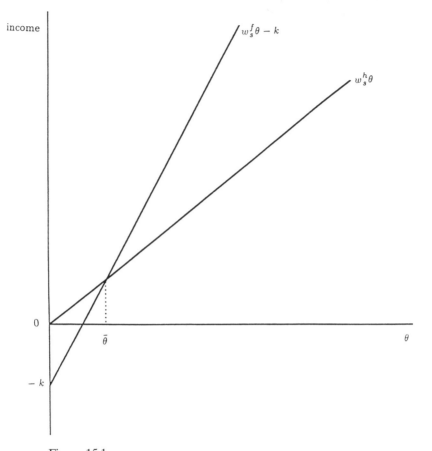

Figure 15.1.

remains in the foreign country. The expected income of such a worker, net of the cost of education, y_t^{rd}, is thus

$$y_t^{rd}(\theta) = m_t w_s^h \theta + (1 - m_t)(w_s^f \theta_t^\alpha - k) - c$$

2. An educated worker of ability θ chooses to migrate. With probability m_t the true ability of the worker is discovered, and the worker remains in the foreign country, receiving $w_s^f \theta$. With the complementary probability $1 - m_t$ the true ability of the worker is not discovered, and the worker remains in the foreign country, in which case he receives $w_s^f \theta_t^\alpha$. In this case, the expected income net of the education cost, $y_t^f(\theta)$, is thus

$$y_t^f(\theta) = m_t(w_s^f \theta - k) + (1 - m_t)(w_s^f \theta_t^a - k) - c$$

3. An educated worker of ability θ chooses to migrate. With probability m_t the true ability of the worker is discovered, and the worker remains in the foreign country, receiving $w_s^f \theta$. With the complementary probability $1 - m_t$ the true ability of the worker is not discovered, and the worker return-migrates. The expected income of such a worker, net of the cost of education, $y_t^{ru}(\theta)$, is thus

$$y_t^{ru}(\theta) = m_t(w_s^f \theta - k) + (1 - m_t)w_s^h \theta - c$$

4. An educated worker of ability θ chooses not to migrate and receives a net income, $y_t^h(\theta)$, of

$$y_t^h(\theta) = w_s^h \theta - c$$

with probability one.[7]

Figure 15.2 depicts these four options and the choices among them. Given θ_t^a and M_{t-1}, the expected income schedules in the four regimes, $y_t^i(\theta) + c$ ($i = rd, f, ru, h$), are illustrated by the lines $R^d R^d$, FF, $R^u R^u$, and HH, respectively. $R^d R^d$ is the income schedule of migrant workers who return upon discovery. $R^u R^u$ represents the income schedule of migrant workers who return if their true abilities remain undiscovered. HH and FF denote the income schedules of permanent home-country workers and permanent migrants, respectively. Note in particular that $R^d R^d$ and FF coincide with the horizontal income schedule $w_s^f \theta_t^a - k$, and $R^u R^u$ coincides with the home wage schedule HH whenever $m_t = 0$. In addition, $R^d R^d$ coincides with the home wage schedule, and $R^u R^u$ and FF coincide with the foreign wage schedule whenever $m_t = 1$, the case of perfect information elaborated earlier.

Observe from Figure 15.2 that when $0 < m_t < 1$, the maximum second-period expected income of an educated worker (indicated by the bold segmented line) is demarcated by two critical values of innate abilities: $\bar{\theta}$ and θ_t^i, where the former (latter) denotes the innate ability

[7] In general, there can be two additional migration regimes for educated home-country workers: (5) An educated worker migrates. With probability m_t the true ability of the worker is discovered, and the worker remains in the foreign country to engage in u-sector employment. With probability $1 - m_t$ the worker receives $w_s^f \theta_t^a$ in the foreign country. (6) An educated worker migrates. With probability m_t the true ability of the worker is discovered, and the worker return-migrates to engage in u-sector employment in the home country. With probability $1 - m_t$, he receives $w_s^f \theta_t^a$ in the foreign country. Later, we show that neither of these options will be pursued by educated migrant workers as long as w_u^h is sufficiently small and k is sufficiently large.

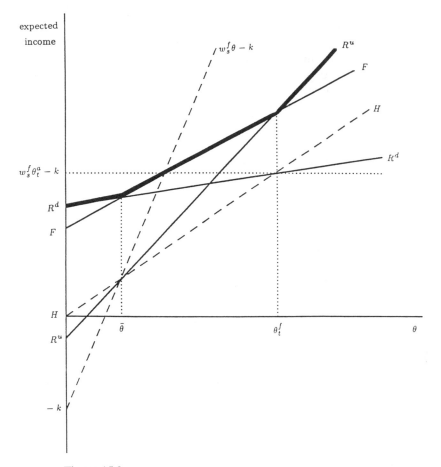

Figure 15.2.

of a migrant who is indifferent between regimes 1 and 2 (regimes 2 and 3). A comparison of the migration patterns shown in Figures 15.1 and 15.2 reveals that under asymmetric information, the most talented workers (with $\theta > \theta_t^f$) will return-migrate with strictly positive probability $1 - m_t$. The inability of foreign employers to decipher the true ability of migrant workers thus acts as a tax on the returns to migration for the most talented workers. In particular, the innate ability of a migrant who is indifferent between regimes 2 and 3, θ_t^f, can be found by noting that

$$(1 - m_t)\left(w_s^f \theta_t^a - k\right) + m_t\left(w_s^f \theta - k\right) = (1 - m_t)w_s^h \theta + m_t\left(w_s^f \theta - k\right)$$

$$\Leftrightarrow \theta = \frac{w_s^f \theta_t^a - k}{w_s^h} \equiv \theta_t^f$$

Note further that because $R^d R^d$ and FF intersect only once, all educated migrants with ability $\theta \leq \theta_t^f$ can be classified into one of two groups once their true capabilities are detected: return migrants and permanent migrants. This follows from the definition of $\bar{\theta}$, the critical innate-ability level at which the home and the foreign wage schedules intersect. Once his true ability is discovered, an educated worker with low ability $\theta < \bar{\theta}$ will choose to work in the home country, where the per-period return is the highest. To see this, note that a migrant with innate ability θ is indifferent between regimes 1 and 2 if and only if

$$(1 - m_t)\left(w_s^f \theta_t^a - k\right) + m_t w_s^h \theta = (1 - m_t)\left(w_s^f \theta_t^a - k\right) + m_t\left(w_s^f \theta - k\right)$$

$$\Leftrightarrow w_s^h \theta = w_s^f \theta - k$$

$$\Leftrightarrow \theta = \frac{k}{w_s^f - w_s^h} \equiv \bar{\theta}$$

Finally, HH lies below the bold segmented line for all values of θ. As long as $\theta_t^a > \bar{\theta}$ and m_t is strictly between zero and unity, the probability that an educated migrant will earn a higher wage in the foreign country is strictly positive. In particular, from the definition of $\bar{\theta}$, if $\theta \leq \bar{\theta}$, $w_s^f \theta_t^a - k > w_s^h \theta$. In addition, $w_s^f \theta - k > w_s^h \theta$ if $\theta > \bar{\theta}$. It follows that if return migration is always an option open to migrant workers, an educated worker will never choose to work only in the home country. We summarize this discussion in the following proposition:

Proposition 1. *If $\theta_t^a > \bar{\theta}$*

1. *Educated workers with innate ability $\theta \leq \bar{\theta}$ migrate. In addition, return migration yields the maximum second-period income once the true ability of such educated workers is discovered.*
2. *Educated workers with innate ability $\theta \in (\bar{\theta}, \theta_t^f]$ migrate. In addition, employment in the foreign country yields the maximum second-period income once the true ability of such educated workers is discovered.*
3. *Educated workers with innate ability $\theta > \theta_t^f$ migrate. In addition, return migration yields the maximum second-period income if the true ability of such educated workers is not discovered.*

Proof.   All proofs are relegated to the Appendix.

We now proceed to the first-stage education choice by comparing the expected utilities for an educated worker and an uneducated worker over the two periods. To focus on the analysis of migration of skilled workers, we assume that k is sufficiently large, with $w_u^f - k < w_u^h$: The per-period foreign income, net of the migration cost, for an uneducated worker is lower than his unskilled wage in the home country. It follows that

$$w_u^h > w_u^f - k \Rightarrow w_u^h(1 + \beta) > (w_u^f - k) + \beta w_u^h$$
$$\Rightarrow w_u^h(1 + \beta) > w_u^h + \beta(w_u^f - k)$$

The inequality on the right-hand side in the first line states that the lifetime utility from working at home is higher than the utility from migrating in the first period of life and the utility from working at home in the second period. The inequality on the right-hand side in the second line states that the lifetime utility from working at home is higher than the utility from working at home in the first period of life and the utility from migrating in the second period. Because $(1 + \beta)w_u^h > (1 + \beta)(w_u^f - k)$ follows from $w_u^h > w_u^f - k$, it follows that migration of the unskilled always yields a lower lifetime utility, irrespective of the timing and duration of migration.

With that in mind, we denote the expected lifetime utility $u_{t-1}(\theta)$ of a worker with innate ability θ born at time $t - 1$ as

$$u_{t-1}(\theta) = E_{t-1}\{\max[\beta y_t(\theta), (1 + \beta)w_u^h]\}$$

where $y_t(\theta) = \max[y_t^{rd}(\theta), y_t^f(\theta), y_t^{ru}(\theta), y_t^h(\theta)]$, and $E_{t-1}(\cdot)$ denotes the expectation operator, with the expectation taken over all possible values of m_t at time $t - 1$. The expected lifetime utility $u_{t-1}(\theta)$ can be determined by comparing the expectation of the discounted lifetime income of an educated worker, $E_{t-1}[\beta y_t(\theta)]$, and the discounted lifetime income of an uneducated worker, $(1 + \beta)w_u^h$. To do so, additional assumptions regarding the determination of the expected future foreign wage offers, θ_t^a, and the probability of discovery, m_t, are required. In what follows, we endow individuals with the faculty of rational expectations, such that $E_{t-1}(x_t) = x_t$.

Consider, then, the lifetime utility of an individual born at time $t - 1$, with $\theta < \bar{\theta}$. From Proposition 1, such a worker strictly prefers regime 1 if educated, and hence the expectation of his discounted lifetime income is just $\beta y_t^{rd}(\theta)$. Education therefore yields a higher lifetime utility than no education if and only if $\beta y_t^{rd}(\theta) > (1 + \beta)w_u^h$, or if and only if

$$\beta\left[m_t w_s^h \theta + (1 - m_t)(w_s^f \theta_t^a - k) - c\right] > (1 + \beta)w_u^h$$

$$\Leftrightarrow \theta > \left[\frac{1 + \beta}{\beta} w_u^h - (1 - m_t)(w_s^f \theta_t^a - k) + c\right]\frac{1}{m_t w_s^h}$$

$$\equiv \theta_t^{er}$$

Note that θ_t^{er} is strictly increasing in w_u^h, c, and k. We thus have the following result: All else remaining constant, *the higher is the unskilled wage and the higher is the cost of education, the smaller will be the fraction of the home-country population acquiring education* $[1 - F(\theta_t^{er})]$. Interestingly, *an increase in the cost of migration k also deters education by home-country workers*. Education not only varies wage earnings at home and abroad, it also renders migration a feasible option. An increase in the cost of migration weakens the migration incentive for acquiring education. Finally, θ_t^{er} is also increasing in m_t whenever $\partial\theta_t^{er}/\partial m_t = (1/w_s^h m_t)(w_s^f \theta_t^a - k - w_s^h \theta_t^{er}) > 0$, which in turn holds because $\theta_t^{er} < \bar{\theta}$. An increase in the probability of discovery m_t lowers the education incentives of low-ability workers – the probability that these workers will be pooled with high-ability workers is lower, and therefore the expected returns to their acquisition of skills are lower. It follows that the fraction of the home-country workers who remain uneducated rises as m_t rises, all else remaining constant.

Similarly, the lifetime utility of an educated individual with $\theta \in [\bar{\theta}, \theta_t^f)$ is higher than the utility of an unskilled worker if and only if $\beta y_t^i(\theta) > (1 + \beta)w_u^h$, or if and only if

$$\beta\left[m_t(w_s^f \theta - k) + (1 - m_t)(w_s^f \theta_t^a - k) - c\right] > (1 + \beta)w_u^h$$

$$\Leftrightarrow \theta > \left[\frac{1 + \beta}{\beta} w_u^h - (1 - m_t)(w_s^f \theta_t^a - k) + c + m_t k\right]\frac{1}{m_t w_s^f}$$

$$\equiv \theta_t^{ef}$$

where θ_t^{ef} is increasing in w_u^h, c, and k and also in m_t, provided that $\partial\theta_t^{ef}/\partial m_t = (1/w_s^f m_t)(w_s^f \theta_t^a - w_s^f \theta_t^{ef}) > 0$.

With θ_t^{er} and θ_t^{ef} now established, there are two critical levels of innate ability that further divide the home-country population into two groups: uneducated and educated.[8] Simple manipulation of the definitions of θ_t^{er} and θ_t^{ef} yields the following result:

[8] Given θ_t^{er} and θ_t^{ef}, we are now in a position to demonstrate the conditions under which no educated return migrant will be employed in the u sector of the home country. To this end, note that in equilibrium, $\beta y_t^{rd}(\theta_t^{er}) = (1 + \beta)w_u^h$. An educated worker is strictly better off working in the skilled sector if and only if $w_s^h \theta_t^{er} > w_u^h$ as the skill level of all educated workers is no less than θ_t^{er}. From the definition of θ_t^{er} we have

Proposition 2

1. *If $\theta_t^{er} < \bar{\theta}$: Workers with innate ability $\theta > \theta_t^{er}$ are better off acquiring education. The lifetime utility of workers with $\theta \le \theta_t^{er}$ is maximized by remaining uneducated.*
2. *If $\theta_t^{er} \ge \bar{\theta}$: Workers with innate ability $\theta > \theta_t^{ef}$ are better off acquiring education. The lifetime utility of workers with $\theta \le \theta_t^{ef}$ is maximized by remaining uneducated.*

If $\theta_t^{er} < \bar{\theta}$, θ_t^{er} defines a critical ability level that divides the home-country population into educated and uneducated workers. Now the home-country population consists of four groups of individuals: uneducated home-country workers (with $\theta < \theta_t^{er}$), educated workers who migrate and return upon discovery (with $\theta_t^{er} \le \theta < \bar{\theta}$), educated permanent migrants (with $\bar{\theta} \le \theta < \theta_t^{f}$), and educated workers who migrate and return if their true ability is not discovered (with $\theta \ge \theta_t^{f}$). This partitioning is as follows:

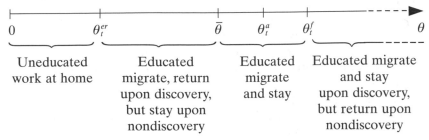

Note again that under asymmetric information, all individuals with $\theta \ge \bar{\theta}$ do not permanently migrate. As noted earlier, asymmetric information penalizes high-ability migrant workers, because with probability $1 - m_t$ such migrants do not receive the foreign wage that accords with their abilities. More important, upon return migration, the home-country population consists of individuals with the lowest and highest ability levels.

If $\theta_t^{er} > \bar{\theta}$, then workers with $\theta < \bar{\theta}$, as well as workers with $\bar{\theta} < \theta <$

$$w_s^h \theta_t^{er} = \frac{1}{m_t}\left[\frac{(1+\beta)w_u^h}{\beta} - (1-m_t)(w_s^f\theta_t^a - k) + c\right]$$

$$= w_u^h + \frac{1}{m_t}\left[\frac{[1+\beta(1-m_t)]w_u^h}{\beta} - (1-m_t)(w_s^f\theta_t^a - k) + c\right]$$

$$> w_u^h$$

if w_u^h is sufficiently small. In addition, because $w_u^f - k < w_u^h$, by transitivity, $w_s^h\theta_t^{er} > w_u^h > w_u^f - k$. Hence, migration regimes 5 and 6, as discussed in footnote 7, will not be pursued by any educated migrant worker.

θ_t^{ef}, remain uneducated. Therefore, the home-country population consists of only three groups: uneducated home-country workers (with $\theta \le \theta_t^{ef}$), educated permanent migrants (with $\theta_t^{ef} \le \theta < \theta_t^f$), and educated home-country workers who return upon nondiscovery (with $\theta \ge \theta_t^f$). Again, the partitioning is as follows:

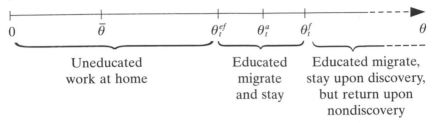

Uneducated work at home

Educated migrate and stay

Educated migrate, stay upon discovery, but return upon nondiscovery

As in the previous case, home-country workers consist of individuals with the lowest ability levels and the highest ability levels upon return migration. The possibility of migration leads to the home country's permanent loss of all migrant workers with skill levels $\theta_t^{ef} < \theta < \theta_t^f$, because, from part 2 of Proposition 1, $y_t^f(\theta) > y_t^{rd}(\theta)$ for every $\theta_t^{ef} \le \theta \le \theta_t^f$. Note also that because, by definition, θ_t^a is the average skill level for all undiscovered migrant workers at time t, while θ_t^{ef} is the skill level for the lowest-ability migrant worker, it must be the case that $\theta_t^a > \theta_t^{ef}$, as shown in the preceding diagram.

Comparisons of θ^* and θ_t^{er}, and of θ^* and θ_t^{ef} yield the following:

Proposition 3. *The fraction of the home-country population pursuing education in the presence of migration opportunities is always higher than the fraction of the home-country population pursuing education in the absence of migration opportunities.*

Proposition 3 reveals that the increase in the incentive to pursue education when migration offers a more attractive wage to the educated leads the home country to a higher degree of educational attainment. Yet it should also be noted that the increase in the fraction of educated workers in the home country due to the prospect of migration does not necessarily imply that the number of educated workers who *stay and work* in the home country increases. To see this, consider the case of $\theta_t^{er} > \bar{\theta}$. From the definitions of θ_t^{ef} and θ^* we have

$$w_s^h \theta^* = m_t(w_s^f \theta_t^{ef} - k) + (1 - m_t)(w_s^f \theta_t^a - k)$$
$$\Leftrightarrow w_s^h \theta^* = m_t(w_s^f \theta_t^{ef} - w_s^f \theta_t^a) + w_s^f \theta_t^a - k$$
$$\Leftrightarrow w_s^h \theta^* < w_s^f \theta_t^a - k$$

where the last inequality follows because $\theta_t^{ef} < \theta_t^a$. In addition, because, by definition, $w_s^f \theta_t^a - k = w_s^h \theta_t^f$, we have $w_s^h \theta^* < w_s^h \theta_t^f$, or $\theta^* < \theta_t^f$. Hence, the group of workers who acquire education in response to the prospect of migration (with skill levels $\bar{\theta} < \theta_t^{ef} \le \theta < \theta^* < \theta_t^f$) belongs to the group of permanent migrants. As a result, the prospect of migration not only leads to a loss for the home country of those educated workers with $\theta > \theta_t^f (> \theta^*)$ who stay in the foreign country upon discovery, it also leads to the preclusion of any increase in the educated workforce in the home country, as a result of the possibility of migration. In what follows, we therefore focus our attention on the case in which $\theta_t^{er} < \bar{\theta}$, where the four "modes of employment" are present simultaneously.[9] As we elaborate further, the possible return migration of those workers who would not have had the incentive to acquire education in the absence of migration opportunities allows a possible economy-wide gain in spite of, and along with, a brain drain.

4   The Dynamics of Migration

With θ_t^{er} and θ_t^f defined, we now analyze the process of migration and the evolution of wage offers as experience with employing migrants accumulates over time. Given an initial experience associated with M_0, migration from the home country in subsequent periods can be summarized by the vector $\{\theta_t^a, \theta_t^{er}, \theta_t^f\}$, the elements of which are in turn solutions to the following system of simultaneous equations:

$$\theta_t^a = \frac{\int_{\theta_t^{er}}^{\theta_t^f} \theta f(\theta)\, d\theta}{F(\theta_t^f) - F(\theta_t^{er})} \tag{15.2}$$

$$\theta_t^f = \frac{w_s^f \theta_t^a - k}{w_s^h} \tag{15.3}$$

---

[9] For $\theta_t^{er} < \bar{\theta}$, we require that

$$m_t w_s^h \bar{\theta} + (1 - m_t)(w_s^f \theta_t^a - k) - c \ge \frac{(1 + \beta) w_u^h}{\beta}$$

Because $\theta_t^a > \bar{\theta}$, the left-hand side of the preceding inequality is greater than $m_t w_s^h \bar{\theta} + (1 - m_t)(w_s^f \bar{\theta} - k) - c = w_s^h \bar{\theta} - c = w_s^h k/(w_s^f - w_s^h) - c$. It follows that

$$m_t w_s^h \bar{\theta} + (1 - m_t)(w_s^f \theta_t^a - k) - c > w_s^h \frac{k}{w_s^f - w_s^h} - c \ge \frac{(1 + \beta) w_u^h}{\beta}$$

whenever w_u^h is sufficiently small and k is sufficiently large.

$$\theta_t^{er} = \frac{1}{m_t w_s^h}\left[\frac{1+\beta}{\beta}w_u^h - (1-m_t)(w_s^f\theta_t^a - k) + c\right] \tag{15.4}$$

On multiplying both sides of equation (15.2) by w_s^f, the equation can be interpreted as requiring the wage offer to each migrant with unknown ability at time t to be equal to the average ability of the migrant cohort with unknown individual ability at time t, multiplied by the wage rate per efficiency unit of labor. Equations (15.3) and (15.4) require, respectively, that the extent of migration and the education decision follow from the expected utility maximization described in Section 3.[10] From equation (15.3) we observe further that

$$\theta_t^a = \frac{w_s^h \theta_t^f + k}{w_s^f} \tag{15.5}$$

and on rewriting equation (15.2),

$$\theta_t^a = \frac{\int_{\theta_t^{er}}^{\theta_t^f} \theta f(\theta)\,d\theta}{F(\theta_t^f) - F(\theta_t^{er})} \tag{15.6}$$

Equation (15.5) captures the supply side of the migrant labor market, that is, the foreign-country wage of an undiscovered migrant worker at time t, $w_s^f\theta_t^a$, is just sufficient to induce the supply of educated workers with ability $\theta \le \theta_t^f$ who are willing to stay and work in the foreign country at the wage $w_s^f\theta_t^a$. Equation (15.6) holds that if θ_t^f represents the ability of the most able migrant worker who prefers $w_s^f\theta_t^a - k$ to his home wage, and θ_t^{er} represents the ability of the least able migrant worker, $1/w_s^f$ of the wage offer at time t (which reflects the willingness to pay for migrant work) is equal to the average ability of the migrant workforce, with unknown individual abilities, at time t.

Figures 15.3 and 15.4 depict the supply (SS) and demand (DD) relationships spelled out in equations (15.5) and (15.6) respectively. The intersection points A in Figure 15.3 and B in Figure 15.4 depict equilibrium combinations of θ_t^a and θ_t^f that simultaneously satisfy equations (15.2)–(15.4), given m_t. It can be confirmed that both DD and SS are upward-sloping.[11] Note also that, in general, DD can be flatter or steeper

[10] A natural question is whether or not a solution to the preceding system exists. In the Appendix we provide an existence proof and spell out the required assumptions.
[11] From equation (15.5), the slope of the supply relationship $(\partial\theta_t^a/\partial\theta_t^f)\mid_{SS}$ can be written as:

$$\frac{\partial\theta_t^a}{\partial\theta_t^f}\Big|_{SS} = \frac{w_s^h}{w_s^f} > 0$$

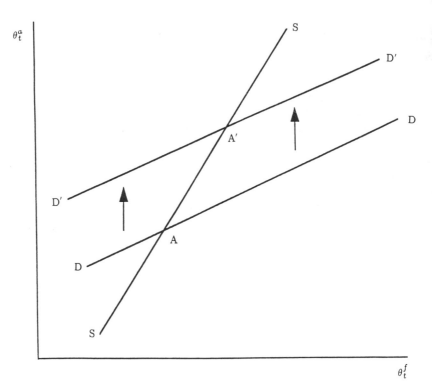

Figure 15.3.

than SS, depending on the exogenous parameters of the model. Consider, for example, the effect of an exogenous increase in the probability of discovery m_t when SS is steeper than DD, as in Figure 15.3. An increase in m_t shifts the DD curve upward, while the SS curve remains unchanged.[12]

From the demand relationship in equation (15.6), we confirm, in the Appendix, that the slope $(\partial \theta_t^a / \partial \theta_t^f) \mid_{DD}$ is

$$\frac{\partial \theta_t^a}{\partial \theta_t^f}\bigg|_{DD} = \frac{(\theta_t^f - \theta_t^a)f(\theta_t^f)/[F(\theta_t^f) - F(\theta_t^{er})]}{1 + \{(\theta_t^a - \theta_t^{er})f(\theta_t^{er})/[F(\theta_t^f) - F(\theta_t^{er})]\}[(1 - m_t)w_s^f/m_t w_s^h]} > 0$$

[12] To see this, note from equation (15.6) that for any given value of θ_t^f, an increase in m_t leads to an upward shift of the DD curve, because

$$\frac{\partial \theta_t^a}{\partial m_t}\bigg|_{\theta_t^f \text{ const.}} = \frac{(\theta_t^a - \theta_t^{er})f(\theta_t^{er})}{F(\theta_t^f) - F(\theta_t^{er})} \frac{\partial \theta_t^{er}}{\partial m_t}$$

$$= \frac{(\theta_t^a - \theta_t^{er})f(\theta_t^{er})}{F(\theta_t^f) - F(\theta_t^{er})} \frac{w_s^f \theta_t^a - k - w_s^h \theta_t^{er}}{m_t w_s^h} > 0$$

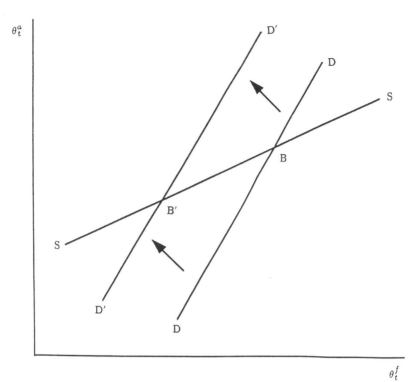

Figure 15.4.

An increase in m_t reduces the number of workers with low ability who acquire education at time $t - 1$ $[1 - F(\theta_t^{er})]$ because workers endowed with rational expectations correctly anticipate the future value of m_t in their human-capital calculus. As a result, the average ability (and hence the demand price) of migrants rises for any given θ_t^f because an increase in m_t shifts the skill composition of the migrant population in the foreign country to the right.

Note further that an increase in m_t has no direct effect on the supply side of the migrant labor market. θ_t^f divides the home-country popula-

where the first equality follows from equation (15.A1) in the Appendix, and the second equality follows from equation (15.A3) in the Appendix. It follows, therefore, that DD shifts upward when m_t increases, or $(\partial \theta_t^a / \partial m_t) |_{\theta_t^f \text{const.}} > 0$. In addition, from equation (15.5),

$$\frac{\partial \theta_t^a}{\partial m_t} \bigg|_{\theta_t^f \text{const.}} = 0$$

Hence, SS is independent of m_t.

tion into two subgroups: a subgroup that consists of low-ability individuals (with $w_s^h\theta < w_s^f\theta_t^a - k$) who are better off remaining in the foreign country only if their true abilities are *not* discovered, and a subgroup that consists of individuals (with $w_s^h\theta \ge w_s^f\theta_t^a - k$) who receive a higher home wage than $w_s^f\theta_t^a - k$. It follows that θ_t^a alone determines the value of θ_t^f, given the wage schedules in the home country and the foreign country.

The new equilibrium pair θ_t^a and θ_t^f is depicted as point A' in Figure 15.3, where both the average ability of migrants and θ_t^f rise as a result of an increase in m_t. In contrast, starting from a point such as B in Figure 15.4, where SS is flatter than DD, an increase in m_t, together with the associated shift of the DD curve, implies reductions in both θ_t^a and θ_t^f, as depicted by point B'. We denote the solutions to the system of simultaneous equations (15.2)–(15.4) as $\theta_t^j(m_t, c, w_u^h)$, $j = a, f, er$. Applying our preceding arguments for the case of an increase in c and for the case of an increase in w_u^h, we obtain the first two parts of the following result; the third part will be reasoned momentarily.

Proposition 4

1. $\theta_t^a(m_t, c, w_u^h)$ is increasing in m_t, c, and w_u^h if and only if SS is steeper than DD or, equivalently, if and only if

$$1 - \frac{(\theta_t^f - \theta_t^a)f(\theta_t^f)}{F(\theta_t^f) - F(\theta_t^{er})}\frac{w_s^f}{w_s^h} + \frac{(\theta_t^a - \theta_t^{er})f(\theta_t^{er})}{F(\theta_t^f) - F(\theta_t^{er})}\frac{(1 - m_t)w_s^f}{m_t w_s^h} > 0 \quad (15.7)$$

2. $\theta_t^f(m_t, c, w_u^h)$ is increasing in m_t, c, and w_u^h if and only if equation (15.7) is satisfied.

3. $\theta_t^{er}(m_t, c, w_u^h)$ is increasing in m_t if and only if

$$\frac{w_s^f\theta_t^a - k - w_s^h\theta_t^{er}}{(1 - m_t)w_s^f} > \frac{\partial\theta_t^a}{\partial m_t} \quad (15.8)$$

Regarding part 3 of Proposition 4, note that from equations (15.2)–(15.4),

$$\frac{\partial\theta_t^{er}}{\partial m_t} = \frac{(w_s^f\theta_t^a - k - w_s^h\theta_t^{er}) - (1 - m_t)w_s^f(\partial\theta_t^a/\partial m_t)}{m_t w_s^h}$$

In general, therefore, an increase in m_t has an ambiguous effect on the incentives of workers with low ability levels to acquire education and migrate. The term $(w_s^f\theta_t^a - k - w_s^h\theta_t^{er}) > 0$, which is equal to the reduction in wages when the true ability of the marginal educated worker (the worker whose skill level is θ_t^{er}) is discovered, captures the negative incentive that an increase in m_t has on the education-cum-migration decision of low-ability workers. This negative incentive, however, coincides with the positive incentive that arises due to the increase in θ_t^a that, contingent on equation (15.7) holding, occurs as more high-ability workers migrate abroad because of an increased m_t. It follows that the negative incentive effect of an increase in m_t dominates the positive incentive effect whenever the increase in θ_t^a with respect to m_t is sufficiently low, as in equation (15.8), in which case $\partial \theta_t^{er} / \partial m_t > 0$.

Proposition 4 completely summarizes the intertemporal variations of θ_t^a, θ_t^f, and θ_t^{er} for any given probability of discovery m_t. Because migrant employment experience is cumulative, and the probability of discovery at any time $t + 1$ depends on the accumulation of migrant employment experience until time $t - 1$ $[m^{-1}(m_t)]$ plus the increment in the total volume of migration at time t

$$\mathcal{M}_t = N[(1 - m_t)\{F(\bar{\theta}) - F[\theta_t^{er}(m_t, c, w_u^h)]\} + F[\theta_t^f(m_t, c, w_u^h)]$$
$$- F(\bar{\theta}) + m_t\{1 - F[\theta_t^f(m_t, c, w_u^h)]\}]$$

the law of motion governing the process of migration therefore depends only on the evolution of m_t, with

$$m_{t+1} = \begin{cases} m[m^{-1}(m_t) + \mathcal{M}_t] & \text{if } m_t < \hat{m} \\ \hat{m} & \text{otherwise} \end{cases} \tag{15.9}$$

where $m^{-1}(m_1) = M_0$ is given.

A steady state of equation (15.9) is denoted m^* such that $m_t = m_{t+1} = m^*$. The steady-state values of θ_t^j will be denoted as $\hat{\theta}^j, j = a, f, er$. The values of $\hat{\theta}^j$ are determined using equations (15.2)–(15.4) once m^* is determined.

Proposition 5. *If equation (15.7) is satisfied and the initial probability of discovery m_1 is such that $\theta_1^a(m_1, c, w_u^h) > \bar{\theta}$, then the only steady-state-equilibrium probability of discovery m^* is equal to $\hat{m}$.*

This result is straightforward, from Proposition 4.[13] In essence, the requirement that equation (15.7) be satisfied guarantees that accumulation of migrant employment experience and hence the probability of

---

[13] We are grateful to Yoram Weiss for pointing out that the steady-state assumption can also be supported by an alternative experience-accumulation formulation in which a per-period depreciation rate can be used to capture the fact that recent migrants provide more information on the quality of the current wave of migrants.

discovery will lead to a sequence of migratory moves from the home country over time. In the process, the average productivity of the migrants improves, not only because of an increase in the incentive for brighter individuals to migrate as the probability of discovery rises but also because of the simultaneous decline in the willingness of the lowest-ability individuals to acquire education and migrate. Such a cumulative process implies that the only long-run equilibrium consistent with an initial condition that yields a positive rate of migration is such that the probability of discovery no longer improves even when $\mathcal{M}_t$ increases.[14]

5   The Possibility of a Welfare Gain

Denote by $\hat{\theta}^{er}$ and $\hat{\theta}^f$ the solutions derived from the system of simultaneous equations (15.2)–(15.4), given $\hat{m}$.

At any time period, the total home-country population $2N$ is distributed as follows: The N young individuals are divided into two groups: $NF(\hat{\theta}^{er})$ who are uneducated and work, and $N[1 - F(\hat{\theta}^{er})]$ who acquire education and do not work. The N old individuals are divided into two groups: $NF(\hat{\theta}^{er})$ who are uneducated and work in the home country, and the rest who engage in migration. These workers, in turn, are divided into three groups: migrants who, with probability $\hat{m}$, will return-migrate and, with probability $1 - \hat{m}$, will remain in the foreign country (consisting of $N[F(\bar{\theta}) - F(\hat{\theta}^{er})]$ individuals); permanent migrants ($N[F(\hat{\theta}^f) - F(\bar{\theta})]$); migrants who, with probability $1 - \hat{m}$, will return-migrate and, with probability $\hat{m}$, will remain in the foreign country ($N[1 - F(\hat{\theta}^f)]$). There are thus $N\{\hat{m}[F(\bar{\theta}) - F(\hat{\theta}^{er})] + (1 - \hat{m})[1 - F(\hat{\theta}^f)]\}$ workers at home who are return migrants, and there are $N\{(1 - \hat{m})[F(\bar{\theta}) - F(\hat{\theta}^{er})] + [F(\hat{\theta}^f) - F(\bar{\theta})] + \hat{m}[1 - F(\hat{\theta}^f)]\} \equiv \hat{\mathcal{M}}^p$ workers who remain abroad.

Therefore, national output accrues from $2NF(\hat{\theta}^{er})$ workers who each produce w_u^h, from $\hat{m}N[F(\bar{\theta}) - F(\hat{\theta}^{er})]$ workers who each produce w_s^h times their individual θ, and from $(1 - \hat{m})N[1 - F(\hat{\theta}^f)]$ workers who each produce w_s^h times their individual θ.

---

[14] It bears emphasis that Proposition 5 also relies on an assumption made in Proposition 1, that is, that $\theta_t^a > \bar{\theta}$. Otherwise, from equation (15.3),

$$\theta_t^f - \theta_t^a = \frac{w_s^f \theta_t^a - k}{w_s^h} - \theta_t^a$$

$$= \frac{w_s^f \theta_t^a - k - w_s^h \theta_t^a}{w_s^h} < 0$$

as $\theta_t^a < \bar{\theta}$. It follows that equation (15.2), which requires that θ_t^f be no smaller than θ_t^a, can never be satisfied, and accordingly migration never takes off.

Denote by $V^m(\hat{\theta}^{er}, \hat{\theta}^f)$ the long-run equilibrium value of the per-period national output in the home country, net of the cost of education. It follows that

$$V^m(\hat{\theta}^{er}, \hat{\theta}^f) = 2NF(\hat{\theta}^{er})w_u^h + N\hat{m}\int_{\hat{\theta}^{er}}^{\theta}(w_s^h\theta - c)f(\theta)\,d\theta$$

$$+ N(1-\hat{m})\int_{\hat{\theta}^f}^{\infty}(w_s^h\theta - c)f(\theta)\,d\theta$$

$$= N\left[2F(\hat{\theta}^{er})w_u^h + \hat{m}\int_{\hat{\theta}^{er}}^{\theta}(w_s^h\theta - c)f(\theta)\,d\theta\right.$$

$$\left. + (1-\hat{m})\int_{\hat{\theta}^f}^{\infty}(w_s^h\theta - c)f(\theta)\,d\theta\right]$$

$$= N\left[2F(\hat{\theta}^{er})w_u^h + \int_{\hat{\theta}^{er}}^{\infty}(w_s^h\theta - c)f(\theta)\,d\theta\right.$$

$$- (1-\hat{m})\int_{\hat{\theta}^{er}}^{\theta}(w_s^h\theta - c)f(\theta)\,d\theta - \int_{\theta}^{\hat{\theta}^f}(w_s^h\theta - c)f(\theta)\,d\theta$$

$$\left. - \hat{m}\int_{\hat{\theta}^f}^{\infty}(w_s^h\theta - c)f(\theta)\,d\theta\right]$$

$$= N\left[2F(\hat{\theta}^{er})w_u^h + \int_{\hat{\theta}^{er}}^{\infty}(w_s^h\theta - c)f(\theta)\,d\theta - (w_s^h\hat{\theta}^p - c)\frac{\hat{\mathcal{M}}^p}{N}\right]$$

where

$$\hat{\theta}^p = \frac{N}{\hat{\mathcal{M}}^p}\left[(1-\hat{m})\int_{\hat{\theta}^{er}}^{\theta}\theta f(\theta)\,d\theta + \int_{\theta}^{\hat{\theta}^f}\theta f(\theta)\,d\theta + \hat{m}\int_{\hat{\theta}^f}^{\infty}\theta f(\theta)\,d\theta\right]$$

is the average ability of all migrant workers who stay abroad. The term $(w_s^h\hat{\theta}^p - c)\hat{\mathcal{M}}^p$ thus refers to the home-country output, net of the cost of education, that the home country forgoes when $\hat{\mathcal{M}}^p$ of its workers migrate and stay in the foreign country. To recall, $\hat{\mathcal{M}}^p$ is the per-period number of home-country workers employed abroad in a steady state. Therefore, per-capita output at home is

$$v^m(\hat{\theta}^{er}, \hat{\theta}^f) = \frac{V^m(\hat{\theta}^{er}, \hat{\theta}^f)}{2N - \hat{\mathcal{M}}^p}$$

Thus, $v^m(\hat{\theta}^{er}, \hat{\theta}^f) > v(\theta^*)$ if and only if

$$\frac{1}{2 - \hat{\mathcal{M}}^p/N}\left[2F(\hat{\theta}^{er})w_u^h + \int_{\hat{\theta}^{er}}^{\infty}(w_s^h\theta - c)f(\theta)\,d\theta - (w_s^h\hat{\theta}^p - c)\frac{\hat{\mathcal{M}}^p}{N}\right]$$

$$> \frac{1}{2}\left[2w_u^hF(\hat{\theta}^*) + \int_{\theta^*}^{\infty}(w_s^h\theta - c)f(\theta)\,d\theta\right] \equiv v(\theta^*)$$

or if and only if

$$\frac{1}{2-\hat{\mathcal{M}^p}/N}\left[2F(\hat{\theta}^{er})w_u^h+\int_{\hat{\theta}^{er}}^{\infty}(w_s^h\theta-c)f(\theta)\,d\theta\right.$$

$$+\int_{\theta^*}^{\infty}(w_s^h\theta-c)f(\theta)\,d\theta-(w_s^h\hat{\theta}^p-c)\frac{\hat{\mathcal{M}^p}}{N}\right]$$

$$>\frac{1}{2}\left[2w_u^hF(\hat{\theta}*)+\int_{\theta^*}^{\infty}(w_s^h\theta-c)f(\theta)\,d\theta\right]$$

On manipulating the preceding equation, we obtain the following necessary and sufficient condition for $v^m(\hat{\theta}^{er},\hat{\theta}^f)>v(\theta^*)$:

$$\left\{\int_{\hat{\theta}^{er}}^{\theta^*}(w_s^h\theta-c-2w_u^h)f(\theta)\,d\theta+\frac{\hat{\mathcal{M}^p}}{N}\left[v(\theta^*)-(w_s^h\hat{\theta}^p-c)\right]\right\}\frac{1}{2-\hat{\mathcal{M}^p}/N}>0$$

$$(15.10)$$

The first term in the curly brackets on the left-hand side of equation (15.10) reflects the gain in per-capita output when the number of educated workers in the home country increases from $N[1-F(\theta^*)]$ to $N[1-F(\hat{\theta}^{er})]$ as a result of the prospect of migration. In particular,

$$\int_{\hat{\theta}^{er}}^{\theta^*}(w_s^h\theta-c-2w_u^h)f(\theta)\,d\theta\equiv(w_s^h\hat{\theta}^d-c-2w_u^h)[F(\theta^*)-F(\hat{\theta}^{er})]>0$$

if and only if $w_s^h\hat{\theta}^d-c>2w_u^h$, where $\hat{\theta}^d$ denotes the average skill level of workers in the range $[\hat{\theta}^{er},\theta^*]$. Hence, the first term of equation (15.10) is positive if and only if the average product of the increase in the educated workforce in the s sector, net of the cost of education, is higher than the forgone output in the u sector. In particular, a sufficient condition for the foregoing is that $w_s^h\hat{\theta}^{er}-c-2w_u^h>0$. From the definition of $\hat{\theta}^{er}$, this requires that

$$\left(2\hat{m}-\frac{1+\beta}{\beta}\right)w_u^h<(1-\hat{m})(c+k-w_s^f\hat{\theta}^a)$$

which, for example, is satisfied for sufficiently small $\hat{m}$ and/or sufficiently large c and k. From Proposition 3, it follows that $w_s^h\hat{\theta}^{er}-c<w_s^h\theta^*-c$, and from the definition of θ^*, it follows that when $\beta=1$, $w_s^h\theta^*=2w_u^h+c$. Therefore, when $\beta=1$, $w_s^h\hat{\theta}^{er}-c<2w_u^h$. But if $w_s^h\hat{\theta}^{er}-c-2w_u^h<0$, the sufficient condition just referred to may not hold. That is, a gain in per-capita income is less likely to occur. Recall our discussion in Section 2.3 in which we pointed out that when $\beta=1$, individual utility maximization corresponds with the social optimum. Here again we find that when $\beta=1$, it is less likely that the migration prospect will lead to an improvement. However, if $\beta<1$, the smaller the β, the larger the gain that will result from the increase in education prompted by the prospect of migration. This is nicely reflected by the increased likelihood that equation (15.10) will hold.

The second term in the curly brackets on the left-hand side of equation (15.10) reflects the change in per-capita income resulting from a reduction in total population due to the loss of educated workers. In particular, this term is positive whenever the per-capita home-country income of steady-state migrant workers, $w_s^h \hat{\theta}^p - c$, is less than the per-capita home-country income in the absence of migration, $v(\theta^*)$. Note that the larger the total number of workers abroad in a steady state ($\hat{M}^p$), the more significant will be the effect of this source of change in per-capita output.

Proposition 6. *The per-capita output in a country vulnerable to migration of skilled workers is higher than the per-capita output in a country that is immune to migration if and only if equation (15.10) is satisfied.*

6 Conclusions

When an economy opens up to migration, workers in the economy are presented with a new set of opportunities and a new structure of incentives. Although the expansion of opportunities results in human-capital depletion, the revised incentives induce human-capital formation: Higher returns to skills in the foreign country prompt more skill-formation in the home country. We have shown that the fraction of the home-country workforce acquring education in the presence of migration opportunities is higher than the fraction of the home-country workforce undertaking education in the absence of migration opportunities.

Migration is also associated with a changing information environment, implying, in particular, that foreign-country employers are imperfectly informed about the skill levels of individual migrant workers. Consequently, migrants with different skill levels are pooled together, and all are paid the same wage, which is based on the average product of the entire cohort of migrants. The imperfect but nonzero capability of employers to decipher true skill levels of individual migrants – captured in the probability of discovery – results in return migration of both the highest- and lowest-skilled migrant workers, whereas permanent migrants are not drawn from the extremes of the skill distribution. Employers nevertheless become less ignorant over time. As their experience with employing migrants builds up, the probability of discovery rises. This progressive rise prompts a sequence of migratory moves characterized by a rising average level of skills, until the probability of discovery reaches its steady-state equilibrium.

Accounting for the steady-state goings, comings, and skill formation, we have shown that under well-specified conditions, per-capita output in the home country is higher than what would have obtained had the country been immune to migration altogether. An intriguing implication of this is that if migration of skilled workers is allowed (rather than hindered), the home-country population can enjoy higher welfare.[15] A drain of brains and a welfare gain need not be mutually exclusive, and, as we have demonstrated, the former can be the very cause of the latter.

APPENDIX

Proof of Proposition 1.   We proceed by stating the conditions under which $y_t^f(\theta) > y_t^{rd}(\theta)$ and $y_t^f(\theta) > y_t^{ru}(\theta)$. Now,

$$y_t^f(\theta) - y_t^{rd}(\theta) = (1 - m_t)(w_s^f \theta_t^a - k) + m_t(w_s^f \theta - k)$$
$$- (1 - m_t)(w_s^f \theta_t^a - k) - m_t(w_s^h \theta)$$
$$= m_t(w_s^f \theta - k - w_s^h \theta) > 0$$

if and only if $\theta > \bar{\theta}$. Similarly,

$$y_t^f(\theta) - y_t^{ru}(\theta) = (1 - m_t)(w_s^f \theta_t^a - k) + m_t(w_s^f \theta - k)$$
$$- (1 - m_t)(w_s^h \theta) - m_t(w_s^f \theta - k) > 0$$

if and only if $\theta < \theta_t^f$, with

$$\theta_t^f = \frac{w_s^f \theta_t^a - k}{w_s^h}$$

It remains to be shown that $\theta_t^f > \bar{\theta}$ and that $y_t^h(\theta) < \max[y_t^{rd}(\theta), y_t^f(\theta), y_t^{ru}(\theta)]$ for all θ. Now,

$$\theta_t^f - \bar{\theta} = \frac{w_s^f \theta_t^a - k}{w_s^h} - \frac{k}{w_s^f - w_s^h}$$
$$= \frac{w_s^f \theta_t^a}{w_s^h} - \frac{kw_s^h + k(w_s^f - w_s^h)}{w_s^h(w_s^f - w_s^h)}$$
$$= \frac{w_s^f \theta_t^a}{w_s^h} - \frac{w_s^f}{w_s^h} \frac{k}{w_s^f - w_s^h}$$
$$= \frac{w_s^f \theta_t^a}{w_s^h} - \frac{w_s^f \bar{\theta}}{w_s^h}$$
$$> 0$$

---

[15] Note that this outcome holds independently of migrants remitting some or none of their higher foreign earnings.

if and only if $\theta_t^a > \bar{\theta}$ [where the first and the fourth equalities follow from the definition of $\bar{\theta} = k/(w_s^f - w_s^h)$].

In addition, for $\theta < \theta_t^f$,

$$y_t^{rd}(\theta) - y_t^h(\theta) = (1 - m_t)(w_s^f\theta_t^a - k) + m_t w_s^h\theta - w_s^h\theta$$
$$= (1 - m_t)(w_s^f\theta_t^a - k) - (1 - m_t)w_s^h\theta$$
$$= (1 - m_t)(w_s^f\theta_t^a - k - w_s^h\theta) > 0$$

Hence $y_t^{rd}(\theta) > y_t^h(\theta)$ for $\theta < \theta_t^f$. Also, because $y_t^f(\theta) > y_t^{rd}(\theta)$, it must also be the case that $y_t^f(\theta) > y_t^h(\theta)$ for $\theta \in [\bar{\theta}, \theta_t^f)$. Finally, for $\theta \geq \theta_t^f$,

$$y_t^{ru}(\theta) - y_t^h(\theta) = (1 - m_t)w_s^h\theta + m_t(w_s^f\theta - k) - w_s^h\theta$$
$$= m_t(w_s^f\theta - k) - m_t w_s^h\theta$$
$$= m_t(w_s^f\theta - k - w_s^h\theta) > 0$$

It follows, therefore, that for all $\theta < \bar{\theta}, y_t(\theta) = y_t^{rd}(\theta); \theta \in [\bar{\theta}, \theta_t^f), y_t(\theta) = y_t^f(\theta)$; otherwise, $y_t(\theta) = y_t^{ru}(\theta)$, where $y_t(\theta)$, recall, is equal to $\max[y_t^{rd}(\theta), y_t^f(\theta), y_t^{ru}(\theta), y_t^h(\theta)]$. ∎

Proof of Proposition 2

1. The case of $\theta_t^{er} < \bar{\theta}$: We need to show that $\beta y_t(\theta) > (1 + \beta)w_u^h$ for every $\theta > \theta_t^{er}$. From the proof of Proposition 1, we have, for all $\theta < \bar{\theta}$, $y_t(\theta) = y_t^{rd}(\theta); \theta \in [\bar{\theta}, \theta_t^f), y_t(\theta) = y_t^f(\theta)$; and otherwise, $y_t(\theta) = y_t^{ru}(\theta)$. Hence, it is sufficient to show the following: (A) for $\theta \in [\theta_t^{er}, \bar{\theta}), \beta y_t^{rd}(\theta) > (1 + \beta)w_u^h$; (B) for $\theta \in [\bar{\theta}, \theta_t^f), \beta y_t^f(\theta) > (1 + \beta)w_u^h$; (C) $\beta y_t^{ru}(\theta) > (1 + \beta)w_u^h$ for $\theta \geq \theta_t^f$.

(A) By the definition of θ_t^{er},

$$\frac{1 + \beta}{\beta}w_u^h = m_t w_s^h\theta_t^{er} + (1 - m_t)(w_s^f\theta_t^a - k) - c$$

$$\Leftrightarrow \frac{1 + \beta}{\beta}w_u^h < m_t w_s^h\theta + (1 - m_t)(w_s^f\theta_t^a - k) - c$$

$$\Leftrightarrow (1 + \beta)w_u^h < \beta y_t^{rd}(\theta)$$

for any $\theta \geq \theta_t^{er}$. Clearly, it must also be the case that $(1 + \beta)w_u^h < \beta y_t^{rd}(\theta)$ for any $\theta \in [\theta_t^{er}, \bar{\theta})$.

(B) Making use of the definition of θ_t^{er}, suppose that $\theta_t^{er} < \bar{\theta}$. We have

$$\left[\frac{1 + \beta}{\beta}w_u^h - (1 - m_t)(w_s^f\theta_t^a - k) + c\right]\frac{1}{m_t w_s^h} < \bar{\theta}$$

$$\Leftrightarrow \frac{1 + \beta}{\beta}w_u^h - (1 - m_t)(w_s^f\theta_t^a - k) + c < m_t w_s^h\bar{\theta}$$

$$\Leftrightarrow \frac{1+\beta}{\beta} w_u^h < m_t w_s^h \bar{\theta} + (1 - m_t)(w_s^f \theta_t^a - k) - c$$

$$\Leftrightarrow \frac{1+\beta}{\beta} w_u^h < m_t (w_s^f \bar{\theta} - k) + (1 - m_t)(w_s^f \theta_t^a - k) - c$$

$$\Leftrightarrow \frac{1+\beta}{\beta} w_u^h < m_t (w_s^f \theta - k) + (1 - m_t)(w_s^f \theta_t^a - k) - c = y_t^f(\theta)$$

for every $\theta > \bar{\theta}$. Note that the next-to-last inequality follows from the definition of $\bar{\theta}$ ($w_s^f \bar{\theta} - k = w_s^h \bar{\theta}$). It follows, therefore, that for every $\theta > \bar{\theta}$, $(1 + \beta)w_u^h < \beta y_t^f(\theta)$ whenever $\theta_t^{er} < \bar{\theta}$.

(C)   Because $y_t^f(\theta) < y_t^{ru}(\theta)$ for $\theta > \theta_t^f$, it follows from (B) that $(1 + \beta)w_u^h < \beta y_t^f(\theta) < \beta y_t^{ru}(\theta)$ for every $\theta > \bar{\theta}$. In the proof of Proposition 1 we have that $\theta_t^f > \bar{\theta}$. Hence, for every $\theta > \theta_t^f(>\bar{\theta})$, $(1 + \beta)w_u^h < \beta y_t^f(\theta) < \beta y_t^{ru}(\theta)$.

2.   The case of $\theta_t^{er} \geq \bar{\theta}$: We need to show that $\beta y_t(\theta) > (1 + \beta)w_u^h$ for every $\theta > \theta_t^{ef}$. In particular, we need to show the following: (D) for all $\theta < \bar{\theta}$, $(1 + \beta)w_u^h > y_t^{rd}(\theta)$; (E) for $\theta \in [\bar{\theta}, \theta_t^{ef})$, $(1 + \beta)w_u^h > \beta y_t^f(\theta)$; (F) for $\theta \in [\theta_t^{ef}, \theta_t^f]$, $(1 + \beta)w_u^h < \beta y_t^f(\theta)$; (G) for $\theta > \theta_t^f$, $(1 + \beta)w_u^h < \beta y_t^{ru}(\theta)$.

(D)   Suppose that $\theta_t^{er} \geq \bar{\theta}$. By the definition of θ_t^{er} we have

$$\left[\frac{1+\beta}{\beta} w_u^h - (1 - m_t)(w_s^f \theta_t^a - k) + c \right] \frac{1}{m_t w_s^h} \geq \bar{\theta}$$

$$\Leftrightarrow \frac{1+\beta}{\beta} w_u^h - (1 - m_t)(w_s^f \theta_t^a - k) + c \geq m_t w_s^h \bar{\theta}$$

$$\Leftrightarrow \frac{1+\beta}{\beta} w_u^h \geq m_t w_s^h \bar{\theta} + (1 - m_t)(w_s^f \theta_t^a - k) - c$$

$$\Leftrightarrow \frac{1+\beta}{\beta} w_u^h > m_t w_s^h \theta + (1 - m_t)(w_s^f \theta_t^a - k) - c = y_t^{rd}(\theta)$$

for $\theta < \bar{\theta}$. It follows, therefore, that for $\theta < \bar{\theta}$, $(1 + \beta)w_u^h > \beta y_t^{rd}(\theta)$.

(E)   We shall first establish that $\theta_t^{ef} \geq \bar{\theta}$. If $\theta_t^{er} \geq \bar{\theta}$, we have

$$\left[\frac{1+\beta}{\beta} w_u^h - (1 - m_t)(w_s^f \theta_t^a - k) + c \right] \frac{1}{m_t w_s^h} \geq \bar{\theta}$$

$$\Leftrightarrow \frac{1+\beta}{\beta} w_u^h - (1 - m_t)(w_s^f \theta_t^a - k) + c \geq m_t w_s^h \bar{\theta}$$

$$\Leftrightarrow \frac{1+\beta}{\beta} w_u^h \geq m_t w_s^h \bar{\theta} + (1 - m_t)(w_s^f \theta_t^a - k) - c$$

$$\Leftrightarrow \frac{1+\beta}{\beta}w_u^h \geq m_t\left(w_s^f\bar{\theta} - k\right) + (1-m_t)\left(w_s^f\theta_t^a - k\right) - c = y_t^f(\bar{\theta})$$

$$\Leftrightarrow y_t^f(\theta_t^{ef}) = \frac{1+\beta}{\beta}w_u^h \geq y_t^f(\bar{\theta})$$

$$\Leftrightarrow \theta_t^{ef} \geq \bar{\theta}$$

where the next-to-last line follows from the definition of θ_t^{ef}. Now, we can make use of the definition of θ_t^{ef} once more to establish that for $\theta \in [\bar{\theta}, \theta_t^{ef})$, $(1+\beta)w_u^h > \beta y_t^f(\theta)$. From the definition of θ_t^{ef} we have

$$\frac{1+\beta}{\beta}w_u^h = m_t\left(w_s^f\theta_t^{ef} - k\right) + (1-m_t)\left(w_s^f\theta_t^a - k\right) - c$$

$$\Leftrightarrow \frac{1+\beta}{\beta}w_u^h > m_t\left(w_s^f\theta - k\right) + (1-m_t)\left(w_s^f\theta_t^a - k\right) - c$$

for every $\theta < \theta_t^{ef}$. It follows, therefore, that for every $\theta < \theta_t^{ef}$, $(1+\beta)w_u^h > \beta y_t^f(\theta)$. This includes, of course, all $\theta \in [\bar{\theta}, \theta_t^{ef})$.

(F)   Making use of the definition of θ_t^{ef},

$$\frac{1+\beta}{\beta}w_u^h = m_t\left(w_s^f\theta_t^{ef} - k\right) + (1-m_t)\left(w_s^f\theta_t^a - k\right) - c$$

$$\Leftrightarrow \frac{1+\beta}{\beta}w_u^h < m_t\left(w_s^f\theta - k\right) + (1-m_t)\left(w_s^f\theta_t^a - k\right) - c$$

for every $\theta > \theta_t^{ef}$. It follows, therefore, that for every $\theta > \theta_t^{ef}$, $(1+\beta)w_u^h < \beta y_t^f(\theta)$. This includes, of course, all $\theta \in [\theta_t^{ef}, \theta_t^f]$.

(G)   Recall that (F) states that $\beta y_t^f(\theta) > (1+\beta)w_u^h$ for every $\theta > \theta_t^{ef}$. This includes, as a subset, $\theta > \theta_t^f$ so that for $\theta > \theta_t^f$, $\beta y_t(\theta) > (1+\beta)w_u^h$. But for $\theta > \theta_t^f$, $y_t^{ru}(\theta) > y_t^f(\theta)$ or $\beta y_t^{ru}(\theta) > \beta y_t^f(\theta)$. Therefore, for $\theta > \theta_t^f$, $\beta y_t^{ru}(\theta) > \beta y_t^f(\theta) > (1+\beta)w_u^h$. ∎

Proof of Proposition 3.   We need to show that $\theta_t^{er} < \theta^*$. From Figure 15.2, observe that to the left of $\bar{\theta}$, $y_t^{rd}(\theta) > y_t^h(\theta)$. Take $\theta = \theta_t^{er}$. Because

$$y_t^{rd}(\theta_t^{er}) = m_t w_s^h \theta_t^{er} + (1-m_t)(w_s^f\theta_t^a - k) - c$$

then

$$y_t^h(\theta_t^{er}) = w_s^h\theta_t^{er} - c$$

In addition

$$w_s^h\theta_t^{er} - w_s^h\theta^* < m_t w_s^h\theta_t^{er} + (1-m_t)(w_s^f\theta_t^a - k) - w_s^h\theta^*$$

$$= \frac{w_u^h(1+\beta)}{\beta} + c - w_s^h\theta^* = 0$$

where the next-to-last equality follows from the definition of θ_t^{er}, and the last equality follows from the definition of $\theta*$. Thus, $w_s^h \theta_t^{er} < w_s^h \theta*$ or $\theta_t^{er} < \theta*$.

To show that $\theta_t^{ef} < \theta*$, observe from Figure 15.2 that to the left of θ_t^f, $y_t^f(\theta) > y_t^h(\theta)$. Taking $\theta = \theta_t^{ef}$, we have

$$y_t^f(\theta_t^{ef}) = m_t(w_s^f \theta_t^{ef} - k) + (1 - m_t)(w_s^f \theta_t^a - k) - c$$

$$y_t^h(\theta_t^{ef}) = w_s^h \theta_t^{ef} - c$$

Hence

$$w_s^h \theta_t^{ef} - w_s^h \theta* < m_t(w_s^f \theta_t^{ef} - k) + (1 - m_t)(w_s^f \theta_t^a - k) - w_s^h \theta*$$

$$= \frac{w_u^h(1 + \beta)}{\beta} + c - w_s^h \theta*$$

$$= 0$$

where the next-to-last equality follows from the definition of θ_t^{ef}, and the last equality follows from the definition of $\theta*$. Thus, $w_s^h \theta_t^{ef} < w_s^h \theta*$ or $\theta_t^{ef} < \theta*$. ∎

The Slope of the Curve DD. Because the DD curve depends on both θ_t^f and θ_t^{er}, we first make use of equation (15.4) to determine that

$$\frac{\partial \theta_t^{er}}{\partial \theta_t^a} = -\frac{(1 - m_t)w_s^f}{m_t w_s^h}$$

Differentiation of equation (15.6) yields

$$\frac{\partial \theta_t^a}{\partial \theta_t^f}\bigg|_{DD} = \frac{\theta_t^f f(\theta_t^f)}{F(\theta_t^f) - F(\theta_t^{er})} - \frac{\theta_t^{er} f(\theta_t^{er})}{F(\theta_t^f) - F(\theta_t^{er})} \frac{\partial \theta_t^{er}}{\partial \theta_t^a}\left(\frac{\partial \theta_t^a}{\partial \theta_t^f}\bigg|_{DD}\right)$$

$$- \frac{\int_{\theta_t^{er}}^{\theta_t^f} \theta f(\theta)\, d\theta}{[F(\theta_t^f) - F(\theta_t^{er})]^2}\left[f(\theta_t^f) - f(\theta_t^{er}) \frac{\partial \theta_t^{er}}{\partial \theta_t^a}\left(\frac{\partial \theta_t^a}{\partial \theta_t^f}\bigg|_{DD}\right)\right]$$

$$= \frac{\theta_t^f f(\theta_t^f)}{F(\theta_t^f) - F(\theta_t^{er})} - \frac{\theta_t^{er} f(\theta_t^{er})}{F(\theta_t^f) - F(\theta_t^{er})} \frac{\partial \theta_t^{er}}{\partial \theta_t^a}\left(\frac{\partial \theta_t^a}{\partial \theta_t^f}\bigg|_{DD}\right)$$

$$- \frac{\theta_t^a}{F(\theta_t^f) - F(\theta_t^{er})}\left[f(\theta_t^f) - f(\theta_t^{er}) \frac{\partial \theta_t^{er}}{\partial \theta_t^a}\left(\frac{\partial \theta_t^a}{\partial \theta_t^f}\bigg|_{DD}\right)\right]$$

$$= \frac{(\theta_t^f - \theta_t^a)f(\theta_t^f)}{F(\theta_t^f) - F(\theta_t^{er})} - \frac{(\theta_t^{er} - \theta_t^a)f(\theta_t^{er})}{F(\theta_t^f) - F(\theta_t^{er})} \frac{\partial \theta_t^{er}}{\partial \theta_t^a}\left(\frac{\partial \theta_t^a}{\partial \theta_t^f}\bigg|_{DD}\right)$$

$$= \frac{1}{\Delta} \frac{(\theta_t^f - \theta_t^a)f(\theta_t^f)}{F(\theta_t^f) - F(\theta_t^{er})}$$

where the second-to-last equality follows from the definition of θ_t^a in equation (15.2). Hence, because $\theta_t^f > \theta_t^a$, a necessary and sufficient condition for DD to be upward-sloping is that $\Delta > 0$. To see that this is indeed the case, note that

$$\Delta = 1 + \frac{(\theta_t^{er} - \theta_t^a)f(\theta_t^{er})}{F(\theta_t^f) - F(\theta_t^{er})} \frac{\partial \theta_t^{er}}{\partial \theta_t^a}$$

$$= 1 + \frac{(\theta_t^a - \theta_t^{er})f(\theta_t^{er})}{F(\theta_t^f) - F(\theta_t^{er})} \frac{(1 - m_t)w_s^f}{m_t w_s^h} > 0$$

Proof of Proposition 4

1. We need to determine the relationships between θ_t^j, $j = a, f, er$, and the exogenous variables m_t, c, and w_u^h, which are implicit in equations (15.2)–(15.4). By totally differentiating equation (15.2), we get

$$d\theta_t^a = \frac{\theta_t^f f(\theta_t^f)}{F(\theta_t^f) - F(\theta_t^{er})} d\theta_t^f - \frac{\theta_t^{er} f(\theta_t^{er})}{F(\theta_t^f) - F(\theta_t^{er})} d\theta_t^{er}$$

$$- \frac{\int_{\theta_t^{er}}^{\theta_t^f} \theta f(\theta) \, d\theta}{[F(\theta_t^f) - F(\theta_t^{er})]^2} [f(\theta_t^f)d\theta_t^f - f(\theta_t^{er})d\theta_t^{er}]$$

$$= \frac{\theta_t^f f(\theta_t^f)}{F(\theta_t^f) - F(\theta_t^{er})} d\theta_t^f - \frac{\theta_t^{er} f(\theta_t^{er})}{F(\theta_t^f) - F(\theta_t^{er})} d\theta_t^{er}$$

$$- \frac{\theta_t^a}{F(\theta_t^f) - F(\theta_t^{er})} [f(\theta_t^f)d\theta_t^f - f(\theta_t^{er})d\theta_t^{er}]$$

$$= \frac{(\theta_t^f - \theta_t^a)f(\theta_t^f)}{F(\theta_t^f) - F(\theta_t^{er})} d\theta_t^f + \frac{(\theta_t^a - \theta_t^{er})f(\theta_t^{er})}{F(\theta_t^f) - F(\theta_t^{er})} d\theta_t^{er} \qquad (15.A1)$$

where the next-to-last line follows from the definition of θ_t^a in equation (15.2). Because $(\theta_t^f - \theta_t^a) > 0$ and $(\theta_t^{er} - \theta_t^a) < 0$, θ_t^a is increasing in θ_t^f and θ_t^{er}. The foregoing derivation, of course, also confirms our claim in Section 4 that θ_t^a is strictly increasing in θ_t^f.

By totally differentiating equation (15.3), we obtain

$$d\theta_t^f = \frac{w_s^f}{w_s^h} d\theta_t^a \qquad (15.A2)$$

Hence θ_t^f is increasing in θ_t^a.

Turning now to the determination of θ_t^{er}, we get, by totally differentiating equation (15.4),

$$d\theta_t^{er} = \frac{1+\beta}{\beta m_t w_s^h} dw_u^h + \frac{1}{m_t w_s^h} dc - \frac{(1-m_t)w_s^f}{m_t w_s^h} d\theta_t^a + \frac{w_s^f \theta_t^a - k}{m_t w_s^h} dm_t$$

$$- \frac{1}{(m_t w_s^h)^2}\left[\frac{1+\beta}{\beta} w_u^h - (1-m_t)(w_s^f \theta_t^a - k) + c\right] w_s^h dm_t$$

$$= \frac{1+\beta}{\beta m_t w_s^h} dw_u^h + \frac{1}{m_t w_s^h} dc - \frac{(1-m_t)w_s^f}{m_t w_s^h} d\theta_t^a + \frac{w_s^f \theta_t^a - k}{m_t w_s^h} dm_t$$

$$- \frac{w_s^h \theta_t^{er}}{m_t w_s^h} dm_t$$

$$= \frac{1+\beta}{\beta m_t w_s^h} dw_u^h + \frac{1}{m_t w_s^h} dc - \frac{(1-m_t)w_s^f}{m_t w_s^h} d\theta_t^a$$

$$+ \frac{w_s^f \theta_t^a - k - w_s^h \theta_t^{er}}{m_t w_s^h} dm_t \qquad (15.A3)$$

It follows that θ_t^{er} is increasing in w_u^h and c, but decreasing in θ_t^a. Also, because $\theta_t^a > \bar\theta$, by the assumption in Section 3.2, $w_s^f \theta_t^a - k > w_s^f \bar\theta - k = w_s^h \bar\theta > w_s^h \theta_t^{er}$, where the last inequality follows from our assumption that $\theta_t^{er} < \bar\theta$ in Section 3.2. Hence, θ_t^{er} is increasing in m_t, all else remaining constant.

We next examine the relationship between θ_t^a and m_t, holding all else constant. By substituting equations (15.A2) and (15.A3) into equation (15.A1), we obtain

$$d\theta_t^a = \frac{(\theta_t^f - \theta_t^a)f(\theta_t^f)}{\mathcal{M}_t/N} \frac{w_s^f}{w_s^h} d\theta_t^a$$

$$- \frac{(\theta_t^a - \theta_t^{er})f(\theta_t^{er})}{F(\theta_t^f) - F(\theta_t^{er})}\left[\frac{(1-m_t)w_s^f}{m_t w_s^h} d\theta_t^a - \frac{w_s^f \theta_t^a - k - w_s^h \theta_t^{er}}{m_t w_s^h} dm_t\right]$$

$$= \frac{1}{\Omega}\left[\frac{(\theta_t^a - \theta_t^{er})f(\theta_t^{er})}{F(\theta_t^f) - F(\theta_t^{er})} \frac{w_s^f \theta_t^a - k - w_s^h \theta_t^{er}}{m_t w_s^h}\right] dm_t \qquad (15.A4)$$

where

$$\Omega = 1 - \frac{(\theta_t^f - \theta_t^a)f(\theta_t^f)}{F(\theta_t^f) - F(\theta_t^{er})} \frac{w_s^f}{w_s^h} + \frac{(\theta_t^a - \theta_t^{er})f(\theta_t^{er})}{F(\theta_t^f) - F(\theta_t^{er})} \frac{(1-m_t)w_s^f}{m_t w_s^h}$$

The numerator in the last line of equation (15.A4) is positive, because $w_s^f \theta_t^a - k - w_s^h \theta_t^{er} > 0$. Therefore, θ_t^a is increasing in m_t if and only if $\Omega > 0$, as stated in Proposition 4.

Substituting equation (15.A3) into equation (15.A1), keeping m_t and w_u^h constant, we obtain

$$d\theta_t^a = \frac{1}{\Omega} \frac{(\theta_t^a - \theta_t^{er})f(\theta_t^{er})}{F(\theta_t^f) - F(\theta_t^{er})} \frac{1}{m_t w_s^h} dc \qquad (15.A5)$$

It follows that θ_t^a is increasing in c if and only if $\Omega > 0$. Finally, holding m_t and c constant, we obtain, on substituting equation (15.A3) into (15.A1),

$$d\theta_t^a = \frac{1}{\Omega} \frac{(\theta_t^a - \theta_t^{er})f(\theta_t^{er})}{F(\theta_t^f) - F(\theta_t^{er})} \frac{1 + \beta}{\beta m_t w_s^h} dw_u^h \qquad (15.A6)$$

Hence θ_t^a is also increasing in w_u^h if and only if $\Omega > 0$.

2. Turning now to θ_t^f, from equation (15.A2) we obtain

$$d\theta_t^f = \frac{w_s^f}{w_s^h} \frac{\partial \theta_t^a}{\partial m_t} dm_t$$

Hence, a necessary and sufficient condition for θ_t^f to be increasing in m_t is that $\partial \theta_t^a / \partial m_t > 0$. From equation (15.A4) we have already determined that θ_t^a is increasing in m_t if and only if $\Omega > 0$. It follows that $\Omega > 0$ is necessary and sufficient for θ_t^f to be increasing in m_t.

In a similar fashion, we can determine, using equations (15.A2) and (15.A5), that

$$d\theta_t^f = \frac{w_s^f}{w_s^h} \frac{\partial \theta_t^a}{\partial c} dc$$

It follows that θ_t^f is also increasing in c under the condition $\Omega > 0$, because $\partial \theta_t^a / \partial c > 0$, from equation (15.A5). Finally,

$$d\theta_t^f = \frac{w_s^f}{w_s^h} \frac{\partial \theta_t^a}{\partial w_u^h} dw_u^h$$

From equation (15.A6), $\partial \theta_t^a / \partial w_u^h > 0$ if $\Omega > 0$; hence θ_t^f is increasing in w_u^h under the condition $\Omega > 0$.

3. To determine the relationship between θ_t^{er} and m_t, note, from equation (15.A3), that, all else remaining constant,

$$d\theta_t^{er} = -\frac{(1 - m_t)w_s^f}{m_t w_s^h} \frac{\partial \theta_t^a}{\partial m_t} dm_t + \frac{w_s^f \theta_t^a - k - w_s^h \theta_t^{er}}{m_t w_s^h} dm_t$$

From equation (15.A4), we obtain the result that $\partial \theta_t^a / \partial m_t > 0$ if and only if $\Omega > 0$. Because $(w_s^f \theta_t^a - k - w_s^h \theta_t^{er}) > 0$, as already pointed out in our discussion following equation (15.A3), we have that θ_t^{er} is increasing in m_t if and only if

$$\frac{w_s^f \theta_t^a - k - w_s^h \theta_t^{er}}{m_t w_s^h} > \frac{(1 - m_t) w_s^f}{m_t w_s^h} \frac{\partial \theta_t^a}{\partial m_t}$$

or if and only if

$$\frac{w_s^f \theta_t^a - k - w_s^h \theta_t^{er}}{(1 - m_t) w_s^f} > \frac{\partial \theta_t^a}{\partial m_t}$$

as stated in equation (15.8). ∎

Proof of Proposition 5.   Because $\theta_1^a > \bar{\theta}$,

$$\theta_1^f - \theta_1^a = \frac{w_s^f \theta_1^a - k}{w_s^h} - \theta_1^a$$

$$= \frac{w_s^f \theta_1^a - k}{w_s^h} - \frac{w_s^h \theta_1^a}{w_s^h}$$

$$= \frac{w_s^f \theta_1^a - k - w_s^h \theta_1^a}{w_s^h} > 0$$

and hence there is positive migration at $t = 1$ with $M_1 = M_0 + \mathcal{M}_1 > M_0$ or, equivalently, $m_2 = m(M_1) > m(M_0) = m_1$. Also, because M_t can be no less than M_0, satisfaction of equation (15.6) implies that $\theta_t^a(m_t, c, w_u^h) > \theta_1^a(m_1, c, w_u^h)$, and hence $\theta_t^a(m_t, c, w_u^h) > \bar{\theta}$ for all $t = 2, 3, 4, \ldots$ In addition, equation (15.6) also guarantees that $\theta_t^f(m_t, c, w_u^h) > \theta_1^f(m_1, c, w_u^h)$, because θ_t^f is increasing in m_t for any t.

Finally, because $\theta_t^{er} < \bar{\theta}$, we have $\theta_t^f > \theta_t^a > \bar{\theta} > \theta_t^{er}$ and $M_t = M_{t-1} + \mathcal{M}_t > M_{t-1}$ for all t. It follows immediately that $M_{t+i} \ge M_t, i = 1, 2, \ldots$ Hence, the only long-run equilibrium probability of discovery must correspond to the upper bound $\hat{m}$. ∎

Existence.   To determine whether or not there exists at least one set of solutions θ_t^j $(j = a, f, er)$ to equations (15.2)–(15.4), for every m_t that satisfies the requirement in Proposition 1 that $\theta_t^a > \bar{\theta}$, we need only show that there exists at least one θ_t^f for every m_t at which the SS and DD curves intersect. Once θ_t^f is determined, equation (15.5) can be used to determine θ_t^a. Finally, the value of θ_t^{er} can also be calculated from equation (15.4) once θ_t^a is determined.

Consider the right-hand side of equation (15.5). Note that as $\theta_t^f \to \infty$, $\theta_t^a \to \infty$. In addition, as $\theta_t^f \to \infty$, the right-hand side of equation (15.6) is finite because, by assumption, θ has a finite expectation. It follows that for sufficiently large θ_t^f, SS lies above DD. By the intermediate-value theorem, existence is guaranteed if and only if DD lies above SS for some $\theta_t^f > \bar{\theta}$, or if and only if

$$\frac{\int_{\theta_t^{er}}^{\theta_t^f} \theta f(\theta) \, d\theta}{F(\theta_t^f) - F(\theta_t^{er})} > \frac{w_s^h \theta_t^f}{w_s^f}$$

The requirement that there exist a $\theta_t^f > \bar{\theta}$ such that DD lies above SS guarantees that the *equilibrium* value of θ_t^a is strictly greater that $\bar{\theta}$. From the definition of θ_t^f in Section 3, $\theta_t^f > \bar{\theta}$ implies that

$$\frac{w_s^f \theta_t^a - k}{w_s^h} > \bar{\theta}$$

$$\Leftrightarrow w_s^f \theta_t^a > w_s^h \bar{\theta} + k$$

$$\Leftrightarrow w_s^f \theta_t^a > w_s^h \bar{\theta} + (w_s^f - w_s^h)\bar{\theta}$$

$$\Leftrightarrow w_s^f \theta_t^a > w_s^f \bar{\theta}$$

$$\Leftrightarrow \theta_t^a > \bar{\theta}$$

REFERENCES

Berry, A. R., and Soligo, R. (1969). Some welfare aspects of international migration. *Journal of Political Economy* 77:778–94.

Bhagwati, J., and Wilson, J. D. (1989). *Income Taxation and International Mobility*. Cambridge, MA: Massachusetts Institute of Technology Press.

Borjas, G. J. (1987). Self-selection and the earnings of immigrants. *American Economic Review* 77:531–53.

Carrington, W. J., Detragiache, E., And Vishwanath, T. (1996). Migration with endogenous moving costs. *American Economic Review* 86:909–30.

DaVanzo, J. (1983). Repeat migration in the United States: Who moves back and who moves on? *Review of Economics and Statistics* 65:552–9.

Grubel, H. G., and Scott, A. (1966). The international flow of human capital. *American Economic Review* 56: 268–74.

Katz, E., and Stark, O. (1987). International migration under asymmetric information. *Economic Journal* 97:718–26.

Katz, E., and Stark, O. (1989). International migration under alternative informational regimes: a diagrammatic analysis. *European Economic Review* 33:127–42.

Kwok, P. V., and Leland, H. (1982). An economic model of the brain drain. *American Economic Review* 72:91–100.

LaLonde, R. J., and Topel, R. H. (1997). Economic impact of international migration and the economic performance of migrants. In: *Handbook of Population and Family Economics*, ed. M. R. Rosenzweig and O. Stark. Amsterdam: North Holland, 799–850.

Ravenstein, E. G. (1885). The laws of migration. *Journal of the Royal Statistical Society* 48:167–227.

Razin, A., and Sadka, E. (1997). International migration and international trade. In: *Handbook of Population and Family Economics*, ed. M. R. Rosenzweig and O. Stark. Amsterdam: North Holland, 851–87.

Reilly, B. (1994). What determines migration and return? An individual level analysis using data for Ireland. Unpublished manuscript, University of Sussex.

Stark, O. (1991). *The Migration of Labor*. Oxford: Blackwell.

Stark, O. (1995). Frontier issues in international migration. In: *Proceedings of the World Bank Annual Conference on Development Economics, 1994*. Washington, DC: The International Bank for Reconstruction and Development, 361–86.

PART VIII

Fiscal Aspects of Monetary Unification

CHAPTER 16

The Interaction of Fiscal Policy and Monetary Policy in a Monetary Union: Balancing Credibility and Flexibility

Roel M. W. J. Beetsma and A. Lans Bovenberg

1 Introduction

The plans for a European monetary union (EMU) have motivated a growing body of research on the optimal design for a European central bank (ECB). A large part of that literature has drawn on the seminal work of Rogoff (1985), who showed that an optimally designed central bank would involve a trade-off between credibility and flexibility. Extending that type of analysis to a monetary union, Laskar (1989) investigated how the optimal degree of conservatism of the central bank would depend on the relative importance of common and idiosyncratic shocks. Alesina and Grilli (1992) focused on the degree of political independence of an ECB and the voting rules for appointment of the ECB board members. Von Hagen and Süppel (1994) also explored how the members of the central bank's council should be appointed or selected.

In contrast to monetary policy, fiscal policy will remain largely a national responsibility within the EMU. The analytical literature on European monetary unification has paid relatively little attention to the role of national fiscal policies and their interactions with the common monetary policy.[1] The interaction between monetary policy and fiscal

Part of this chapter was written when the first author was a postdoctoral fellow at DELTA (joint research unit CNRS-EHESS-ENS), Paris. He thanks DELTA for the stimulating research environment. He also thanks the Nederlandse Organisatie voor Wetenschappelijk Onderzoek (NWO) for financial support (Dossiernummer 400-70-015/11-3).

[1] Levine and Pearlman (1992) and Levine (1993) performed a numerical analysis of the interaction between fiscal and monetary policies in an EMU. Bryson, Jensen, and Van Hoose (1993) and Bryson (1994) studied monetary and fiscal coordination in a model of two interdependent economies that produced imperfectly substitutable goods. To keep the analysis of the trade-off between credibility and flexibility tractable, we shall assume perfectly substitutable goods.

policy in a closed-economy setting with national monetary policy-making has been analyzed by Alesina and Tabellini (1987), Debelle (1993), and Debelle and Fischer (1994). This chapter draws on that literature to investigate how national fiscal policies will interact with the common monetary policy in an EMU. In fact, in the tradition of Phelps (1973) and Alesina and Tabellini (1987), we shall explore the role of monetary policy from a public-finance perspective. In particular, the Barro-Gordon model of nominal wage contracting employed by Rogoff (1985) to investigate the trade-off between credibility and flexibility will be extended to a monetary union with decentralized fiscal policy-making. Within such a framework with endogenous fiscal policy, adverse output shocks are stabilized not only through the traditional channel of inflation surprises (Barro and Gordon, 1983; Rogoff, 1985; Laskar, 1989) but also through lower taxes financed by additional seigniorage revenues and lower public spending.[2] In this way, stabilization policy involves not only monetary policy but also fiscal policy. We find, in contrast to Rogoff (1985), that an optimally designed central bank, which ignores the social role of seigniorage, may be less conservative than society.

We shall show that compared with the case of national monetary policy-making, stabilization policy in a monetary union will rely more heavily on fiscal policy, because country-specific shocks cannot be stabilized by standard monetary policy. The reduced stabilization role for monetary policy in a monetary union implies that, compared with the case of national monetary policies, the optimally designed central bank will be more conservative, in that it will attach a higher priority to price stability. Whereas monetary unification thus will reduce both expected inflation and the variance of inflation, it will harm overall welfare by reducing average output and public spending and increasing the variability in those parameters. However, a properly designed system of international transfers may enable a union to avoid that decline in welfare. In fact, countries may prefer to enter an economic and monetary union if that union involves international transfers geared toward stabilizing country-specific shocks. Intuitively, compared with national monetary and fiscal policies, international transfers provide a more effective device to insure countries against adverse shocks.[3]

---

[2] Also, Calvo and Guidotti (1993), in a model with monetary-policy precommitment, highlighted the role of seigniorage revenues in macroeconomic stabilization for a variety of shocks.

[3] Morales and Padilla (1995) studied the role of a supranational transfer system in attaining a Pareto-efficient cooperative outcome in a world composed of self-interested countries whose monetary policies yield international spillovers.

The remainder of this chapter is structured as follows: Section 2 presents the model. To analyze the effects of an EMU, we shall analyze two intermediate cases in Section 3, assuming that monetary policy is selected at the national level by a dependent central bank. Hence, monetary policy is effectively under the control of the government. Section 4 presents the case in which monetary policy is still conducted at the national level, but is delegated to an instrument-independent central bank. Section 5 investigates the interaction between a union-wide monetary policy set by an instrument-independent ECB and decentralized fiscal policies set by the member states of the monetary union. The analyses in Sections 4 and 5 are conducted in three steps. First, we study the macroeconomic effects on the levels and variabilities of inflation, output, and public spending. Second, the welfare impacts are explored. Finally, we analyze the optimal design of the monetary institutions. Section 6 illustrates how country-specific shocks can be stabilized by international transfers. Section 7 concludes the discussion.

2 The Model

This section presents the model for the benchmark case of monetary policy-making at the national level. There are n countries. Whereas labor is immobile internationally, there is a single commodity that is perfectly substitutable and perfectly tradable.

Consider some country i ($i = 1, \ldots, n$). The private sector, the fiscal authority, and the central bank of country i are involved in a game. The assumptions about the timing are as follows: First, nominal wages are concluded. Second, output shocks occur, as discussed later. Third, policy decisions are implemented. Finally, firms set their levels of output and employment.

Following, among others, Alesina and Tabellini (1987), Debelle (1993), Debelle and Fischer (1994), and Jensen (1994), we assume that workers in country i are represented by trade unions whose sole objective is to achieve their real-wage-rate target, the logarithm of which we normalize to zero. Therefore, the (log) of the nominal wage rate is set equal to the expected (log) price level, $E(p_i)$. Expectations are rational. Hence the subjective price expectation of wage-setters, p_i^e, equals the mathematical expectation that follows from the model [i.e., $p_i^e = E(p_i)$]. The output of a representative firm in country i is given by

$$Y_i = L_i^\eta \exp(\xi_i) \qquad (0 < \eta < 1) \tag{16.1}$$

where L_i is labor and ξ_i is an idiosyncratic shock with finite variance that hits the economy of country i only. The shocks are identically distributed for all countries. We assume that $E(\xi_i) = 0 \; \forall \; i$ and that $E(\xi_i\xi_j) = 0 \; \forall \; i, j$ such that $i \neq j$.

Output in country i is taxed at a rate τ_i. The firm maximizes profits, $(1 - \tau_i)P_iL_i^\eta\exp(\xi_i) - W_iL_i$, where P_i and W_i represent, respectively, the price level and the wage rate. Hence, (log) output is given by $y_i = [\eta/(1 - \eta)](\pi_i - \pi_i^e - \tau_i + \log \eta) + \xi_i/(1 - \eta)$, where π_i denotes the inflation rate, π_i^e represents the expected (by wage-setters) inflation rate, and $\log(1 - \tau_i)$ has been approximated by $-\tau_i$. For convenience, we normalize output by subtracting the constant $[\eta/(1 - \eta)]\log \eta$ from y_i. Moreover, we redefine the shocks as $\omega_i \equiv \xi_i/(1 - \eta)$.[4] The variance of ω_i is denoted by σ_i^2. Normalized output x_i thus amounts to

$$x_i = v(\pi_i - \pi_i^e - \tau_i) + \omega_i \quad \text{where } v \equiv \eta/(1-\eta) > 0 \qquad (16.2)$$

A favorable supply shock, $\omega_i > 0$, raises the marginal productivity of labor, thereby inducing firms to hire more labor. Thus output increases not only because of the direct effect of the positive supply shock but also because of the expansion of employment.

In the absence of tax distortions and stochastic shocks, $x_i = 0$ in a rational-expectations equilibrium (where $\pi_i = \pi_i^e$ and $\omega_i = 0$); see equation (16.2). In addition to distortionary output taxes, we allow for other, non-tax distortions due to, for example, union control of the labor market or monopoly control over commodity markets. The first-best output level (i.e., output with neither tax nor non-tax distortions) is denoted by $\tilde{x}_i$. Thus $\tilde{x}_i > 0$ measures the non-tax distortions and can be interpreted as an *implicit* tax on output.

Society i's welfare-loss function differs from that of the trade unions because it accounts for the preferences of workers as well as nonworkers. Society i's preferences, which are defined over inflation, output, and public spending, are represented by the following loss function:

$$V_{S,i} = 1/2\left[\alpha_{\pi S}\pi_i^2 + (x_i - \tilde{x}_i)^2 + \alpha_{gS}(g_i - \tilde{g}_i)^2\right] \qquad (\alpha_{\pi S}, \alpha_{gS} > 0) \qquad (16.3)$$

Welfare losses increase in the deviations of inflation, (log) output, and government spending (g_i is government spending as a share of nondistortionary output) from their targets. The target level of inflation corresponds to price stability, whereas the target for output is given by its nondistortionary level, $\tilde{x}_i$. The target for government spending, $\tilde{g}_i$, can be interpreted as the optimal share of nondistortionary output to be spent on public goods if sufficient lump-sum taxes are available (Debelle and

---

[4] From the definition of ω_i and the properties of ξ_i, we have that $E(\omega_i) = 0 \; \forall \; i$ and that $E(\omega_i\omega_j) = 0 \; \forall i, j$, such that $i \neq j$.

Fischer, 1994). Parameters $\alpha_{\pi S}$ and $\alpha_{g S}$ stand for the weights of the price-stability and public-spending objectives, respectively, relative to the weight of the output objective, which is normalized to unity. All countries feature the same relative-preference weights. Targets for employment and public spending, in contrast, are allowed to vary across countries, reflecting different labor-market institutions and preferences for public goods.

Each country has a fiscal authority or government. The loss function for the government of country i is given by (16.3). Appendix A derives the government budget constraint:

$$g_i + (1+\rho)d_i = \tau_i + \varkappa\pi_i \tag{16.4}$$

where ρ denotes the (constant) real interest rate, $d_i \geq 0$ represents the stock of single-period indexed government debt, and $\varkappa \geq 0$ stands for the constant ratio of real-money holdings as a share of output (in the absence of distortions and stochastic shocks).[5] Seigniorage revenues are given by $\varkappa\pi_i$.

Using (16.2), we can rewrite the government budget constraint (16.4) as follows:

$$\text{GFR}_i \equiv \tilde{K}_i - \omega_i/\nu = [(\tilde{x}_i - x_i)/\nu] + \varkappa\pi_i + [\tilde{g}_i - g_i] + [\pi_i - \pi_i^e] \tag{16.5}$$

where

$$\tilde{K}_i \equiv \tilde{g}_i + (1+\rho)d_i + \tilde{x}_i/\nu \tag{16.6}$$

The government financing requirement, GFR_i, consists of a deterministic component $\tilde{K}_i$ and a stochastic component $-\omega_i/\nu$.[6] The deterministic component amounts to the government spending target $\tilde{g}_i$, debt-servicing costs $(1 + \rho)d_i$, and a labor subsidy aimed at offsetting the implicit tax on output, $\tilde{x}_i/\nu$. The last four terms on the right-hand side of (16.5) represent the four sources of finance. The first three terms correspond to the three components of the loss function, indicating that financing the GFR is costly in terms of society's welfare. An inflation surprise is the fourth source of finance.

---

[5] Alesina and Tabellini (1987), Debelle (1993), Debelle and Fischer (1994), and Jensen (1994), among others, assumed that $\varkappa = 1$. However, as will become clear later, a nonunitary value for $\varkappa$ plays an important role in our analysis.

[6] As will be shown later, the relative magnitudes of the deterministic and stochastic components of the GFR are important factors in the optimal design of monetary institutions, which typically involves a trade-off between credibility and flexibility (Rogoff, 1985; Cukierman, 1992).

**3   National Monetary Policy-Making with
a Dependent Central Bank**

As in a study by Beetsma and Bovenberg (1997a), the first-best equilibrium (which yields zero welfare losses) will be attained if a single benevolent policy-maker, who sets both monetary policy and fiscal policy, can freely employ lump-sum taxation (Debelle and Fischer, 1994). In the absence of lump-sum taxation, the resulting equilibrium will be second-best as long as the policy-maker can commit to the optimal state-contingent rule. Here, however, we assume, rather realistically, that policy-makers cannot commit. The absence of commitment gives rise to additional welfare losses.

This section explores the case of national monetary policy-making by a dependent central bank. Hence, monetary policy in country i ($i = 1, \ldots, n$) is effectively under the control of its government.

3.1   *Macroeconomic Effects*

The equilibrium outcomes for $\varkappa \pi_i$, $\tilde{g}_i - g_i$, and $(\tilde{x}_i - x_i)/v$ are derived in Appendix B and are shown in Table 16.1. Compared with the stochastic component, the deterministic component of GFR$_i$ exerts larger adverse impacts on price stability, output, and public spending. The reason for the relatively large negative impact of the deterministic component on the three determinants of welfare (i.e., inflation, output, and public spending) is that inflation surprises [i.e., the fourth source of finance on the right-hand side of (16.5)] contribute to the financing of only the stochastic component of the GFR. Indeed, the coefficients of the deterministic component $\tilde{K}_i$ in the expressions for $\varkappa \pi_i$, $\tilde{g}_i - g_i$, and $(\tilde{x}_i - x_i)/v$ sum to unity, whereas the corresponding coefficients of the stochastic component ω_i/v sum to less than unity in absolute value. Only if the coefficient for the inflation surprise is added do these latter coefficients add up to unity (in absolute value), as required by the GFR, equation (16.5).

Inflation surprises cannot contribute to the financing of the deterministic component, because wage-setters have rational expectations and thus anticipate the effect of the expected GFR, $\tilde{K}_i$, on inflation when setting wages. Accordingly, a larger deterministic component will raise inflation expectations. However, wage-setters cannot anticipate the stochastic component of the GFR because the stochastic shocks occur only after wage constracts have been signed. Accordingly, as far as the stochastic part of the GFR is concerned, inflation expectations are exogenous. Inflation surprises, therefore, can contribute to the financing of the stochastic component.

Table 16.1. *Outcomes of the output gap and the policy instruments*

| Variable | National monetary policy-making | |
	Dependent central bank	Independent central bank
$(\tilde{x}_i - x_i)/v$	$\left(\dfrac{1/v^2}{D_1}\right)\tilde{K}_i - \left(\dfrac{1/v^2}{D_1^*}\right)\left(\dfrac{\omega_i}{v}\right)$	$\left(\dfrac{1/v^2}{D_2}\right)\tilde{K}_i - \left(\dfrac{1/v^2}{D_2^*}\right)\left(\dfrac{\omega_i}{v}\right)$
$\varkappa\pi_i$	$\left(\dfrac{\varkappa(\varkappa+1)/\alpha_{\pi S}}{D_1}\right)\tilde{K}_i$ $-\left(\dfrac{\varkappa(\varkappa+1)/\alpha_{\pi S}}{D_1^*}\right)\left(\dfrac{\omega_i}{v}\right)$	$\left(\dfrac{\varkappa/\alpha_{\pi M}}{D_2}\right)\tilde{K}_i - \left(\dfrac{\varkappa/\alpha_{\pi M}}{D_2^*}\right)\left(\dfrac{\omega_i}{v}\right)$
$\tilde{g}_i - g_i$	$\left(\dfrac{1/\alpha_{gS}}{D_1}\right)\tilde{K}_i - \left(\dfrac{1/\alpha_{gS}}{D_1^*}\right)\left(\dfrac{\omega_i}{v}\right)$	$\left(\dfrac{1/\alpha_{gS}}{D_2}\right)\tilde{K}_i - \left(\dfrac{1/\alpha_{gS}}{D_2^*}\right)\left(\dfrac{\omega_i}{v}\right)$
$\pi_i - \pi_i^e$	$-\left(\dfrac{(\varkappa+1)/\alpha_{\pi S}}{D_1^*}\right)\left(\dfrac{\omega_i}{v}\right)$	$-\left(\dfrac{1/\alpha_{\pi M}}{D_2^*}\right)\left(\dfrac{\omega_i}{v}\right)$

Variable	Monetary union
$(\tilde{x}_i - x_i)/v$	$\left(\dfrac{1/v^2}{D_2}\right)\tilde{K}_A + \left(\dfrac{1/v^2}{1/v^2 + 1/\alpha_{gS}}\right)(\tilde{K}_i - \tilde{K}_A) - \left(\dfrac{1/v^2}{D_2^*}\right)\left(\dfrac{\omega_A}{v}\right)$ $-\left(\dfrac{1/v^2}{1/v^2 + 1/\alpha_{gS}}\right)\left(\dfrac{\omega_i - \omega_A}{v}\right)$
$\varkappa\pi$	$\left(\dfrac{\varkappa/\alpha_{\pi M}}{D_2}\right)\tilde{K}_A - \left(\dfrac{\varkappa/\alpha_{\pi M}}{D_2^*}\right)\left(\dfrac{\omega_A}{v}\right)$
$\tilde{g}_i - g_i$	$\left(\dfrac{1/\alpha_{gS}}{D_2}\right)\tilde{K}_A + \left(\dfrac{1/\alpha_{gS}}{1/v^2 + 1/\alpha_{gS}}\right)(\tilde{K}_i - \tilde{K}_A) - \left(\dfrac{1/\alpha_{gS}}{D_2^*}\right)\left(\dfrac{\omega_A}{v}\right)$ $-\left(\dfrac{1/\alpha_{gS}}{1/v^2 + 1/\alpha_{gS}}\right)\left(\dfrac{\omega_i - \omega_A}{v}\right)$
$\pi - \pi^e$	$-\left(\dfrac{1/\alpha_{\pi M}}{D_2^*}\right)\left(\dfrac{\omega_A}{v}\right)$

Note: $D_1 \equiv [\varkappa(\varkappa+1)/\alpha_{\pi S}] + 1/v^2 + 1/\alpha_{gS} > 0$; $D_1^* \equiv [(\varkappa+1)^2/\alpha_{\pi S}] + 1/v^2 + 1/\alpha_{gS}$ > 0; $D_2 \equiv \varkappa/\alpha_{\pi M} + (1/v^2 + 1/\alpha_{gS}) > 0$; $D_2^* \equiv [(\varkappa+1)/\alpha_{\pi M}] + 1/v^2 + 1/\alpha_{gS} > 0$.

An adverse output shock is stabilized through three channels, corresponding to the three nonoutput sources of financing on the far right-hand side of (16.5): additional seigniorage, a cut in public spending that will raise the spending gap ($\tilde{g}_i - g_i$), and an inflation surprise. The first and second channels allow for lower explicit taxes, and the third channel operates like an implicit output subsidy financed by employees. This latter channel has received scant attention in the literature, and the first two channels, which involve fiscal policy, have been largely ignored.

3.2   Welfare

Society i's equilibrium expected welfare loss (see Appendix B) amounts to

$$E(V_{s,i}) = \left[\frac{\left\{(\varkappa+1)^2 / \alpha_{\pi S}\right\} + 1/\nu^2 + 1/\alpha_{gS}}{2D_1^2} \right] \tilde{K}_i^2 + \left[\frac{1}{2D_1^*} \right] \left[\frac{\sigma_i^2}{\nu^2} \right] \quad (16.7)$$

where $D_1 \equiv [\varkappa(\varkappa + 1)/\alpha_{\pi S}] + 1/\nu^2 + 1/\alpha_{gS}$ and $D_1^* \equiv [(\varkappa + 1)^2/\alpha_{\pi S}] + 1/\nu^2 + 1/\alpha_{gS}$. Society's welfare loss is thus composed of a term arising from the deterministic component of the GFR and a term associated with the corresponding stochastic component. The coefficient preceding σ_i^2/ν^2 is smaller than that preceding the deterministic component (because $D_1^* > D_1$). Intuitively, financing the stochastic component is least costly, because it can be financed in part through inflation surprises, as inflation expectations are not affected. The deterministic component, in contrast, is especially costly in terms of additional welfare losses, because it raises inflation expectations as wage-setters anticipate its inflationary consequences.

4   National Monetary Policy-Making with an Independent Central Bank

Whereas fiscal policy (the choices of taxes and spending) is still determined by the government, monetary policy is now delegated to a central bank.[7] Although the central bank is not free to choose its objectives, it is instrument-independent (Fischer, 1995) in the sense that it is free to select the inflation rate needed to attain the assigned objectives. The

---

[7] The objectives of the government have been assumed to coincide with society's objectives. Therefore, in the context of this model, it does not matter whether the "principal" in delegating monetary policy is the government or the legislature.

central bank of country i cares about price-stability and deviations of output from its target. Its loss function is given by

$$V_{M,i} = 1/2 \left[\alpha_{\pi M} \pi_i^2 + (x_i - \tilde{x}_i)^2 \right] \qquad (\alpha_{\pi M} > 0) \qquad (16.8)$$

We allow for the central bank's price-stability weight $\alpha_{\pi M}$ to be different from society's price-stability weight $\alpha_{\pi S}$ because, as shown by Rogoff (1985), society may be better off by appointing a central banker whose preferences diverge from those of society.

The central bank and the government are involved in a Nash game. Thus the two policy-makers determine their policies simultaneously, taking each other's policies as given. The central bank's reaction function (see Appendix C) is

$$\pi_i = \left[\frac{v^2}{\alpha_{\pi M} + v^2} \right] \left[\pi_i^e + \tau_i + \left\{ \frac{\tilde{x}_i - \omega_i}{v} \right\} \right] \qquad (16.9)$$

Larger (tax and non-tax) distortions in output and labor markets and higher expected inflation cause the monetary authority to increase inflation in order to protect employment. Adverse supply shocks act like implicit taxes on output and thus induce the central bank to offset those "taxes" through unanticipated inflation.

4.1   Macroeconomic Effects

As in the case of a dependent central bank, inflation surprises contribute to the financing of only the stochastic component of GFR$_i$. Therefore the coefficients of the deterministic component in the equilibrium outcomes for $\varkappa \pi_i$, $\tilde{g}_i - g_i$, and $(\tilde{x}_i - x_i)/v$ add up to unity, and the coefficients of the stochastic part of GFR$_i$ sum to less than unity (Table 16.1).

If the price-stability weight of the central bank coincides with that of the government (i.e., $\alpha_{\pi M} = \alpha_{\pi S}$), average inflation will be lower, and the average output gap [i.e., $(\tilde{x}_i - x_i)/v$] and the average spending gap will be larger than with a dependent central bank. Seigniorage, in contrast, will on average be smaller than with a dependent central bank. The reason is that an independent central bank fails to internalize the government budget constraint and thus ignores the role of seigniorage in financing the GFR. The macroeconomic outcomes under a dependent and an independent central bank will coincide only if real-money holdings are zero, so that seigniorage revenues are absent.

Table 16.2 shows the variances of inflation, public spending, and output. These variances indicate that inflation will be less variable with

Table 16.2. *Variances of output and policy instruments*

	National monetary policy-making	
Variable	Dependent central bank: $* \sigma_i^2/v^2$	Independent central bank: $* \sigma_i^2/v^2$
π_i	$\left(\dfrac{(\varkappa+1)/\alpha_{\pi S}}{D_1^*}\right)^2$	$\left(\dfrac{1/\alpha_{\pi M}}{D_2^*}\right)^2$
g_i	$\left(\dfrac{1/\alpha_{gS}}{D_1^*}\right)^2$	$\left(\dfrac{1/\alpha_{gS}}{D_2^*}\right)^2$
x_i	$\left(\dfrac{1/v}{D_1^*}\right)^2$	$\left(\dfrac{1/v}{D_2^*}\right)^2$

Variable	Monetary union ($\sigma_i^2 = \sigma^2, i = 1,\ldots,n$)
π	$\left(\dfrac{1/\alpha_{\pi M}}{D_2^*}\right)^2\left(\dfrac{\sigma^2/n}{v^2}\right)$
g_i	$\left(\dfrac{1/\alpha_{gS}}{D_2^*}\right)^2\left(\dfrac{\sigma^2/n}{v^2}\right) + \left(\dfrac{1/\alpha_{gS}}{1/v^2 + 1/\alpha_{gS}}\right)^2\left(\dfrac{n-1}{n}\right)\left(\dfrac{\sigma^2}{v^2}\right)$
x_i	$\left(\dfrac{1/v}{D_2^*}\right)^2\left(\dfrac{\sigma^2/n}{v^2}\right) + \left(\dfrac{1/v}{1/v^2 + 1/\alpha_{gS}}\right)^2\left(\dfrac{n-1}{n}\right)\left(\dfrac{\sigma^2}{v^2}\right)$

Note: For definitions, see Table 16.1.

an independent central bank (assuming $\alpha_{\pi M} = \alpha_{\pi S}$). Output will be less successfully stabilized, although fiscal policy will play a more important role in stabilization policy, as indicated by a higher variance of public spending.

4.2   Welfare

Society i's expected welfare loss (see Appendix C) amounts to

$$E(V_{S\,i}) = -\left[\frac{\alpha_{\pi S}/\alpha_{\pi M}^2 + 1/v^2 + 1/\alpha_{gS}}{2D_2^2}\right]\tilde{K}_i^2 + \left[\frac{\alpha_{\pi S}/\alpha_{\pi M}^2 + 1/v^2 + 1/\alpha_{gS}}{2\left(D_2^*\right)^2}\right]\left[\frac{\sigma_i^2}{v^2}\right]$$

$$(16.10)$$

where $D_2 \equiv \varkappa/\alpha_{\pi M} + 1/v^2 + 1/\alpha_{gs} > 0$ and $D_2^* \equiv (\varkappa + 1)/\alpha_{\pi M} + 1/v^2 + 1/\alpha_{gs} > 0$. As with a dependent central bank, the deterministic component of the GFR is relatively costly because it raises inflation expectations and thus cannot be financed through inflation surprises. Consequently, the coefficient in front of $\tilde{K}_i$ in (16.10) exceeds that in front of σ_i^2/v^2.

Whether or not delegation of monetary policy to an instrument-independent central bank will be welfare-enhancing will depend on $\varkappa$ and on the relative sizes of $\tilde{K}_i$ and σ_i. Suppose that $\alpha_{\pi M} = \alpha_{\pi S}$. Thus the central bank attaches the same relative weight to price-stability as does society. The welfare losses associated with the deterministic component of the GFR will be lower with an independent central bank if real-money holdings are low (Beetsma and Bovenberg, 1997a). In this case, losses due to the fact that the independent central bank ignores the role of seigniorage in financing the GFR are outweighed by the gains from a reduction in the inflation bias due to the lack of commitment achieved through the delegation of monetary policy. Stabilization policy is efficient with a dependent central bank,[8] but not with an independent central bank (unless $\varkappa = 0$). Therefore, the coefficient in front of σ_i^2/v^2 in the welfare-loss expression is higher with an independent central bank. Hence, if it is not possible to adjust the central bank's objectives, delegation of monetary policy to an independent central bank will be welfare-enhancing if neither the real-money holding nor the ratio $\sigma_i^2/\tilde{K}_i$ is large.

4.3   The Optimal Central Bank

Delegation of the task to control inflation to a central bank may be a (partial) substitute for commitment in monetary policy-making. In particular, Rogoff (1985) has shown that welfare can be improved by assigning monetary policy to a conservative central banker who attaches relatively more weight to low and stable inflation than society does. This improves the trade-off between credibility (the reduction in the inflation bias) and flexibility (the capacity to stabilize the economy in the presence of stochastic shocks). In practice, "conservatism" could be interpreted as choosing someone who is known to be relatively inflation-averse as a central banker. Alternatively, it could be interpreted as a stronger emphasis on monetary stability in the central bank's constitution.

---

[8] This is the case because commitment problems are absent in financing the stochastic component of GFR_i while the government effectively controls all the policy instruments, taking the budget constraint into account.

To find the optimal price-stability weight for the central bank, we differentiate (16.10) with respect to $\alpha_{\pi M}$ to obtain

$$\partial E(V_{S,i})/\partial\alpha_{\pi M} = (1/\alpha_{\pi M}^2)(1/v^2 + 1/\alpha_{gS})[T_1\tilde{K}_i^2 + T_2\,\sigma_i^2/v^2] \qquad (16.11)$$

where

$$T_1 \equiv \left[\frac{\varkappa - \alpha_{\pi S}/\alpha_{\pi M}}{D_2^3}\right], \qquad T_2 \equiv \left[\frac{(\varkappa + 1) - \alpha_{\pi S}/\alpha_{\pi M}}{\left(D_2^*\right)^3}\right]$$

The welfare loss arising from the deterministic component of the GFR will be minimized if $\alpha_{\pi M} = \alpha_{\pi S}/\varkappa$. The welfare loss arising from the stochastic component of the GFR will reach its minimum for $\alpha_{\pi M} = \alpha_{\pi S}/(\varkappa + 1)$. The optimal price-stability weight $\alpha_{\pi M}^{\text{opt}}$ balances credibility and flexibility and thus lies between the two extremes $\alpha_{\pi S}/(\varkappa + 1)$ and $\alpha_{\pi S}/\varkappa$.[9] Moreover, the optimal price-stability weight will decline if stochastic shocks become relatively more important (as indicated by a larger ratio $\sigma_i^2/\tilde{K}_i^2$).[10]

The social value of seigniorage causes our result to differ from that obtained by Rogoff (1985). He found that the optimal central bank should always be more conservative than society. Intuitively, the only distortion in his model is the absence of commitment. In our model, in contrast, another distortion is present, namely, the failure of the independent central bank to account for the social value of seigniorage. The optimal central bank will be more conservative than society only if the distortions implied by the absence of commitment are large compared with the distortions due to the failure to internalize the social value of seigniorage. This is the case if, first, the deterministic component of the GFR is large compared with the stochastic component and, second, real-money holdings are small. The first condition ensures that commitment problems are relatively serious. The second condition implies that the social value of seigniorage is very small. Indeed, if money holdings are zero (i.e., $\varkappa = 0$), we reproduce Rogoff's result that the optimal central bank is unambiguously more conservative than society. Debelle (1993) and Debelle and Fischer (1994) assumed that the money–output ratio

---

[9] This can be seen from (16.11) by noting that T_1 is negative (positive) if $\alpha_{\pi M}$ is less than (is greater than) $\alpha_{\pi S}/\varkappa$, while T_2 is negative (positive) if $\alpha_{\pi M}$ is less than (is greater than) $\alpha_{\pi S}/(\varkappa + 1)$.

[10] The implicit-function theorem yields $\partial\alpha_{\pi M}^{\text{opt}}/\partial(\sigma_i^2/\tilde{K}_i^2) = -[\partial\text{RHS}_{(16.11)}/\partial(\sigma_i^2/\tilde{K}_i^2)]/[\partial\text{RHS}_{(16.11)}/\partial\alpha_{\pi M}]$, evaluated at $\alpha_{\pi M} = \alpha_{\pi M}^{\text{opt}}$, where RHS stands for "right-hand side." The conditions for an internal minimum at $\alpha_{\pi M}^{\text{opt}}$ require that $\partial\text{RHS}_{(16.11)}/\partial\alpha_{\pi M} > 0$ at $\alpha_{\pi M} = \alpha_{\pi M}^{\text{opt}}$. Moreover, $\partial\text{RHS}_{(16.11)}/\partial(\sigma_i^2/\tilde{K}_i^2) = (1/\alpha_{\pi M}^2)(1/v^2 + 1/\alpha_{gS})T_2\tilde{K}_i^2/v^2 > 0$ at $\alpha_{\pi M} = \alpha_{\pi M}^{\text{opt}}$, because $\alpha_{\pi S}/(\varkappa + 1) < \alpha_{\pi M}^{\text{opt}} < \alpha_{\pi S}/\varkappa$.

was unity (i.e., $\varkappa = 1$). With these relatively large money holdings, the optimal central bank should be less conservative than society (unless stochastic shocks are absent). If $0 < \varkappa < 1$, the central bank should be more conservative than society from the point of view of minimizing the deterministic loss (because $\varkappa < 1$), but less conservative than society from the point of view of minimizing the loss associated with the stochastic shocks (because $\varkappa > 0$). Accordingly, the optimal central bank may be more or less conservative than society depending on the relative importance of the stochastic component versus the deterministic component of the GFR.

5   A Monetary Union

In the contemplated EMU, the ECB will select the inflation rate, which will be uniform across the union. Fiscal policy will continue to be selected at the national level. Policy-makers again will determine their policies simultaneously, taking each other's policies as given.

Output in country i is now given by

$$x_i = v(\pi - \pi^e - \tau_i) + \omega_i \qquad (16.2')$$

The total seigniorage revenues collected by the ECB are to be distributed equally over the participants in the union.[11] Therefore the government budget constraint and the GFR of country i are now given by, respectively,

$$g_i + (1 + \rho)d_i = \tau_i + \varkappa\pi \qquad (i = 1,...,n) \qquad (16.4')$$

$$\tilde{K}_i - \omega_i/v = [(\tilde{x}_i - x_i)/v] + \varkappa\pi + [\tilde{g}_i - g_i] + [\pi - \pi^e] \qquad (i = 1,...,n)$$

$$(16.5')$$

The ECB attaches the same relative weight to the objectives of each participating country. Again, the relative weight attached to price stability may differ from the societies' relative weight. The ECB thus features the following loss function:

$$V_{\text{ECB}} = \frac{1}{2}\left\{\alpha_{\pi M}\pi^2 + \sum_{i=1}^{n}(x_i - \tilde{x}_i)^2/n\right\} \qquad (\alpha_{\pi M} > 0) \qquad (16.12)$$

---

[11] Aizenman (1992, 1993) and Sibert (1994) assumed that the distribution of seigniorage in the monetary union would not be fixed ex ante. That yields suboptimally high inflation. According to the Maastricht treaty, seigniorage revenues will be distributed to EMU participants according to some fixed scheme (depending on relative population sizes and relative incomes).

The ECB minimizes (16.12) subject to (16.2)′, $i = 1, \ldots, n$, taking as given not only tax rates and public-spending ratios but also expected inflation π^e. The resulting reaction function amounts to [compare to (16.9)]:

$$\pi = \left[\frac{v^2}{\alpha_{\pi M} + v^2} \right] \left[\pi^e + \frac{1}{n} \sum_{i=1}^{n} \left(\tau_i + \left\{ \frac{\tilde{x}_i - \omega_i}{v} \right\} \right) \right] \tag{16.13}$$

An increase in country i's tax rate or a bad shock to its economy ($\omega_i < 0$) will raise the union-wide inflation rate, but only by the factor $1/n$.

5.1   Macroeconomic Effects

Table 16.1 shows the equilibrium outcomes that are derived in Appendix C. The expression for inflation is of the same general form as that under national monetary policy-making. However, in a monetary union, inflation cannot be attuned to country-specific circumstances. Instead, it is determined by union averages.

The expressions for the spending gap and the output gap, $(\tilde{x}_i - x_i)/v$, are a bit more complicated. In interpreting these expressions, we distinguish between the average and the country-specific components of the GFR. Monetary policy can finance only the average components $\tilde{K}_A$ and ω_A/v. Indeed, in an EMU, policy will respond in the same way to average variables as national policies do to country-specific variables with national monetary policy-making. Hence the coefficients associated with the average components of the GFR in the expressions for the spending and output gaps coincide with the corresponding coefficients under national policy-making.

In an EMU, monetary policy cannot contribute to financing the country-specific components $\tilde{K}_A - \tilde{K}_i$ and $(\omega_A - \omega_i)/v$. Indeed, $\tilde{K}_A - \tilde{K}$ and $(\omega_A - \omega_i)/v$ do not appear in the expression for inflation. The loss of monetary policy as an instrument to finance these country-specific components has implications for the levels and variances of output and public spending. In particular, output is more sensitive to country-specific components than to average components. Accordingly, the coefficients in front of $\tilde{K}_A - \tilde{K}_i$ and $(\omega_A - \omega_i)/v$ in the expression for output exceed the corresponding coefficients in front of $\tilde{K}_A$ and ω_A/v. Moreover, the variance of output is larger in an EMU, because neither seigniorage nor inflation surprises can help to stabilize country-specific shock components (Table 16.2).

Another implication of the loss of monetary policy for financing country-specific components is that fiscal policy has to bear the entire burden of financing these components. Indeed, public spending is more sensitive to the country-specific components of the GFR than to the corresponding average components (Table 16.1). The larger stabilization role of fiscal policy is reflected also in the larger variance of the public-spending gap in an EMU (Table 16.2).

We can use the results in Table 16.1 to order the sensitivities of the output and spending gaps with respect to the four components of the GFR. In particular, the average stochastic component is stabilized best in the sense that it exerts the smallest impact on output and spending. The reason is that not only seigniorage but also inflation surprises contribute to the financing of this component. The average deterministic component is an intermediate case as far as its impact on output and spending is concerned. Union-wide monetary policy contributes to the financing of this component by generating seigniorage.[12] However, with rational wage-setters anticipating inflation, monetary policy cannot generate inflation surprises and thus is less effective in reducing the variations in output and spending than for the average stochastic component. The country-specific (stochastic and deterministic) components exert the largest impact on the output and spending gaps, because monetary policy cannot play any role in financing these components (neither through seigniorage nor through inflation surprises).

5.2   Welfare

Except where explicitly stated otherwise, beginning here the deterministic components of the GFRs and the variances of the shocks are assumed to be uniform across the EMU (i.e., $\tilde{K}_i = \tilde{K}$ and $\sigma_i^2 = \sigma^2$ for all i). Under these assumptions, the equilibrium welfare loss (see Appendix C) amounts to[13]

$$E(V_{S,i}) = \left[\frac{\alpha_{\pi S}/\alpha_{\pi M}^2 + 1/v^2 + 1/\alpha_{gS}}{2D_2^2} \right] \tilde{K}_i^2 + \left[\frac{1}{2(1/v^2 + 1/\alpha_{gS})} \right] \left[\frac{\sigma^2}{v^2} \right] +$$

$$\left\{ \left[\frac{\alpha_{\pi S}/\alpha_{\pi M}^2 + 1/v^2 + 1/\alpha_{gS}}{\left(D_2^*\right)^2} \right] - \left[\frac{1}{1/v^2 + 1/\alpha_{gS}} \right] \right\} \left[\frac{\sigma^2/n}{2v^2} \right] \quad (i = 1,...,n)$$

$$(16.14)$$

---

[12] With very small money holdings (i.e., $\varkappa = 0$, which corresponds to the case of Rogoff, 1985), the average deterministic component exerts the same impact on output and spending as the country-specific components. However, even if $\varkappa = 0$, monetary policy continues to perform a useful role in stabilizing average stochastic shocks.

[13] If $n = 1$, (16.14) reduces to (16.10), the welfare loss under national monetary policy-making.

If it leaves $\alpha_{\pi M}$ unaffected, monetary unification, or an increase in the number of countries, n, will raise welfare if the coefficient of $(\sigma^2/n)/2\nu^2$ in the last term on the right-hand side of (16.14) is positive. This condition can be reduced to

$$\alpha_{\pi M} < \left[\frac{\alpha_{\pi S}}{2(\varkappa+1)}\right] - \left[\frac{\varkappa+1}{2(1/\nu^2+1/\alpha_{gS})}\right] \qquad (16.15)$$

Thus monetary unification will enhance welfare only if the central bank is substantially less conservative than society. Intuitively, if condition (16.15) is met, inflation will play an excessive role in stabilizing output. Monetary unification will act as an indirect instrument to reduce the excessive stabilization, because in a monetary union monetary policy can no longer be used as effectively to stabilize country-specific shocks, $(\omega_A - \omega_i)/\nu$.

In practice, the central bank is not likely to be less conservative than society. For example, if the price-stability weight of the central bank coincides with society's corresponding preference weight ($\alpha_{\pi M} = \alpha_{\pi S}$), monetary unification will unambiguously harm welfare. In this case, the central bank's price-stability weight exceeds the optimal price-stability weight from a stabilization point of view under national monetary policy-making, $\alpha_{\pi S}/(\varkappa + 1)$. Accordingly, by reducing the stabilization role of monetary policy, monetary unification will move the degree of stabilization even further from its optimum, thereby harming welfare. These adverse welfare effects of unification can be avoided only if idiosyncratic shocks are absent (i.e., $\sigma^2 = 0$).[14]

Expression (16.14) indicates when the less effective use of monetary policy as an instrument to stabilize shocks in a monetary union is particularly serious. That is the case if, first, shocks are relatively important (as indicated by large values for σ^2), second, monetary policy is an effective instrument to stabilize output, and, third, compared with monetary policy fiscal policy is relatively costly as an instrument of stabilization policy. The second condition is met if the short-run Phillips curve is steep, in which case inflation surprises will be effective instruments for stabilizing output. The third condition is met if a small price-stability weight $\alpha_{\pi S}$ indicates that fluctuations in inflation are not costly, while a large public-spending weight α_{gS} indicates that fluctuations in public spending are especially costly.

If the deterministic parts of the GFRs are allowed to diverge, countries may differ on their relative preferences whether or not to join a monetary union. This has been analyzed in more detail by Beetsma and

---

[14] If shocks are absent, the GFRs in all countries will coincide. With perfect convergence of GFRs, monetary policy does not need to be attuned to country-specific circumstances.

Bovenberg (in press-b) for the case without shocks. With an unchanged, but not too high, degree of central-bank conservatism, a relatively "undisciplined" country (a country with a relatively high value of $\tilde{K}$) will benefit from joining a monetary union, through a lower inflation bias. As average inflation increases for relatively disciplined countries, these countries will be even worse off than in the case of all countries having equal deterministic components of their GFRs.

5.3   The Optimal ECB

The optimal price-stability weight of the ECB is found by differentiating (16.14) with respect to $\alpha_{\pi M}$:

$$\partial E(V_{S,i})/\partial \alpha_{\pi M} = (1/\alpha_{\pi M}^2)(1/v^2 + 1/\alpha_{gS})[T_1 \tilde{K}^2 + T_2 (\sigma^2/n)/v^2]$$
$$(i = 1,...,n) \tag{16.16}$$

where T_1 and T_2 are as defined in (16.11). Just as with national monetary policy-making, the optimal price-stability weight lies between $\alpha_{\pi S}/(\varkappa + 1)$ and $\alpha_{\pi S}/\varkappa$. Monetary unification (i.e., an increase in the number of participants in the union, n) will raise the optimal price-stability weight by reducing the variance of the common shock component, σ^2/n, and thus the ratio $(\sigma^2/n)/\tilde{K}$ (see footnote 10). With monetary policy becoming a less effective stabilization device, the union members should appoint a more conservative central banker so that monetary policy will be focused more on credibility and less on flexibility.[15]

Enlarging an EMU while optimally adjusting monetary arrangements not only will promote price stability by reducing the average level of inflation but also will reduce the variability of inflation. However, the other components of welfare (i.e., output and public spending) will suffer as monetary policy contributes less to the financing of the GFR. Moreover, the variability in both output and spending will increase as monetary policy provides less stabilization and fiscal policy takes over part of the stabilization task.[16]

---

[15] This result is reminiscent of the work of Laskar (1989), who analyzed the optimal degree of central-bank conservatism in open economies with imperfectly substitutable commodities and national monetary policies. He showed that the national central banks should be made more conservative if shocks become more idiosyncratic.

[16] The expressions for the variabilities of output and public spending in Table 16.2 are increasing in both n and the price-stability weight of the central bank. Accordingly, this variability increases, for two reasons. First, with given preferences of the central bank, the central bank is less effective in stabilization if the EMU grows in size. Second, the union members find it optimal to raise the price-stability weight of the central bank. This reduces the stabilization role of monetary policy further, thereby increasing the variability of output and spending.

The overall effect of these changes on the various components in welfare is that monetary unification will unambiguously reduce welfare, even given the optimal adjustment of monetary institutions.[17] Intuitively, the optimally designed central bank, which trades off credibility and flexibility, does not provide sufficient stabilization. By further reducing stabilization, a larger EMU will yield a first-order welfare loss.

6   International Transfers

Because inflation can no longer be used to stabilize the country-specific shock components in an EMU, this situation has the potential to create a role for a supranational transfer system to insure countries against such shocks. In the presence of such a transfer system, not only monetary policy but also segments of fiscal policy can be centralized at a supranational level. This section explores such a transfer system.

In this model, transfer payments are made after shocks have materialized, but before policies have been selected. The payments are set by a supranational authority, which weighs each of the countries equally. Accordingly, the optimal transfer scheme $\{t_i\}_{i=1}^n$ minimizes $(1/n)\Sigma_{i=1}^n V_{S,i}$ subject to the condition that $\Sigma_{i=1}^n t_i \leq 0$ (i.e., feasibility), the modified GFRs

$$\tilde{K}_i - \omega_i/\nu - t_i = [(\tilde{x}_i - x_i)/\nu] + \varkappa\pi + [\tilde{g}_i - g_i] + [\pi - \pi^e] \qquad (i = 1,...,n)$$

$$(16.5)''$$

(thus allowing for $\tilde{K}$ values to be different across countries), and the participation constraints of the individual countries. These require that, ex ante, each of the countries be at least as well off in an EMU with a transfer scheme as with national monetary policy-making in the absence of a transfer scheme. Appendix C gives the formal derivation of the optimal transfer scheme.

With the deterministic components of the GFRs being equal for all countries, the optimal transfer scheme equates ex-post welfare losses across the union. The optimal scheme thus amounts to setting

$$t_i = (\omega_A - \omega_i)/\nu \qquad (i = 1,...,n) \qquad (16.17)$$

---

[17] To see this more formally, write $E(V_{S,i})$ as a function V of $\alpha_{\pi M}$ and n, and let $\alpha_{\pi M}^{\text{opt}}(p)$ denote the optimal $\alpha_{\pi M}$ for an EMU of size p. Hence, by definition of $\alpha_{\pi M}^{\text{opt}}(p)$ we have that $V[\alpha_{\pi M}^{\text{opt}}(m), m] < V[\alpha_{\pi M}^{\text{opt}}(m + 1), m] < V[\alpha_{\pi M}^{\text{opt}}(m + 1), m + 1]$, which is the welfare loss under an optimal EMU of size $m + 1$. The last inequality holds because the coefficient of $(\sigma^2/n)/2\nu^2$ in (16.14) is negative at $\alpha_{\pi M} = \alpha_{\pi M}^{\text{opt}}(m + 1)$ [which lies between $\alpha_{\pi M}/(\varkappa + 1)$ and $\alpha_{\pi M}/\varkappa$].

This implies that individual countries are perfectly insured against the country-specific shock components. The associated expected welfare loss is given by

$$E(V_{S,i}) = \left[\frac{\alpha_{\pi S}/\alpha_{\pi M}^2 + 1/v^2 + 1/\alpha_{gS}^{-1}}{2D_2^2} \right] \tilde{K}^2$$

$$+ \left[\frac{\alpha_{\pi S}/\alpha_{\pi M}^2 + 1/v^2 + 1/\alpha_{gS}^{-1}}{2(D_2^*)^2} \right] \left[\frac{\sigma^2/n}{v^2} \right] \qquad (i = 1,...,n) \qquad (16.18)$$

We assume that all countries want to join the EMU. With fixed preference weights (including a given $\alpha_{\pi M}$), a larger EMU will raise welfare because it will increase the potential to insure against idiosyncratic shocks. Thus, whereas monetary unification without international transfers will harm welfare, it will raise welfare if it is accompanied by a properly designed transfer system.[18]

Just as in the absence of international transfers, the optimal central bank becomes more conservative in a larger EMU. The reason is that a larger EMU implies more effective stabilization through international transfers. This reduces the role of monetary policy in stabilizing the economy. Hence, in trading off credibility and flexibility, the optimal central bank should focus more on credibility. In contrast to the case without international transfers, the variabilities of output and spending are reduced because the enhanced stabilization provided by the transfers decreases output variability. Moreover, it reduces the need to employ national fiscal policy as a stabilization tool, thereby decreasing the variability of public spending.

The enhanced insurance offered by an international transfer system implies that a larger EMU with optimally designed monetary institutions and international transfers would enhance welfare. Hence, just as with unchanged preference weights, a larger EMU will be welfare-enhancing only if it involves international transfers.

For the case in which the deterministic components of the GFR are allowed to differ, the optimal transfer scheme depends on the degree of divergence between these components relative to the variance of the idiosyncratic shocks. If the $\tilde{K}_i$ $(i = 1, \ldots, n)$ do not differ significantly, the

---

[18] This welfare gain is due to the international transfer system rather than monetary unification. With national monetary policy-making, the international transfer system would yield the same welfare gain. However, in the presence of such an optimally designed transfer system, transferring monetary policy to the central level of the union would not yield any welfare losses, because international transfers rather than national monetary policy would stabilize country-specific shocks.

participation constraints are not binding, and the optimal transfer scheme is given by

$$t_i = (\tilde{K}_i - \tilde{K}_A) + (\omega_A - \omega_i)/\nu \qquad (i = 1, ..., n) \tag{16.19}$$

This transfer scheme results in equal welfare losses ex post and is composed of a deterministic component $(\tilde{K}_i - \tilde{K}_A)$ and a component that insures against the country-specific components of the shocks. In particular, the countries with the lower financing requirements will systematically transfer resources to the countries featuring higher financing requirements. If the differences among the $\tilde{K}_i$ $(i = 1, ..., n)$ are sufficiently large, the participation contraints of countries with relatively low $\tilde{K}$ values will become binding. However, there still will be a systematic, but relatively smaller, flow of transfers away from those countries to the other members of the EMU.

7   Conclusions

In investigating the macroeconomic implications of an EMU, this chapter has focused on the links between fiscal policy and monetary policy in stabilizing and boosting employment. In the presence of endogenous fiscal policies, output (or employment) is stabilized not only through the traditional channel of inflation surprises but also through variations in seigniorage revenues and public spending. With national monetary policy-making, we found that, in contrast to Rogoff (1985), the optimally designed central bank may be less conservative than society if real-money holdings are large and supply shocks are important compared with the deterministic component of the GFR (which is affected by spending targets, public-debt service, and non-tax distortions in output and labor markets).

In the absence of international transfers, an EMU implies less effective stabilization of country-specific shocks. This raises the variability not only of output but also of public spending as national fiscal policies bear more of the burden of stabilizing country-specific shocks. Unless national central banks attach a very low priority to price stability and thus focus too much on stabilization, less effective stabilization in an EMU will reduce overall welfare, compared with national monetary policy-making.

We have also studied the optimal design of monetary institutions. We have found that, compared with the national central banks, the optimally designed ECB should place more emphasis on price stability, because monetary policy becomes a less effective stabilization tool in an EMU.

This explains why European central bankers generally favor European monetary unification.

The analysis in this chapter can be extended in several ways. An important extension would be to allow governments to run deficits or surpluses. In another study (Beetsma and Bovenberg, 1997b), we employed a two-period deterministic, single-country model to study the relationship between monetary institutions and debt accumulation. That study indicated that discretionary monetary policy-making induces the government to reduce current-debt accumulation in order to mitigate the future inflation bias; see also Obstfeld (1997). With a benevolent government, inflation will thus be too high, while debt accumulation will be too low. By making the central bank sufficiently conservative, society can eliminate the inflation bias and ensure optimal debt accumulation. However, if, in addition to the absence of commitment, political distortions yield a myopic government, the second-best alternative can be adopted only by supplementing a conservative central bank with ceilings on public debt. In this way, institutional adjustments can be targeted at the origins of the distortions.

Monetary unification will exacerbate the debt bias arising from myopic governments (Beetsma and Bovenberg, 1995). The reason is that governments in a monetary union have less incentive to reduce future inflation through unilateral debt reductions. This reflects the public-good character of lower inflation: whereas the costs of such actions in terms of fiscal policy are borne entirely by each individual government, the benefits in terms of a lower common inflation rate are spread over the entire union. Therefore, debt ceilings are particularly useful in a monetary union with myopic policy-makers. Also, Aizenman (1994) found that restrictions on decentralized fiscal policy may enhance welfare in a monetary union. By imposing ceilings on public debt, the central administration induces decentralized decision-makers to internalize the externalities they impose on each other.

Thus, in light of the foregoing discussion, a natural extension of the current analysis would be to allow for debt dynamics. Within such a framework, stabilization would occur not only through the channels discussed in this chapter but also through public-debt policy. With more instruments available to stabilize the economy, the ECB could be designed so as to further alleviate the credibility problem. Accordingly, the optimal ECB would be even more conservative. Our basic findings here on international transfers, however, would continue to hold. In particular, international transfers would still play a useful role. Although debt policy could assume part of the stabilization task of national monetary policy, sooner or later the additional debt would have to be repaid by the citizens of the country. An adverse shock thus would cause a fall in the country's permanent income. To reduce the variability of their income, countries still find it attractive to participate in a transfer scheme. International transfers would be particularly useful if governments were myopic. In that case, debt ceilings would be needed to prevent governments from running excessive debts, but would at the same time reduce the extent to which debt could be used as an instrument to stabilize shocks.

A second extension of the current model would be to change the strategic interactions. In another study (Beetsma and Bovenberg, in press-a), fiscal authorities were Stackelberg leaders vis-à-vis the central bank. The fiscal authorities exploited their strategic advantage by increasing the tax rate so as to induce the central bank to raise the inflation rate in order to protect employment. The resulting higher tax and seigniorage revenues gave rise to a spending bias. Within that setting, entry into a monetary union acted as a disciplinary device for the fiscal authorities because it weakened their strategic position vis-à-vis the central bank. Therefore, taxes, public spending, and inflation will be lower in a monetary union.

It would also be interesting to study alternative institutional arrangements for monetary policy, such as giving the ECB an inflation contract (Persson and Tabellini, 1993; Walsh, 1995) or imposing an inflation target on the ECB (Lockwood, 1996; Svensson, 1997). Inflation contracts, however, may be difficult to implement in practice, in part because the government may renege on the contract (McCallum, 1995). Inflation targets are becoming more popular: The central banks of New Zealand, Canada, and the United Kingdom are operating under such targets, although their inflation targets may be subject to credibility problems (Beetsma and Jensen, 1997).

Our results should not be interpreted as implying that monetary unification would not be justified in the absence of international transfers. To keep the analysis tractable, we have ignored other factors that might tilt the balance in favor of an EMU (such as increased trade, reduced transactions costs, and unified payments systems). Moreover, even if monetary unification would not be justified on economic grounds, it might still take place for political reasons. Even then, our analysis should be useful in that it provides insights about the interactions between monetary policy and fiscal policy in an EMU and about the optimal design of an ECB.

If an EMU is accompanied by an optimally designed international transfer system, the implied insurance of the country-specific components of the shocks will actually result in more effective rather than less effective stabilization, thereby reducing the variability not only of inflation but also of output and spending. Accordingly, in our model, monetary unification raises welfare only if it is accompanied by a properly designed system of international transfers. This result suggests an important relationship between monetary and political integration, because international transfers (i.e., centralization not only of monetary policy but also of segments of fiscal policy) are likely to be feasible only in an EMU with sufficient political integration.

In addition to political obstacles, a related barrier to an international transfer system is that country-specific shocks may be difficult to observe. In particular, individual countries are likely to possess more information about such shocks than is the supranational authority responsible for the transfers. That could give rise to moral-hazard; for example, see Persson and Tabellini (1996).

However, by enhancing the transparancy of the European market and building trust between the various countries, monetary unification is likely to alleviate the moral-hazard problems associated with risk-sharing arrangements within the union. Accordingly, whereas it is often argued that monetary unification would reduce the scope for stabilization policy, it may actually facilitate the development of new instruments and institutions that could help to stabilize country-specific shocks. As a result, a monetary union might enhance not only monetary stability but also the stabilization of country-specific shocks.

APPENDIX A: DERIVATION OF EQUATION (16.4), THE GOVERNMENT BUDGET CONSTRAINT FOR COUNTRY i

Real-money balances are given by $M_i/P_i = \varkappa\tilde{X}_i$, where $\tilde{X}_i$ is the (constant) output level in the absence of any distortions or shocks (the antilog of $\tilde{X}_i$), and M_i is the nominal money supply. It follows immediately that $(M_i - M_{i,-1})/M_i = (P_i - P_{i,-1})/P_i$. If distortions and shocks are not too large, tax revenues can be approximated by $\tau_i P_i \tilde{X}_i$.[19] In nominal terms, the government budget constraint is

$$P_i G_i + (1 + \rho)P_i D_i = \tau_i P_i \tilde{X}_i + (M_i - M_{i,-1})$$

where G_i is the level of government spending and D_i is the outstanding stock of (indexed) public debt. Finally, $(M_i - M_{i,-1})$ is the increase in the nominal money supply. Dividing both sides by $P_i \tilde{X}_i$ yields the government budget constraint in shares of $\tilde{X}_i$:

[19] Most of the literature (e.g., Alesina and Tabellini, 1987; Debelle, 1993) has implicitly used the approximation $\tilde{X} \approx X$.

$$g_i + (1+\rho)d_i = \tau_i + \varkappa\pi_i$$

where we approximate π_i by $(P_i - P_{i,-1})/P_i$.

APPENDIX B: DERIVATION OF THE OUTCOMES UNDER A DEPENDENT CENTRAL BANK

Substitute (16.2) for x_i into (16.3). The Lagrangian for the government of country i is

$$L_{F,i} = 1/2\left\{\alpha_{\pi S}\pi_i^2 + \left[\nu(\pi_i - \pi_i^e - \tau_i) + \omega_i - \tilde{x}_i\right]^2 + \alpha_{gS}(g_i - \tilde{g}_i)^2\right\}$$
$$+ \lambda_i[g_i + (1+\rho)d_i - \tau_i - \varkappa\pi_i] \tag{16.B1}$$

The first-order conditions for π_i, τ_i, and g_i are, respectively,[20]

$$\alpha_{\pi S}\pi_i + \nu\left[\nu(\pi_i - \pi_i^e - \tau_i) + \omega_i - \tilde{x}_i\right] = \varkappa\lambda_i \tag{16.B2}$$

$$-\nu\left[\nu(\pi_i - \pi_i^e - \tau_i) + \omega_i - \tilde{x}_i\right] = \lambda_i \tag{16.B3}$$

$$\alpha_{gS}(g_i - \tilde{g}_i) = -\lambda_i \tag{16.B4}$$

We eliminate λ_i from the system (16.B2)–(16.B4) and add the government budget constraint to the system to obtain

$$\alpha_{\pi S}\pi_i = -(\varkappa+1)\nu\left[\nu(\pi_i - \pi_i^e - \tau_i) + \omega_i - \tilde{x}_i\right] \tag{16.B5}$$

$$\nu\left[\nu(\pi_i^e - \pi_i - \tau_i) + \tilde{x}_i - \omega_i\right] = \alpha_{gS}(\tilde{g}_i - g_i) \tag{16.B6}$$

$$g_i + (1+\rho)d_i = \tau_i + \varkappa\pi_i \tag{16.B7}$$

The solution of this system is derived in two steps. In the first step we compute the deterministic components of the policy instruments (i.e., we compute the expected values for the policy instruments). In the second step we compute the stochastic components of the policy instruments.

As for the first step, we take expectations (denoted by superscript e; note that we assume rationality of expectations, so that subjective and model-induced expectations are equal to each other) of both sides of the equations of the system (16.B5)–(16.B7):

$$\alpha_{\pi S}\pi_i^e = -(\varkappa+1)\nu(-\nu\tau_i^e - \tilde{x}_i) \tag{16.B5'}$$

$$\nu(\nu\tau_i^e + \tilde{x}_i) = \alpha_{gS}(\tilde{g}_i - g_i^e) \tag{16.B6'}$$

---

[20] The linear-quadratic structure of the model ensures that the optimal policy mix follows uniquely from the first-order conditions.

$$g_i^e + (1 + \rho)d_i = \tau_i^e + \varkappa \pi_i^e \tag{16.B7}'$$

We rewrite (16.B5)'–(16.B7)' as

$$\varkappa \pi_i^e = [\varkappa(\varkappa + 1)\nu^2/\alpha_{\pi S}](\tau_i^e + \tilde{x}_i/\nu) \tag{16.B8}$$

$$\tilde{g}_i - g_i^e = (\nu^2/\alpha_{gS})(\tau_i^e + \tilde{x}_i/\nu) \tag{16.B9}$$

$$\tilde{K}_i = (\tau_i^e + \tilde{x}_i/\nu) + \varkappa \pi_i^e + (\tilde{g}_i - g_i^e) \tag{16.B10}$$

We substitute the right-hand sides of (16.B8) and (16.B9) for $\varkappa \pi_i^e$ and $\tilde{g}_i - g_i^e$, respectively, into (16.B10). The result can be solved for $(\tau_i^e + \tilde{x}_i/\nu)$ as a function of $\tilde{K}_i$. Using this result, the solutions for $\varkappa \pi_i^e$ and $\tilde{g}_i - g_i^e$ then follow from (16.B8), and (16.B9), respectively. Hence, the solution of the system (16.B8)–(16.B10) is given by

$$\varkappa \pi_i^e = \{[\varkappa(\varkappa + 1)/\alpha_{\pi S}]/D_1\}\tilde{K}_i \tag{16.B11}$$

$$\tau_i^e + \tilde{x}_i/\nu = [(1/\nu^2)/D_1]\tilde{K}_i \tag{16.B12}$$

$$\tilde{g}_i - g_i^e = [(1/\alpha_{gS})/D_1]\tilde{K}_i \tag{16.B13}$$

where $D_1 \equiv \varkappa(\varkappa + 1)/\alpha_{\pi S} + 1/\nu^2 + 1/\alpha_{gS}$, as defined in the main text.

We denote by superscript d the deviation of a variable from its expected value (i.e., $x^d \equiv x - x^e$, where x is an arbitrary variable). We subtract equations (16.B5)'–(16.B7)' from their counterparts in the system (16.B5)–(16.B7) to yield

$$\alpha_{\pi S}\pi_i^d = (\varkappa + 1)\nu^2(-\pi_i^d + \tau_i^d - \omega_i/\nu) \tag{16.B5}''$$

$$\nu^2(-\pi_i^d + \tau_i^d - \omega_i/\nu) = -\alpha_{gS}g_i^d \tag{16.B6}''$$

$$g_i^d = \tau_i^d + \varkappa \pi_i^d \tag{16.B7}''$$

We substitute (16.B7)'' into (16.B6)'' to yield

$$\nu^2(-\pi_i^d + \tau_i^d - \omega_i/\nu) = -\alpha_{gS}(\tau_i^d + \varkappa \pi_i^d) \tag{16.B14}$$

We combine (16.B5)'' and (16.B14) to yield

$$[\alpha_{\pi S}/(\varkappa + 1)]\pi_i^d = -\alpha_{gS}(\tau_i^d + \pi \varkappa_i^d) \tag{16.B15}$$

which can be rewritten as

$$\tau_i^d = -[(\alpha_{\pi S}/\alpha_{gS})/(\varkappa + 1) + \varkappa]\pi_i^d \tag{16.B16}$$

Hence the system to be solved consists of equations (16.B5)'', (16.B7)'', and (16.B16). We substitute the right-hand side of (16.B16) for τ_i^d into (16.B5)''. The resulting equation can be solved for π_i^d to yield

$$\varkappa\pi_i^d = -\{[\varkappa(\varkappa+1)/a_{\pi S}]/D_1^*\}\omega_i/\nu \tag{16.B17}$$

where $D_1^* \equiv (\varkappa+1)^2/a_{\pi S} + 1/\nu^2 + 1/a_{gS}$, as defined in the main text. We combine (16.B17) with (16.B16) to yield

$$\tau_i^d = \{[\varkappa(\varkappa+1)/a_{\pi S} + 1/a_{gS}]/D_1^*\}\omega_i/\nu \tag{16.B18}$$

Next we combine (16.B7)″, (16.B17), and (16.B18) to yield

$$g_i^d = \{(1/a_{gS})/D_1^*\}\omega_i/\nu \tag{16.B19}$$

The solution of $\varkappa\pi_i$, as given in Table 16.1, is the sum of the right-hand sides of (16.B11) and (16.B17). Similarly, the solution of $\tau_i + \tilde{x}_i/\nu$ is the sum of the right-hand sides of (16.B12) and (16.B18), and $\tilde{g}_i - g_i$ follows upon subtracting the right-hand side of (16.B19) from the right-hand side of (16.B13). Finally, we can write

$$(\tilde{x}_i - x_i)/\nu = -\pi_i^d + (\tau_i + \tilde{x}_i/\nu) - \omega_i/\nu \tag{16.B20}$$

The solution of $(\tilde{x}_i - x_i)/\nu$ follows upon combining (16.B20) with (16.B17) and the solution for $(\tau_i + \tilde{x}_i/\nu)$.

Society's expected welfare loss follows upon substitution of the solutions for π_i, $\tilde{x}_i - x_i$, and $\tilde{g}_i - g_i$ into (16.3):

$$E(V_{S,i}) = \frac{1}{2}E\left[\frac{(\varkappa+1)^2}{a_{\pi S}} + \frac{1}{\nu^2} + \frac{1}{a_{gS}}\right]\left[\left[\frac{1}{D_1}\right]\tilde{K}_i + \left[\frac{1}{D_1^*}\right]\left[\frac{\omega_i}{\nu}\right]\right]^2 \tag{16.B21}$$

Expression (16.7) follows immediately from the facts that $\tilde{K}_i$ is nonstochastic and that the shocks have zero expected value and are uncorrelated with each other.

APPENDIX C: DERIVATIONS FOR AN INDEPENDENT CENTRAL BANK (EMU AND NATIONAL MONETARY POLICY-MAKING)

We consider the most general setting of an EMU with a transfer scheme. The outcomes in Section 5 follow by setting $t_i = 0$, and the outcomes in Section 4 also follow by setting $n = 1$.

Derivation of the Outcomes. Substitute (16.2)′, $i = 1, \ldots, n$, into (16.12). Hence the ECB selects π to minimize

$$\frac{1}{2}\left[a_{\pi M}\pi^2 + \sum_{i=1}^{n}\{[\nu(\pi - \pi^e - \tau_i) + \omega_i - \tilde{x}_i]^2\}/n\right] \tag{16.C1}$$

The first-order condition for the inflation rate selected by the ECB is

$$\alpha_{\pi M}\pi + (1/n)\sum_{i=1}^{n} v\left[v(\pi - \pi^e - \tau_i) + \omega_i - \tilde{x}_i\right] = 0 \tag{16.C2}$$

This can be solved to yield the ECB's reaction function (16.13):

$$\pi = \left[\frac{v^2}{\alpha_{\pi M} + v^2}\right]\left[\pi^e + \frac{1}{n}\sum_{i=1}^{n}\left[\tau_i + \left[\frac{\tilde{x}_i - \omega_i}{v}\right]\right]\right] \tag{16.C3}$$

The Lagrangian associated with government i's problem is

$$L_{F,i} = \frac{1}{2}\left\{\alpha_{\pi S}\pi^2 + \left[v(\pi - \pi^e - \tau_i) + \omega_i - \tilde{x}_i\right]^2 + \alpha_{gS}(g_i - \tilde{g}_i)^2\right\}$$
$$+\lambda_i[g_i + (1+\rho)d_i - t_i - \tau_i - \varkappa\pi] \tag{16.C4}$$

The first-order conditions with respect to τ_i and g_i are, respectively,

$$-v\left[v(\pi - \pi^e - \tau_i) + \omega_i - \tilde{x}_i\right] = \lambda_i \tag{16.C5}$$

$$\alpha_{gS}(g_i - \tilde{g}_i) = -\lambda_i \tag{16.C6}$$

We eliminate λ_i from the system (16.C5) and (16.C6) to yield

$$\alpha_{gS}(\tilde{g}_i - g_i) = v\left[v(\pi^e - \pi + \tau_i) + \tilde{x}_i - \omega_i\right] \tag{16.C7}$$

The system that determines the equilibrium policy choices is thus given by (16.C3), (16.C7), and the modified GFR (16.5)″. We can rewrite (16.2)′ as

$$(\tilde{x}_i - \omega_i)/v + \tau_i = (\tilde{x}_i - x_i)/v + (\pi - \pi^e) \tag{16.C8}$$

Using (16.C8), we can rewrite (16.C3) as

$$\pi = \left[\frac{v^2}{\alpha_{\pi M}}\right]\frac{1}{n}\sum_{j=1}^{n}\left[\frac{\tilde{x}_j - x_j}{v}\right] \tag{16.C9}$$

and (16.C7) can be written as

$$\tilde{g}_i - g_i = \left[\frac{v^2}{\alpha_{gS}}\right]\left[\frac{\tilde{x}_i - x_i}{v}\right] \tag{16.C10}$$

We substitute (16.C9) and (16.C10) into (16.5)″ to obtain

$$\tilde{K}_i - t_i - \left[\frac{\omega_i}{v}\right] + \pi^e = \left[1 + \frac{v^2}{\alpha_{gS}}\right]\left[\frac{\tilde{x}_i - x_i}{v}\right]$$
$$+ \left[\frac{(\varkappa + 1)v^2}{\alpha_{\pi M}}\right]\frac{1}{n}\sum_{j=1}^{n}\left[\frac{\tilde{x}_j - x_j}{v}\right] \tag{16.C11}$$

Taking averages, for $j = 1, \ldots, n$, of the left- and right-hand sides of (16.C11) and using the assumption that the sum of the transfers over all countries equals zero, we obtain

$$\tilde{K}_A - \left[\frac{\omega_A}{\nu}\right] + \pi^e = \left[1 + \frac{\nu^2}{\alpha_{gS}} + \frac{(\varkappa+1)\nu^2}{\alpha_{\pi M}}\right]\frac{1}{n}\sum_{j=1}^{n}\left[\frac{\tilde{x}_j - x_j}{\nu}\right] \qquad (16.C12)$$

We combine (16.C12) with (16.C9) to obtain

$$\tilde{K}_A - \left[\frac{\omega_A}{\nu}\right] + \pi^e = \left[1 + \frac{\nu^2}{\alpha_{gS}} + \frac{(\varkappa+1)\nu^2}{\alpha_{\pi M}}\right]\left[\frac{\alpha_{\pi M}}{\nu^2}\right]\pi \qquad (16.C13)$$

Under the assumption of rational expectations, (16.C13) implies

$$\pi^e = \left[\frac{1/\alpha_{\pi M}}{D_2}\right]\tilde{K}_A \qquad (16.C14)$$

We substitute (16.C14) into (16.C11) to yield

$$\tilde{K}_i - t_i - \left[\frac{\omega_i}{\nu}\right] + \left[\frac{1/\alpha_{\pi M}}{D_2}\right]\tilde{K}_A = \left[1 + \frac{\nu^2}{\alpha_{gS}}\right]\left[\frac{\tilde{x}_i - x_i}{\nu}\right]$$
$$+ \left[\frac{(\varkappa+1)\nu^2}{\alpha_{\pi M}}\right]\frac{1}{n}\sum_{j=1}^{n}\left[\frac{\tilde{x}_j - x_j}{\nu}\right] \qquad (16.C15)$$

Taking averages of the left- and right-hand sides of (16.C15), for $j = 1,$ $\ldots, n$, yields

$$\tilde{K}_A - \left[\frac{\omega_A}{\nu}\right] + \left[\frac{1/\alpha_{\pi M}}{D_2}\right]\tilde{K}_A = \left[1 + \frac{\nu^2}{\alpha_{gS}} + \frac{(\varkappa+1)\nu^2}{\alpha_{\pi M}}\right]\frac{1}{n}\sum_{j=1}^{n}\left[\frac{\tilde{x}_j - x_j}{\nu}\right]$$
$$(16.C16)$$

This can be rewritten as

$$\frac{1}{n}\sum_{j=1}^{n}\left[\frac{\tilde{x}_j - x_j}{\nu}\right] = \left[\frac{1/\nu^2}{D_2}\right]\tilde{K}_A - \left[\frac{1/\nu^2}{D_2^*}\right]\left[\frac{\omega_A}{\nu}\right] \qquad (16.C17)$$

We plug (16.C17) back into (16.C15) and rewrite to yield

$$\tilde{K}_i - t_i + \left[\frac{(\varkappa+1)/\alpha_{\pi M}}{D_2^*}\right]\left[\frac{\omega_A}{\nu}\right] - \left[\frac{\omega_i}{\nu}\right] - \left[\frac{\varkappa/\alpha_{\pi M}}{D_2}\right]\tilde{K}_A = \left[1 + \frac{\nu^2}{\alpha_{gS}}\right]\left[\frac{\tilde{x}_i - x_i}{\nu}\right]$$
$$(16.C18)$$

This can be rewritten as

$$\frac{\tilde{x}_i - x_i}{\nu} = \left[\frac{1/\nu^2}{D_2}\right]\tilde{K}_A + \left[\frac{1/\nu^2}{1/\nu^2 + 1/\alpha_{gS}}\right](\tilde{K}_i - t_i - \tilde{K}_A)$$
$$- \left[\frac{1/\nu^2}{D_2^*}\right]\left[\frac{\omega_A}{\nu}\right] - \left[\frac{1/\nu^2}{1/\nu^2 + 1/\alpha_{gS}}\right]\left[\frac{\omega_i - \omega_A}{\nu}\right] \qquad (16.C19)$$

Combination of (16.C9) and (16.C19) yields

$$\pi = \left[\frac{1/\alpha_{\pi M}}{D_2}\right]\tilde{K}_A - \left[\frac{1/\alpha_{\pi M}}{D_2^*}\right]\left[\frac{\omega_A}{v}\right] \tag{16.C20}$$

Combination of (16.C10) and (16.C19) yields

$$\tilde{g}_i - g_i = \left[\frac{1/\alpha_{gS}}{D_2}\right]\tilde{K}_A + \left[\frac{1/\alpha_{gS}}{1/v^2 + 1/\alpha_{gS}}\right](\tilde{K}_i - t_i - \tilde{K}_A)$$

$$- \left[\frac{1/\alpha_{gS}}{D_2^*}\right]\left[\frac{\omega_A}{v}\right] - \left[\frac{1/\alpha_{gS}}{1/v^2 + 1/\alpha_{gS}}\right]\left[\frac{\omega_i - \omega_A}{v}\right] \tag{16.C21}$$

Setting $t_i = 0$ in (16.C19)–(16.C21), we obtain the outcomes in the lower panel of Table 16.1. If, in addition, we set $n = 1$, we have that $\tilde{K}_A = \tilde{K}_i$ and $\omega_A = \omega_i$, and the outcomes reduce further to those in the last column of the upper panel of Table 16.1.

Derivation of the Welfare Losses. Using (16.C19) and (16.C21), we can write country i's welfare loss as

$$V_{S,i} = \frac{1}{2}\alpha_{\pi S}\pi^2 + \frac{1}{2}(1/v^2 + 1/\alpha_{gS})A_i^2 \tag{16.C22}$$

where

$$A_i \equiv \left[\frac{1}{D_2}\right]\tilde{K}_A + \left[\frac{1}{1/v^2 + 1/\alpha_{gS}}\right]\left[\tilde{K}_i - t_i - \tilde{K}_A + \frac{\omega_A - \omega_i}{v}\right] - \left[\frac{1}{D_2^*}\right]\left[\frac{\omega_A}{v}\right]$$

Using (16.C20) in (16.C22) and setting $t_i = 0$ and $\tilde{K}_i = \tilde{K} \; \forall \; i$, we have that $E(V_{S,i})$ equals half its expected value of

$$\alpha_{\pi S}\left(\left[\frac{1/\alpha_{\pi M}}{D_2}\right]\tilde{K} - \left[\frac{1/\alpha_{\pi M}}{D_2^*}\right]\left[\frac{\omega_A}{v}\right]\right)^2 +$$

$$\left(\left[\frac{1/v}{D_2}\right]\tilde{K} - \left[\frac{1/v}{D_2^*}\right]\left[\frac{\omega_A}{v}\right] - \left[\frac{1/v}{1/v^2 + 1/\alpha_{gS}}\right]\left[\frac{\omega_i - \omega_A}{v}\right]\right)^2 +$$

$$\alpha_{gS}\left(\left[\frac{1/\alpha_{gS}}{D_2}\right]\tilde{K} - \left[\frac{1/\alpha_{gS}}{D_2^*}\right]\left[\frac{\omega_A}{v}\right] - \left[\frac{1/\alpha_{gS}}{1/v^2 + 1/\alpha_{gS}}\right]\left[\frac{\omega_i - \omega_A}{v}\right]\right)^2 \tag{16.C23}$$

From this point, we assume that $\sigma_i^2 = \sigma^2 \; \forall \; i$. Hence

$$E(V_{S,i}) = \left[\frac{\alpha_{\pi S}/\alpha_{\pi M}^2 + 1/v^2 + 1/\alpha_{gS}}{2D_2^2}\right]\tilde{K}^2 +$$

$$\left[\frac{\alpha_{\pi S}/\alpha_{\pi M}^2 + 1/v^2 + 1/\alpha_{gS}}{2(D_2^*)^2}\right]E\left[\frac{\omega_A}{v}\right]^2 + \left[\frac{1}{2(1/v^2 + 1/\alpha_{gS})}\right]E\left[\frac{\omega_i - \omega_A}{v}\right]^2$$

$$\tag{16.C24}$$

where we have made use of the fact that ω_A/v and $(\omega_i - \omega_A)/v$ are uncorrelated if $\sigma_i^2 = \sigma^2 \; \forall \; i$.[21] From (16.C24) it follows that

$$E(V_{S,i}) = \left[\frac{\alpha_{\pi S}/\alpha_{\pi M}^2 + 1/v^2 + 1/\alpha_{gS}}{2D_2^2} \right] \tilde{K}^2 +$$

$$\left[\frac{\alpha_{\pi S}/\alpha_{\pi M}^2 + 1/v^2 + 1/\alpha_{gS}}{2\left(D_2^*\right)^2} \right] \left[\frac{\sigma^2/n}{v^2} \right] + \left[\frac{1}{2\left(1/v^2 + 1/\alpha_{gS}\right)} \right] \left[\frac{(n-1)\sigma^2/n}{v^2} \right]$$

(16.C25)

where we have made use of the assumption that the shocks are uncorrelated with one another. Expression (16.C25) can be rewritten as (16.14), which reduces further to (16.10) if $n = 1$.

Derivation of the Optimal Transfer Scheme. The optimal transfer scheme is found by minimizing $(1/n) \sum_{i=1}^n V_{S,i}$ over $\{t_i\}_{i=1}^n$ subject to the feasibility constraint and the participation constraints for each of the n countries. Clearly, under the optimal scheme, the feasibility constraint holds with equality, that is, $\sum_{i=1}^n t_i = 0$. The participation constraint of, say, country i requires that, ex ante, country i be at least as well off in expected value by joining a monetary union with a transfer scheme as it would be under national monetary policy-making in the absence of a transfer scheme. The expected welfare loss under the latter alternative is given by expression (16.10), which we repeat here:

$$\left[\frac{\alpha_{\pi S}/\alpha_{\pi M}^2 + 1/v^2 + 1/\alpha_{gS}}{2D_2^2} \right] \tilde{K}_i^2 + \left[\frac{\alpha_{\pi S}/\alpha_{\pi M}^2 + 1/v^2 + 1/\alpha_{gS}}{2\left(D_2^*\right)^2} \right] \left[\frac{\sigma^2}{v^2} \right]$$
(16.C26)

where we have used the assumption that $\sigma_i^2 = \sigma^2$.

It is convenient first to ignore the participation constraints when optimizing. The appropriate Lagrangian is

$$\frac{1}{2} \alpha_{\pi S} \pi^2 + \frac{1}{2} \left(1/v^2 + 1/\alpha_{gS}\right) \sum_{i=1}^n A_i^2/n + \lambda\left(\sum_{i=1}^n t_i\right)$$
(16.C27)

Note that π does not depend on the transfer scheme. The first-order conditions associated with the t_i $(i = 1, \ldots, n)$ are

$$\frac{1}{n} \left\{ \left[\frac{1}{D_2} \right] \tilde{K}_A + \left[\frac{1}{1/v^2 + 1/\alpha_{gS}} \right] \left[\tilde{K}_i - t_i - \tilde{K}_A + \frac{\omega_A - \omega_i}{v} \right] - \left[\frac{1}{D_2^*} \right] \frac{\omega_A}{v} \right\} = \lambda$$
$$(i = 1, \ldots, n)$$
(16.C28)

---

[21] Note that $E(\Sigma_j\omega_j/n)(\omega_i - \Sigma_j\omega_j/n) = E(\omega_i\Sigma_j\omega_j/n - \Sigma_j\omega_i^2/n^2) = (1/n)E(\omega_i^2) - (1/n^2)\Sigma_j E(\omega_i^2) = 0$, where we have used the assumption that the shocks are uncorrelated with one another.

Summing (16.C28) over $i = 1, \ldots, n$ and using $\Sigma_{i=1}^{n} t_i = 0$, we obtain

$$\lambda = \frac{1}{n}\left(\left[\frac{1}{D_2}\right]\tilde{K}_A - \left[\frac{1}{D_2^*}\right]\left[\frac{\omega_A}{v}\right]\right) \tag{16.C29}$$

We substitute (16.C29) back into (16.C28) and solve to yield

$$t_i = \tilde{K}_i - \tilde{K}_A + (\omega_A - \omega_i)/v \qquad (i = 1,\ldots,n) \tag{16.C30}$$

Clearly, the feasibility constraint is fulfilled. We substitute (16.C30) into (16.C22) to obtain country i's welfare loss if it joins a monetary union with a transfer scheme:

$$\left[\frac{\alpha_{\pi S}/\alpha_{\pi M}^2 + 1/v^2 + 1/\alpha_{gS}}{2D_2^2}\right]\tilde{K}_A^2 + \left[\frac{\alpha_{\pi S}/\alpha_{\pi M}^2 + 1/v^2 + 1/\alpha_{gS}}{2\left(D_2^*\right)^2}\right]\left[\frac{\sigma^2/n}{v^2}\right] \tag{16.C31}$$

Hence country i is prepared to join if expression (16.C31) is smaller than (16.C26). Therefore, if the differences between the deterministic components of the financing requirements are not too large compared with the variance of the shocks, a monetary union combined with the transfer scheme (16.C30) can be implemented. Moreover, for a given dispersion of the deterministic components of the financing requirements, it is more likely that such a monetary union can be implemented if the number of participants is larger.

The transfer scheme is thus composed of a deterministic component $t_i^S \equiv (\tilde{K}_i - \tilde{K}_A)$ and a component that eliminates the idiosyncratic parts of the shocks in the GFR. If the transfer scheme (16.C30) implies violation of the participation constraints of countries with relatively low $\tilde{K}$ values, then the deterministic components of the transfers made by these countries need to be reduced.

REFERENCES

Aizenman, J. (1992). Competitive externalities and the optimal seigniorage. *Journal of Money, Credit and Banking* 24:61–71.
Aizenman, J. (1993). Soft budget constraints, taxes, and the incentive to cooperate. *International Economic Review* 34:819–32.
Aizenman, J. (1994). On the need for fiscal discipline in a union. NBER working paper 4656. Washington, DC: National Bureau of Economic Research.
Alesina, A., and Grilli, V. U. (1992). The European central bank: reshaping monetary politics in Europe. In: *The Creation of a Central Bank*, ed. M. B. Canzoneri, V. U. Grilli, and P. Masson. Camibridge University Press.
Alesina, A., and Tabellini, G. (1987). Rules and discretion with non-coordinated monetary and fiscal policies. *Economic Inquiry* 25:619–30.

Barro, R. J., and Gordon, D. B. (1983). Rules, discretion and reputation in a model of monetary policy. *Journal of Monetary Economics* 12:101–21.

Beetsma, R. M. W. J., and Bovenberg, A. L. (1995a). Does monetary unification lead to excessive debt accumulation? CEPR discussion paper 1299, Centre for Economic Policy Research, London.

Beetsma, R. M. W. J., and Bovenberg, A. L. (1997a). Designing fiscal and monetary institutions in a second-best world. *European Journal of Political Economy* 13:53–79.

Beetsma, R. M. W. J., and Bovenberg, A. L. (1997b). Central bank independence and public debt policy. *Journal of Economic Dynamics and Control* 21:873–94.

Beetsma, R. M. W. J., and Bovenberg, A. L. (in press-a). Monetary union without fiscal coordination may discipline policymakers. *Journal of International Economics.*

Beetsma, R. M. W. J., and Bovenberg, A. L. (in press-b). Designing fiscal and monetary institutions for a monetary union. *Public Choice.*

Beetsma, R. M. W. J., and Jensen, H. (1997). Optimal monetary policy under output persistence through state-independent delegation. Unpublished manuscript, Universities of British Columbia/Maastricht/Copenhagen.

Bryson, J. H. (1994). Macroeconomic stabilization through monetary and fiscal policy coordination: implications for European monetary union. *Open Economies Review* 5:307–26.

Bryson, J. H., Jensen, H., and Van Hoose, D. D. (1993). Rules, discretion, and international monetary and fiscal policy coordination. *Open Economies Review* 4:117–32.

Calvo, G. A., and Guidotti, P. E. (1993). On the flexibility of monetary policy: the case of the optimal inflation tax. *Review of Economic Studies* 60:667–87.

Cukierman, A. (1992). *Central Bank Strategy, Credibility, and Independence.* Massachusetts Institute of Technology Press.

Debelle, G. (1993). Central bank independence: a free lunch? Unpublished manuscript, Department of Economics, Massachusetts Institute of Technology.

Debelle, G., and Fischer, S. (1994). How independent should a central bank be? CEPR publication 392. Stanford University.

Fischer, S. (1995). Modern approaches to central banking. In: *The Future of Central Banking,* ed. F. Capie, S. Fischer, C. Goodhart, and N. Schnadt, pp. 262–308. Cambridge University Press.

Jensen, H. (1994). Loss of monetary discretion in a simple dynamic policy game. *Journal of Economic Dynamics and Control* 18:763–79.

Laskar, D. (1989). Conservative central bankers in a two-country world. *European Economic Review* 33:1575–95.

Levine, P. (1993). Fiscal policy co-ordination under EMU and the choice of monetary instrument. *The Manchester School (Suppl.)* 41:1–12.

Levine, P., and Pearlman, J. (1992). Fiscal and monetary policy under EMU: credible inflation target or unpleasant monetarist arithmetic? CEPR discussion paper 701, Centre for Economic Policy Research, London.

Lockwood, B. (1996). State-contingent inflation contracts and output persistence. CEPR discussion paper 1348, Centre for Economic Policy Research, London.

McCallum, B. T. (1995). Two fallacies concerning central-bank independence. *American Economic Review Papers and Proceeedings* 85:207–11.

Morales, A. J., and Padilla, A. J. (1995). Designing institutions for international monetary policy cooperation. CEPR discussion paper 1180, Centre for Economic Policy Research, London.

Obstfeld, M. (1997). Dynamic seigniorage theory: an exploration. *Macroeconomic Dynamics* 1:588–614.

Persson, T., and Tabellini, G. (1993). Designing institutions for monetary stability. *Carnegie-Rochester Series on Public Policy* 39:53–84.

Persson, T., and Tabellini, G. (1996). Federal fiscal constitutions: risk sharing and moral hazard. *Econometrica* 64:623–46.

Phelps, E. S. (1973). Inflation in the theory of public finance. *Swedish Journal of Economics* 75:67–82.

Rogoff, K. (1985). The optimal degree of commitment to an intermediate monetary target. *Quarterly Journal of Economics* 99:1169–89.

Sibert, A. (1994). The allocation of seigniorage in a common currency area. *Journal of International Economics* 37:111–22.

Svensson, L. E. O. (1997). Optimal inflation targets, "conservative" central banks, and linear inflation contracts. *American Economic Review* 87:98–114.

von Hagen, J., and Süppel, R. (1994). Central bank constitutions for federal monetary unions. *European Economic Review* 38:774–82.

Walsh, C. (1995). Optimal contracts for independent central bankers. *American Economic Review* 85:150–67.

Name Index

407

Subject Index